The Deployment and Payment of the Clergy

A Report by

LESLIE PAUL

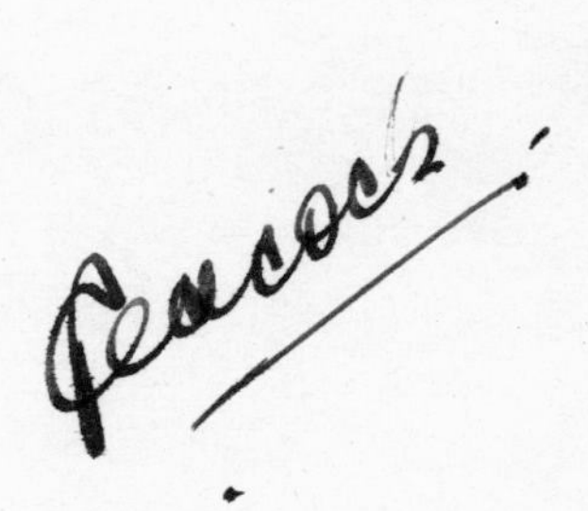

CHURCH INFORMATION OFFICE
Church House, Westminster, SW1

This report has been published by
the Church Information Office for the
Central Advisory Council for the Ministry
9 Tufton Street, Westminster, SW1

First published January 1964

Printed in Great Britain by
W. & J. Mackay & Co Ltd, Chatham

FOREWORD

On 14th July, 1960, the Church Assembly, after a long debate initiated by Lt-Col H. E. Madge of Winchester, passed the following resolution:

> That the Central Advisory Council for the Ministry be instructed to consider, in the light of changing circumstances, the system of the payment and deployment of the clergy, and to make recommendations.

After deliberation about the best way to undertake this formidable task, the Council asked Mr Leslie Paul to make a fact-finding inquiry and submit a report to them.

The report now published is the result of nearly two years' intensive work by Mr Paul, and the Central Advisory Council for the Ministry is deeply indebted to him. His sociological and literary experience, and his wide knowledge of the Church from the inside, are clearly shown throughout the report. As a result the Church is presented with a factual survey of the present situation which cannot be disregarded.

The views of the Council on the report are being published separately and simultaneously.[1] It is intended that the whole subject should be debated by the Church Assembly in February and July, 1964. I shall not comment here on the contents of the report, beyond saying that the Council warmly supports its main recommendations. The debate in the Church Assembly in February will begin a debate which must be carried on in the dioceses and parishes throughout the country. I pray God that out of it will come a new understanding of the role the Church must play in the changing world of 1964 if it is to be faithful to its Lord and Master.

KENNETH LINCOLN
Chairman,
Central Advisory Council for the Ministry

November, 1963

[1] *A Study of the Paul Report*. CIO. 1s. 6d.

ACKNOWLEDGEMENTS

Though it is unfortunately impossible to acknowledge or thank individually everyone who has contributed to the making of this report, I must cordially thank the Rev. H. D. F. Fayers for his statistical analysis of Mr Geoffrey Heawood's CACTM records, the Rev. A. B. Miskin for the papers contributed by him which he so often discussed with me, and Mr R. F. Neuss, head of the Statistical Unit, for the paper specially written on the way recruitment to the clergy is likely to go, and for checking many of my figures and giving me the latest of his. I am much indebted to Mr Anthony P. M. Coxon and Mr David H. J. Morgan for making available and coming to explain to me some of the findings of their independent research; also to Dr James W. B. Douglas and to Mr John Greve, both of the London School of Economics, for letters to me confirming and expanding their research findings.

I am much indebted too for valuable information freely given by the Church Commissioners, the Civil Service Pay Research Unit, the Establishment Division of the Board of Trade, the University Grants Committee, the Deputy Chief Planner and Senior Research Officers of the Ministry of Housing and Local Government, the AA and their auditors Messrs Lord, Foster and Co.

I have to express my thanks for the permissions granted to me to use copyright material as follows: to the University of Cambridge Appointments Board and to Mrs Christine Craig for permission to reproduce Table 25 from *The Employment of Cambridge Graduates, 1963*; to the Editor of *New Society* and Dr John Barron Mays for permission to quote from the article 'New Hope in Newtown' in the issue of 22nd August 1963; to the Editor of *New Society* and Mr Colin MacInnes to quote from 'A Godless Nation' in the issue of 29th August 1963; to Mr Mervyn Jones and Messrs Secker and Warburg for permission to quote from *Potbank*; to Mr P. R. Kaim-Caudle for permission to quote from his report, *Religion in Billingham, 1957–59*; to Professor R. K. Kelsall and Messrs Routledge & Kegan Paul Ltd for permission to quote from *Higher Civil Servants in Britain from 1870 to the Present Day*.

I have to thank Mr and Mrs Mark Cornwall-Jones for their most timely and voluntary help at especially critical points in the research, and Miss H. J. Nutter for reading the proofs. I have to thank the Council and Staff of CACTM and of my Advisory Committee for their continuous encouragement and readiness to help, and in so doing I must offer my thanks to the staff of Church Assembly generally.

I must also thank the Primate of Canada, the Archbishops of Jerusalem and Wales, the Secretaries of the Provinces of Scotland, Ireland and South Africa, and the Registrar of Calcutta Diocese for their clear and helpful letters.

I wish to thank all those who came to see me or received me individually or corporately, or wrote to me on their own initiative or by my invitation, particularly those bishops, dignitaries and parish priests who fully and candidly filled in my questionnaires or sent me documents and diaries. Lastly, and most warmly, I must thank my secretary, Mrs Jean Henderson, B.Sc., whose indefatigable and unstinted labours at every stage have made the report possible.—L.P.

TABLE OF CONTENTS

LIST OF TABLES

LIST OF MAPS

LIST OF GRAPHS

LIST OF DIAGRAMS

LIST OF ABBREVIATIONS

ASA	=	Average Sunday attendance
CACTM	=	Central Advisory Council for the Ministry
CIO	=	Church Information Office
CBF	=	Central Board of Finance
CEMS	=	Church of England Men's Society
DBF	=	Diocesan Board of Finance
DSF	=	Diocesan Stipends Fund
EC	=	Easter communicants
MQ	=	Main Questionnaire
OW	=	Overworked
PCC	=	Parochial Church Council
SE	=	Summary of Evidence
TLTD	=	Too little to do
UE	=	Underemployed

DIOCESE REFERENCE NUMBERS

In certain tables the dioceses are referred to by numbers, as follows:

1 Canterbury
2 London
3 Winchester
4 Bath and Wells
5 Birmingham
6 Bristol
7 Chelmsford
8 Chichester
9 Coventry
10 Derby
11 Ely
12 Exeter
13 Gloucester
14 Guildford
15 Hereford
16 Leicester
17 Lichfield
18 Lincoln
19 Norwich
20 Oxford
21 Peterborough
22 Portsmouth
23 Rochester
24 St Albans
25 St Edms. and Ips.
26 Salisbury
27 Southwark
28 Truro
29 Worcester

30 York
31 Durham
32 Blackburn
33 Bradford
34 Carlisle
35 Chester
36 Liverpool
37 Manchester
38 Newcastle
39 Ripon
40 Sheffield
41 Sodor and Man
42 Southwell
43 Wakefield

INTRODUCTION

TOWARDS A CRITICAL POINT

IN the country as a whole, though not everywhere to the same degree, the Church of England is facing a loss of membership and the attrition of its power and influence. It is not a new and surprising development, coming overnight, but the steady accumulation of pressures and processes which are at least as old as the century itself. In some cases they can be traced back to the beginning of the industrial revolution; in others to the '80s, when the religious revivals of the nineteenth century passed their peak and a recession began. Certainly they bear the mark of two world wars and a multitude of social changes. It might be wise to speak of the Church as being thrust by these developments towards a critical point rather than to use that overworked word, crisis, to describe what is happening, for the process is a slow one. Perhaps the rejection of emotive terms will enable us to keep a certain coolness and objectivity in assessing the evidence.

There are many facets of the decline: one concerns the displacement of the Church of England from the centre of affairs. The apparatus of its once central position remains, but emptied of power; the fact of establishment is manifest to everyone in the crowning of kings and queens, in the bench of bishops in the Lords, in the magnificent cathedrals, in the special role of the Church in television and radio and even in the attentiveness of the press to what bishops say and clergymen do. Despite the imposing apparatus, the Church is not the pacemaker in the moral and disciplinary life of the nation it once was. On the whole, it fights rearguard actions rather than promotes new crusades. The parliament upon which it is dependent is no longer inevitably filled with members of Christian upbringing and commitment. It is not now the laity legislating, and by its remoteness makes the lonely dependence of the Church upon its will the more poignant. But the massive shift of the Church from the centre to the periphery of affairs simply and perhaps properly reflects the shift which has taken place in the faith of ordinary men and women. The Church is not at the heart of *their* affairs as once it was, despite popular attachment to it as an historical and picturesque institution.

Historians have left us in no doubt that the decline in the influence of the Church is the other side of the medal of the increasing secularisation of society. Since the Middle Ages, one learned pursuit after another has escaped from under the wing of the Church: the disciplines of pure science—its objectivity and disinterestedness—have become the norms of the schools, replacing those of a doctrinally committed theology. Secularisation has made itself master in almost every walk of life: charity for the poor was long ago taken from parish vestries and placed in the hands of local government unions; in the end the State itself has become the greatest charity for those in need and today all of us are its beneficiaries. Education has moved largely from the hands of the Church into those of local authorities and the State. The trade unions and employers' associations which the Industrial Revolution flung up were far from the obediently Christian Guilds of masters and journeymen of the Middle Ages. The unions, and the left-wing political parties everywhere associated with them, added a militant quality to the growing secularisation: for them the Church was an instrument of an oppressing ruling class as for others it was the means of suppressing or extinguishing scientific truth. Though of England one has to say that the peculiar nature of the churches prevented the growth of a rabid anti-clericalism, there is no doubt that the belief that the Church was always 'against the men' was a factor in estranging it from the rising working-class movement in the nineteenth century. From the time of David Hume much English philosophy has been sceptical, empirical, pragmatic. Despite a brief flowering of idealism and of Christian evolutionary philosophy, to which the Church's own thinkers, such as William Temple, made a distinct contribution, empiricism, positivism, and utilitarianism have dominated so much of the intellectual life of England as to appear even to define its limits! Contemporary linguistic philosophy seems to be the end point of this development. It is inevitably critical of the language of liturgy and theology, and at this moment powerfully shapes theological self-criticism within the Church itself.

During the making of this survey great controversies and great events have moved the Church. The succinct report, *Conversations between the Church of England and the Methodist Church*, properly roused high ecumenical hopes. It also sobered the Church by its prediction of the need for extensive legal and constitutional changes, equivalent to 'the granting of complete self-government' for the Church of England and a form of establishment no more onerous than that possessed by the Church of Scotland. The unexpected plan accepted by the Toronto Congress, called *Mutual Responsibility and Interdependence in the Body of Christ*, startled the Church at home into serious understanding of the need to bring order and organised interdependence into the Anglican Communion throughout the world. The new mood Pope John brought to Christianity and movements of the Roman Church towards reunion have, after Delhi, stirred every Christian communion. The Christian world everywhere burgeons with hope. It has therefore been easy to conceive of this report as a contribution to the understanding of the tasks of a new Christian order.

Of the controversies, rather more domestic, the most important was set going by *Soundings*, *Objections to Christian Belief* and *Honest to God*. It was caught up with such related themes as the Quaker report on sex and Professor Carstairs' 1962 Reith Lectures, and prompted in part by the fear of some churchmen that the Church had not (and perhaps never would) come to terms with enlightened secular teaching on sex, or else that it had nothing valid to say on some moral and many intellectual matters. The debate on Christian images had its origin in the belief of some that the great Christian words and images which have fed a hundred generations no longer say anything to contemporary men. At the heart therefore of such controversies seems to be an agonising consciousness of failure to communicate. National apostasy is assumed to be the consequence. A defence of those who felt so was made by Mr Nicholas Mosley writing an editorial in *Prism* (itself a focus of controversy, too) and saying that,

> We are now in the curious situation in which the parable of the lost sheep is almost precisely reversed: there is now statistically one sheep safe in the fold and ninety and nine have gone into the mountains. So what do we do? Are not our instructions clearly to set off for the mountains, and to leave the one sheep for a while to fend for itself?

It would not be proper to enter into these controversies here; one simply points to them as part of that spirit of critical self-examination roused by a sense of the decline of the Church's influence and confidence, and likely to lead to a radical reappraisal of its mission. There are many precedents for this situation: in all of them an external secular discovery or movement of thought exercises a powerful, even explosive, pressure on the Church until it is assimilated or rejected. Such an intellectual overhaul is painful at any time: it is made more excoriating today by the haunting sense that intellectual failure to come to terms with contemporary thought may be the cause of pastoral failure.

Yet this would be to assume too much. It would be wrong to attribute national apostasy (if such it is) wholly to the social and intellectual movements which appear to sum it up, for then the Church's declining influence would seem to rest on the conscious decisions of intellectually awakened people, which would be as blatant a rationalisation as one could find. Every worker on religious censuses and surveys is struck by the number of people who are ready to declare themselves Christians and even to name their denominations without ever going to church. They believe themselves to be good Christians and will often assert that one can be a good Christian without churchgoing, which they will sometimes protest is an irrelevance. Have they, then, reached the state of 'religionless Christianity' Bonhoeffer tentatively spoke of, which has become a new 'cause' in some quarters of the Church? If so, and they speak the truth about their personal faith, the Church's relationship with them must be far different from that with those who have intellectually rejected Christianity. We often classify them, just the same, in the category of those whom the Church fails to reach with its communication, those who reject the gospel: yet it is conceivable one is totally wrong in doing so.

The conscious intellectual decision to reject Christianity, though significant and influential, may be rarer than we sometimes suppose. There are unconscious decisions, too, not always about faith so much as about the priorities of home and workaday life, which determine whether one goes to church. They can be given rational explanations of quite another sort. It may, for instance, seem more dignified, or give one more status, to say that one is Christian without needing to go to church than to say one prefers motoring on Sunday to listening to the parson. There was a smell of rationalisation about the negatively couched replies given as 'reasons for non-churchgoing' by some 1,829 listeners and non-listeners to religious broadcasts in the course of an inquiry made by the Audience Research Department of the BBC a few years ago.[1] The greater part said they had too much to do, or had lost the habit. Other reasons given were: 'Don't see any point in going', 'The services are boring', 'No one else in the family goes', 'It is too far to go'. The answers might be said to disguise laziness about going to church, or to serve as euphemisms for disbelief. All the same, only 9 per cent of non-listeners and 3 per cent of the whole sample said openly: 'Don't believe in Christianity any more.'

It must be said about this sad negativism that, though there is something in the contemporary climate which prevents men from believing, there is also something which discourages men from being what they want to be, and feel they need to be: certainly when that climate is a packed and clogged conurbation. Men can be discouraged from being active in the Church, and for the Church, even when they do believe and for the same reasons which discourage other creative initiatives in society: the source and nature of the discouragement (or disincentive, to use modern jargon) may never consciously be known to those most influenced by it. And this is a sociological rather than an academic matter and can only be uncovered by

[1] *Religious Broadcasts and the Public*, BBC, 1955.

sociological techniques designed to reveal *what* is actually happening before one comes to the *why*. Canon Boulard, the French priest-sociologist, in his classic *Introduction to Religious Sociology*, has shown the obduracy of social and religious patterns which persist across the centuries despite all missions and changes of ecclesiastical policy. One of the necessary tasks today is to see the pastoral charge of the Church over against the social patterns and demographic groupings given by history. Their capacity to be darkly and unyieldingly themselves, impervious to argument because they are not decided at the level of argument, tells us that here are positions to be taken by attrition rather than assault: they also tell us, on the credit side, why elsewhere the Church survives long years of persecution and terror. The deeper the movement of the soul the harder it must be to swing it from this side to that. The first acceptance of Christianity by a people produces great spiritual changes in folk or race feelings and attitudes: a few generations of apostasy do not easily eradicate them. But similarly a long period of apostasy, with all its hidden rejections, is not reversed overnight by a mission or campaign: one has to count in generations. If I speak of these things it is because I am conscious of the complexity and stubbornness of issues beneath such more (arguably) superficial matters as the payment and deployment of the clergy. They present a challenge at once marvellous and thrilling and perhaps in the very fact that they must extend us so fully one sees the hand of the Holy Spirit.

THE SCOPE OF THE SURVEY

In the making of this absorbing survey the first difficulty I foresaw was the breaking down of such large and unmanageable fields as 'payment', 'deployment', 'changing circumstances' into reasonably tidy sections of study and inquiry. 'Changing circumstances' seemed to me of two kinds, the first concerned the way the world at large was going, the second what was happening within the Church itself to its daily life and organisation, and order. But lest I should find myself embarked on a new anatomy of Britain (not to say of the Church as well), I thought that it would be sufficient to sketch in the social backgrounds against which the major problems of payment and deployment could be considered. This I have done, but the weight of that social evidence is such that however briefly sketched it broods over every page of the report.

As to 'payment' and 'deployment', I thought it quite imperative to consult clergy of every rank, the laity, and church organisations, as widely and as thoroughly as possible, and to classify and analyse the evidence provided for me in this way. The Summary of Evidence describes how this has been done and sets out the main results where they are not already presented in the report. Over payment I have been concerned to gather and set out the evidence collected and to contrast the status of the clergy as a group with other professions. Over deployment it was necessary to see first what the real situation is at this moment, and so I sought to understand the structure of the ministry as well as the actual facts of deployment. This done, I felt it necessary to look at the pressing missionary tasks of the Church in the light especially of the dominant social tendencies earlier discussed, and to ask what structure of ministry and what pattern of deployment might enable the Church the better to fulfil them. The first seven chapters set out the evidence and assess it. Chapters VIII and IX discuss the pros and cons of a number of theories and proposals. From Chapter X onwards I seek to make and to justify my own contribution to the solution of problems the evidence raises.

This is perhaps the point to say that the limited time available for the survey precluded certain forms of inquiry. I could not in the time available summarise and analyse the many contributions which commissions and committees of the Church have made to these very matters here discussed, though I have read and pondered most of them. I could not conduct a full-scale inquiry into how overseas provinces of the Anglican Communion controlled payment and deployment, though much evidence has come to me from them. I thought the Church would best be served by a fresh and to some extent sociological approach in an inquiry ultimately concerned with the day-to-day effectiveness of the ordained ministry of the living Church, rather than with its long history.

CHAPTER I

A First Look at the Evidence

STATISTICS OF DECLINE

It is necessary to look at some of the evidence for what is perhaps too readily accepted as national apostasy. At this stage it will not be mine, and it will be mostly figures.[1] Out of a home population of 40 million people in the provinces of Canterbury and York in 1958[2], 27 million had been baptised, which was 67 per cent of the population. Of baptised members aged 3 to 14, only 26 per cent (1,161,000) were in Sunday school. Confirmation provided a better picture. Of baptised members aged 13 and over, 9·7 million (45 per cent) had come forward for confirmation. To have been baptised and reached 17 are the only legal qualifications for inclusion on electoral rolls. Their membership was 2·9 million in 1958, which was 14 per cent of baptised persons aged 17 and over. Easter communicants in that year were 2·2 million, which was 23 per cent of confirmed members: Christmas communicants in the same year were 1·9 million (approx.) or 19 per cent.

The figures spotlight the dilemma of the Church over its membership. What is its real membership? The 27 million baptised or the 2·9 million—a tenth of that—on electoral rolls? Or, since membership of electoral rolls is the most distrusted of all Church of England statistics, ought one to say membership has been truly embraced by those who confirmed the baptismal vows their godparents gave? This is a handsome total of 9·7 million. Most people, however, are confirmed at 15 or under (Canterbury 56·4 per cent; York 62·6 per cent). Can they really be regarded as finally and responsibly committed? Few would say so: every parish priest grieves over the young people who lapse. If one falls back on Easter communicants this gives 2·2 million—1 in 4 of confirmed members, 1 in 12 of baptised members, *1 in 17* of the home population. Realistically one must speak of a progressive reduction of membership from the impressive multitude of the baptised to the thin minority of Easter or Christmas communicants, the last only 1 in 20 of the home population.

Whether we base membership most broadly on infant baptism or more narrowly upon confirmation figures, there is in both cases

[1] Taken unless otherwise stated from that first-class statistical compilation, *Facts and Figures about the Church of England, 1962*, CIO.

[2] *Total* population, 42·6 million, includes approx. 2 million people born outside the two provinces.

Table I. Church of England Infant Baptism Rates per 1,000 Live Births, 1956–60, Provinces of Canterbury and York

C.B.F. Ref. Nos.	Dioceses	Infant baptism rates per 1,000 live births			1960 rate expressed as a percentage of the 1956 rate
		1956	1958	1960	
(1)	(2)	(3)	(4)	(5)	(6)
1	Canterbury	665	628	648	97·4
2	London	464	444	413	89·0
3	Winchester	651	602	620	95·2
4	Bath and Wells	704	648	645	91·6
5	Birmingham	626	565	522	83·4
6	Bristol	549	562	523	95·3
7	Chelmsford	653	626	620	94·9
8	Chichester	692	709	700	101·2
9	Coventry	595	564	552	92·8
10	Derby	578	573	573	99·1
11	Ely	647	611	552	85·3
12	Exeter	709	637	616	86·9
13	Gloucester	675	658	595	88·1
14	Guildford	688	638	630	91·6
15	Hereford	801	747	750	93·6
16	Leicester	575	565	552	96·0
17	Lichfield	674	641	601	89·2
18	Lincoln	713	717	694	97·3
19	Norwich	714	671	658	92·2
20	Oxford	635	605	576	90·7
21	Peterborough	607	557	528	87·0
22	Portsmouth	609	561	557	91·5
23	Rochester	718	661	620	86·4
24	St Albans	560	538	505	90·2
25	St Edmundsbury and Ipswich	632	589	560	88·6
26	Salisbury	681	663	649	95·3
27	Southwark	538	536	483	89·8
28	Truro	604	556	533	88·2
29	Worcester	718	727	628	87·5
Means:	Province of Canterbury	614	587	561	91·4
30	York	601	589	573	95·3
31	Durham	617	589	578	93·7
32	Blackburn	554	535	519	93·7
33	Bradford	532	514	491	92·3
34	Carlisle	753	713	697	92·6
35	Chester	596	577	546	91·6
36	Liverpool	477	468	453	95·0
37	Manchester	541	532	501	92·6
38	Newcastle	601	555	547	91·0
39	Ripon	572	527	505	88·3
40	Sheffield	700	702	661	94·4
41	Sodor and Man	669	603	543	81·2
42	Southwell	581	571	530	91·2
43	Wakefield	587	589	575	98·0
Means:	Province of York	580	564	541	93·3
Means:	Provinces of Canterbury and York	602	579	554	92·0

Notes:

1. The statistics in col. (3) are taken from col. (16) of Table 29 in *Facts and Figures about the Church of England, 1959*, and those in col. (4) are taken from col. (16) of Table 64 in the 1962 edition of that book.

2. The figures in col. (5) are taken from col. (15) of Table I of the Statistical Section of *The Church of England Year Book, 1964*.

3. All the baptism rates have been calculated by the Statistical Unit from the numbers of infant baptisms obtained from the parochial returns, and from the Unit's estimated numbers of live births in the dioceses, derived from the Registrar General's Statistical Reviews for England and Wales.

4. Infant baptisms in extraparochial places of worship have not been included, unless incumbents included them in their parish registers in the parochial returns.

serious evidence of decline. Table I opposite, prepared by the Statistical Unit of the CBF, contrasts the Church of England rate of infant baptisms per 1,000 live births for the years 1956, 1958 and 1960. In only one diocese, Chichester, has the rate improved (to 101·2 per cent). For all other dioceses the fall averages 8 per cent: and if a contrast is made first between the drop from 1956 to 1958, then of that between 1958 to 1960, an accelerating fall is evident. Infant baptisms were 623 per 1,000 live births in 1885 and reached 717 in 1927: the figure of 554 in 1960 shows therefore how considerable the decline has been over a generation.

The overall figures just quoted mask the individual failures the table reveals. In London, Southwark, Bradford and Liverpool dioceses under half the babies are baptised at Anglican fonts: in that sense there the Church of England is no longer in a majority position. Another urban diocese, Birmingham, shows a very sharp drop. No less than twelve dioceses in Canterbury province and two in York province show results ten or more per cent poorer than 1956. Surprisingly and perhaps ominously, certain rural dioceses, Exeter and Ely for example, also show a decline. Whether one is able to explain this away in terms of a declining countryside or not, the steadiness of the total fall since 1927 points to a continual erosion in the sphere of the Church's greatest statistical success.

Confirmation figures are no more encouraging. The returns for 1962 for the provinces of Canterbury and York show a total of 180,284 persons confirmed, a decline of 5·6 per cent in one year; 1962, however, is a bulge year and the mere existence of so much greater an adolescent population might have guaranteed that the overall figure of the previous year (191,042) was at least maintained if not exceeded. The rate of decline per 1,000 of the population between 12 and 15 is of this order, 1960—68·4: 1961—67·9: 1962—62·6. It is quite serious. The following table shows how the confirmation picture has changed since 1957:

Table II. Changes in Confirmation Figures, 1957–62

Year	Confirmations (all ages)	Estimated population aged 12 to 20 incl.	No. of confirmations per 1,000 pop. aged 12–20
1957	172,288	4,997,000	34·5
1958	173,177	5,092,000	34·0
1959	182,721	5,382,000	34·0
1960	190,713	5,587,000	34·1
1961	191,042	5,756,000	33·2
1962	180,284	5,914,000	30·5

The other pointers to the decline of the Church's outreach to the whole population may be given briefly:

Marriages solemnised by the Church of England fall steadily from 907 per 1,000 marriages in 1844 to 496 in 1957 (civil and Roman Catholic ceremonies rise);

Easter Day Communicants fall from 98 per 1,000 population over 15 in 1911 to 63 in 1958;

Electoral Rolls fall from 140 per 1,000 of population of appropriate age in 1924 to 91 per 1,000 in 1959;

Sunday School numbers fall from 303 per 1,000 population aged 3–14 in 1897 to 149 in 1958.

The statistics of decline might, if one were perverse enough, be interpreted favourably. It can be argued that it was once necessary to conform to social fashion by going to church at least occasionally, by having one's babies baptised, children confirmed, sons and daughters married in church. Therefore, it is said, all that the declining figures show is that the Church has lost its social conformists; but this is too complacent a solution. The reduction is taking place all along the line, and the gap, even in the most favourable times, between the main membership groups—baptism, confirmation and Easter communicants—has never been explicable in conformity terms. In any case, if the collapse of social conformity is the cause it cannot be said to be operating everywhere with the same pressure. Has it gone twice as far in London as in Hereford diocese? Hereford has an infant baptism rate of 750 per 1,000 live births as against 413 in London (a contrast to be found elsewhere between rural and urban dioceses). If so, is the spread of freedom from conformity eventually to reduce Hereford to London's figures? What *makes* Hereford conform? And why should industrial Sheffield have a score (661) nearly as high as rural Carlisle (697) and vastly greater than London? One is wise to turn away from superficially bright answers like the collapse of social conformity. They have a double cutting edge anyway in Christian terms: if we persuade the majority of people to attend Church because it is spiritually necessary to them, and they do, shall we simply have persuaded them to conform socially? For they will be conforming to a social pattern. It has not escaped ironical notice that the Americans are criticised for attending church in great numbers, the English for failing to. One has to probe beneath conformity. In any case, conformism, in the pejorative meaning of the acceptance of an empty routine of churchgoing, probably ceased to work as an incentive after 1914, yet infant baptisms, it is worth remembering, continued to rise per 1,000 live births to 1927. They reached their apogee therefore in a decade in which open dissociation from the Church had become both intellectually respectable and socially acceptable!

THE DEPLOYMENT OF THE CLERGY

Only one part of the malaise or sense of growing crisis in the Church has its origin in the decline of its membership and congregations or in its failure to make the impact upon the nation it feels it ought to make. The other part concerns its internal organisation and the proper use and deployment of resources, including clergy, of which it ought, by its own profession of faith, to be a good, not a wasteful, steward. The interior problems are as tangled, as resistful of simplification, as any other group of social problems we are likely to find, and with origins as mixed: but certain things may be pointed out at this stage which illuminate the use we make as a Church of a ministry increasingly precious.

In 1851 there were 16,194 clergy for a population of 16·9 million, that is, one clergyman for every 1,043 persons in the two provinces: by 1901 the clergy numbers had reached a peak of 23,670, but the population had climbed faster, to 30·6 million, giving a ratio of one clergyman to 1,295 persons. By 1951 the population had jumped to 41·3 million: but the number of clergy had fallen to 18,196: the ratio was now 1:2,271. This is not quite the whole story. During the century covered by these figures the number of clergy over 65 rose from 1,480 to 5,530: the number of persons per clergyman below 65 years rose correspondingly from 1,148 to 3,263. Figures show that the clergy has become an older age group: in 1851, 78 per cent of the clergy were under 55; in 1959, 54 per cent. In 1851, 9 per cent were 65 and over, and in 1959, 29 per cent. Despite the increase in the expectation of life since 1851, a rising average age, of course, means rising annual losses through death or retirement. However, the changes in the rising average age are difficult to assess exactly. In 1851 the average age was 44, in 1951, 55: since retirement pensions were augmented by state old age pensions in 1958 the number of non-active or partly active clergy has increased and this has reduced the average age of 'clergy working full time' in both provinces. In 1959 it was 50, in 1961, 49. The average age for the whole clergy in 1961 (perhaps the only figure really comparable with that of 1851) was 55. For *incumbents* in both provinces in 1961 it was 53·2. The possible shrinkage of the numbers of the ministry, as well as its tendency as a group to age, caused great concern in the last decade, locally as well as nationally. A report of the Rural Parishes' Committee made to the Bishop of Gloucester in 1960 included this hypothetical table, which demonstrated diocesan alarm:

Probable Reduction of Manpower in the Diocese

	1960	*1970*	*1980*
Number of incumbents	215	199	165
Average age of incumbents	51·2	55·3	62·5

The problem of replacement of the clergy became most acute in 1958 when the rising gap between entrants to the ministry and losses from it reached 127. The gap has closed since, indeed the lines have crossed over: entrants for 1961 were 686, losses were 494.[1] The Church may not therefore, as was once feared, face an actual shrinkage of men in the active ministry, but rather an increase. However with the population of the two provinces 'exploding', as the statisticians say, it is likely to continue to see the ratio of parson to population move against it. The 1963 population of the two provinces was 44·08 million: by the year 2001 it is expected to be 59·36 million, a 34·7 per cent increase. There is no proof yet that clergy figures will keep in step.

School teachers are distributed roughly in ratio to the population, though often with difficulty. When the population increases in an area, new schools are built and teachers recruited: when it declines, schools are closed and teachers sent elsewhere. The Ministry of Education, by agreement with local educational authorities, fixes, a year ahead, a 'teacher quota' for each authority, which it ought not to exceed. Effectively, this puts a brake on recruitment to the well-served areas and deflects teachers in search of posts to the more poorly-served areas. The clergy are not deployed even on this basis, though the establishment of new conventional districts and the making of united benefices and pluralities is part of the business of adapting the Church to population changes. They certainly are not 'posted' to duties, like policemen or soldiers. Clergy still are deployed by parish, and a parish means an actual area with legally established boundaries, one or more churches and a benefice income by which the parson can at least *begin* to be paid. Such was the basis on which 16,194 clergy were deployed in 1851; just so were 10,390 incumbents deployed in 1961. Traditionally therefore a man goes to where there is a legal parish and an actual building—a physical, consecrated church: the parish church is the basis of the appointment

---

[1]

	1959	*1960*	*1961*	*1962 (prov.)*
All entrants	601	676	686	*716*
Total losses	612	556	494	*582*

of assistant clergy, too. This very strong and very ancient ecclesiastical system, slowly built up since St Augustine's mission to Canterbury and even today not entirely divorced from the social and political pattern of the country, has served the Church well in this sense: it has provided the territorial 'coverage' necessary to fulfil its task as pastor to the nation, it has fostered and promoted communities and it has sharply defined the responsibilities of the parish priest. There was no inch of territory and therefore no place where anyone could live beyond reach of the spiritual ministrations of a priest or a place to worship. However adapted and chopped about in the course of time, it was a system inherently more suitable to a country where the population was dispersed over the countryside than to one where, as now, it is concentrated in towns: the increasing urbanisation of England has more and more revealed the inadequacies of deploying clergy territorially irrespective, for the most part, of population concentrations. What originally was the common-sense policy of providing one priest for every natural community has become in effect in our time a haphazard distribution of men. The result is that in certain dioceses like Hereford, Norwich, Exeter, there is one clergyman for between 1,000 and 2,000 population, but in others such as London, Southwark, Manchester, there is only one clergyman to about 4,500 to 5,500 persons, while in the worst served, Birmingham, Liverpool, Sheffield, the ratio is about one to 6,000. Put another way (1958 figures), some 4,630 clergy are in charge of parishes each of 1,500 population or less, while a roughly equal number, 4,794, are concerned with parishes which rise from 5,000 to over 20,000 in population. In fact, in 1958 figures, 41·7 per cent of clergy deal with 11·2 per cent of the population and at the other end of the scale 14·6 per cent deal with 34·7 per cent of the population. The inevitable effect of the parochial system of deployment is at present to place most of the parsons in the country while most of the population lives in the towns.

There is other evidence which can be gleaned from *Facts and Figures about the Church of England 1962*: the increasing brevity of a priest's tenure of his living; the drift of the clergy from north to south of the country, for example, which is slowly denuding the York province of the priests it so badly needs. The ratio of parochial clergy to population in York province is 1:3,986 persons, while in Canterbury province it is 1:2,966. The York province has on the whole a much higher rate of offering to the priesthood than the Canterbury province, as subsequent evidence shows, and would have fewer manpower problems if its clergy stayed where they were ordained and served their titles. That they do not and join the drift south is additional evidence of what in personnel management terms might be bluntly argued to indicate 'low job satisfaction'. The uneven distribution of assistant curates, at least in terms of actual need, is also important evidence of poor use of manpower. The facts look bad. It would be premature to say that failure to use manpower more skilfully is the cause of declining membership and support of the Church: there are certainly deeper causes: but some relationship we may reasonably expect to find. If priests are not where the people live one must expect this to reflect itself in pastoral results. However, before we subject these hypotheses to more rigorous testing it seems proper to look first at other analyses of the Church's power and influence, and then at that broader picture of the nation's life against which inevitably the Church's mission will be judged. It is essential to ask what is happening socially and demographically to England. If we can see what is happening, perhaps we shall be able to say not only where the clergy are most wanted now, but where they are most likely to be wanted in the future.

CHAPTER II

The Church in its Social Aspect

If we turn from a study of the Church's decline from its once high estate to ask what the Church actually is, statistically, socially, at this moment in the life of the nation, the answers are not all discouraging. It is necessary to explain what one means by the Church 'statistically, socially'. If one speaks of the Church, as one must, as the Body of Christ, as the spiritual communion and devotion of the faithful in Christ, as the Church in its fellowship and worship, there are always critics who raise impatient questions about the Church in society, in its social and political outreach so to speak, or as, principally, *kerygma*, or the preaching Church. If, on the other hand, one speaks of the Church as a social force, involved and soiled in the sweat of the world, there are those who point to the apparently neglected transcendence of the Church, to its place out of time, above this particularly hurly-burly, herald of the Heavenly City of God and only pilgrim through the earthly one. There is a real and not to be resolved tension here. Since this report must, by its terms of reference, concentrate on the Church in its social impact and look at it as one social institution among many, it is as well to state the ground upon which one does so. Briefly, it is this: however we may describe or define the Church, it is *also* and *always* a social institution affected by and in its turn affecting the social patterns within which it operates. More, the more successful it is as spiritual mentor of its congregation the more important it becomes as a social influence. Perhaps the corollary is also true. The more successful it is as a social influence, the more it has to struggle to prevent its spiritual life from being subjected to society, or made the instrument of society; the more it must labour self-critically to keep its sources pure. Equally, the more it fails in its religious tasks, the feebler its social impact becomes. Within the terms of such an understanding it is sensible, and even obligatory, to look at the Church first as an earthly institution, asking the questions one would ask of other institutions, and then as a social institution rooted in a particular society at a particular time, seeking to change its behaviour patterns, but also limited and conditioned by them.

THE CHURCH AS A SOCIAL INSTITUTION

Viewed as a social institution the Church at this particular moment of time is no mean force. If one takes infant baptism and church marriage as, for some residual religious reason, necessary to those participants who never go religiously beyond them, then some two-thirds of the people of England need the services of the Church in baptism and over half in marriage; possibly the greatest percentage at burial. If we take a more real figure of commitment—confirmation, 9·8 million in 1960, this is larger than the membership of the TUC, which in 1961 was 8·1 million. Or again if we take such a figure as the Christmas communicants, which is approximately 2·1 million in 1960, it is perhaps not ludicrous to point out that this is of a higher order than those who in 1961 were attending evening institutes in England and Wales (1·7 million). One of the facts incumbents were asked to supply in the Main Questionnaire addressed to them at the beginning of this survey was 'Average Sunday Attendance, all services'. Their answers produced a total average Sunday attendance of 205,990 for 885 livings. Of course, this includes—it is intended to—those who go to church twice, or even three times, on Sunday, for it was asked in order to secure a picture of the Sunday duties of the incumbents. If this is any sort of a guide, then for 11,470 livings of both provinces the average Sunday attendances, all services, ought to be in the region of 3 millions, a total understandably larger than that for Easter communicants. Yet the MQ figures take no account of those attending school, college and institution chapels, royal peculiars, and other non-parochial places of worship, or of children in Sunday school. The real figure, then, of those attending Church of England worship on Sunday could be very much higher. The results of some of the surveys I discuss below suggest that it is. Viewed religiously, the number of worshippers may be held to be unsatisfactory, but considered socially it is formidable, and makes the Church of England by far and away the most important social institution in the land. Other statistical exercises strengthen this picture of the Church's human riches and social potentiality. It is in touch with some 800,000 confirmed young people between 14 and 20. In the same age group it has approximately 273,000 young people (1960 figures) enrolled in church youth organisations. The two groups overlap, but are not identical. The figures show it as by far and away the largest organiser of youth in the country: moreover, it is most successful in the organisation of young adolescents (211,000 aged 14 to 17) where so many youth movements signally fail. Perhaps we ought to add nearly a quarter of a million members of choirs, 50,000 altar servers, 1,161,000 members of Sunday schools, 182,000 adults enrolled in religious education groups, the 830,000 children in church schools, and over 3 million readers of parish magazines, to indicate some of the ways in which the Church in its manifold activities ramifies away into the fibres of the society of which it is a part. It has some 781 'local associations' in the shape of rural deaneries, each with a titular head, though not yet each with its professional secretary. The Church may properly be scandalised that only a quarter of its 9·8 million confirmees come to church regularly, but it need not on that account undervalue the loyalties that it does enjoy. It reaches a larger group than any other voluntary organisation which depends for its existence upon the regular attendance of its members at a place of meeting, their participation in a variety of voluntary activities and their voluntary contributions. No political party commands such a weekly 'audience' or has the services of so large a professional body. The Church is only surpassed in audience figures by the organs of mass communication—the press, television and radio. But those audiences are passive ones, membership of them involves no one in any personal commitment whether organisational, doctrinal, moral or spiritual: merely in the ability to pay for the service.

THE ROSEWORTH SURVEY

It is proper also to speak of the continued hold of the Church over the nation, at least in idea, if not in activity such as churchgoing, as it shows itself locally, too. A survey was made at my request in the Roseworth Estate, Stockton-on-Tees, by a team of 70 Anglicans and 70 Methodists. They were 'paired up' and given a briefing as to how to use a simple inquiry form, and each pair was given one or two roads to cover. During the course of a fortnight every house in the parish was visited. The estate comprised 2,189 houses and some 8,190 individuals. Here are some of the results:

1. Declared religious denomination of 2,189 households:

	No.	%
(*a*) Church of England	1,328	60·7
(*b*) Roman Catholic	405	18·5
(*c*) Free Church	294	13·4
(*d*) Mixed C. of E./R.C.	101	4·6
(*e*) Mixed C. of E./Free Church	53	2·4
(*f*) Jehovah's Witnesses or no professed belief	8	·4
	2,189	100·0

2. Place of baptism of individuals

		No.	%
(*a*)	Church of England	5,312	64·9
(*b*)	Roman Catholic	1,800	22·0
(*c*)	Free Church	1,060	12·9
(*d*)	Unbaptised	18	·2
		8,190	100·0

The contrast between declared allegiance and activity was considerable. Of 731 Church of England confirmed individuals, 257 were regularly or occasionally in attendance at church, but active Church of England families numbered only 142. However, it is the size of the declared allegiances and the absence of non-allegiance to which it is important to draw attention at this stage of the argument. The evidence is the same from surveys I did not promote. In that BBC Survey of 1959 of adult listeners and non-listeners to religious broadcasts in Great Britain, to which reference has already been made, 993 (54 per cent) declared themselves Anglican and only 130 (7 per cent) stated no denomination at all. A Gallup Poll, *Religion in Britain* (1957), rather suspect for the inadequacy of its sampling and of its questions, produced the information that 55 per cent of the adult population 'belong to' the Church of England. The Roseworth declarations of Church of England allegiances are of the same order of magnitude.

INDEPENDENT SURVEYS

In 1961, a team of the Cambridge Movement for Church Reform undertook a pilot survey of the attitudes of some 500 families at Longleven, a new suburb of Gloucester with a population of 14,000, mostly of young families whose wage-earners were described as following these kinds of occupations: 'skilled machine operators, machine inspectors, civil servants, clerks, teachers, travelling representatives, shop assistants, etc.' Two groups were chosen:

Group 'A'—400 families selected at random from the 729 families who had been visited during the initial stage of the Stewardship Campaign.

Group 'B'—100 families in a door-to-door canvass in one street, omitting those questioned under Group 'A'.

The first four questions, together with the two groups' answers, are as follows:

1. *Have you been confirmed?*

	'A'	'B'
Yes	67%	61%
No	33%	39%
Average age at confirmation	16 yrs	14 yrs

2. *Does worship make any difference to you?*

	'A'	'B'
Yes	76%	62%
No	21%	35%
Don't know	3%	3%

3. *Do you think death is the end?*

	'A'	'B'
Yes	14%	14%
No	64%	63%
Don't know	22%	23%

4. *Are you glad to see your parson when he visits you in your home?*

	'A'	'B'
Yes	92%	84%
No	5%	3%
Don't know	3%	13%

The degree of conformity of view between churchgoing Group 'A' and (presumably non-churchgoing) Group 'B' is remarkable.

The Morpeth Council of Churches produced the following analysis of a canvass:

Declared religious denominations of 3,473 families

	No.	%
Church of England	2,334	67·2
Roman Catholic	486	14·0
Methodist	243	7·0
Presbyterian	243	7·0
Congregational	117	3·4
Other denominations	43	1·2
No denomination or uncommitted	7	·2

A similar census of 602 houses of the Fleet Downs Estate, Dartford, Kent, by a group of young Anglicans, gave this rough and ready result: Total houses, 602; Church of England allegiance, 300 (49·8 per cent); Methodist, 48 (8 per cent); Roman Catholic, 26 (4·3 per cent); Presbyterian, 16 (2·7 per cent); Baptist, 9 (1·5 per cent);

Congregational, 3 (·5 per cent); uncommitted, 200 (33·2 per cent). The results as between Morpeth and Fleet Downs differ considerably in the number of uncommitted. However, Morpeth rested its canvass on a form each household was asked to fill in and hand to a visitor when he called, Fleet Downs firstly relied on a door-to-door canvass. Morpeth visited 3,894 homes and received no answers or refusals from about 400 of them. The analysis is based only on those who did reply: the larger proportion of the 400 must therefore rank as uncommitted. The 400 no answers or refusals to answer from Morpeth bear a relation to the 200 uncommitted of Fleet Downs. For whatever reason, 'Jehovah's Witnesses' or 'no professed belief' at Roseworth Estate constitute a negligible quantity. Virtually *all* are committed.

At Sedgley, Dudley, Worcester, five laymen and the incumbent of All Saints' Church made a survey of three small new housing estates. At each of 608 households they left a leaflet which invited the head of the household to give details of his household and to state its religion. 537 replies were received. The results were as follows:

Distribution by religion of 537 households

	No.	%
Church of England	349	65·0
Mixed Church of England and other	29	5·4
Methodist	80	14·9
Roman Catholic	34	6·3
Baptist	8	1·5
Miscellaneous	9	1·7
Congregationalist	4	·7
Jews	2	·4
None	22	4·1

Even if we have to assume that the 71 who did not give a reply or a classifiable reply were all either uncommitted or of no religious faith, the massive commitment on the other side speaks for itself.

BILLINGHAM AND OTHER SURVEYS

It is to be noted that all these censuses were conducted in housing estates which everywhere constitute a pastoral problem. In the same year (1962) as most of the surveys quoted, Mr P. R. Kaim-Caudle, a tutor in Social Studies at Durham University, published a survey, *Religion in Billingham, 1957–59*, undertaken for the Billingham Community Association. Statistically it showed, among other things, the exetnt of Billingham's religious commitment in baptism, burials and marriages.

The number of children baptised (659) in 1957 represents 94 per cent of the children born that year. It is not claimed that this percentage is absolutely correct, rather that it is almost certainly conservative. Not all children baptised in 1957 were necessarily born in that year (and vice versa); some children born in Billingham may have been baptised outside the town, say at their grandparents' church, a small number at the point of death were baptised in hospital. . . .
Baptism of infants is certainly, whatever may be the parents' religious views, a practice virtually universal in Billingham.[1]

As to burials, statistics indicate that of the 243 who died only 207 received a religious funeral. Mr Kaim-Caudle says this is certainly incorrect. The out-of-town locations of the nearest crematorium and of the hospital probably lead to the 36 discrepancies.

The four undertakers who conduct practically all the funerals in the town do not know of any burial or cremation without religious rites . . . religious rites at burials are universal.[2]

Only in weddings is there a greater gap, but still church weddings constitute the overwhelming majority. The share of the Church of England in these rites is shown by the following table. The Roman Catholic Church is strong in Billingham (3,500 of the population of 20,000 over 15) and this accounts for the excellent showing it makes.

	Baptisms		*Burials*		*Weddings*	
	No.	*%*	*No.*	*%*	*No.*	*%*
Anglican churches	430	65	149	72	89	52
Free churches	76	12	31	15	36	21
Roman Catholic churches	153	23	27	13	46	27
All churches	659	100	207	100	171	100
	Births		*Deaths*		*Marriages*	
Registrar General's returns	702		243		237	
Therefore no religious rites recorded	43		36		66	

As to the general picture, the size of the congregations going to church at Easter in Billingham constituted about 20 per cent of the population above school-leaving age. On Sunday 12 April 1962,

[1] Op. cit., p. 4. [2] Ibid.

it was about $15\frac{1}{2}$ per cent.[1] If we turn from busy industrial towns or new housing estates to remote villages or decaying town parishes, the picture does not greatly alter. The Rev. A. Motion, Rector of St Andrew in the centre of Newcastle upon Tyne, a parish of old and new housing blocks, which has suffered a decline of population, conducted a house-to-house survey. He reported that there was a strong Roman Catholic group in the population which produced a reversal of the usual dominant Anglican position: other denominations (Roman Catholic principally) were declared in the case of 137 out of 424 families, Church of England 86. The religiously committed in the parish outnumbered the uncommitted by 52·5 per cent to 47·5 per cent. Two tiny little parishes perched on the coast of Northumberland, near the border with Scotland, which have stayed stable since 1801 and where the last new building was a school in 1896, and where Presbyterianism is strong, produced evidence, through a new domesday survey made by the Rector, of membership of the Church through the electoral roll of 1 in 4 of the adult population of approximately 260. The figure is made more significant by the presence of 32 old-age pensioners and 49 agricultural workers in the two parishes, classes which, though they may come to church, do not so readily 'put their names to bits of paper'. The Easter communicants of the two parishes were 37 in 1962, a ratio of 142 per 1,000 adults.

Right at the other extreme of the social spectrum an investigation into the Crown Street district—largely slummy—of Liverpool 'showed that 45 per cent of the 574 households interviewed claimed to have attended church within the last month . . . 56 per cent claimed that they had been visited by a church representative . . . and 51 per cent of the children of these households attended Sunday school'.[2]

This high rate of church attendance was achieved in a district with a large Roman Catholic element (71·6 per cent of those claiming attendance 'in the last month' were R.C.). Perhaps here there is a lesson in loyalty for the Church of England.

In producing this fresh and varied evidence from so many different communities my intention has not been to weigh one denomina-

[1] The Gallup Poll, *Religion in Britain*, 1957, stated that asked what they did the previous Sunday, 14 per cent of British adults said they had been to church.

[2] *Churches in the Crown Street District*, preliminary report, November 1959, by J. A. Jackson, M.A., privately circulated. What happened religiously to the Crown Street residents transported to the new estate at Kirkby is told by Dr John Barron Mays in 'New Hope in Newtown', *New Society*, 22 August 1963. Reference to his article is made below, pp. 42 and 45.

Cf. also *Urban Redevelopment and Social Change: A Study of Social Conditions in Central Liverpool 1955-56* by Dr. Charles Vereker, Dr. John Barron Mays and others, Liverpool, 1961.

tion against another, but to draw attention to a basic religious commitment to Christian churches generally, and to the Church of England in particular, behind all figures of decline.

The fact is, I think [wrote Mr Colin MacInnes,[1] a shrewd and sympathetic observer], that there exists, in England, a kind of 'church' outside the churches, which consists of hundreds of thousands of persons who are not without belief, who accept certain moral imperatives, who expect the churches to go on functioning like a kind of insurance company for the public conscience, but who are repelled by, or uninterested in, the actual manifestations of organized Christianity.

In the light of that remark the figures from such different urban areas are particularly impressive witnesses. They show that a majority demand the rites of churches to mark the most elemental events of life—birth, marriage, death. Though they themselves may be inarticulate about their reasons, it looks as though they feel that human dignity in these events is manifested in and vindicated by a religious ceremony. We ought not to despise a lingering sense of the numinous our secular society attaches to them.

Only a minority of those interviewed are not prepared to declare an allegiance, however tenuous, to one church or another. A majority still declare themselves Church of England and their recourse to it for the basic rites confirms that their allegiance is just that much more than nominal. We have the right to deplore our failure to bring this formidable group to church, or their failure to come, but we cannot ignore it. Its potentiality and its goodwill remain. The overall conclusion must be that however much the Church may be oppressed by a sense of decline, or of national apostasy, there remains a broad platform of faith and works which always makes possible its renewal and recovery.

Mr Kaim-Caudle said of Billingham what I have tried to say of England:

However inadequate the impact of religion and churches may appear to people who hold strong religious views, there is no doubt that the impact, as far as it is capable of quantitative assessment, is not only greater than is often thought, but is greater than that of any other activity which requires any degree of active participation. The nominal membership of the two major political parties in the town is about 300 and many of these are card holders who never attend a meeting. There are no party political organisations catering for either children or adolescents. The number of people registered for non-vocational evening classes run by the Local Education Authority is about 500 and another fifty people take WEA and University courses. Students at vocational part-time (not day release) classes are measured in dozens rather than hundreds.

[1] 'A Godless Nation', *New Society* (No. 48), 29 August 1963.

The impact of the Roman Catholic Church on its members as measured by church attendances and children going to church schools is strong and needs no discussion. The impact of the Anglican and Free Churches on their members is on average much weaker but even so virtually all children are baptised, all funerals are conducted with religious rites, almost three-quarters of all couples are married in church, nearly half of all children between 4 and 13 go to Sunday school and a seventh of all adults attend church at least occasionally.

There is also a great deal of voluntary work done in and for the churches. About 200 people participate in the administration of the Anglican and Free Churches as councillors, stewards, deacons, trustees or elders. As many as 170 take Sunday school classes and a good many more take part in sales of work and other money-raising efforts. On the social side of church life, women's clubs have 550 members and about a sixth of all children of school age (excluding Roman Catholics)—some 700—are in uniformed youth organisations affiliated to the churches, 400 of their elders are members of youth clubs. . . .

It has been shown that in a prosperous working-class town where social roots are not very deep, the impact of religion and churches is still one of the strongest in the life of the community.[1]

[1] *Religion in Billingham, 1957–59*, pp. 15–16.

CHAPTER III

The Social Background

THE POPULATION EXPLOSION

IT is sometimes said that Britain is now passing through a second industrial revolution. If by this we mean that there is a spurt of industrial production marked by new enterprises and techniques, a rising standard of living, new mobility of labour and the explosion of population to which attention has already been drawn, then it is true. Between the censuses of 1951 and 1961 population in the United Kingdom increased by 2·5 million (according to preliminary estimates) and reached an average density of 564 persons to the square mile. In England and Wales alone that density is now 790. According to the Registrar General's return, the population of England and Wales in mid-1962 was 46·7 million. It is estimated that in the next four years there will be an average of 870,000 births per year—more than the population of Liverpool—but that by the end of the century births per year will rise to just over 2 million, equivalent to perhaps the population of two new Birminghams every year. This is an upward revision of previous estimates made necessary by the rising birth-rate, which is 20 per cent greater than it was ten years ago.

The increasing population is not being evenly distributed. There are areas which are losing population or changing hardly at all—the border counties with Scotland, the centre and north of Wales, the more remote areas of Devon and Cornwall, parts of East Anglia, the County of London and parts of Middlesex, and the centres of other conurbations. There are zones which are gaining: the Tyne and Tees, the Merseyside and Manchester, the Birmingham-Wolverhampton zone, and the Midlands around Leicester, the Bristol area, and above all the metropolis and the south-east corner of England, which is drawing population to itself at an extraordinary rate.

The new industrial growth has been mainly in the Midlands and the South. The old primary industries on which the first industrial revolution was based were for the greater part located in the North. Coalfields have been worked out in the course of time, iron-ore sources are exhausted and competition has had to be met from new sources of power such as oil, electricity, nuclear power. The importance of the older industries and the towns dependent on them has diminished. All this is common knowledge, and has given rise to the theme of the geographical Two Nations, a declining North struggling for survival against a rising prosperous South. Though it has elements

MAP 1
THE POPULATION EXPLOSION

The map shows the relative increases or decreases in population the dioceses have undergone between 1931 and 1959. The çentres of great conurbations lose population to the outskirts.

Diocese	Per cent increase (+) or decrease (−)
York	+12·3
Durham	+ 1·4
Blackburn	+ 6·8
Bradford	+ 1·9
Carlisle	+ 6·0
Chester	+21·9
Liverpool	+ 7·1
Manchester	− 4·5
Newcastle	+ 7·7
Ripon	+10·2
Sheffield	+ 7·5
Sodor and Man	+12·6
Southwell	+24·7
Wakefield	+ 0·1

Diocese	Per cent increase (+) or decrease (−)
Canterbury	+13·4
London	− 4·3
Winchester	+27·0
Bath & Wells	+25·7
Birmingham	+19·0
Bristol	+20·8
Chelmsford	+27·5
Chichester	+34·0
Coventry	+48·2
Derby	+16·9
Ely	+26·1
Exeter	+11·2
Gloucester	+33·3
Guildford	+65·4
Hereford	+12·4
Leicester	+22·8
Lichfield	+21·7
Lincoln	+16·9
Norwich	+10·1
Oxford	+56·9
Peterborough	+27·1
Portsmouth	+21·3
Rochester	+49·6
St Albans	+82·8
St Ed. & Ipswich	+19·1
Salisbury	+32·4
Southwark	− 5·8
Truro	+ 6·7
Worcester	+26·5

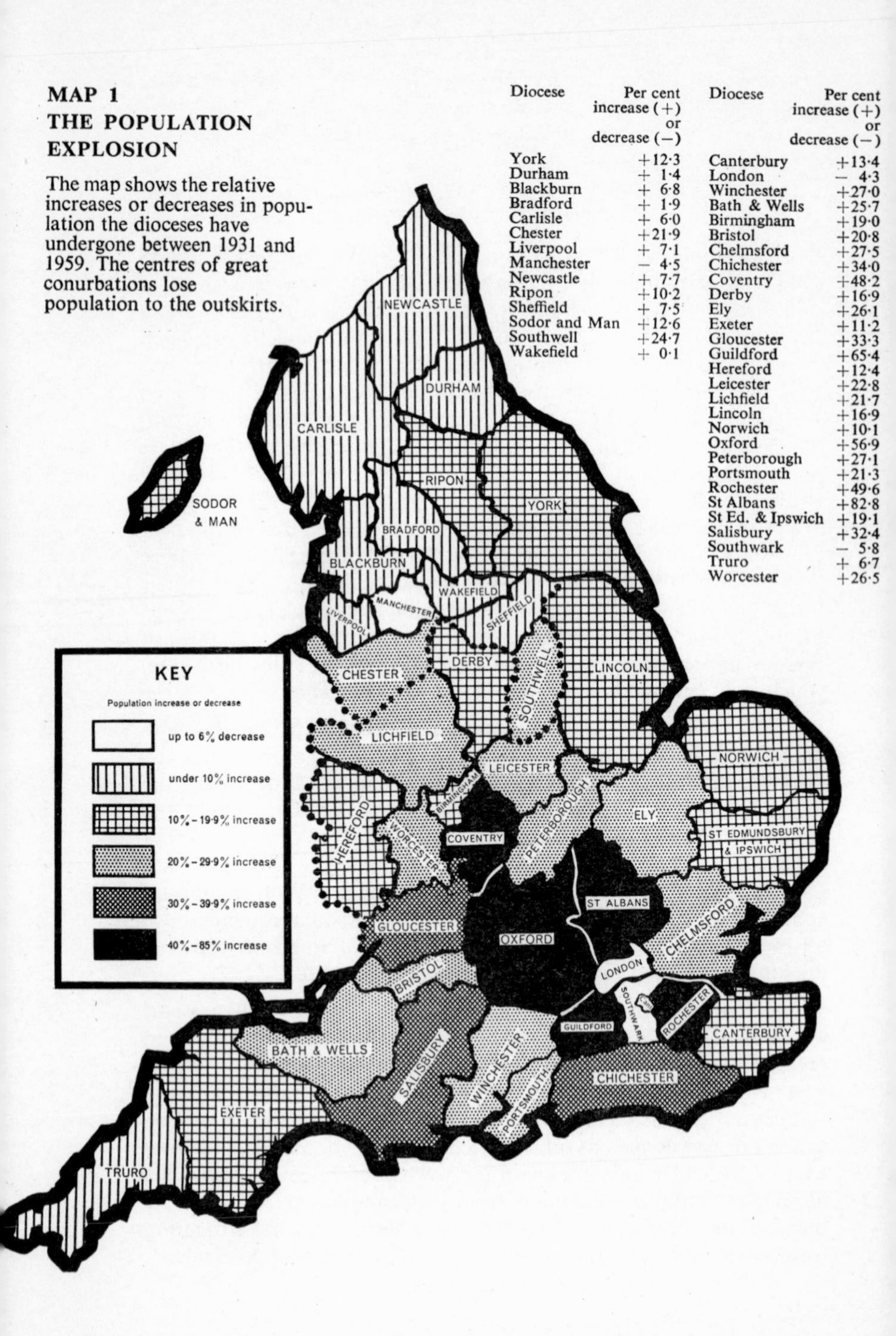

of truth, it is not the whole story. It is rather, as *The Times* special correspondents pointed out,[1] 'a question of differential net growth'. 'The increase in the southern population was about five times what it was in the North' between 1951 and 1961. But it did increase in the North, which has its own centripetal forces at work in and around its own great conurbations and both loses and gains workers. It is a fact in any case that nearly two-thirds of the population of England and Wales lives in six major conurbations: of these, four are in the North—Manchester, Merseyside, West Yorkshire, the North East. Despite the difficulties under which the North is labouring a hasty judgment about its decline would be unwise: nor could any government permit it and survive.

This does not alter the fact that the growth in and around the metropolitan area has been phenomenal. The area bounded roughly by a line from the Wash to the Solent contains about one quarter of the country's population: it has increased its population—and its jobs—at a rate round about 50 per cent *above* national average. Of the million new jobs created in the last ten years, 400,000 have been in London and the South East. In the heart of the capital jobs are still growing at the rate of 20,000 a year, despite government efforts to check office growth and encourage administrative and industrial decentralisation or redistribution. The population of this south-eastern triangle is 'expected to grow by 2½ million in the next twenty years and by at least 4 million by the end of the century. In view of the steadily rising birth rate therefore, total population in this region is likely to turn out to be even greater. In terms of housing it means building 2½ Birminghams in the next twenty years, or 4 new Birminghams by the end of the century.'[2] Many years ago H. G. Wells and other social reformers spoke of their fear that London would simply spread south till it reached the sea, and asked for a reform of London government to cope with it. Now the fear is that the midland and south-eastern conurbations marching to meet each other in the diocese of St Albans will ultimately form 'one huge built-up zone 50 miles wide and 250 miles from north to south'.[3] Experts agree that if Britain ultimately joins the Common Market the conurbanisation of the South East will be greatly accelerated.

[1] 10 December 1962.

[2] Mr John Greve, Lecturer in Social Administration at the London School of Economics, in a lecture on 'Housing in London' given to Southwark Diocesan Conference, 12 June 1963, and in a letter to me. Cf. also *London: Employment, Housing, Land*, the joint white paper of the Ministry of Housing and Local Government and Minister for Welsh Affairs, Cmd 1952, 1963, to which this chapter is also indebted.

[3] *The Times*, 10 December 1962.

To speak in such large, grand terms is apt to stun rather than stimulate unless one gets down to actual cases of what this increase means in the next few years. To take examples almost at random, Oxford diocese, which lies half in and half out of the south-eastern triangle, has to face population changes of which the following Table III gives ten examples only out of twenty-three expected centres of population change between 1961 and 1971+. I have omitted any figures at present confidential. It will be noted that many of the towns listed below were once small market and county towns which are now in the process of becoming cities (by American definition a central area of 50,000 population: there are now 157 such in Britain).

Table III. Planned Population Changes: Oxford Diocese

Towns	Existing population	Planned population (1971+)
Oxfordshire		
Banbury	20,000	40,000
Bicester	6,000	10,000
Thame	4,000	8,000
Witney	9,000	15,000
Berkshire		
Abingdon	15,000	21,000
Bracknell	21,000	54,000 (*extension of new town*)
Ascot	15,000	20,000
Sandhurst-Crowthorne	13,000	16–20,000
Buckinghamshire		
Aylesbury	25,000	42,000
Bletchley	16,500	24,000

The overall total increase the diocese can expect in about ten years for the twenty-three areas is 207,500. For all these new people not only the local authorities but the Church, too, must make varied and complicated provision.

We can carry the story northwards. The West Midlands conurbation centres on Birmingham and Wolverhampton. It both gains and loses population. The natural local area of overflow is the rest of the West Midlands and schemes for the reception of the overspill have been announced for Dawley, Redditch, Daventry and Worcester, and some smaller towns in Staffordshire. Table IV shows how the centre is expected to lose population and the overspill areas to gain it. There will be an overall gain, but a new distribution.

Table IV. Expected Population Changes in Birmingham Area

Area	1961	1981
1. West Midlands conurbation	2,353,000	2,260,000
2. The rest of the West Midlands	1,576,000	2,340,000
Total	3,929,000	4,600,000

The North Merseyside conurbation covers greater Liverpool and its hinterland, and the South Merseyside is the Wirral peninsula. Between 1961 and 1981 the natural increase is expected to add 317,000 people to North and 55,300 to South Merseyside. Planned provision for overspill will send 70,000 people from Liverpool, Bootle, and Kirkby into Widnes, Ellesmere Port, Huyton, Whiston and elsewhere in the next seven years. The effect for the Merseyside conurbations over twenty years is expected to be as follows:

Table V. Expected Population Changes in Liverpool Area

Area	1961	1981
1. North Merseyside	1,206,300	1,332,000
2. South Merseyside	407,500	524,800
Total	1,613,800	1,856,800

The Manchester conurbation area (technically the S.E. Lancashire and N.E. Cheshire conurbation) expects to repeat the pattern of a thinning centre and of rising population on the periphery. Here is how the area is expected to change:

Table VI. Expected Population Changes in Manchester Area

Area	1961	1981
1. Central (Manchester and Salford)	815,100	676,000
2. Northern periphery	1,332,000	1,439,000
3. Southern periphery	395,900	477,000
Total	2,543,000	2,592,000

It is hardly necessary to say that a similar story could be told of all the dioceses fringing on the metropolitan ones and of several in the Midlands and North. Chelmsford, St Albans, Oxford, Guildford, and

Rochester dioceses all include areas of planned overspill and natural migration from Central London. The inner areas of the counties of London and Middlesex are losing population, partly by housing policies designed to reduce the density per acre and partly by a seemingly irresistible tide which forces middle and lower income groups to move even farther out as the rents and prices of homes and flats in the centre soar out of their reach. London in particular (but Birmingham and Manchester also, as we have seen) presents the spectacle of a centre thinning out and of growing congestion at the periphery of its vast metropolitan zone. Housing for those who work in the metropolis extends forty to fifty miles from the centre. The London County Council is prepared to finance the buying of houses by its citizens within a radius of fifty miles of the centre.

These demographic changes have produced a new sort of homeless. Though the *Census 1961, England and Wales, County Report, London*, shows that 80 per cent of Londoners pay rent, in the County of London alone some 20,000 dwellings a year come out of rent control, about half of which are then sold. Thousands of houses are pulled down every year for slum clearance (7,500 in 1961 in the County of London). Mr John Greve has made the important point that the privately rented sector of housing grows smaller each year and competition for it grows more intense. The effect on rents can be foreseen. The result is a new and growing group of homeless, not, as in the 'thirties, of down-and-outs, but of young married couples with two or three young children where the husband is earning round about average wages and is not yet eligible for a council house and incapable of a deposit on a new house. For such a group the new rents are out of the question even if accommodation which will accept young children can be found. It is significant that the County Report speaks of young married couples moving out and single young persons, who can live in one room, moving in.

JOBS AND TRANSPORT

Population redistribution in the great conurbations does not often mean, unfortunately, the redistribution of jobs as well as housing, except perhaps where new towns are developed on the fringes. The centripetal power of London over jobs grows year by year. Nearly 1·5 million people come into London each day, most of them to jobs. Despite increasing use of private cars and motor cycles (85,000 a day in the rush hour, a 46 per cent increase in six years), the vast majority come by public transport (1·2 million per day by London Transport, an increase of 73,000 since 1955). Nearly two-thirds of these voyagers through acute discomfort arrive between 8.30 and

9.15 every morning: transport sometimes nearly reaches total stoppage through saturation. We pay an appalling and increasing human price for the peculiar centripetal power of the Central London areas, where office floor space has increased by 32 per cent since pre-war days and looks like increasing by nearly as much again in the next ten years, despite attempts at restriction.

In truth, side by side with a new industrial revolution there is a new transport revolution: the symbol of it is Dr Beeching's plan for reorganising the railway system by cutting it back to its axial lines out of the metropolis and between the great conurbations. Railways no longer have the monopoly they possessed even fifty years ago. Traffic on the inter-urban roads, which increased for private cars by 8·9 per cent per annum and for all motor vehicles by 6·6 per cent between 1959 and 1961, is expected to increase over the whole decade between 1960 and 1970 at nearly the same annual rate. A Ministry of Transport report[1] says it expects an increase of total road traffic of 60 or 70 per cent by 1970. Beyond that it cannot prophesy, because traffic conditions may act by then as a disincentive to road travel. The report says that 'quite small additions to an overloaded system can produce disproportionate damage'. It hardly dares calculate the cost in terms of destruction of amenity and environment imposed on those living and working in areas of great and increasing traffic congestion.

THE IMPERSONAL SOCIETY

The new and sometimes culturally disastrous patterns of life imposed by the urban growth, and the increasing mobility the various travel facilities make possible, led Dr Gibson Winter to write that, 'The sundering of communities of production and consumption may well prove to be the most important single change produced by the industrial revolution.'[2] The old natural communities, in which the places where people went to work were by and large close to the places where they lived, are gone. They linger on in some way in village and market or county town, but even these tend to become dormitories for workers of every sort who bus or motor-cycle or go by car to the nearest great work centre; or, if that is too far, they lose their younger population to the nearest car plant or chemical works. We have therefore to see the social changes not only in terms of growth and redistribution of population, but of a changing way of

[1] *The Transport Needs of Great Britain in the Next Twenty Years*, 1963, p. 15.

[2] *The Suburban Captivity of the Churches*, New York, 1961, p. 60.

life of which the main feature is urbanisation and conurbanisation. Dr John Barron Mays wrote of the 4½ million new homes built in new towns and housing estates since the war:

What has been taking place, and is, indeed, still going on, is nothing less than a gigantic nation-wide social experiment, involving whole neighbourhoods and vast populations on the move and under constraint of enforced change. The happiness and even the mental health of hundreds of thousands of people depend on the way in which these large-scale migrations take place.[1]

One is reminded, by the sheer scale of the movement Dr Mays is describing, of Hendrick Kraemer's judgment:

Outstanding traits of modern society are loneliness and massification. Both belong together. They imply an irrepressible drift towards virtual or actual nihilism, inner emptiness and loss of real sense of direction.[2]

The old clear distinction between town and country—in the sense dear to schoolmasters who set essays asking, 'Do you prefer living in the town or the country?'—has gone, perhaps for ever. There is not even the abrupt landscape change there once was: the motorways and their signs carry the town to the ends of the island. One can no longer speak of the city, the ring of suburbs, *then* the country, though this was possible until the predominance of the motor-car. Now there is the emptying city centre: then zones around it with railway termini, bus and coach stations, road flyovers and one-way networks, decayed residential and new industrial zones all indiscriminately mixed; then the suburbs of the late nineteenth and early twentieth centuries; then new suburbs in plots and patches which are largely enclaves decided by income brackets; then areas which are indeterminate, sometimes housing, sometimes new industry reaching along highways and motorways to dormitory villages and feeder satellite towns set in a still surviving countryside but hardly part of it—and then on to the next conurbation sweeping out to meet it! This is the image of universal subtopia of the Midlands and South East of England.

Dr Gibson Winter wrote: 'Market, shop, office, store and factory are spheres of impersonal dealings and manipulations; but a person's social identity—who he is in the human community of persons, *as a person*—is rooted primarily in the residential sphere of personal

[1] 'New Hope in Newtown', *New Society* (No. 47), 22 August 1963. Incidentally, Kirkby St Chad is the largest C of E parish in the two provinces—52,177 population.

[2] *A Theology of the Laity*, 1958, p. 178. He goes on to give a warning: 'The direct approach to these deep-seated diseases has no great promise, because the de-religionising of vast sectors of people in modern society has deep-seated and long-range historical causes.'

association.'[1] But in the conurbation that sphere is going to be a suburb, and a suburb and more particularly a housing estate (whether of high or low income bracket) can be an 'insulated enclave', in Dr Winter's phrase, a homogeneous, claustrophobic area in which people have much the same income, interests and limitations, which in a cultural sense dies of inbreeding, and certainly lacks the fertilising influence of constant personal mixing with other social groups, classes, occupations and interests, something which naturally occurred in village or market town or ancient city. 'The most obvious illustration of this commonplace is the stripping of leadership from many areas of the central cities.'[2] And not simply from the central areas. The process is said to have its lesson for the Church in this sense: 'The metropolis is inclusive. Churches that identify with local areas become exclusive and anti-metropolitan.'[3]

There are three areas, I would argue, which suffer most from conurbation: (1) the decayed inner areas, (2) the new housing estate, but particularly the council estate and the lower income group estate, (3) the village or small town, which is swallowed up.

DECAYED INNER AREAS

The decayed inner areas, once packed, slummy but lively areas, like pre-war Poplar or the nineteenth-century Elephant and Castle and the Old Kent Road, or the Scotswood Road district at Newcastle upon Tyne, the Moor in Sheffield, lose at some point their indigenous populations through slum clearance, bombing, general decay or the spread of industry and commerce. *Family and Kinship in the East End of London*[4] tells much of the story of what happens humanly speaking when the older inhabitants move out.

The area shedding its settled older group suffers a sea change. Decaying old property is taken over by coloured people or other migrants, or in solid Victorian areas gets chopped into flats and bed-sitters. A new population moves in—students, immigrants, young married couples without children who cannot find other housing, single young people from the provinces at their first metropolitan jobs, all of whom will presently float away and never develop a sense of belonging. It is in these decayed downtown centres that we find many historic old churches from which the *raison d'être* has departed, like old hulks silted up in a bay from which the sea has receded.

[1] *The Suburban Captivity of the Churches*, p. 24.

[2] Op. cit., p. 65. [3] Ibid., p. 28.

[4] Michael Young and Peter Willmott, 1957.

HOUSING ESTATES

A young witness to the Albemarle Committee spoke of his housing estate as a graveyard with lights. Unfair though this is to the town planner who seeks to combine low-density housing with gardens and amenities and contour building, we see exactly what the young witness meant. His estate had neither the natural life and justification of a town centre nor the plushy prestige of a well-to-do neighbourhood with Jaguars in the garages and swimming baths on the lawns. Outside the home it had the sense of emptiness—probably no one actually *chose* to live there, though many perhaps (and with reason) came to love it when a sense of neighbourhood grew: it seems agreed that there is less neurosis and unhappiness and itch to be gone in a low-density housing estate than in blocks of flats. Even so it may be impossible to create a new permanent community if the housing estate is preserved as the dormitory for the overspill of the neighbouring conurbation to which it belongs. Such is the case, for example, at St Helier Estate, Morden, in Surrey, which belongs to the LCC. No child born on the estate can ever marry and settle in it, following in the footsteps of his parents, for the simple but dismal reason that being born in Surrey he cannot qualify for London housing. St Helier can never have its own second generation inhabitants.

What the housing estate can mean at its (possible) worst is described by Mervyn Jones in *Potbank*, a study of the Potteries which mentions *inter alia* that 'one-tenth of the city's area is described as derelict'.

> Bentilee is the largest of the outlying estates. It consists of hundred of red brick houses, all exactly alike. One long street—the numbers go up to 550—is the backbone, and the other streets branch off it at regular intervals. I suppose there must have been some sort of plan, but the effect is as if the Council had started to cater for the current waiting list and added a bit more whenever it had a suitable number of names. You can tell when the houses were built by their colour: those nearest the city are darker, those further along are bright pink. At the very end, a road had been thrust into the countryside and was waiting for its houses. Because of the hilly ground, there is some open space; but it has been completely neglected. Scrub grass, nettles and thistles grow up to the walls of the houses, on land which is dusty in summer and no doubt muddy in winter. A dirty stream, blocked in places with rubbish and rotting vegetation, wanders through the estate. There are no trees. . . .[1]

A picture of this sort could have prompted the young man's bitter remark to the Albemarle Committee.

[1] *Potbank*, London, 1961, p. 86.

However, it would be improper merely to speak of the poorest estates. New towns, despite growing pains, can count imaginative and social successes. Even estates not numbered as new towns (with all the prestige and concentrated effort such a status brings) can claim victories. Dr John Barron Mays, in the *New Society* article from which I have already quoted, describes what happened in Kirkby, a new estate on the outskirts of Liverpool fed by slum dwellers from, among other places, the Crown Street district of Liverpool. Kirkby has passed from being a tiny rural village to the proportions of an entire New Town—though without its status—in less than a decade. But it has become a place of hope and confidence, Dr Mays explains, and social and family life, far from being denuded, have probably been enriched, not simply by new amenities but by a growing sense of communal pride.

The churches clearly play a dominant role in the developing community life of the neighbourhood. . . . Undoubtedly one of the reasons why the religious association and practice of the ex-Crown Streeters was so satisfactorily maintained was that the churches themselves, were, in the main, ready for the invasion and got the nucleus of their organisation in being *before* all the new population arrived. In particular, the Roman Catholic churches evidenced considerable foresight and vitality. Not only has the Roman Catholic Church concentrated on building the necessary schools and chapels to meet the residents' needs, they have gone much further by establishing the necessary halls and clubs so that the parish has become as much a focus of the social life of the neighbourhoods as for the more narrowly religious activities. Immense energy has been devoted to this achievement and funds have been raised on an impressive scale. The Church of England has also, though at a somewhat slower pace, striven to meet the needs of its people at all levels. In 1963–4, for example, they are to put up an entirely new Youth Centre for the use of the original parish church, St Chad's.

Had the Catholic Church not been ready for the waves of new arrivals who descended upon Kirkby from its inception in 1952 to its virtual completion in the early 1960s social life might well have broken down entirely. No less than half the entire population is Catholic.[1]

There are lessons for all the churches in that story.

'VERTICAL RECEPTACLES'

If horizontal housing has its problems, so has the vertical. Blocks of flats seem the only low-density answer to land shortage in the central areas, but they break up the existing community pattern

[1] 'New Hope in Newtown', *New Society* (No. 47), 22 August 1963.

without necessarily providing a new one. What an ordinary back street does is to clothe an area with houses. The house doors open on to the street, the best rooms look out on it and on their neighbours across the way. Everyone living in the street, old or young, passes and repasses endlessly through it on their many kinds of business, and children play in it. The small street in which houses are close together becomes to its inhabitants what the quadrangle is to the college, a common area which all share, but carrying no obligations except those of friendliness and neighbourliness. When a block of flats is built what we have really done is to set a street on end. But it is now a cul-de-sac, not a thoroughfare. Hardly anyone ever goes the whole length of the street in the sky. The common space of the street is gone: other blocks are usually too far away to form with it a common wall round a common area. It is perhaps most revealing that we can never easily use the word 'house' for a pile of flats. Our vernacular word is the hard unemotive 'block'. A poem by Berthold Brecht speaks of such blocks as 'vertical receptacles'. The experience and tasks of a parish priest walking down a village street or down the back street of a suburb are far different from one scaling in anonymity the vertical streets of flatland. In the one he is the man among neighbours, the pastor in the midst of his flock. In the other he is the man on the door knocker who would not trouble to be there at all, up on the sixth floor, if he wasn't selling something, like the man with encyclopaedias.

THE VILLAGE

The village or small country town swamped by overspill from the conurbations must not be forgotten. It is fighting a losing battle: if too near a conurbation it will be overwhelmed, if too far away its population may decline. In the past it preserved for us, and still sometimes does, the mixed community—gentry, farmers, professional folk, shopkeepers, labourers, ne'er-do-wells, mechanics, farriers, chapel pastors—which provided varied local leadership and with which the Church always seemed happiest and at its socially most useful. The doubling or trebling of its population in perhaps as little as ten years by private and council building completely transforms it socially: the old clubs and societies and meetings and village enterprises like amateur dramatics, flower shows, charities, Christmas parties for the children, based on face-to-face relations of a primary community sometimes remain as part of the life of a privileged inner group from which 'estate' people are excluded, or else they break down in a gallant effort to be inclusive. The area tends to lose its *raison d'être* as a community and perhaps finally accepts its role as a passive secondary community, the life of which is really sucked in to the metropolis ten miles away. Nothing is more certain than that scores and scores of such old and once independent communities will disappear into spreading conurbations: not just in the South East, but wherever a conurbation is to be found.

OTHER SOCIAL CHANGES

There are other social changes which must be remembered: for instance, the rise of new zones for the retired, mostly in the South. Their concentration in certain areas creates special problems. An internal memorandum[1] of the Board for Social Responsibility said:

> The survivors of the late Victorian and Edwardian large families are still with us (their lives prolonged by increased medical and social care) to create the 'problem of old people'. One in seven people in England and Wales will be aged 65 and over by 1975. It is estimated that by 1980 we shall have 9 million pensioners, making the very high proportion of 17·4 per cent of the population. (It is already about 15 per cent.) Economically these depend for their livelihood on the wealth created by the generation below them, in their working years—which generation constitutes a *small* proportion of the population, because it is the product of the restricted family era, reduced still further by the second war.

Older seaside resorts always seemed well adapted in their life and institutions to the summer flood of visitors, but the transformation of small seaside villages and hamlets for six months of the year by holiday and caravan camps, whose visitors will outnumber local residents by as much as ten to one, puts the life of these little communities right out of balance. Ancient communities can be revived or destroyed by new motorways and by-passes.

In personal living we cannot forget the well-documented changes in standards and attitudes brought by rising general affluence (personal incomes have doubled since 1952) and supported by the provisions of the welfare state. All who remember the 'thirties are struck by the changes for the good these have brought to our society. It seems both unwise and unjust to brush them into a general condemnation as materialistic. We have to note the greater freedom, greater candour, and greater economic independence of young people, particularly working-class young people,[2] but to remember that the working class has benefited least from the educational revolution brought about by Mr Butler's Act of 1944, and that for them today educational deprivation turns out to be

[1] *Social Changes and their Significance for the Strategy of the Church*, 1962.

[2] See *The Youth Service in England and Wales, 1960*, Cmd. 1929.

another sort of social deprivation, a fast one 'they' have pulled, to which we have not yet learnt the answer. We have to accept a new balance between the members of the sexes. The old 'surplus' of women has gone. For the first time in history as far as we know 'males now outnumber females in our population up to 30; in the age group 15 to 30, this excess now amounts to 2½ per cent, and it is expected to rise to 5 per cent by the end of the century'.[1] The spinster-of-necessity, devoted to good works, upon whom the Church has so much depended, is likely to disappear. We have to note that earlier marriage, earlier and smaller families, smaller and more efficient houses, have changed the basic institution of society, the family. Married women may have twenty or thirty years left *after* they have brought up their children in which to serve society: during the years the children are growing up they may still work, and do, in increasing numbers. A new and dominant figure in the social pattern is the young husband earning about £1,000 a year, saddled with a thirty-year mortgage for the semi-detached he is buying, paying off weekly for his furniture, saving for a second-hand car and too preoccupied with painting the window frames and decorating the bathroom at week-ends to go to church. He is a changed husband socially, spending more of his spare time helping his wife, who may also have to work, than his father ever did, and much less often going out to the pub and the league football games. But he may have a degree, or a higher national certificate, and read the *New Scientist*, and he will get promoted and in five years' time motor his family across the Continent for a three-week holiday. His great-grandfather never left his village, his grandfather went on trips on the Golden Eagle to Margate, his father belonged to a youth organisation which camped and hiked on the hills of England. The 'Orpingtons' of England are full of such able, aspiring, honourable but limited young fathers.

PATTERNS OF GROUP BEHAVIOUR

In speaking of such a young man we have left the field of demographic patterns and moved over to patterns of individual behaviour. Yet at the same time we have identified the young man as a member of a technological group in society. Paradoxically, one has only to speak of individual behaviour to thrust into relief the importance of group patterns even to the most individualistic of men.

The greybeard who goes to the park to play football with small boys or the little boy who spends his evenings in the public libraries

[1] *Social Changes and their Significance for the Strategy of the Church.*

reading up the law of torts is behaving out of his age group, and would be regarded as eccentric unless he were a member of another group which specifically authorised such behaviour—the greybeard is a Scouter or professional coach, perhaps; the small boy is swotting as part of a school quiz team. Behaviour outside one's group is by no means impossible but it needs a strong or obsessive personality. But what *is* one's group? In fact, we are members of many. Even the small boy is a member of many—of his class, itself a member of a larger group, the school; of his family; of his street friends; of the church; of the choir; of the quiz team. Some such groups are central and permanent, others peripheral and ephemeral. Yet each group tends to be dominant during the moments he is a member of it. His father is a member of his family, of his work group, of his recreational group, of his trade union or professional society, of his educational group, his speech group and so on. He, like his son, moves from one age group to another with his contemporaries, and for each age group certain patterns of behaviour are given or not given, though they continually change by influences improperly understood. The economist might speak of the influence of a man's work, of earnings and spendings on his group-behaviour pattern, the sociologist of the influences of school and speech and neighbourhood. But quite often what appears to overcome the inertia of one group, its resistance to change, is the impact of another more dynamic group. When we urgently want to change or defend certain things we form a society to do so. The society is a pressure group. But not all groups are pressure groups. Some are natural groups—the family, the age group—some like the nation with a common frontier and language, or an ethnic group, come close to natural groups or are based on them. The church in its primitive form is a pressure group intent on change. When it achieved the conversion of an empire and became responsible for the pattern of life of a people it became very much the natural group in which conformity to social usage is strong: the tension between the church as the explosive group within society and the church as supporting, protecting, 'establishing' the society of which it is part is always there. It simply becomes more acute when the social order is disturbed or corrupted or the church declines. The pressure group tends to be small, congregational, fervent. The natural groups large, sometimes vaguely defined, inarticulate but nevertheless deciding social usages and exerting inertial pressure on their members to conform.

It would seem that the Church is still the focus of a natural group in a natural rural community, that in the town it is a congregational group and that in the suburb it plays an ambivalent role. We can best understand its role in the natural community by looking at the great conurbations where the local community has almost vanished and if there is a natural community it is the whole metropolitan area itself. Here the resident male is a member of several groups, geographically and in other ways distinct—he works in one place, lives in another, enjoys physical recreation in a third, entertainment or cultural recreation in a fourth, goes to a pub or club or evening institute in a fifth. His community is broken down into a series of separate but interlocking functional groups and institutions. The church which he attends is one among many of such specialist groups: it provides for his religious needs. But like other groups it is divisive in that it adds another dimension to his life which needs time, energy and planning if it is to be enjoyed. To all these group activities there is a contractual aspect. He *joins* his football club, or his trade union. He is under contract to his employer who specifies his place and times of work. He *elects* when to go to the pub or a dance: no particular social usage compels it. His life therefore is fragmented: the satisfaction of its fragments demands a series of conscious decisions sometimes of an intellectual order, for, as it were, nothing in this situation is given, not even finally his job of work. At any rate, mere social usage is not enough: it may not even exist.

THE FAMILY

The family, however, is not a fragmenting group but a unifying group: it is at the centre of a handful of related lives which strike out towards work, recreation, social and religious commitments. Each member of the family above infancy will have his or her star of lines of commitment, and each will be different, the mother, particularly if she goes to work, the schoolboy, the schoolgirl, the sibling at work. It would seem natural in these circumstances to cut down the lines of commitment before life becomes too confused or exacting and to concentrate on the family, which is the centre of personal life; on the work group, which is obligatory; and on the recreational groups which are often closely related to family (holidays, car outings) and work (clubs, savings). 'If there is a danger in this, it is of an inward-looking absorption with the family, and an almost pathological fixation on "inter-personal relationships" such as has bemused some sections of American society.'[1]

It is also true that each additional line of commitment is an added expense: there is a point beyond which the means available limit loyalties against a man's will. Possibly everything the conurban resident does beyond his central commitment to family and work has

[1] *Social Changes and their Significance for the Strategy of the Church.*

the air of being contrived and easily terminable when it becomes a burden or interest is lost—evening institutes, trade union branch meetings, amateur dramatics, tennis, Church, the lot. The Rev. Conor K. Ward, writing in another connexion, produced the right phrase for conurban men and women: 'They might be said to have manifested a sense of involvement rather than a sense of belongingness.'[1] He also said that an individual seems to be able to sustain only a certain number of social relations. The Church appears as one of a number of organisations competing on the periphery for the conurbanised man's time, loyalty, money. But nothing appears changed for him if he refuses participation, except that to himself his life is thankfully simplified. He can still, as we have seen, believe himself Christian and Anglican. No powerful group social usage sends him to church in England, though it appears to do so among the middle classes of the United States: nor does some great metropolitan loyalty or sense of belonging urge him to go as a matter of duty: the Church does not appear to him as the heart of the metropolis as it so often appears the heart and the soul of a village, the disappearance of which would impoverish life there.

It is, of course, more possible in urban than in rural society for a family to shrink within itself and to refuse all commitments or loyalties or contacts except the basic ones and otherwise to rest upon the impersonal and anonymous elements in city life. It is easier. The newspapers and the milk will be on the doorstep, television keeps contact with the world, shopping can be as impersonal and wordless as the delivery of the post. It was Durkheim who saw in the growth of this impersonalisation a kind of *anomie*, that is a state of mind in which people are consumed with a meaningless anxiety; in which they feel themselves isolated, but they know not from what, and lack purpose because their condition of life does not appear to be one over which purpose can have any influence. It seems to affect deeply those who are widowed or old in cities and have lost purpose through loneliness: but the young and alone can be just as deeply affected by this contemporary form of medieval *accidie*. For the old, the Church is often the only 'club' open to them still. 'Pastoral strategy would require that ordinands and their pastoral allies in social and parish work should be prepared for an exceptionally demanding ministry to the aged, for the rest of this century.'[2]

[1] *Priest and People*, p. 110.

[2] *Social Changes and their Significance for the Strategy of the Church.*

THE COMMUNITY

In the village or market town, which is still in some sense a natural community, the role of the Church seems far different. The church itself is often at the centre of lines of commitment which stretch out through church day school and Sunday school, church hall with its many social functions, fêtes, outings, parties, charitable efforts, even protests against traffic menace. Vestries and rural district councils are often pale shadows compared with the real leadership exercised by rector and vicar, the village schoolmaster, churchwardens who are farmers or gentry, prominent citizens, bank managers, hotel owners, and where no local effort or enterprise seems complete without the vicar's name on it. Indeed, it often begins in his study and when it flowers outside, there he is in the chair. In such conditions, where many must work close to where they live and even if of independent means must find much of their social life within the parish, it is socially as well as religiously meaningful to be a member of the Church and to attend its services. Attendance becomes an expression of belonging. The great words of the Book of Common Prayer really speak to an 'us' which has a geographical and social unity upon whom the Lord's mercy and blessing may be entreated to fall. The meaningful 'us' is usually absent in cities: it would be easier to feel if a visual image could be attached to the 'us'. But to try to do so about the swarming streets is to induce vertigo.

It would seem that the suburb has elements both of the village and the city. When the city predominates, as in decaying inner suburbs, sucking life out of areas which once possessed a sense of neighbourhood, then all that has been said of the conurban collapse makes sense. In other areas, particularly outer ones, the suburb still plays a formative role. New houses, new schools, new roads, new institutions are springing up. There is a sense of something creative going on of which the resident is part and of which the Kirkby story reminds us. He may have the exhilaration of moving up in his income bracket, and so experience a release of energies. He may seek out that to which he ought to belong to mark his new status. It might be both the Church and the golf club. The housing estate, more contrived, less a matter of choice, initially sullenly entered, may nevertheless itself move into the stage where it elicits a sense of pride and belongingness. The Church as a new outlet for energies and as an important element, sometimes the only element, in the formation of a community out of a collection of dwellings, reaps a harvest in the shape of goodwill and of congregations. However, there is no single kind of suburb: there are those which are social-class enclaves, collections of people of one income group turning their backs on the metropolis, 'insulated residential communities' as Dr Winter calls them, where 'neighbourhood comes to mean an island of homogeneous people'. There are suburbs which because of their remoteness from the metropolis where everyone works are deserts during the day and streets of anonymity behind shut doors at night. There are others where the conurbation floods over the old natural village community, presenting the incumbent with three or four new housing areas, each sharply distinguished socially and by income levels from the rest, and all unwilling to mix. The incumbent must seek to mould them into one Christian community against the resistance of all. What then happens is that the Church often seems the Church 'for the others, not for us': it is identified with a particular class, or way of speech and dress.

It is important to remember that as the tides of building flow outwards from the great conurbations the problems we have just examined will be multiplied. More rural parishes will be engulfed, more town centres will decay because their amenities decay and their *raison d'être* disappears, more suburban parishes will struggle to reach the new thousands pouring into their estates.

I conclude by saying that this discussion of social changes has been of necessity brief. It is necessarily tentative, too, for one of the hardest tasks is to see the permanent shapes crystallising in the society on the move around one. It was important to concentrate on demographic factors, for these present in the boldest way the problems the second Industrial Revolution presents to the Church. It will be seen presently, from what incumbents have reported to me, how sharply they feel themselves faced with so many of the social problems I have touched upon. The deployment or redeployment of the clergy, assuming it is possible, only makes sense if it is undertaken in the light of the considerable social changes transforming England. As late as the outbreak of the Second World War, England seemed still a strong, even rigidly traditional society in which the class and role of a citizen at death was largely determined by his class at birth and the social milieu and schooling of his childhood. It is a socially fluid society to which a traditionally inflexible church organisation, fashioned for more stable times, has now to adapt itself.

Graph 1. Easter Communicants

The heavy line shows Easter communicant figures per 1,000 of the population, diocese by diocese, from MQ figures. It follows closely the lighter line plotted from Easter communicant figures per 1,000 of the population *over* 15 given in Table 64, Col. 12, of *Facts and Figures, 1962*. The dioceses are arranged in population density order. The graph shows clearly how pastoral results decline as population density rises.

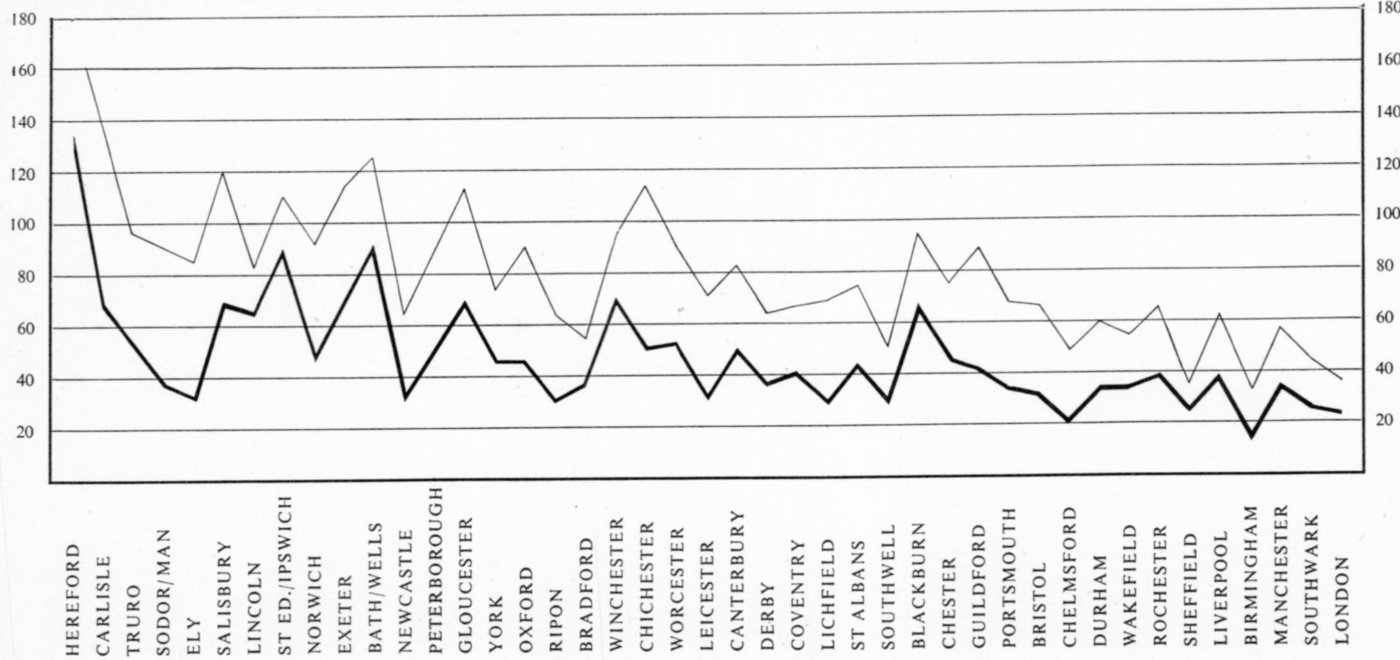

CHAPTER IV

Social Change in the Parishes

It is fortunately possible to move from a somewhat large and general survey of social changes to their actual impact on the parishes of the two provinces. One of the first undertakings of this inquiry was the dispatch of a Main Questionnaire (MQ) to a 10 per cent sample of the parishes of the two provinces. The sample was prepared by the Statistical Unit of the Central Board of Finance. The text of the Questionnaire is given in the Summary of Evidence, p. 228 f, together with a breakdown of such replies as lent themselves to statistical treatment. All the important findings will be discussed presently, but the point must be made here that some of the material drawn from the replies was both unexpected and highly important. The MQ aimed at what was really a 'work-study' of the parish priest's life. It asked him for details of the weight and extent of his parochial cure, and what help he had from the laity and other clergy in pursuit of it. It asked for a breakdown of his Sunday duties and his weekday activities. It tried to elicit what were the pressures upon his daily life, for what tasks he wanted help and for what spiritual and pastoral exercises he needed more time. In asking these questions what I had in mind was to arrive at a picture of the professional life of the clergy in order that it might be contrasted with the work-pattern of other professions. If men were to be deployed or redeployed it was important to discover where they were overworked or underworked and if possible why, and how they themselves judged their situation. It was not initially my intention to subject evidence such as this to a statistical analysis: I had expected it to be too personal and idiosyncratic, a guide to my thinking rather than evidence demonstrating a significant pattern. Yet the evidence of pattern presently became overwhelming and the report presents it statistically as well as in other ways.

PASTORAL RESULTS AND POPULATION DENSITY

A study of *Facts and Figures about the Church of England 1962*, reveals that the pastoral results of dioceses stand in inverse relation to the density of population. The greater the density of population the poorer the results (per 1,000 of the population) on the whole, in baptismal, confirmation and Easter communicant figures. With some important exceptions the table of baptismal figures on p. 18

Graph 2. Sunday Attendances and Confirmations

The graph contrasts by dioceses, Average Sunday Attendances per 1,000 pop. (1962) (heavy line) with Annual Confirmations per 10,000 pop. (1958) (light line). It shows that in ten years confirmations can recreate the congregation all over again, but that the wastage must be very high; in ten years roughly each church will lose as many communicants as it gains. Again, pastoral results fall as population rises.

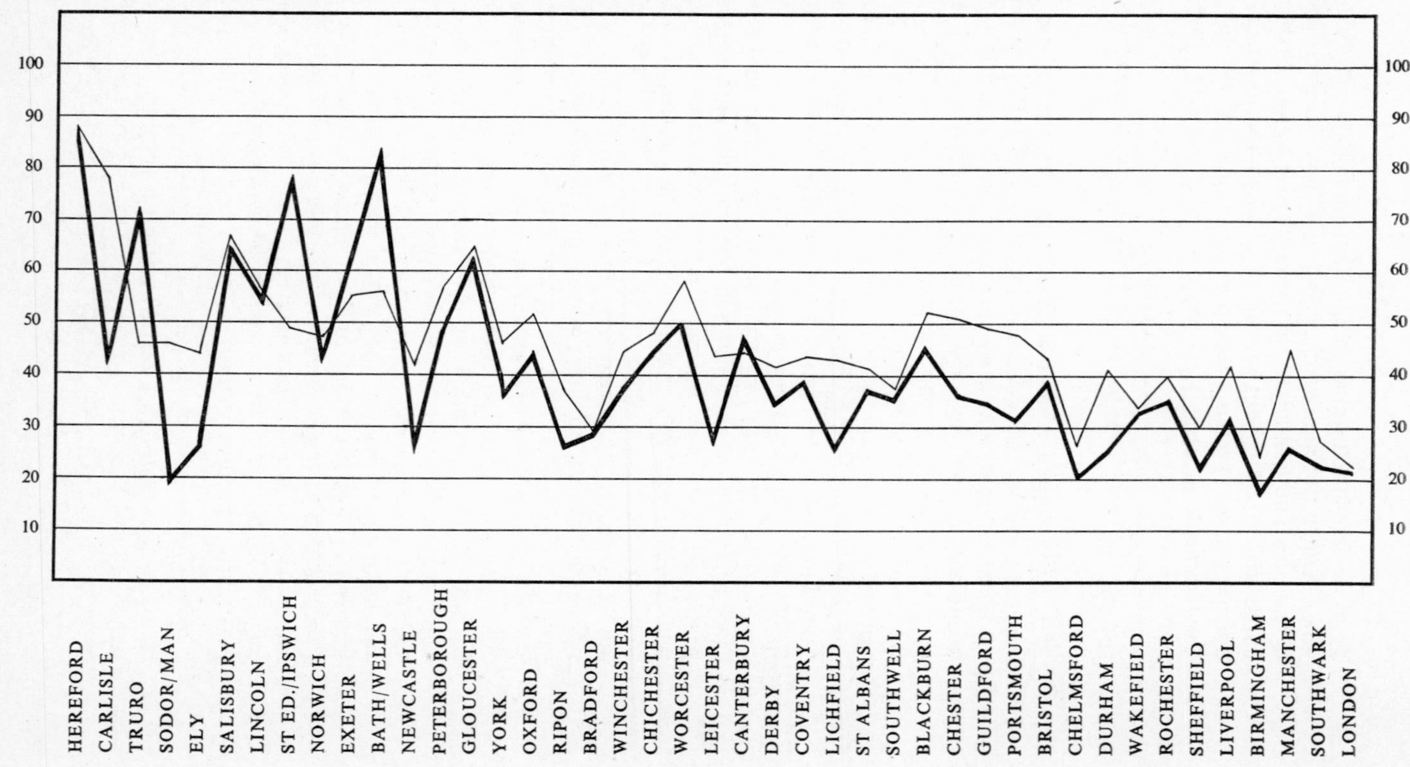

confirms this. What so strikingly emerged from the analysis of such Main Questionnaire returns as could be handled statistically is that time and time again a correlation inexorably established itself, even between such apparently personal matters as serious reading and population density. The strongest example of this correlation appears in average Sunday attendances which the Main Questionnaire asked for: in these, for example, Hereford, with the lowest density, touches 1 in 9 of the population every Sunday; London, with the highest density, 1 in 46. When these figures had been totalled per diocese they were averaged against other figures—population, number of churches and number of clergy—and then confirmed quite remarkably the expected correlation. The graph opposite relates two sets of figures, diocese per diocese. The dioceses are arranged in population density rank according to *Facts and Figures about the Church of England 1962.* The first set (heavy line) are the average Sunday attendances (ASA) per diocese per 1,000 population from MQ returns and the second set are confirmation figures per 10,000 population of 15 and over from *Facts and Figures* (Table 61). The two lines fall with a striking similarity and regularity as population density increases. Not only do the figures confirm each other but they show that a church, on this basis, re-creates its congregation in ten years. But if in ten years it has brought in confirmands equal in number to the original congregation, it has also lost communicant members to the same degree. Were it not for this steady erosion every congregation, though losing perhaps one to two members per 100 by death and removal each year, would steadily grow. Other graphs tell similar stories. The total result of these statistical studies can be expressed simply and strongly: the greater the density of population, the higher the failure rates of the Church, the more acute the problems of the clergy. The areas of highest density are the areas of the greatest missionary need in the Church.

EVIDENCE OF SOCIAL CHANGE

Because I viewed the Main Questionnaire as a professional inquiry, not a statistical one, nor even a social one, I asked no questions about the social background of the parishes in the sample. I soon found, however, that many clergy were most deeply involved in and troubled by the social changes in their parishes and were giving me accounts of them which bore out most remarkably the statistical conclusions already described. Page 4 of MQ, for example, asked about parish plans, what was growing and what was not, and Question 32 said 'Most parishes seem unique. Do please add sheets to explain the parish situation and/or your life and work if the questionnaire appears inadequate in any way.' It invited extended answers, and got them, and I decided to classify them.

It was obvious that mostly under Question 32, but often in response to the whole of p. 4, incumbents were reporting:

1. The changing social conditions of the parish;

2. The state of parochial life (i.e. whether it was flourishing, or in decay, was happy or beset with personal problems);

3. The pattern of a man's own ministry since his ordination, sometimes in such detail that it constituted a 'case-history'.

A system of classifying returns on the basis of their evidential value was instituted and it produced among other results, the figure of 278 livings 'reporting considerable social change' which is 30·73 per cent of the sample. The Pilot schemes which preceded the MQ yielded twenty-six such livings, or 31 per cent of the returns, a most interesting correspondence.

At the same time a further system of classification was established which broke down the livings in the sample into rural (R), suburban (S), town (T) and mixed (R+T, R+S, etc.). The Statistical Unit classification into rural or urban was not regarded as sensitive enough. The results of the breakdown are given in Table 15 of the Summary of Evidence. Briefly the sample totals and percentages turned out to be:

	No. of livings	*% of 905*
Rural	379	41·88
Suburban	246	27·18
Town	255	28·18
Mixed	25	2·76

Yet again, within these four categories, an effort was made to classify those parishes or livings which by the general tenor of the answers it was permissible to regard as (*a*) busy and successful, (*b*) in decay. The overall picture is given in Table 16 of the Summary of Evidence. The main point here is that 102 parishes were classified as in decay (11·26 per cent of the sample) and 57 (6·29 per cent) as successful. The majority of the successful parishes were suburban (38) and the majority of the decaying (69) were town. Cross-reference with the 'social change' parishes showed that just about *one in four* of the 'social change' parishes was also classified as decaying (Table 17). Or put another way, eight out of ten of the parishes classified as decaying were also reporting considerable social change. It was certainly striking to discover that *almost one in three of the parishes in the sample were reporting social change* and that it seemed the most common factor in what appeared to be the decay of parishes.

What were the grounds on which parishes were classified as 'reporting considerable social change'? It must be said that the classification depended entirely upon the remarks made on returned questionnaires. The following kind of evidence—much of it urban decay and/or urban renewal—was accepted as a fair basis of classification:

1. New housing estates and/or great increases in population.
2. Temporary decline of an area through slum clearance.
3. Closing of factories or pits and loss of population in consequence.
4. Movement of white people out of and coloured people into an area.
5. Transformation or re-zoning of an area, i.e. residential area into industrial belt, older family residential area into a flat and bed-sitter-land, slums into council estates.
6. Social destruction of an area by motorways or flyovers, opencast mining, land subsidence.
7. Transformation of a rural parish by caravan camps and/or holiday camps.
8. Decline of a parish through continual loss of population, particularly of the younger folk, for whatever reason.
9. Transformation of parishes (in the South mostly) by rise in number of the retired.
10. Changes in the social basis or rural parishes (i.e. from simple village to stockbroker village, or to residential area of technologists from a nuclear plant, etc.).
11. Changes brought to remote parishes by transport—railway closings, or road access improvement.

Evidence about new housing was by far and away the most general and therefore the most numerous basis of classification: it was certainly the most widely spread in both provinces. This is to be expected from what has been said in the previous chapter of the population explosion and inevitable housing expansion outside the great conurbations.

The evidence incumbents themselves give is most illuminating. To throw additional light on the examples below, where thought valuable, population, average Sunday attendances all services (ASA), number of churches and staff are given: the staff number includes the incumbent, of course.

CLERGY COMMENTS

New Housing

Ex. 1. An incumbent from a Midlands diocese reports that he has a parish which has grown from 1,000 to 3,000 in about twenty-five years. 'During the period two additional churches and one mission room have been built . . . there has been no very realistic approach to the problem of clerical staffing [but] a procession of curates staying two to two and a half years. A reorganisation is being considered which will result in clergy coming for longer periods and having particular responsibility centred round church. [It] may result in division . . . into a number of parishes. Should this happen it is hoped that they will be held in unity by some form of a Group Ministry . . . all very tentative, but this area has certainly been a casualty of the failure of the Church to meet rapid urbanisation with rapid redistribution of diocesan manpower and resources. . . .'

Ex. 2. An incumbent from a northern diocese, single-handed, with a population of 6,000 and an average Sunday attendance of 350, writes: 'An assistant curate is necessary, as the parish grows from 6,000 to 10,000 in the next five years. The scattered nature of the parish makes constant use of a car essential for ordinary visiting. People here welcome their priest into their homes and incoming parishioners need to be welcomed into the church family.'

Ex. 3. From a northern diocese (pop. 30,000, ASA 900, 3 churches, 3 staff): 'This parish has grown so quickly in the last ten years: one council estate of about 7,000 persons, one private building, 6,000; a third one in process of about 4,000 and much other house and flat building in other parts of the parish. We built a new church eight years ago and have another church (formerly a mission building) near completion.'

Ex. 4. From the North West (pop. 18,000, ASA 700, 2 churches, 3 staff): 'A happy sphere of work. . . . A new township of middle class (lower) private building round a village church seating 500 in the very centre of a compact parish. . . . Social attitudes make churchgoing easy and on any sort of "occasion" morning services are duplicated for lack of room. Much family churchgoing—men often coming alone with their children. . . .'

Ex. 5. From the North West (pop. 30,000, ASA 700, 3 churches, 4 staff): 'This parish is increasing by 1,000 a year: it will probably end at 45,000. I dread the time when the death-rate begins to catch up with the birth-rate, and it is doing now. We baptised 280 children last year and buried 135 people. . . .'

Ex. 6. From the Home Counties: '1951—10,353; 1962—14,000; expect to be 1970—25,000.'

Ex. 7. From the South Coast: 'Population has increased in the last fifteen years from 1,000 to 15,000 and is largely of new building estates. . . . Parish church and mission church as far as could be from centres of population.'

Ex. 8. From the Midlands: 'Five new housing estates in eight years.' And from another in the same diocese: 'Population from 200 to 9,000 in twenty years.'

Perhaps in a nutshell the problems and opportunities of housing developments are shown by the incumbent who wrote that the boundaries of his parish were much the same as in Saxon times and till the 'thirties the population had only marginally increased. However, over the past thirty years a large housing estate had grown up four miles from his little Norman parish church and separated from it by a 'no man's land' sparsely populated. The vast estate is served therefore, as best it may be, by a mission church.

Other Forms of Social Change

Ex. 9. From the North (pop. 11,000, ASA 300, 3 churches, 4 staff): 'Three churches once all flourishing set in an area which over the past fifteen years has been subject to *rapid* slum clearance and *slow* rebuilding as a light industrial area, dockland, flats . . . in process of erection three blocks of eleven-storey flats. . . . Constant demolition, ugly scars of undeveloped debris-strewn sites. Lots of children. Poor home life, no sense of community.'

Ex. 10. From the North (pop. 1,600, ASA 55, 1 church, 1 staff): 'Typical of areas with rapidly falling population, little work and a sense of ceasing to exist. They are therefore psychologically dying, a fact which makes all activity very difficult. This has quite changed the nature of life and work since 1955. In truth I continue now chiefly because of the memory of, and attachments formed before, that time. . . .'

Ex. 11. From the South: 'Fourteen whole roads at present levelled. Roughly 2,000 residents compulsorily moved to other districts. Rebuilding in flats probable two to three years.'

Ex. 12. From the East Coast (res. pop. 900, summer 30,000; ASA 120, 1 church, 1 staff): 'This parish is the biggest caravan centre in the world so far as we know. There are 8,000 caravans along our coastline, housing some 30,000 people from Easter to October. All the local people are engaged in the holiday industry and work seven days a week. In addition, Butlin's. . . .'

Ex. 13. From the Midlands (two parishes, (1) 8,000, (2) 1,500; 2 churches, 1 staff): 'St X Church has lost many of its congregation through slum clearance and road-widening schemes. . . . St X Church itself is to be demolished for road improvements, but we are negotiating for a new site near to the (new) flats, as St Y Church will be cut off from [the main part of its parishes] by the same road development which will incorporate a flyover.'

MAP 2
PARISHES SUFFERING CHANGE OR DECAY

The distribution of parishes in the MQ sample classified as undergoing social change or parochial decay is shown here. The true density of these two sorts of parish could be about ten times as great, though there is considerable overlap.

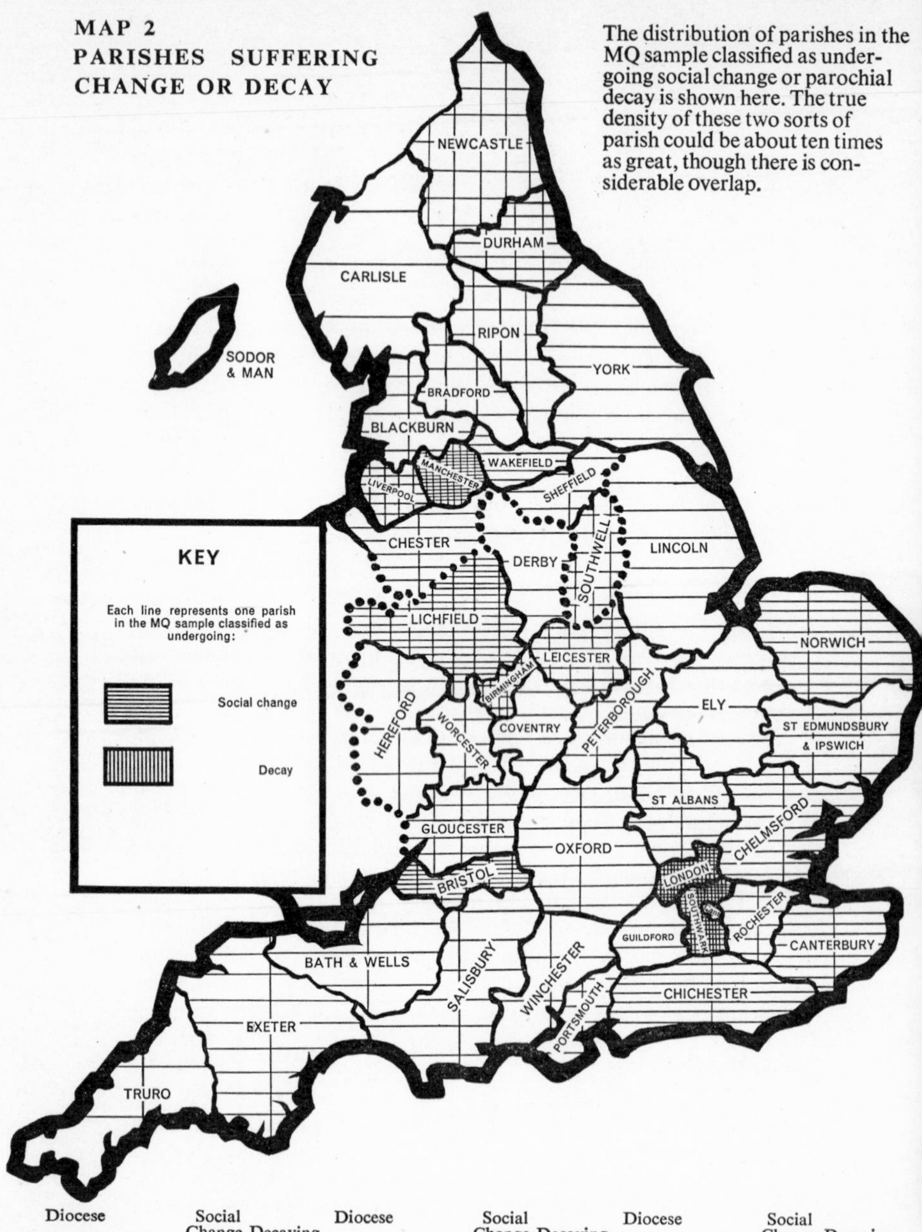

Diocese	Social Change Parishes	Decaying Parishes
Canterbury	8	1
London	14	15
Winchester	2	1
Bath & Wells	3	1
Birmingham	5	5
Bristol	9	5
Chelmsford	10	1
Chichester	7	1
Coventry	4	—
Derby	4	—
Ely	3	—
Exeter	8	1
Gloucester	5	3
Guildford	2	—
Hereford	3	1
Leicester	8	4
Lichfield	19	7
Lincoln	6	—
Norwich	11	2

Diocese	Social Change Parishes	Decaying Parishes
Oxford	7	1
Peterborough	4	2
Portsmouth	6	1
Rochester	5	1
St Albans	10	1
St Ed. & Ipswich	4	2
Salisbury	6	1
Southwark	17	11
Truro	2	1
Worcester	3	1
Totals Province of Canterbury	195	70

Diocese	Social Change Parishes	Decaying Parishes
York	8	—
Durham	7	3
Blackburn	5	1
Bradford	4	2
Carlisle	3	—
Chester	6	1
Liverpool	6	4
Manchester	15	9
Newcastle	7	5
Ripon	6	3
Sheffield	4	1
Sodor and Man	—	—
Southwell	6	3
Wakefield	6	—
Totals Province of York	83	32
Totals Provinces of Canterbury & York	278	102

Ex. 14. From the Midlands: 'When I first came to this parish seven years ago we had a morning congregation of 200. Eleven o'clock is still our best service . . . [but] nothing has grown during my tenure due to closure of R.A.O.C. factory and removal from parish of educational institutions. The population has gone away. I am left with villagers half of whom are R.C.'

Ex. 15. From the South West: 'We are a dying parish. The population is decreasing. We are surrounded by open-cast coal sites, etc., which threaten to increase. We have very few children. Any kind of youth work is impossible. Most of our church members are aged people incapable of doing anything to help in the work of the church.'

Ex. 16. From the South: 'The two parishes really consist of a number of scattered hamlets over an area of approximately 1 × 4 miles. Both parishes are bisected by the X—— arterial road.'

Ex. 17. From the West: 'We tend to be sent problem families [to our new housing estate], as we have a Family Service Unit and other welfare bodies at work in the parish. Our chronic need is for leaders with initiative. We have few "black-coated" workers, no doctors live in the parish; we have eight schools but only two teachers live in the parish. Many of our young people come from houses where promises and appointments are not kept. Shift work . . . do-it-yourself . . . H.P. . . . and lassitude. . . .'

Ex. 18. From the Metropolis: 'Used to be a pleasant riverside parish with small houses, flats and some large houses by the river and round a square. The new road has taken away a large proportion of small family houses. In others the children leave when they grow up; the parents remain as rent protected. After they are both dead the house is done up and occupied by new people, often television or professional artists or designers. . . .'

Ex. 19. From inner London: 'An international transit camp.'

Ex. 20. From the North West (pop. 8,000, ASA 200, 1 church, 1 staff): 'A varied and movable population—many in flats—all coloured —no sense of community—wild youth and indifferent. Absence of key people from Church life and worship . . . a grave situation, parishes and areas like this are a challenge to our leading priests. . . .'

Ex. 21. From the North West (pop. 10,000, ASA 200, 1 church, 1 staff): 'The parish has no natural community feeling, no single shopping centre, and the local cricket club recently closed through lack of support. People are moving further out and West Indians and others moving in (some of them members of the Church I am glad to say). The scale of the move may be gathered from the fact that we have had to replace every S.S. Superintendent (four depts.) twice over and over fifty teachers since I came here . . . (but) a happy parish. . . .'

DECAYING PARISHES

The 278 'social change' parishes were so classified upon the reports of the incumbents themselves. No such simple procedure was possible with the 102 decayed parishes: in some cases the classification was awarded upon an incumbent's report, in others upon his congregational figures (average Sunday attendance and so forth) in relation to the reported population. When, for example, an incumbent reported that though he was very fond of the parish and liked the people 'the parish has broken the hearts of both my immediate predecessors. The apathy is appalling—not only in the parish at large but even the majority of the church council are not really keen', I looked for evidence of possible pastoral failure or collapse. In this case, the classification was not awarded, but in another case it was, when the incumbent said that the parishes (he had two) had been unlucky—first a long ministry of thirty-four years, of an old priest, then a ministry for three and a half years of a priest 78 years old when he arrived, two short ministries of two years and one year, then four interregnums of from six months to two years during which a large family broke away and started a Christadelphian sect: in such a case it was easy to accept 'a running down of Church life'. Examples of potential classification by figures are as follows:

Table VII. Some Statistics of Representative Decaying Parishes

Livings	Reported pop.	Easter comm.	Av. Sun. attend.	ASA per 1,000	ASA per church	ASA per clergy
Town	15,000	48	50	3·3	50	17
Suburban	16,000	113	100	6·2	100	100
Town	25,000	80	40	1·6	40	40

When a parish shows only forty people out of 25,000 attending church on Sunday, a rate of less than two per 1,000, or when less than six per 1,000 in other parishes are reported, perhaps parochial decay is too mild a word. Even the possibility that incumbents have exaggerated their populations, say by 25 per cent, and therefore depressed their pastoral results by as much, does not rescue them. A sense of pastoral collapse hangs over them still.

What a slow and steady decay of a parish can mean is shown by these figures of Easter communicants from a church built in 1881 deep in an inner suburb of London. In 1884 there were 310; 1890, 522; 1912, 479; 1920, 510; 1929, 360; 1939, 210; 1946, 167; 1950, 113; 1962, 101. Confirmation candidates fell more steeply in numbers; in the twenty years between 1902 and 1921 there were 839 candidates; between 1942 and 1961, 136. Yet though the population of the parish today (12,000) is far larger than at any time before 1930, the parish and neighbouring areas have been subjected to a most drastic urban renewal and decay—originally a parish of middle to lower middle class private homes, it has become a zone of working-class flats and estates. The cause of decline is therefore, first of all, sociological.

MORE CLERGY COMMENTS

When such a low impact upon the neighbourhood is translated into human terms, these are the results:

Ex. 22. Rural parish (pop. 350, ASA 2): 'I venture to add a few facts about this parish which your questionnaire does not raise. £9,000 are required for the repair of the church: the amount contributed for all church purposes last year was £23. I have had five confirmation candidates in seventeen years. . . . There is no financial benefit to be gained from selling a redundant country church and disposing of the site. But here the only secure income is £200 from the patrons, which has to be made up to £800 by the Church Commissioners and the diocese, who get very poor value for their money. There is no PCC, no organist, no choir and no verger. There is no heating in the winter and evensong is held at 3 p.m. to avoid the cost of lighting. There is no chapel for the disgruntled to attend.'

Ex. 23. Rural parish: 'Parish was ruined by neglect and stupidity of an elderly vicar here over twenty-five years. He wrecked a good choir by forbidding anyone to attend the Chapel Harvest, forgetting that many had chapel cousins. There were no baptisms for three and a half years. No wonder there are difficulties enough to damp the enthusiasm of the most energetic vicar. There is a lost generation here. . . .'

Ex. 24. Eclectic city church, the parish of which has decayed, but which has moved over to 'Guild Church' functions: 'This church was to be closed as there was no longer need for it in this part of town—houses were being demolished to make way for industrial development. I came here at the end of 1955 to establish the church as a catchment church for the town and as a base from which to carry on the work of industrial evangelism. The venture seems to have proved successful and the place now prospers. But it is a large and eclectic congregation and in no sense a parish group.'

Ex. 25. Industrial parish (pop. 20,000, ASA 260, 2 staff, 3 churches): 'There is urgent need for (1) an office; (2) a really good filing system, with cabinets, etc.; a secretary at least five mornings a week. . . . This parish is a large village overtaken by the town—

we have the village church plus a new church, an old mission in what was "the working-class end", and an estate in building with site for church we still have to build and staff shortly. The problem is to reconcile "the villagers" who form the main body of Church people with the "new" people. Both parties tend to resent each other. The "villagers" tend to expect the vicar to do as vicars did in the days when there were 5,000 of them and four curates to help. . . .'

Ex. 26. Town parish, of which incumbent says everything has gone down during his tenure, and that people are moving out: 'This has a large working population . . . mostly friendly but completely apathetic. Very large numbers of children and adults unbaptised. Hence almost year-round baptism instruction. Congregations at present very self-centred and outsiders not really welcomed—and sense it. PCC "appointed" without voting for forty years. Numbers on PCC always too large. Sung services "provincial" and generally uninspiring owing to unskilled organist, poor choir; and people "love to have it so". Parish needs younger man with curate and sisters or lady worker.'

Ex. 27. Suburban parish, struggling with overspill chaos: 'It is a horrid ugly sprawling dormitory for A . . ., from which it is separated by only a few fields, and people (mostly young couples) only come here to get a house. They do not want to belong; they do not participate; most of them are completely tied up financially with HP and mortgage. A good deal of the main road ribbon development was pre-war, but since it has become a town-planner's nightmare. There is no natural centre, everything is scattered and you can't even change your tradesman, for to do so would mean walking a mile to the next shop!

'At the moment it is one of the few areas around A . . . where it is reasonably easy to get a house and this results not only in a constant stream of new residents but quite a remarkable "change-over" rate. A local doctor told me that in one year 700 patients left the area and about that number came in. People seem to come here for courses at the university or in industry [of] about two years' duration, and then they are gone. There is also considerable movement in the quick buying and selling of houses for capital gain.

'The population is an odd mixture of original residents and newcomers, and in addition of various university types and artisans and factory workers. Some of the younger university people attempt something for the community, but they are usually on the left politically and agnostic towards religion. Many sedate dons live in the older houses, but never mix in community life. On the whole the Church lives on a small, good-hearted faithful body of artisans.

'Apart from the foregoing, church life is only just moving out of its old village tradition with worship and activities geared to that sort of community. It is desperately trying to "catch up" with the growing community, developing church organisations, extending church work and life. The pastoral and administrative burdens are very heavy ones, and the two of us find we can hardly cope. We need at least another full-time member of staff, clerical or lay, and a complete reorganisation of parish administration. At the moment I do all the secretarial work . . . or what little there is done, and the parish does not even provide a typewriter.'

SUCCESSFUL PARISHES

The successful parishes were more easy to classify. If an incumbent reported high average Sunday attendances, and many reported 500–1,000, one knew that here was pastoral success in the sense at least of a thriving congregational life. Here are four such:

Table VIII. Some Statistics of Representative Successful Parishes

Livings	Reported pop.	Easter comm.	Av. Sun. attend.	ASA per 1,000	ASA per church	ASA per clergy
Suburban	23,000	930	600	26	600	300
Suburban	45,000[1]	800	1,000	22	1,000	286
Suburban	30,000	750	900	30	300	300
Rural	1,600	180	135	84	34	90

And finally, here is an eclectic city parish with a population almost gone. The incumbent reported it as 1,000, but the 1961 census showed it as 593:

Eclectic city parish	Pop.	Easter comm.	Av. Sun. attend.	ASA per 1,000	ASA per church	ASA per clergy
	593	379	500	843	500	500

It is most important to note that in the case of the first three, despite their obvious congregational success, their average Sunday attendance per 1,000 falls below the ASA for the whole sample, which is 31·1 per 1,000. One incumbent wrote that he constantly warned his congregation that their vigorous and thriving church life could mislead them—their impact on the parish was still fractional. Nevertheless such parishes deserve to be considered as busy and successful.

[1] Probably nearer 35,000 by latest census figures.

Here are actual reports:

Ex. 28. Suburban parish (reported pop. 36,000, ASA 1,030, 4 churches, 6 staff): 'Our main problem is sheer numbers: 380 funerals, 120 weddings, 200 baptisms, 80+ confirmations per annum. Until the "bulge" passed on we had nearly 2,000 on the Sunday school roll. The parish magazine goes to over 4,000 houses with the help of 130 distributors. I make great use of lay workers, running training courses. Apart from administration much of my time goes in this way.'

Ex. 29. Town parish (pop. 7,500 and growing, ASA 700–750): 'For three years we have had a parish week-end for the PCC. One day silence followed by a day of discussion to plan the year ahead. . . . I have a growing population and a growing congregation. It is well balanced both in age and in income groups and there is an excellent response from the laity. Thanks to a Christian Stewardship campaign and three missions in seven years (teaching and evangelistic), the parish has come to life. *My big difficulty is to know what to shed if I am to get my priorities right. . . .*'

A population growth, apparently accelerating, in the great conurbations, and at the same time a loss of population in certain rural areas must logically impose strains on our relatively rigid territorial parochial framework. Other demographic developments, like housing estates of one income group, or parishes which become enclaves of the retired or the coloured, simply complicate the issue. Basically, into some parishes vast numbers are poured, quarts into pint pots, while others can be slowly drained of people and left to the old. In this connexion it is significant that, despite the uniting of benefices, the number of livings with a population of under 1,000 has increased by sixty-nine since 1958. Since incumbents are appointed upon a territorial, not a population, basis one incumbent may have a cure so huge that he despairs of covering more than a fraction of it, while another finds a cure withering around him and so despairs of his own *raison d'être*. In what manner do these matters reveal themselves in the statistics collected from MQ? They show first of all that it is impossible to define a parish except territorially. It may have no inhabitants or it may have 35,000. It is equally impossible to define it in terms of a congregation. One parish may have a Sunday attendance of only two (the vicar and his wife),[1] another of 1,000: MQ brought to light fifty-two churches where attendance was actually ten or less! It cannot be defined in terms of churches. One church is most common, but united benefices may give a parson care of anything between two and six churches. It cannot be defined in terms of work. One parson will speak of his rural cure as 'a plea-

[1] An actual example.

sant week-end hobby', another in a town is on his own report made grey with fatigue and sweaty with hysteria by an eighty-hour working week. The parish, in fact, defies definition except as a territory, and though, considered historically, we must recognise that it was a marvellous collective achievement to give each community its parson and church, is it today more than an administrative convenience in the deployment of men? It provides each man with a church in which to minister, a house to live in, a benefice to help support him, and these are good and necessary provisions: one cannot imagine a Church which believes it necessary to provide places of worship and a professional ministry fulfilling its mission without them. However much we criticise the institutions of the Church, this kind of provision has everywhere been made since the earliest centuries. But the buildings (church, parsonage house, church hall) become the plant which must be serviced and kept going, often at all costs. The Church gets tied down to its plant and its sense of mission, 'cabin'd, cribb'd, confin'd' by it. A man tends to get sent to where there is a 'plant' to keep going, almost irrespective of whether people use it or not. Other forms of deployment are made exceedingly difficult by the legal obstacles to the disposal of redundant churches.[1] Moreover, the attachment of the Church to its buildings and to the sentiments they generate over the centuries tends to institutionalise the Church heavily. The faithful laity and the people at large come to think of the Church as the buildings it displays, to which the clergy are sent as of necessity. Much evidence has come my way of the tenacity with which the laity will fight to preserve an actual church even when all pastoral justification for it has gone, and really it only encumbers the ground. For them, loyalty to the Church is loyalty to that building. No wonder some parsons ask, 'Why was I ordained? To preach the gospel or to look after this particular set of buildings like a caretaker?' A territorial pastoral system inherited from the past, tied to its buildings, must always be in trouble over the adjustment of its relatively inflexible institutions to the changing pastoral needs of a fluid society.

Figures from various sources show how these considerations affect the parishes. According to the 1961 census there are now 939 parishes with populations between 10,000 and 19,999, 116 with populations over 20,000, and one parish of over 50,000 people. The whole group of parishes of 10,000 population and over shows an (expected) increase of twenty-nine on 1960 figures. Many of these are single-handed parishes. But how many? The MQ returns, checked

[1] A Commission on Redundant Churches reported to the Church Assembly in November 1963 (C.A. 1463).

MAP 3
PARISHES OF POPULATION OF 10,000 OR MORE

Diocese	No. of parishes (census 1961)
York	34
Durham	41
Blackburn	17
Bradford	12
Carlisle	4
Chester	32
Liverpool	55
Manchester	54
Newcastle	26
Ripon	20
Sheffield	42
Sodor and Man	—
Southwell	27
Wakefield	14
Totals Province of York	378

Diocese	No. of parishes (census 196[illegible]
Canterbury	[illegible]
London	[illegible]
Winchester	[illegible]
Bath & Wells	
Birmingham	[illegible]
Bristol	[illegible]
Chelmsford	[illegible]
Chichester	[illegible]
Coventry	[illegible]
Derby	[illegible]
Ely	
Exeter	[illegible]
Gloucester	
Guildford	[illegible]
Hereford	
Leicester	[illegible]
Lichfield	[illegible]
Lincoln	[illegible]
Norwich	[illegible]
Oxford	[illegible]
Peterborough	
Portsmouth	[illegible]
Rochester	[illegible]
St Albans	[illegible]
St Ed. & Ipswich	
Salisbury	
Southwark	[illegible]
Truro	[illegible]
Worcester	
Totals Province of Canterbury	[illegible]
Totals Provinces of Canterbury and York	[illegible]

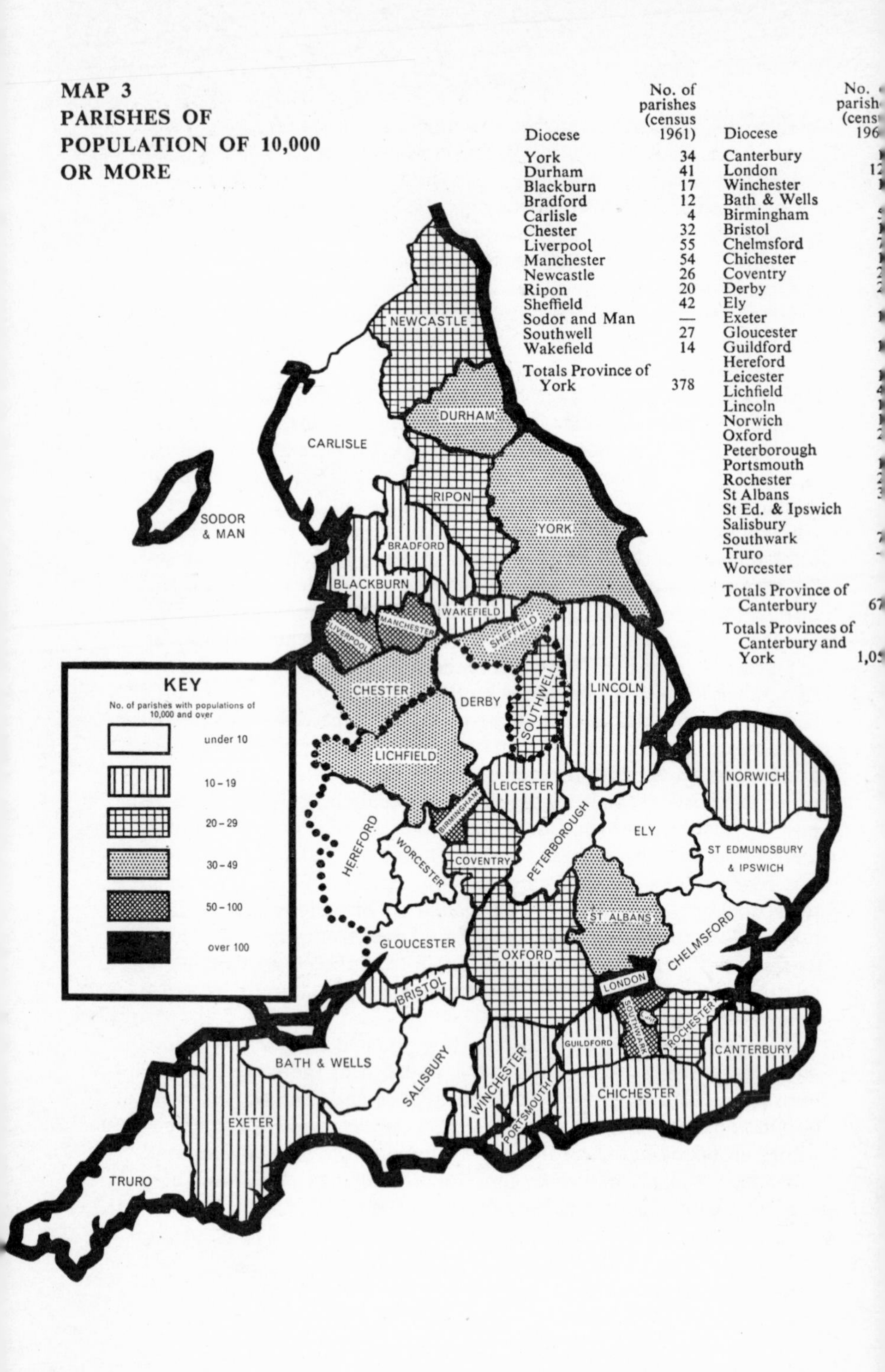

against 1961 census figures, showed that out of 196 parishes in the sample with a population of 10,000 and over, fifty-six were single-handed. The same proportion would give 302 single-handed parishes out of a total of 1,056 for the whole country. That in itself tells how large one particular group of hard-pressed clergy must be.

When parish returns from the MQ were being classified a group of ninety-five was selected for special examination because it consisted of single-handed clergy who had reported populations of 10,000 and over. They constituted, *a priori*, an overworked group and their pastoral results and personal work scores were computed. The average population per living as they reported it was 14,065. However, their own estimates of their parish populations turned out to be inaccurate, for reasons assessed in the Summary of Evidence, p. 224 f. Only some fifty-six of the total sample of 905 parishes were entitled to claim membership of this group. Nevertheless, the ninety-five were single-handed men and their populations were heavy ones. Reassessed in terms of the 1961 census figures, they still yielded an average population of 10,410. And yet another check showed an actual group of ninety-one single-handed men with parishes of 7,500 population and over, and that is 10 per cent of the 905 parishes in the sample! The single-handed group is a very considerable one indeed.

Another group of clergy, half as large, consisted of forty-eight incumbents with livings of a population of 450 or less: the population of the *whole* of this group is 15,050, which is close to the *average parish population*, census figures, of the fifty-six single-handed men (12,680). Of course, rural problems and town problems are different ones—to cover a large territory sometimes creates difficulties as considerable as covering a large population. Nevertheless, the disparities between cures point to the difficulty the Church has in making sensible use of scarce manpower through the existing parochial framework.

UNDERWORKED AND OVERWORKED MEN

One consequence is, of course, to overwork some men and underwork others. A further method of classification of the MQ returns showed this very simply. Some clergy had their returned questionnaires marked, hypothetically, 'overworked' (ninety-nine); others 'underemployed' (ninety-six). Of the 'OW' group only eleven were rural incumbents, of the 'UE' group, eighty-six. The heavily populated town and suburban parishes predispose men to overwork. One can examine this in terms of the two provinces. York province is suffering more acutely than Canterbury province from the shortage of clergy. According to the latest figures of the Statistical Unit, York had (1961) one clergyman to every 3,986 population and Canterbury one to 2,966. The MQ returns just examined showed fifteen underemployed in York to eighty-one in Canterbury, but forty-eight overworked in York to fifty-one in Canterbury. York showed twenty-two highly populated parishes run single-handed as against Canterbury, thirty-four, and this though the population of York province is 14·8 million and Canterbury 28·8 million. The 1961 census figures show 678 parishes in Canterbury province and 378 in York province with populations of 10,000 or over (Map 3).

The pastoral problems created by these great divergences are revealed by the incumbents themselves, first at the overworked and then at the underemployed end of the spectrum:

Ex. 30. A town incumbent, who says 'mine is a glorious parish': 'The parish will quite literally kill me one day and I am quite prepared for this . . . am in a chronic state of perspiration (so people will not approach me) and am so desperately tired. . . . Oh how desperately I need a holiday, or if not that, just a bit of interest on the part of anyone in the utterly impossible task with which I am confronted.'

Ex. 31. A suburban incumbent with a busy parish: 'Being single-handed means . . . that one is tied to the spot. It means . . . that all interviews, visiting, confirmation classes and so forth . . . fall to one's lot. Visiting certainly is not done as it should be. As in the army, there is bound to be a certain amount of . . . "C.O. isolation", but the absence of an assistant intensifies this isolation. To whom can you speak if you think you have an impossible churchwarden? . . . If one's congregation is not, as a whole, a reading or thinking congregation, with whom does one rub such wits as one may happen to possess?'

Ex. 32. An overworked rural incumbent (pop. 2,000, area 16 sq. miles, ASA 90, 1 staff): 'I came here to write and to restore two parishes . . . the previous incumbent had been forced to resign . . . enormous restoration problems at two churches faced the people; they were apathetic and embittered . . . even the bare necessities for services did not exist . . . I had a breakdown through overwork, but was unable to take the three months' rest desiderated by my doctor . . . I have carried on at the same pace and lost no time as a result of illness, but the possibility of full recovery is thereby lessened. . . .'

Ex. 33. A town incumbent, without comment: 'The time sheet shows an average week of 70 hours. When special events come round such as Lent, Christmas, Harvest, Confirmation, etc., this has to be stepped up to 80/90. It is not that one is unwilling to work these long hours, as the whole of one's life is dedicated, but the effect is disastrous. One feels a sense of being held fast in a machine that grinds endlessly on. Hobbies are impossible. Family life is neglected and worse still one becomes uninteresting and dull to other people. This feeling is made worse here by this unhappy parish. As my predecessor has said, he "never knew what the crucifixion really meant until he came to Y. . . ." '

Second, for the underemployed end of the spectrum:

Ex. 34. A rural incumbent (pop. 450, ASA 32, 2 churches): 'The two parishes are typically rural and entirely agricultural. In the two ministering to about 600 people, are two churches and three Methodist churches. This seems to me absurd, and that a working arrangement with the Methodists should be sought. Our relationship with them is good, since we work together in all parish activities. The small country parish no longer provides an adequate sphere of work for one man, since many functions which the parish priest was responsible for are now provided by local authority, Women's Institute, Young Farmers' Club, etc.'

Ex. 35. A rural incumbent who lists some fourteen government and local society posts as his principal work: 'I have never found two small country parishes provided me with enough work and from the start I entered local government work and became a member of the Diocesan Board of Finance. This has developed so that now I am Chairman of the R.D.C.'

Ex. 36. A rural incumbent, who, like another rural incumbent, reminds us that the town parson only meets his successes; the rural parson meets his failures at every turn of the lane: 'No parson has ever had his faith fully tested unless he has experienced a country parish. In my experience it is a far tougher, soul-destroying job than a town parish. People are terribly conservative, sensitive . . . in a town parish you are more conscious of those who come to church. In village life you must be aware of everyone. . . .'

STATISTICAL TESTS

We can analyse the effect of rising density of population upon the lives of incumbents by statistical methods, too. The MQ asked, among other questions, what time incumbents spent on (1) visiting; (2) reading; (3) parish administration. It proved possible to extract and record these times, parish by parish, and strike diocesan averages. Graph 3 shows that as population density rises the time spent on visiting and serious reading falls, while the time spent on parish administration rises.

We must be clear what that means: the greater the population an incumbent has to deal with, the more time spent on 'desk work' and

Graph 3. The Pressure of Administration

The three lines show diocese by diocese the average hours per week the clergy spend on visiting (light); parish administration (heavy); serious reading (broken). The dioceses are arranged in population density order. As the density rises, the serious reading falls, the visiting falls, the time spent on parish administration rises.

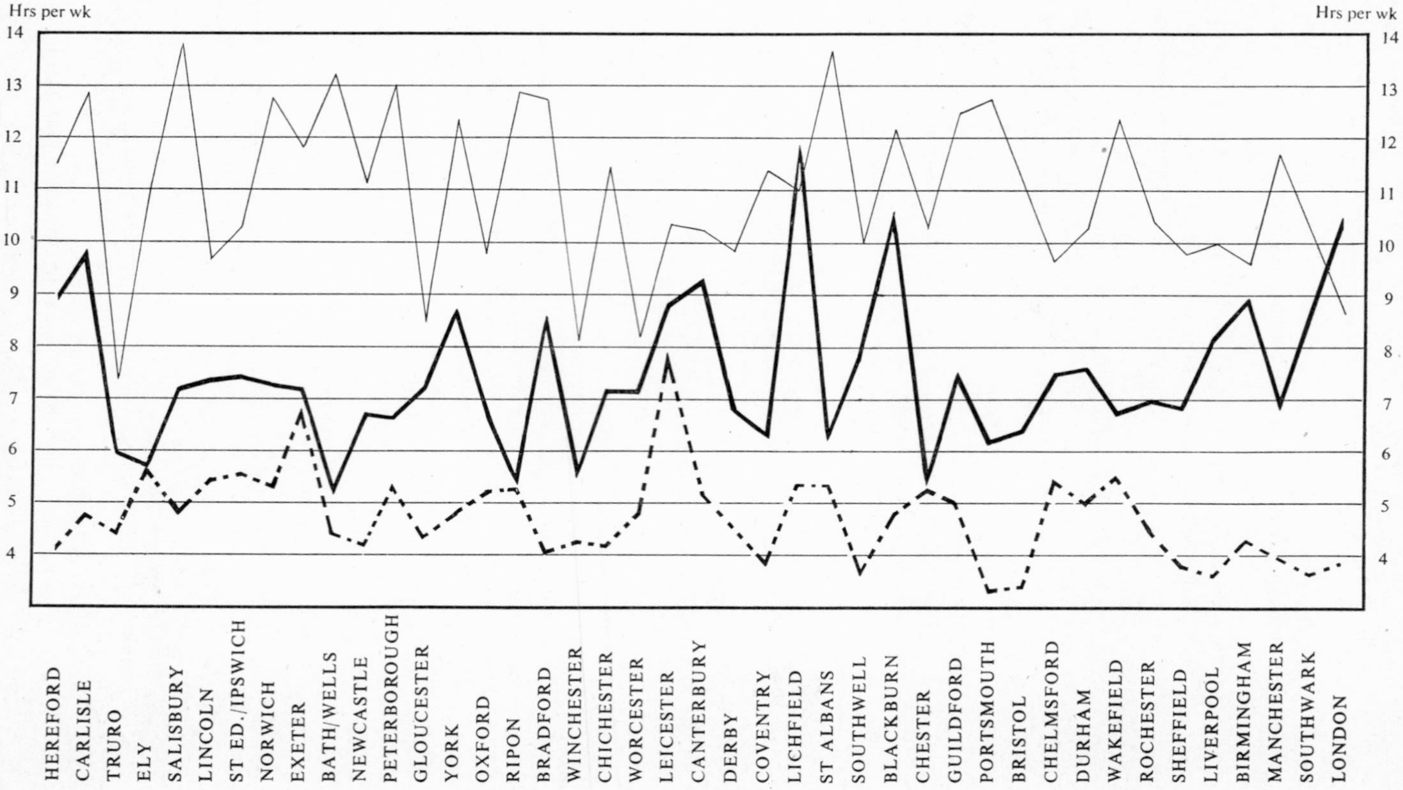

related chores makes inroads into his spiritual, pastoral and intellectual life. It is, of course, a conclusion which applies just as strongly to diocesan bishops and other church dignitaries, though I have no figures to prove it.

The MQ provided other material which enlightens us about the effect of urban density on the weekly work-pattern of the incumbent. By using a points system it proved feasible and instructive to award a weekday and a Sunday score to every incumbent who filled in the appropriate sections of the questionnaire. These two were extracted and averaged diocese by diocese. In Graph 4 they are shown plotted against the population density. They show that with increased population density work scores tend to rise. It is as simple as this, that by and large incumbents appear to meet the challenge of tough urban conditions by harder work, often by overwork. To some extent this is not exactly a matter of choice. An incumbent has responsibilities which automatically grow with increasing population, quite irrespective of the size of his congregation: they spring from the residual social nature of Anglicanism: baptisms, marriages, funerals have to be conducted. The Billingham figures show that funerals with religious rites are almost universal. There, with a population of 32,000, there were 207 funerals in the town in a year, of which 149 (72 per cent) were conducted by Anglican clergy. Elsewhere, one rector with a population of 17,000 reported six funerals, three weddings, a week; another, with a population of 3,200, forty funerals a year, twelve to fifteen weddings; a third with a population of 24,000, 160 funerals, 130 weddings, 250 baptisms every year. Weddings most frequently occur on Saturday, funerals on Monday. These two days otherwise are the most convenient and most usual days on which the incumbent expects to have some time off. It is important to make the point that as the population density rises the more elements over which the incumbent naturally has no control press upon his time-table. In these roles, performing duties quasi-civil, quasi-religious, he is perhaps more like the local registrar than pastor of a flock, though few parsons would want to deny that pastoral opportunities spring from the conduct of these elemental rites.

STRAINS ON THE PAROCHIAL SYSTEM

The evidence seems to be conclusive that the parochial system suffers increasing strain and decreasing pastoral effectiveness with increasing population density, a judgment to some extent modified by relative success in better-class suburbs. The evidence also suggests more strains than townsfolk imagine on the rural ministry, but this

Graph 4. How Hard the Clergy Work

A points system was used to award individual clergy Sunday and weekday work scores. The top graph gives average weekday scores, diocese by diocese; the bottom gives Sunday scores. Both are arranged against dioceses in population density order. As density rises, Sunday and weekday work scores tend to rise too. Of the ten most densely populated dioceses six are above average for Sunday and eight for weekday scores. Of the ten least densely populated only two are above average for Sunday and three for weekday.

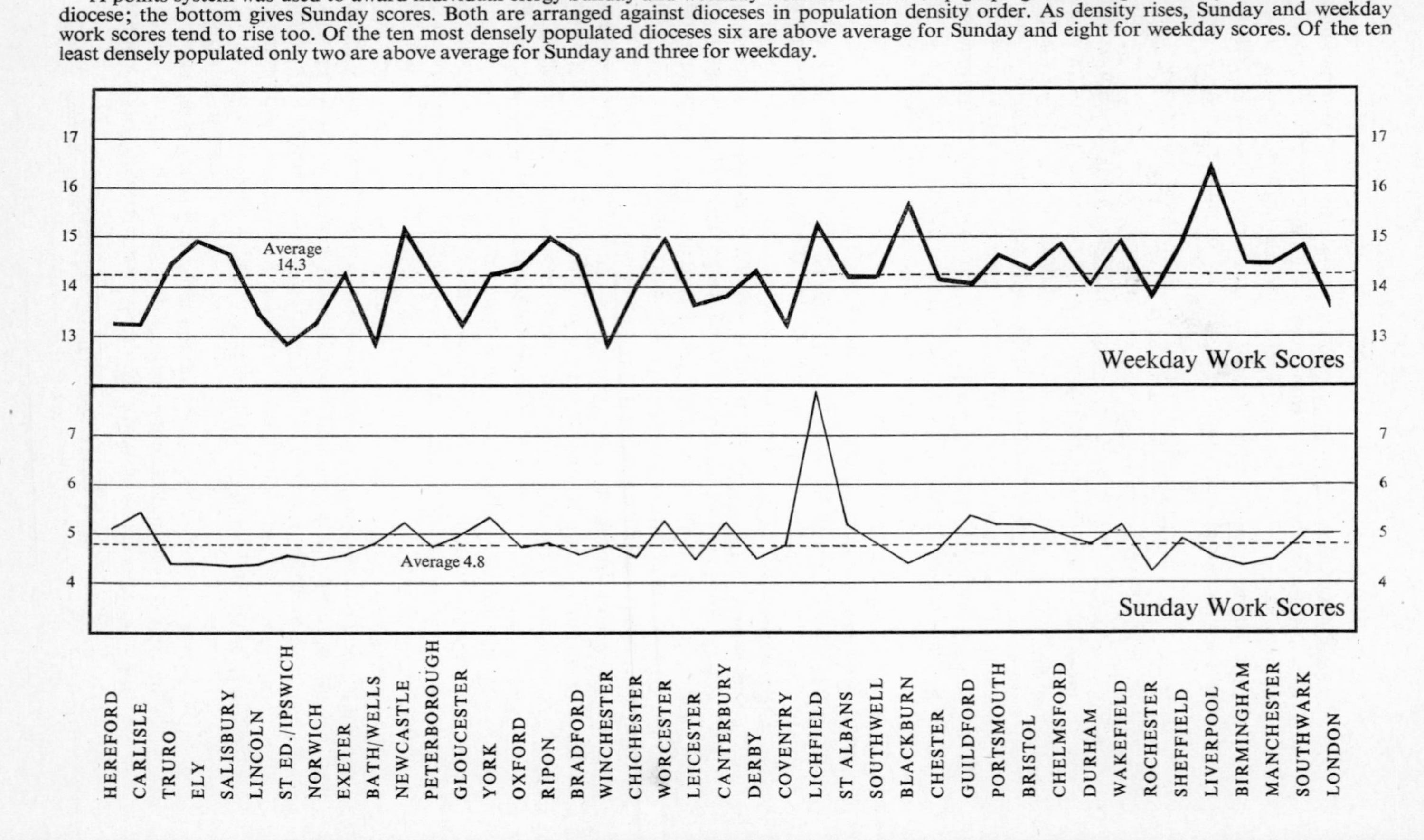

has yet to be unfolded. What is the nature of the urban failure? Are we faced with a problem primarily sociological or primarily spiritual, or can we say that all sociological questions, like political ones, are ultimately theological ones?

A second scrutiny of MQ returns was made to isolate incumbents of livings the circumstances of which it was hoped would reveal their degrees of pastoral success or their own stresses and strains. Of course, it emerged—it is no new discovery—that in areas of high population it is easier to get a congregation to a church than in thinly populated areas, even though the *number per thousand* who attend in the thinly populated area is far greater than in a town, and therefore that the size of the congregation in densely populated areas can mask the failure of impact on the parish as a whole. At the other end of the spectrum, a high rate of attendance per 1,000 quite often masks the smallness of the actual cure in terms of souls. More, it seemed to appear that in the areas of highest density the church congregations do not go on getting larger automatically: a law of diminishing returns operates. One began to grow convinced that arithmetical progression in density produced geometrical progression in pastoral difficulties so that some parishes were swamped by them, easily drifting to hopelessness about the pastoral outreach and beginning to die or to turn inwards and live only in terms of the actual gathered congregation. We need a term for this swamping process—perhaps urban saturation? Social services, roads, transport, hospitals, in conurbations also suffer from urban saturation, though mostly from over use of facilities. Yet the law that applies there applies to the Church, too: if a small effort will make little impact on a big difficulty, it is delayed or not made. If the big effort is needed and cannot be made, then a sense of hopelessness or frustration sets in.

The effort to isolate groups produced a deeper understanding of the rural-urban axis of the Church. What groups had to be isolated, however? Some had already been isolated for me by other efforts at classification—the hypothetically overworked or underemployed for instance, or those who reported too little to do. It was thought most useful to isolate others who for one reason or another might be expected to show pastoral results above or below average: the ill or disabled; the elderly; those with the busiest Sunday or weekday; those with the highest and the lowest populations; and so forth. The final list of these special groups was as follows:

1. Weekday score 18 (Wk. sco. 18).
2. Sunday score 6 or over (Sun. sco. 6+).
3. Largest reported single-handed parishes (Largest rep. s.h.p.).
4. One man to three or more churches (1 man to 3 + ch.).

5. Rural Deans (40 only from MQ sample).
6. Parishes of population under 450 (Par. 450−).
7. Average Sunday attendance under 30 per church (ASA 30−).
8. Clergy over seventy years of age (Clergy 70+).
9. Ill or disabled (Ill or dis.).
10. Case histories (Case hist.).
11. Two little to do (own estimate). (TLTD).
12. Overworked (OW).
13. Underemployed (UE).

The following table shows how many are to be found in each group and what happens when the pastoral results and work indices are averaged and set in population density rank for comparison. The population figures are as reported to me by incumbents and 1961 census figures would considerably revise them. The Summary of Evidence (p. 225 f.) explains why for purposes of this table what the incumbents have reported has been left just as it is. It can be seen at once that a real pattern emerges.

Table IX. Analysis of Special Groups in the Light of Population Density Rank (MQ Figures).

No.	Size of Sample	Name of Group	Av. Pop. per living	ASA per clergy	ASA per 1,000	EC per 1,000	Sun-day Score	Week-day Score	Av. Age of inc.
(1)	(2)	(3)	(4)	(5)	(6)	(7)	(8)	(9)	(10)
1	32	(1) Wk. sco. 18	15,666	192	27	28	5·0	18·0	53
2	95	(3) Largest rep. s.h.p.	14,065	246	18	19	5·2	15·2	49
3	99	(12) OW	12,460	211	29	31	5·2	16·0	50
**4*	*41*	*Manchester dio.*	*10,570*	*161*	*26*	*32*	*4·6*	*14·5*	*47*
5	193	(2) Sun. sco. 6+	9,710	180	32	35	6·5	14·8	50
**6*	*905*	*Entire Sample*	*7,483*	*154*	*31*	*35*	*4·8*	*14·3*	*51*
7	40	(5) Rural Deans	7,438	142	27	22	4·7	14·7	56
8	20	(10) Case hist.	6,955	106	30	38	4·3	13·5	54
9	21	(9) Ill or dis.	4,830	149	23	18	4·0	13·7	58
10	40	(11) TLTD	2,805	69	27	38	4·3	12·3[1]	54
11	80	(4) 1 man to 3+ ch.	2,707	130	46	57	5·3	13·5	51
12	42	(8) Clergy 70+	2,688	110	44	54	4·3	12·6	74
**13*	*29*	*Lincoln dio.*	*2,216*	*97*	*54*	*68*	*4·4*	*13·5*	*52*
14	96	(13) UE	1,414	73	52	71	4·3	12·4[2]	56
15	98	(7) ASA 30−	927	44	49	84	4·6	12·7	55
16	48	(6) Par. 450−	314	54	179	205	4·4	11·8[3]	58

[1] 22 gave no weekday and Sunday scores, therefore the average is extremely unreliable.
[2] 49 gave no weekday scores. [3] 31 gave no weekday scores.

*Included for purposes of contrast.

The diocesan distribution of the members of these special groups and of other MQ figures proved illuminating. It is shown in SE Appendix 4, under the title of Classification of MQ returns by Numerical Count. In that chart the dioceses are arranged in rank of rising population density: the count of special groups against them shows that their (the special groups') distribution is not purely random but is influenced by demographic factors. Indeed, as SE points out, the whole sweep of church pastoral problems is there set out.

It can be seen in Table IX that in general the ASA per clergyman falls with the falling density of population, while ASA and EC per 1,000 simultaneously rise. There is a steady fall in both Sunday and weekday work scores as populations fall, but with expected exceptions. The man with three or more churches scores very highly on Sundays, next in rank to those extracted for highest Sunday score. He certainly scores higher than his population density rank. Equally it is expected that the 'solo' men, with the highest ASA per clergyman, will show the poorest results of ASA and EC per thousand. Interestingly the overwork group does appear to pull its pastoral results slightly above expectation for population density. And in the ninety-eight livings where the ASA is thirty or less per church we have the poorest pastoral results of the lot, because one is really catching dying churches in this particular statistical net. It is perhaps confirmed by the fact that the Sunday and weekday work indices for the parsons in this particular group more than accord with their density group expectations: we cannot therefore easily attribute their pastoral results to laziness. It looks indeed as though there is, on the average, a work-norm imposed on the clergy by the population of the living: it varies according to responsibilities a little (Groups 3 and 4 of the final list), but population appears to exercise an ultimate control. Overwork does not significantly change the pastoral results.

Therefore we have to assume that social or demographic factors exercise a profound influence on religious allegiance and religious observance. Population density is only one of these factors: the type of population is another, or we should not have a higher rate of religious observance in suburban and mixed parishes than in downtown parishes—the incidence of decay and success figures are very significant here.

Of course, a statistical finding does not impose a rule: it merely abstracts into figures and averages certain aspects of the behaviour of men and women. If the finding appears significant we still have to hunt around for the individual and group behaviour patterns which determine the statistical result.

Graph 5. Attendance at Church

The heavy line records average Sunday attendance per church per diocese as taken from MQ returns: the scale of actual numbers of attendances forms the right vertical. It is contrasted with average Sunday attendance per 1,000 (light line) the scale of which is given on the left vertical. The base line is of dioceses arranged in population density order *according to MQ averages*. As density rises attendance per church rises too, but the lines show that in rural areas a high rate of pastoral effectiveness (per 1,000 pop.) can mask a very small actual cure, and on the contrary high church attendances in towns disguise a very low total pastoral impact.

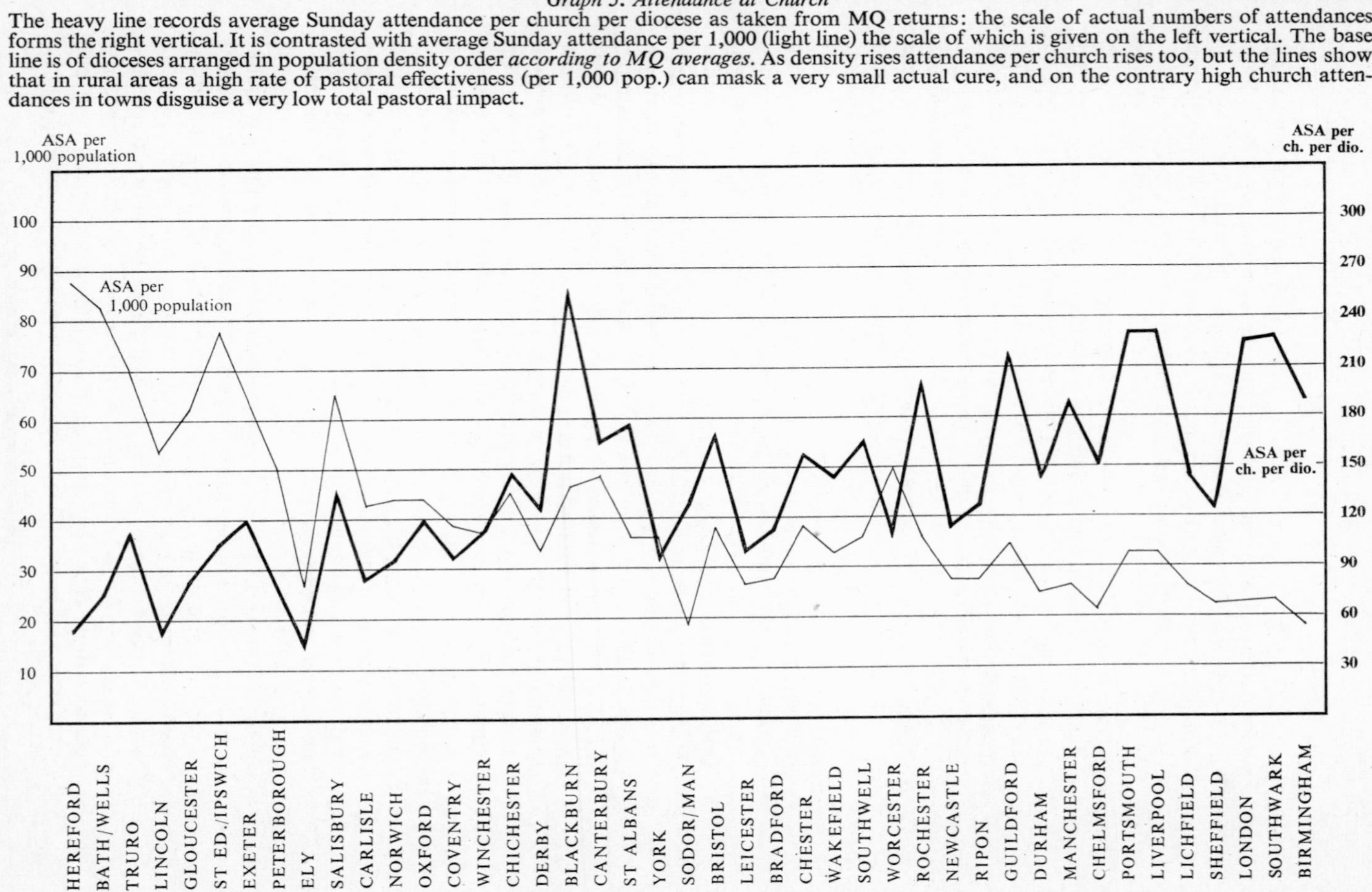

CHAPTER V

The Isolation of the Clergy

THE TOWN PRIEST

IT is easy to see that the parish is a more meaningful entity to rural parsons than town parsons. The town parish quite often makes no sense to its inhabitants; they do not think in terms of the parish; their journeys along their lines of commitment may never even take them past the church doors; the parish is not the neighbourhood, if a neighbourhood exists. The peripheral, optional character of church activities in the town is felt by all, including the parish priest. If he is confronted as well by the decline of his impact in terms of total population—a declining ASA per 1,000, for instance—and a stationary or declining congregation, not in its age structure even representative of the population at large, then he may despair about his ministry. Socially, communally, it may come to look as meaningless to him as the parish as a geographical unit does to his parishioners. He cannot from his isolated and fragmented parish gain much sense of service to and integration into the conurbation which dominates him as it does his parishioners. One suburban incumbent wrote:

> No parish should have less than two clergy. Partnerships—viz. doctors—prove best. Breakdown: most clergy have had one, of one kind or another. Major cause? So grave a responsibility, and the task so often completely misunderstood by the laity who regard the Church as their spare-time job—albeit a fine one.

Another incumbent of a town parish wrote in a sensible analysis of his situation that the incumbent, as an unfortunate result of the daily pressures and pattern of his life,

> does not have time to associate much with his fellow clergy. [I] think that the clergy would be much more effective if they worked a lot more closely together and got to know each other better . . . conferences, meetings [are] not enough; the clergy need to meet each other more informally, perhaps more in each other's homes. I suspect it is unusual for one parson to visit another unless he has some particular business to deal with and I do not think that many priests' wives mix more than on MU deanery committees—and so many wives are now working that the needful contacts become even less. [There is] real need for closer contact between parochial clergy who still work too much in isolation and even in competition. There is an unnatural division between the 'apparently' successful and ditto unsuccessful [and] still too deep a churchmanship cleavage. [I] cannot see any sign yet of 'Group Ministry' becoming the norm . . . but . . . many of us think our work could be done better along such lines. . . .

A rural priest too said, 'I must say I am never lonely, but I sometimes wish my fellow clergy would drop in and have a talk, but this they never do.'

If the suburban and town incumbent is in difficulty over the social unreality of the parish, he is often, it seems, ill at ease over his isolation. It is in the nature of geographical territories not to overlap and for that sheer physical fact to separate one ministry from another, one clergyman from another with a kind of finality. Each parson tends to stay within his territory, and his pastoral authority, except when visiting his sick in hospitals or conducting funerals, officially ends when he leaves it. An incumbent would certainly be alarmed or indignant if he learnt that another priest was visiting or somehow functioning in his own streets without his permission. The parish has one spiritual authority, and is in this sense deliberately separatist. The fact that the incumbent exercises a cure by and under the authority of his bishop does not in practice affect the parson's sovereignty within his territory. The state of separateness is recognised in law, too: the incumbent is placed in legal possession of his freehold and cannot be moved from it without his consent unless he proves guilty of a criminal offence or is proved by a burdensome process of inquiry to have failed in his duties. The parish therefore, whatever its character, is isolated legally as well as geographically. Where the area of its isolation includes a natural community, this isolation is even beneficial, for it helps to define the community. When it is a slice cut artificially out of a tangle of urban streets and meaningless to its inhabitants, its social and spiritual isolation is made difficult to overcome because of the legal separation of the parish from all others. It is an inflexible frame fixed over but failing to hold together a relatively mobile society.

THE RURAL PRIEST

It might seem from what has so far been said that there is an ideal parochial set-up in the countryside and an artificial and impracticable parochial system in the towns and that we move from country conditions where the Church functions happily to urban conditions where parsons are plunged in misery because of their ineffectiveness. It is not so. Where the Church in the country serves a natural community and is supported by all classes, this may be so: but it is more often an ideal condition than a real one. It is even statistically the case that I have more cries of despair from incumbents in the country than in the town and it has something obscurely to do with the changing social status of the clergyman in the country.

It is a little dangerous to generalise about the clergy. They have endured poverty and contempt in the past, particularly at the height of the farming community's hostility to tithes, and sometimes actual persecution of the kind the Rev. A. Tindal Hart's studies[1] tell us about. Yet, historically—we may think of the eighteenth and nineteenth centuries, when the vestry was still a unit of local government—the parson was a member, even if sometimes a despised member, of the dominant social group in the countryside as well as representative and executive officer of an awe-inspiring estate of the realm. He was a graduate of Oxford or Cambridge or privately educated at a great house. He came from the gentry or clergy families or from the minor sons of great families. He was 'related'. He spoke the language of his group and shared their tastes and understandings, their political prejudices. He might be overdominated by the lord of the manor who was his patron, or by the aristocracy of the great house from which perhaps his bishop had sprung, but this confident ruling group sustained him in his ministry to his flock. Their presence gave him special authority in his dealing with all other classes. The support afforded him by a powerful, locally domiciled gentry which itself provided the effective local leadership must have helped to make good for him any sense of isolation he may have felt through lack of contact with other clergy. He did not expect his life to be lived with teams of clergy, but with his social equals, albeit laity, in his neighbourhood. There was at least some society in which he moved as a welcome and accepted equal. And he could always have his curate.

It is this social support for the rural parson which has so often melted away: at least he cannot count on its automatic solidarity any more. The new mobility of people, the new role of the retired and the week-ender in the country, the flood of transport, of housing, the vanishing of the rural gentry and the closing of the great house, all tell *socially* against his position. They produce for the rural clergyman an isolation, often intellectual and cultural, he has never experienced in any century before. His stipend is not high enough to support him on the level of new professions. He is less likely than ever today to have private means. He may be rather a poor man with a growing family. Only the solitary lower-income bracket housing-estate parson in a town experiences an equal isolation. 'To whom can I speak?' both kinds have many times said to me.

It is true that with leadership by the gentry so often disappearing in the countryside as the class itself physically disappears or loses faith, a sense of obligation to support the Church evaporates among

[1] Cf. *The Nineteenth Century Country Parson*, *The Eighteenth Century Country Parson*, etc. etc., and *Country Counting House*, London, 1962.

farm labourers and other rural classes. One parson writes that church attendance by the farmers is much diminished.

> Their fathers were always present. The rising generation are as casual as they are well-to-do [and] not so generous as the poor parishioners to the church and have the means to organise activities on Sundays which leave churchgoing out of account. I pin my hopes for the future on the youth of my parish, who come to church because they want to. . . .

These generalisations seem supported by what the parish priests themselves write and how they speak of their loss of status and of feelings of insecurity. Looking back, 1939 rather than 1914 may ultimately be fixed as the year when the social system in the countryside began to disappear. And historians may decide that mechanised farming, accessibility by motor-car to towns, the closing of village schools, and the spread of urbanisation have had as much to do with the reduction of social status of the countryside as death duties or any other legislation.

A rural parson with a population of 900 speaks of the changing character of his village:

> The Church school was closed in 1949, the primary county school is two miles away, the high school five miles away, served by school buses. The young people are scattered and have no sense of belonging. The 'upper' class are the PCC and church officers. The villagers who work mainly on the farms are very hard to draw to church services and organisations. After 14 and 15 most of the young people move away. . . .'

A rural parson, with a population of 220, resigning because he has too little to do, writes:

> It would appear to me that there are a number of priests like myself in country livings most of whom suffer from a sense of frustration and do so in isolation. There is, I believe, a great need for such priests to meet more often than they do, to plan, discuss, pray and study together. The monthly chapter meeting is . . . little more than a time-waster . . . like most chapters I have attended it suffers from inertia. . . .

He finds—

> a tendency to be busy about trifles. . . . Over the last twelve months I have grown despondent. . . . The parish demanded little except Sunday services, though there would be an outcry if there was no incumbent. A lay reader could perform the majority of the tasks. . . .

Rural parishes, too, can be meaningless socially.

> Most of the congregation come from a distance; there are about twenty cottage homes and three or four larger houses. . . . There is not a shop or even street lighting and we are two miles from nearest transport, i.e. bus.

Isolation and lack of support have their effect. A rector reports:

I am church treasurer, fire lighter, and general handyman in church and rectory. We have no electric light in the rectory in which I have many jobs, fire lighting, cleaning windows and two lead roofs twice a year. . . .

Another rector says:

One is incumbent, secretary, typist, chapter clerk, hospital chaplain, school manager, Inspector of Church Schools, Chairman CEMS. . . .

Another with fifty square miles to cover and four parishes, speaks of four of everything—PCCs, Sunday schools, youth clubs, fêtes, village schools:

I am a Director, rather than a pastor or missionary.

Yet another:

Helping out always needed. Deanery rarely at full strength. . . . Three parishes absolute limit for one man. The Archangel Gabriel could not do more and retain his sanity. . . .

Many speak of the problem of distances—one even of being fifty miles from his cathedral city and four miles and twelve miles from the hospitals his parishioners are taken to. One rural incumbent *without a car* said he had—

six invalids to visit at E— (twelve miles away), D— (five miles), C— (eighteen miles) and B—(ten miles, no bus thither). Apart from D—it takes half a day to visit any of them. C—twice this week to one patient dying. All (apart from B) visited last week.

A rural incumbent reported his revolt at the demands of his parish:

There is or there should be no question of a country parson not having enough to do. He has to do the work of at least two servants as well as his parish work. The more pertinent question is what on earth did his Victorian predecessor do! But it is of course true that there is not enough priestly work in a country parish to fill in a working week. When I first came [here] I worked thirteen hours a day and was never in during the evening. . . . I organised clubs, square dancing, socials, dramatic work, etc. etc. In the end I revolted from it all. So much of it just wasn't my job at all. . . .

Doing his own job, he said, he could run four parishes of the size of his with the help of a lay reader.

The parish is *not* a full-time job. . . . It's very easy to find oneself gently rotting away.

It is permissible to speak of the two kinds of discouragement which fall on the clergy from the circumstances discussed. In the town:

In a *totally* working-class parish (i.e. no resident teachers, doctors or graduates at all and no executives) to deal with one's congregation only would give hope of covering one's work and instructing people in depth—but to care for the whole parish sets problems which can hardly be stated.

In the country:

It is questionable whether it is right to have a resident incumbent in many of these places. A man can easily lose heart when Sunday after Sunday he is ministering to less than six people at any one service.

The first sort of isolation can lead to breakdown:

Last November I had a 'nervous breakdown' and was off duty for four and a half months. Looking back I can see that it was because I was attempting to run my parish in my own strength and that I was trying to get too much done all at once [in my] first parish. One small point, I would like to suggest that at my first-class theological college not enough time was given to the subject of parish administration and too much emphasis was put on visiting as the *only* true part of parish work—consequently I've had an overriding guilty conscience if I have not managed to visit a vast list of people (as a curate this resulted in a private head-hunting foray each day, and a gloating review of visits done recorded on the card index!) . . . I'm thrilled to have been one of those chosen to send in a reply. . . .

The loneliness of a country priest provoked this thoughtful essay:

The trouble with the Church is not lack of efficiency but lack of effectiveness. Many of us clergy are not effective . . . because of causes that are much deeper than any reorganisation can touch. We have been immersed in parish routine and problems for years. Our faith has grown dull. In some ways it has received rude shocks that have shaken it at its foundations. But we have no one to whom we can turn, unless we happen to have some personal friend and adviser, which some of us, for all our efforts to find one, have not got. Fellowship is a word much bandied about in the Church, but the substance of it barely exists. There ought to be a spiritual adviser for clergy to whom they can turn as of right, not as asking a personal favour, and often at that. Let him go round visiting them to be their helper in Christ. Best of all . . . absolutely best of all, surely . . . let the bishop be the bishop. Let the reorganisation, or whatever it is that the present move is seeking, be a setting free of the bishops from all the numerous committees, financial bodies and supervisory administrative duties that at present make it quite impossible for them to be

Fathers-in-God to their clergy. In this diocese it is tragic, for we have a bishop with real pastoral gifts: in the last five years we have had two opportunities to avail ourselves of them, and only in a very limited sort of way. How different life would be if he, or someone like him, were going round the clergy individually . . . sharing their confidences. . . .

A layman who felt himself high and dry in a post in which he was not able to give of his best would 'pull up sticks' and move on.

But after you are instituted they leave you alone. . . . A small living is a pleasant enough life if you are content to simply plod on and minister to the needs of your flock, and spend the rest of your time in the garden or reading. However, if you are young and active—after a few years in such a parish you realise that there is really little else you can do and you begin to chafe at the bit. The problem then arrives, what are you to do? The only thing you can do is to see your bishop and tell him that you would like to move so that you will not stagnate. He simply promises to bear your case in mind, and there the matter rests.

Of course, when all the social conditions of parishes and the personal problems of the clergy have been considered it is understandable if breakdowns occur, and 'case-histories' pile up: this is more particularly so when a clergyman feels that his own power to remedy his situation is severely limited by the existing machinery for filling benefices and by the sense of good form which prevents a parish priest from applying for a post or advertising his abilities. Those who speak with bitterness of the situation are not only those who feel that they are never personally visited but those who believe that their abilities, secular, theological, pastoral, are not used, not even known, and that basically no one cares. This was one of the factors which caused an incumbent already quoted to write of 'spiritually sick clergy' not to be healed just by some ecclesiastical reorganisation.

One conclusion presses itself: the inflexibility of the existing parochial system is an impediment to the exercise of the Church's pastoral ministry, but equally it is productive of despair among the clergy. There is need for a more effective ministry to the whole people, but before that an even greater need for the pastoral care of the ministry itself by the whole Church.

Extracts which show the tensions within the Church and the ministry do not tell the whole story. One must take note of clergy attitudes to the new challenges. If any mood predominates in all the material I have seen it is impatience with the Church at the slowness with which it moves to take up the challenges. Men say often with a moving candour, 'I am a prey to despair', but they also say, 'I am fighting demons.'

I really wonder how you are going to establish the difference between the many . . . clergy who are depressed and fed up and feel that they were never trained to face a situation like the one which faces them now, and those who feel that there is real relief to be found in so much of the changing things, and that so much of what our fathers took for granted is gone.

It would be false to represent all the clergy as critical of the parochial system. Perhaps one-half made no comment in the MQ and so we do not know what they think: to an unknown number the parochial system with all its strains is sacrosanct. Many of the most hard-pressed incumbents, who made some of the most pungent comments of all, wrote in terms of love and devotion about their vocation. What they said showed them often utterly and obliviously at the call of what I (but not necessarily they) might describe as a thankless, secular-minded laity. 'A glorious parish', they cry out. Or 'I couldn't be busier and love every minute of it'. 'We have great spiritual encouragement.' 'I would not change my job for all the world.' Yet sometimes they say, 'We keep going!' 'I just manage to tick over.' 'We stay cheerful.' 'I am not discouraged by the size of my task here and the lack of tools to do the job.' Or 'I battle on.' Then they are a little like soldiers writing home from the front line to cheer up relatives who might otherwise grow uneasy.

CHAPTER VI

The Structure of the Ordained Ministry

THE MINISTRY AS A PROFESSION

WHATEVER else the ordained ministry is, it is also a profession. Like other free professions, it has the means of controlling entry into its ranks, of regulating ethical practices, of determining standards and pressing for their maintenance. An applicant for ordination must be acceptable to a diocesan bishop and can, at the end of his training, only be ordained by one. Even though the bishop elects that the applicant shall pass through the selection machinery of CACTM—he can by-pass it, of course—it is before selection boards largely composed of clergymen that he must pass and it is to theological colleges entirely staffed by clergymen that he must go to be trained. Only in pre-theological colleges may he find lay tutors. Clergy again will be responsible for his post-ordination training. In the sense that the profession itself scrutinises applicants, trains them and ordains and places them, the profession is an autonomous and a self-renewing one.

Its control over its own life and practice is actually greater than this professional structure suggests. The Convocations of Canterbury and York are (at the present moment) entirely bodies of clergy, and in their hands rest the spiritualities, that is to say doctrine and practice of the Church of England subject to Parliament. Church Assembly has three Houses, one of Bishops (43 members), one of Clergy (350 members), one of Laity (346 members). Since 'nothing shall be deemed to be fully passed by the Assembly which has not received the assent of a majority of the members present and voting of each of the Houses sitting together or separately' it is clear that there are two clergy vetoes to one lay veto over proceedings, apart from an absolute clerical majority. Moreover, the Constitution of Church Assembly forbids it to encroach on powers belonging to Convocations or to bishops. Further, of course, the Church has its own courts, which have powers to discipline its clergy, and to decide other legal issues, and 'the lawful sentences of which are enforced by the State', in the words of Archdeacon Guy Mayfield, who also said that this right is fundamental to the establishment of the Church of England.[1]

One should add to these autonomous powers of the profession, the freehold which office confers. The incumbent, the dean, the canon, the archdeacon, the diocesan bishop, the archbishops receive

[1] *The Church of England: Its Members and its Business*, 1958, p. 202.

their offices and dignities as properties from which they cannot be alienated except by processes of law difficult to operate apart from proved criminal offences. No one can simply be *dismissed* either for incompetence or failure or because it was hoped to pursue a different policy in parish or diocese. The clergy therefore are not only placed in control of their own professional life but, individually, have entrenched rights which protect them from one another. In this their professional powers would seem to exceed those of most other professions: a solicitor employed by a company is not *qua* solicitor or a teacher employed by a local authority is not *qua* teacher protected from termination of his contract. The nearest approach to this protection from dismissal is to be found in the Civil Service. But the Civil Service is not *also* a profession in the clerical sense; though it may control entry it does not train its members: it has no real autonomy, it exists to serve the State and is subject to the authority of ministers and Parliament. There is perhaps no exact parallel to be found anywhere to the powers and privileges of the clergy. What Convocations and Church Assembly do is finally subject to the seal of Parliament: but the freehold is a right which could only be abrogated by a change of law. As the law stands at the moment existing freeholders are safe in the enjoyment of it as long as they wish.

Even when all this has been said, it is not enough. The clergy is also the *sacred* ministry. The service of ordination is the gift of the Holy Spirit in the laying-on of hands. 'Receive the Holy Ghost for the office and work of a Priest in the Church of God, now committed unto thee by the imposition of our hands. Whose sins thou dost forgive, they are forgiven; and whose sins thou dost retain, they are retained.' Whether the laying on of hands is *symbolic* of the transmission of divinely granted power from the first Pentecost or is the means of it might be argued. The plain words of the ordinal speak of a real committal, not a symbolic one. The powers conferred in ordination to the priesthood are mighty and holy powers if one accepts that here the priest acts in the name of, and by authority of, Christ. The candidate is, in the words of the bishop, ordained to 'the same office and ministry appointed for the salvation of mankind' as that to which the first apostles, prophets and evangelists were appointed. The only meaning which can be attached to these words and acts is that the priest is a man set apart by God; and that ordination intends this meaning is shown by the ban on certain other callings as dangerous or injurious to the ordained man: a man's life from this moment on is limited and disciplined by his new status.

It is, of course, true that what ordination precisely means today, how it is interpreted, is much debated. Even the title of a book like Eric James's *Odd Man Out* suggests how deeply and with some anguish the priest's 'separation and involvement' are being argued out. My concern here is simply that the approach made to clergy problems in this chapter shall not be misunderstood. I am committed to studying the clergy as a professional group. Needless to say, I accept that it cannot be considered only as this. There cannot be, or at least ought not to be, simply self-selection of the ministry as a role, a profession, a 'career'. There has to be something more than self-selection, something which all selection boards and bishops find hard to measure, a sense of vocation, a call from God, a sacrificial decision. In *Gender and Ministry*[1] the authors spoke of the 'too prevalent attitude towards the clergy as the recipients of some semi-magical status', and in a fervour of alliteration wanted it disclaimed, discouraged, and discarded. Yet though it ought not to be semi-magical, some 'status' is at present conferred which is certainly more than social or professional. The least that priests would affirm, and laymen would assent to, would be that ordination authorises and gives power to a man to fulfil his office, and that this power is of Christ. How it separates a man from the laity and from the world, or even why, is arguable. But the world and the clergy have always felt the cleric to be a man set apart.

There is another sense in which ordination must be understood. A profession like law or medicine or military science is its own source of knowledge over which it often believes it has a monopolistic right. To be a layman in law, medicine or military affairs is first to be at a disadvantage before the professional experts and then to be excluded from their sources of knowledge and techniques of evaluating it. It would not be regarded as professionally or socially wise that the laity should be initiated. The layman is deliberately confronted with professional opacity. Though at times university theological studies are afflicted with this professional exclusiveness, this is a university, not a clerical, professionalism. The clergy, and the ordination service reminds us of it, are intended to be transparent instruments of a Power not themselves, the vehicles of the inrush of divine love into the world, of which they are commanded to be the bearers and evangels. Hence not even the 'sacralising' of the ministry, or erroneous beliefs about its 'semi-magical' status ought really to transform it, while this function remains, into an opaque inward-looking profession, defending itself against the world, and guarding an arcane revelation. The nature of its ministry forces upon it the

[1] A report prepared for the Church Assembly by the Central Advisory Council for the Ministry, 1962, p. 11.

self-effacing burden of communicating Another's word, Another's command, Another's love. The missionary role has another consequence: it should and from time to time does force the ministry to look critically at the high professional self-regard, common to other professions, which though it might preserve the clergy socially would destroy it religiously. Essentially it asks for humble men, and for a ministry which does not finally exclude those who have received a call but by lack of education, or for other reasons, are not yet professionally equipped for fulfilling it.

The historical self-authorisation and self-control of the ministry is plain to see when the ministry is regarded as a professional group. It has to be held in tension with that pentecostal view of it as a special channel of divine grace and revelation. However, there are dangers. The double role, when carried to extremes, leads to the clericalisation of the Church, to the belief that the Church is constituted by its ordained groups who minister to, but are not soiled by, a worldly laity of whom a lesser holiness is expected. Bishop F. R. Barry spoke of this clericalisation of the Church as a 'fatal tendency'. 'This is one of the worst disasters that have befallen it.'[1] And of course, the *reductio ad absurdum* of the creation of an exclusive clerical caste is that 'the Church in more than one place [is] finding herself reduced to the state of a priestly system without a Christian people',[2] an exact description of some Anglican parishes today. The priestly monopoly is made the more powerful if a priest is by birth and upbringing a member of a recognisable ruling class or social caste or, upon ordination, is automatically translated into it. Despite an often very real poverty, the English parish priest was usually accepted at least as on the fringe of the 'gentry'—'carriage folk' class, if not more. To question his professional claims, in such a situation, could be therefore also to threaten his social position. Today much is changed. The social status of the clergyman is under question as society becomes more egalitarian. But the clergyman who loses his social status cannot fall back on his professional status for his basis of authority at a time when clericalisation itself is challenged by a growing demand for a Church which involves the laity as heavily as the clergy in 'the priesthood of all believers'. The new role the laity has to play, and is being asked to play by the ordained ministry, constitutes the religious revolution of the twentieth century.[3]

If subsequently in this chapter the clergy are considered as a professional group and their status, deployment, rewards examined in

[1] *Asking the Right Questions*, 1960, p. 83.
[2] Yves M. J. Congar: *Lay People in the Church*, 1957, p. 41.
[3] See in this connexion the remarkable story of lay initiatives and ministries in *We the People*, Kathleen Bliss, London, 1962.

the light of them, this is not to be taken as meaning that their charismatic role is disregarded or the ambivalence of their role *vis-à-vis* the laity is forgotten.

MEMBERSHIP

According to the latest figures (1961) there are 18,749 Anglican clergymen in the provinces of Canterbury and York. The number represents an advance on previous years (1959, 18,061; 1960, 18,596) not accounted for by new ordinations for the interesting, even amusing, reason that the Church's Statistical Unit tends to discover forgotten clergymen (returned retired missionaries, those who have pursued secular careers and no longer minister, and so forth). These forgotten men swell the statistics, but do not necessarily add to the manpower deployed by the Church. About one clergyman in six is retired. The full-time clergy of both provinces number 15,488. Approximately 1,750 of these hold non-parochial appointments, over 230 are dignitaries without parochial cures, nearly 3,040 are assistant curates. The number of incumbents including dignitaries with parochial cures, is 10,361 (1962) occupying that number of livings. However, the total number of livings is rather higher—11,390—so that just about one living in eleven is vacant at any given time. The effective *parochial* force, however, is the number of incumbents plus the number of unbeneficed clergymen in parochial work (ministers of conventional districts and assistant curates); this now numbers approximately 13,500.

There is, according to the 1961 census figures, an average of one parochial clergyman to 3,261 persons. The average differs strikingly between provinces (Canterbury is 1 : 2,966; York is 1 : 3,986) and even more between dioceses in the manner already discussed in an earlier chapter; Birmingham, Liverpool, Sheffield, Durham, Manchester, London, Southwark, have ratios of 1 : 4,500 or over; Chelmsford is a runner up; Hereford is still at the bottom of the density scale with 1 : 1,120. It has already been argued that these ratios depend on a distribution of the clergy which is basically geographical and unrelated therefore to the distribution of population. The historical reasons for this need not be recapitulated.

AGE STRUCTURE

From the years 1956 to 1959 losses from the ordained ministry through death or retirement exceeded entrants. The peak loss was of 681 in 1958, the year in which clergymen then became entitled to receive the State pension in addition to the pension provided by the

Church: the gap narrowed in 1959 and in 1961 the entrants exceeded losses from the ministry: there were 686 entrants as against 494 losses. Falling rate of entry tends on the whole towards an ageing group; a rising rate of entry, if principally from the young, reverses the process. But it depends on the scale of new entry as to how quickly the average age is reduced. Though the number newly ordained has risen annually from 1954 to 1962 (441 to 632, i.e. 191 above 1954), the number recommended for training has fallen erratically from its 1959 peak of 757 to 673 in 1962. There is therefore some uncertainty about how the ordination figures will move in the next few years. The picture in the long run looks rosier. The Statistical Unit has prepared for me a double prediction: the first is of the numbers of the clergy, which they expect to rise from a total of nearly 20,000

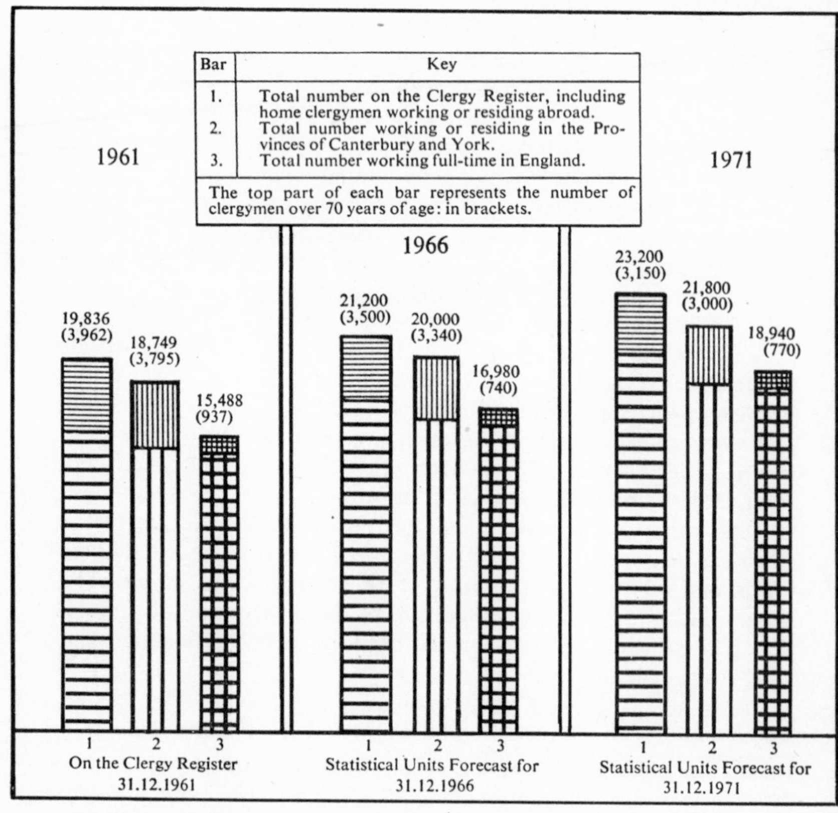

Diagram 1. Clergy Numbers in 1961 contrasted with Predictions for 1966 and 1971.
(Source SE, Table 54)

in 1961 to over 21,000 by 1966 and to over 23,000 by 1971. By that year the *working* clergy alone of the two provinces should have risen almost to 19,000. The second is of the changing age structure in that period. Diagrams 1 and 2 show precisely the expectations.

The present age structure of the clergy is shown again in Diagram 3, which, using the 1961 census figures, contrasts the age structure of the working clergy of the two provinces with teachers, university teachers, and expanding young professions such as scientists and managers. From these it will be seen that at present the clergy fall into a far older age pattern than the other groups and enjoy a longer professional life. By 1971, according to the Statistical Unit, the clergy will have ceased to be quite so elderly. Those under 35 will form the second largest of the six age groups. If Diagrams VII and VIII in *Facts and Figures 1962* are consulted, it will be seen that the

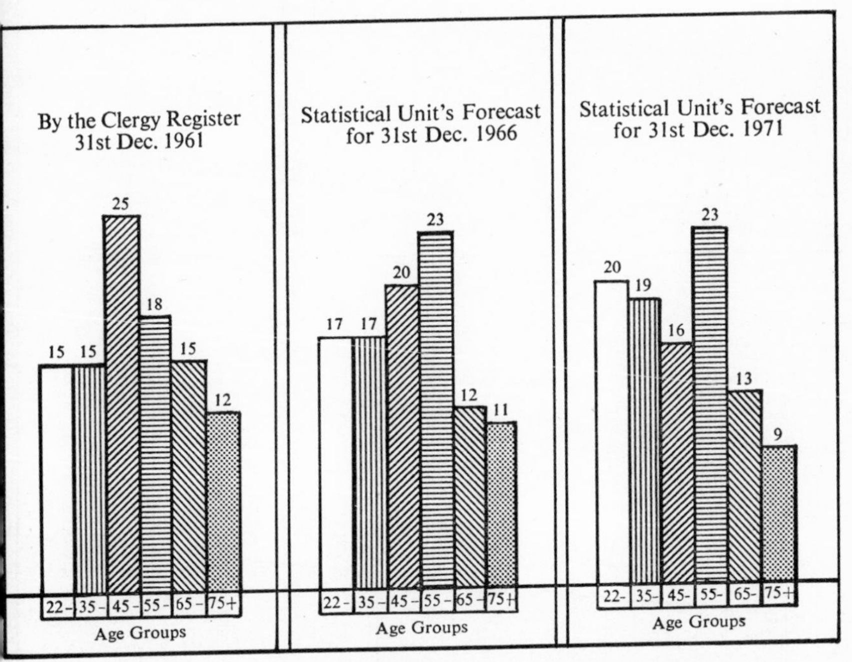

Diagram 2. Clergy Age Groups in 1961 against Expectations for 1966 and 1971.
(Number in each age group per 100 clergymen.)

(Source SE, Table 54a)

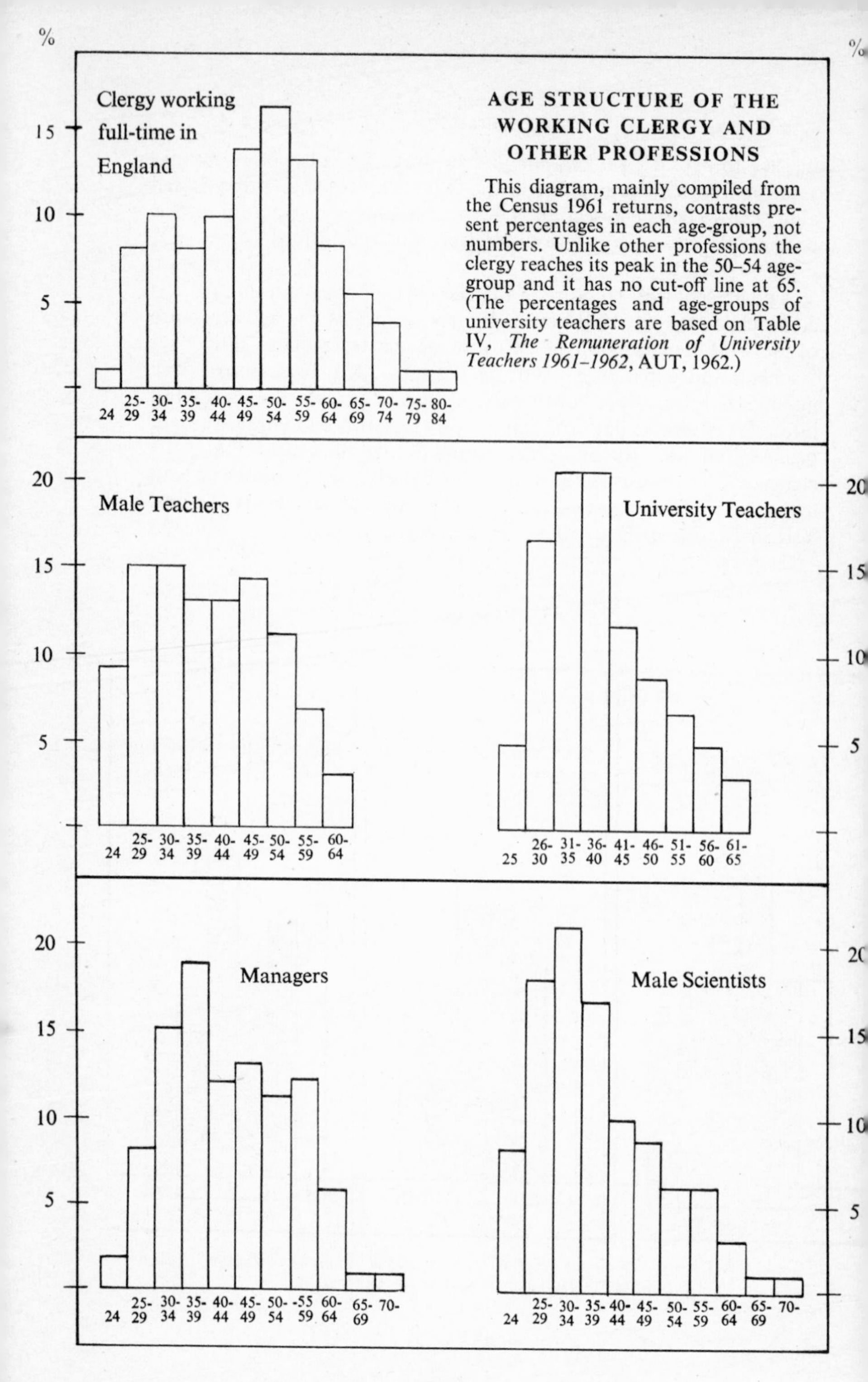
AGE STRUCTURE OF THE WORKING CLERGY AND OTHER PROFESSIONS
This diagram, mainly compiled from the Census 1961 returns, contrasts present percentages in each age-group, not numbers. Unlike other professions the clergy reaches its peak in the 50–54 age-group and it has no cut-off line at 65. (The percentages and age-groups of university teachers are based on Table IV, The Remuneration of University Teachers 1961–1962, AUT, 1962.)
Clergy working full-time in England
Male Teachers
University Teachers
Managers
Male Scientists
%
5
10
15
20
24
25-29
30-34
35-39
40-44
45-49
50-54
55-59
60-64
65-69
70-74
75-79
80-84
25
26-30
31-35
36-40
41-45
46-50
51-55
56-60
61-65
70-

Diagram 3

ageing of the clergy as a group, which has been going on for a century, is at last moving into reverse.

In one respect the clergy is unique as a profession: it recruits new members at almost any age, sometimes over 70 years. There were, in 1962, twenty-nine deacons (4·6 per cent) aged 60 and over. Between the years 1954 and 1962 more than a quarter of all deacons ordained were 35 and over. It is unusual in most professions to enter after 35. In 1961, 24 per cent and in 1962, 30 per cent were 35 and over. Consistent recruitment over more even than the normal span of working life will tend, of course, to keep the average age higher than in other professions. At present it is 54½ for all clergy, and 53 for incumbents by Statistical Unit figures, and 51·3 (incumbents only) by the MQ sample. A further factor enters into the pattern of the ministry. The retired and semi-retired render services which constitute a valuable pastoral aid. More than a thousand clergy are 'retired with permission to officiate'; they constitute an older auxiliary force not to be found in other professions. Their presence and continued service reminds us that a priest is ordained for life and retirement or failure to exercise his ministry does not extinguish holy orders. Retired men, however, are as unevenly distributed as the rest of the clergy, for understandably the clergy retire to the South, where they help to swell resorts more and more given over to those on pension.

ENTRY

The normal process of entering the ordained ministry is through attendance at a theological college and the passing of the General Ordination Examination: these are the expected qualifications, modified or abandoned only for the over-40s. The regulation of the entry requires a great deal more: first that a candidate should satisfy his bishop, then that he should satisfy the CACTM Selection Conference to which he is sent that he is a fit person. At both stages the reality of the vocation as well as intellectual qualifications will be considered. Candidates who are under the age of 25 are expected to read for a university degree if possible, but there is a wide degree of latitude and, in fact, of those ordained between 1953 and 1962 less than 50 per cent were graduates: since 1960 the number of graduates appears to be falling as a percentage of ordinands and must continue to do so. At present those in training without degrees form 56·9 per cent of the whole. A radical transformation of the ministry may be under way. The trend is unmistakable, and at least one part of it can be attributed to the efforts of the Church in post-war years to make provision for those whose vocation is unquestioned and gifts of personality high, but who have proved educational casualties.[1] Brasted Place, the Bernard Gilpin Society and other pre-theological colleges provide special training for such men. The average expected qualification academically, for the non-graduate candidate, is between five GCE 'O' level papers and five 'O' level plus two 'A' level: it is therefore less stringent than normal university entrance qualifications. According to Mr Anthony Coxon's survey of ordinands,[2] more than half of each group of ordinands (those with degrees and those without them) agree that 'if he is capable of it, an ordinand should read for a degree during the course of his training'. But only a small percentage of the whole said an ordinand *ought* to read for a degree, and about one-quarter of the degree group and one-third of the other agreed that it was by no means essential to read for a degree. These are rather remarkable expressions of opinion in a time when the prestige value of a degree is higher than it has ever been in the national life and entry into many professions is now inconceivable without one. That the Church appears to be moving in another direction probably has two causes—that it is placing more value on its own training, and that it has conceded in principle the desirability of recruiting its ministry on a wider basis than graduate status has so far made possible (in part because it was forced to by falling recruitment).

It is interesting confirmation of what has already been said about the wide range of entry by age into the ministry that Mr Coxon's findings show the average age of ordinands under training (in his sample) as 33·5 years.

> The wide dispersion of ages of men in training reflects the fact that there are at least two ages at which ordinands begin training: (1) the usual age of about 24 after University . . . and (2) at about 35 or more after training in, or practice of, other occupations.[3]

Training is not, at least theoretically, completed by ordination. It is the custom to place deacons under incumbents who will train them for pastoral and priestly duties in the parish, and of course they must sit the priest's examination and accept post-ordination training. If a man does two years at a theological college and three years in his first curacy, then his period under training could be argued to be five years. Pre-theological plus theological college training could lengthen the period to six or seven years. Satisfactory, if only it were

[1] The document which virtually reversed qualification policies was the Report of a CACTM Committee, *The Training of Non-Matriculated and Non-Graduate Candidates*, confidentially circulated in 1952.

[2] *Ordinand's Survey 1962:* for a fuller account of this related research see SE, pp. 280–2.

[3] Interim Report, privately circulated July 1963.

possible to assume also some really systematic training in the first curacy, which is not the case.

The Central Advisory Council for the Ministry has said:

Not all are required to read theology for their degrees. It would be a great weakness if none of the clergy of the Church of England had studied anything other than theology at university level, and men are being ordained who have studied in almost every conceivable faculty of our universities.[1]

However, Mr Coxon reports of his sample that of those under training with degrees, 104 are in theology, forty-two in the arts, twenty in natural science, nineteen in history, seven each in classics and social sciences, five each in English and philosophy, others six. Theology heads the list therefore, for reasons not altogether unexpected: it is among other things a further *professional* qualification.

SCOPE

In the present analysis one means by 'scope' whatever in other professions would be described as 'career-structure'. To terms such as 'career' or 'promotion' or 'prestige' applied to the ordained ministry both laity and clergy demur: no one cares to think of the ordained ministry as the instrument of personal ambition. Yet ambition can be noble, too, and incentives need not be dishonourable. Many dioceses use systems of differential stipends by which pastoral cures which include heavy populations, great distances or several churches are rewarded more highly than others with slighter duties: such payments are partly intended to offset heavier expenses, but they are also in effect incentives to a man either to stay in a difficult parish or to transfer to it. Again we speak of preferment and not promotion in the Church; but preferment as generally understood is promotion and none the worse for that; we need not be afraid of the term: if there are heavier and greater responsibilities in the ministry, then we need a system of promotion to fill them. And by 'career-structure' it is not generally meant how does a man become a Cotton or a Clore from being a mere house agent, or even whether every curate carries a mitre in his knapsack, but simply what scope will open out to a man as he gains in years and experience.

The point to be made at once is that for by far the greater majority of the clergy at home there is no 'career-structure' as industry, teaching or other professions might conceive it. The average career of a

[1] *Men for the Ministry*, CIO, 1963, p. 8.

Diagram 4. Promotion Ladders of the Clergy and two other professions compared

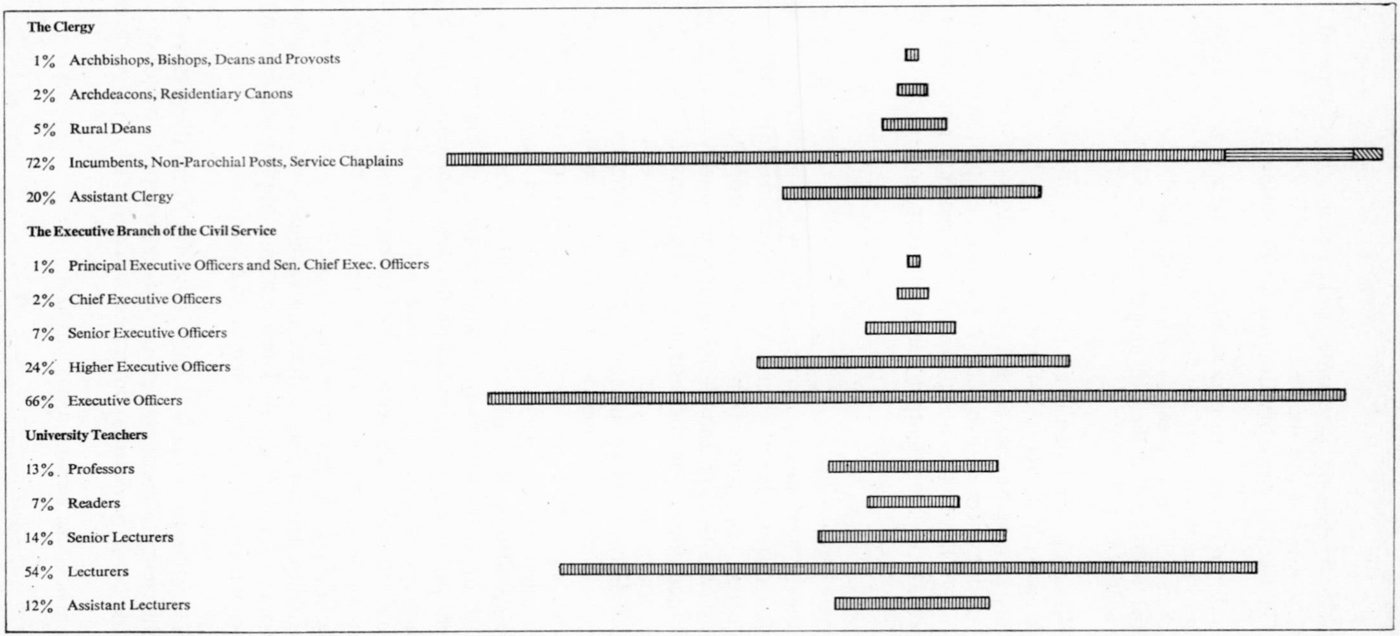

The Clergy

1% Archbishops, Bishops, Deans and Provosts

2% Archdeacons, Residentiary Canons

5% Rural Deans

72% Incumbents, Non-Parochial Posts, Service Chaplains

20% Assistant Clergy

The Executive Branch of the Civil Service

1% Principal Executive Officers and Sen. Chief Exec. Officers

2% Chief Executive Officers

7% Senior Executive Officers

24% Higher Executive Officers

66% Executive Officers

University Teachers

13% Professors

7% Readers

14% Senior Lecturers

54% Lecturers

12% Assistant Lecturers

clergyman has two or three stages: first curacy, second curacy, incumbency. Some move from first curacy to incumbency in one. To become an incumbent is to have 'arrived' professionally. The incumbency is the plateau of the profession: it is for most their career's fulfilment. In 1959 there were 9,386 incumbents and 779 rural deans (also incumbents): higher dignitaries numbered only 427: thus there was one chance in twenty-four of preferment to their ranks. In contrast, of all university teachers in 1961–2, 5,465 were lecturers or assistant lecturers and 2,804 were senior lecturers, readers, or professors: a university teaching career presented more than one chance in two of promotion. Of course, it has immediately to be said that the Church has no promotion ladder as such, not even by seniority, and the diagram opposite, which contrasts the 'promotion ladders' of university teachers, the executive branch of the Civil Service and the clergy shows clearly that the 'top posts' in the Church constitute only 3 per cent on the whole. The incumbency, certainly in the past, when it was more plainly movement into a social rank, whether in town or country, was in itself a sufficient arrival. None sought to be moved out of it: this was where most men expected to stay, only the very exceptional or very well-connected became higher dignitaries. The office of rural dean might be carried by the largest, most important strategically, or wealthiest living of the deanery—though not necessarily so. Translation to it involved a change of status, greater social prestige, but not inevitably a higher stipend. Certainly today the deanery means harder work and greater expenses, some professional prestige, without necessarily extra reward. The nearest parallel professionally to the incumbency is the general practice of a doctor. The doctor usually sinks his capital in a practice and can the less easily move out of it if it is a disappointing affair. The advantage the clergy has always enjoyed (compared with a solicitor or general practitioner) is relative ease of movement from living to living.

Clergy are as other men, on the whole they prefer to work where conditions are congenial or encouraging, the opportunities greater, or private circumstances are less harassing, disappointments fewer. They are not deployed as are front-line soldiers into areas of greatest casualty: they can accept or refuse livings offered to them. Therefore we must assume that for the most part clergy change livings, unless to lighter duties for reasons of health or age, because of the better incentives or greater challenges they offer. They may be mistaken in their hopes, but the hopes are there; they do not consciously downgrade themselves. Of 10,390 incumbents in 1961—clergy of the age disposition already shown—5,327 had held their present livings under five years, and 2,600 from five to nine years. Only 23·7 per cent had an innings of over ten years. There is an expectation of service of about thirty-five years. With an average length of service in a living of about seven years an incumbent could serve in five different livings in the course of his life: more if the average length of service in a living continues to fall. This internal circulation of the clergy, of course, grants them wider experience and constitutes a form of concealed promotion without translation to higher office. But as the turnover rate increases so the historical intention of the freehold and the living are defeated: a man is no longer set down as pastor of his flock for most of his lifetime, the *persona* of the community as the squire was lord of the manor for all his lifetime; and the schoolmaster, passing rich on £40 a year, was teacher of the flock until he died. That sort of social stability the parson himself no longer accepts as inevitable or desirable.

However, so basic has the stability of a living and the income of a benefice been to the Church that it has been the normal practice to award such dignitaries as archdeacons and other diocesan officers with livings. Thus a parish is served with a priest and a diocese provided with an official by one and the same stipend which led one dignitary to remark sadly to me that he had treated his parish with 'calculated neglect' and was now resigning his office to give it the attention it deserved. As far as I could discover from direct enquiries to dioceses and deans and provosts, of some 182 residentiary cathedral posts fifty-eight are held by archdeacons, suffragan and assistant bishops and other diocesan officers. When it comes to diocesan staff generally by far the largest group of clergy serving the diocese is paid by benefice or trust. Thirty-five archdeacons are paid this way as against fifteen on salary. It is only in the latest additions to diocesan staffs, youth officers or chaplains, or directors of education, that the numbers directly remunerated exceed those remunerated by benefice.

THE EXTRAPAROCHIAL MINISTRY

The newer offices remind us that there has been a considerable growth in the extraparochial ministry. The Services, the prisons, public schools and teaching generally have always provided extraparochial posts and livelihoods for clergymen. The Services, which have a chaplaincy establishment ratio, are unlikely to increase the number of chaplains they engage more than marginally in the next few years. The Royal Navy at the end of 1962 was, at 85, three chaplains under strength: the Army in 1961 had 157 chaplains of whom almost a quarter were on short-service commissions: the Royal Air Force at the end of 1962 was, at 95, two below strength. It should be remarked that for men on short-service commissions, usually of four years, a

Forces chaplaincy is no more than a spell of duty away from ordinary parochial cures. On June 1st, 1962, there were 89 full-time hospital chaplains, a number likely to increase only marginally. The Prison Commission, before its demise, reported to me that there were 27 full-time chaplains in the Prison Service proper and another six in approved schools (who also teach). The total of 96 full- and part-time chaplains is expected to increase to 115 in the next four years. Allowing for expansion to full strength and beyond, it is difficult to argue that these traditional forms of the extraparochial ministry will account for more than approximately 480 clergymen, some of whom would return to the parochial ministry after a short term of duty.

The foreseeable increases in the extraparochial ministry are likely to be in youth work, industry, and university and training college chaplaincies and tutorial posts. There is, of course, a considerable imminent expansion in Church training colleges. The following table describes the expansion, actual and hypothetical, and the demands it could make on men in holy orders.

Table X. Church Training College Expansion

Years		Students	Members of staff in orders
Actual	1957–8	6,147	29
Actual	1962–3	9,161	49½
Expected	1967–8	13,000	70

Of course, the clerical members of these staffs are not simply chaplains. Normally they are members of the teaching staff also available for pastoral duties. A case could be argued for having full-time chaplains, were funds available.

With at least seven new universities planned or building and the old under expansion and a tremendous expansion in colleges of advanced technology the pastoral duties of the Church to students are bound to increase. The following diagram illustrates the mounting university figures since 1945 for the whole of Britain. The acceptance by the government of the report of the Robbins committee, *Higher Education* (October 1963), may mean that these targets will be reached sooner. All in all, the Committee's proposals will mean about 560,000 young people in full-time higher education of all kinds in 1980–81, compared with 216,000 in 1962–63. 560,000 is rather more than the population of Sheffield.

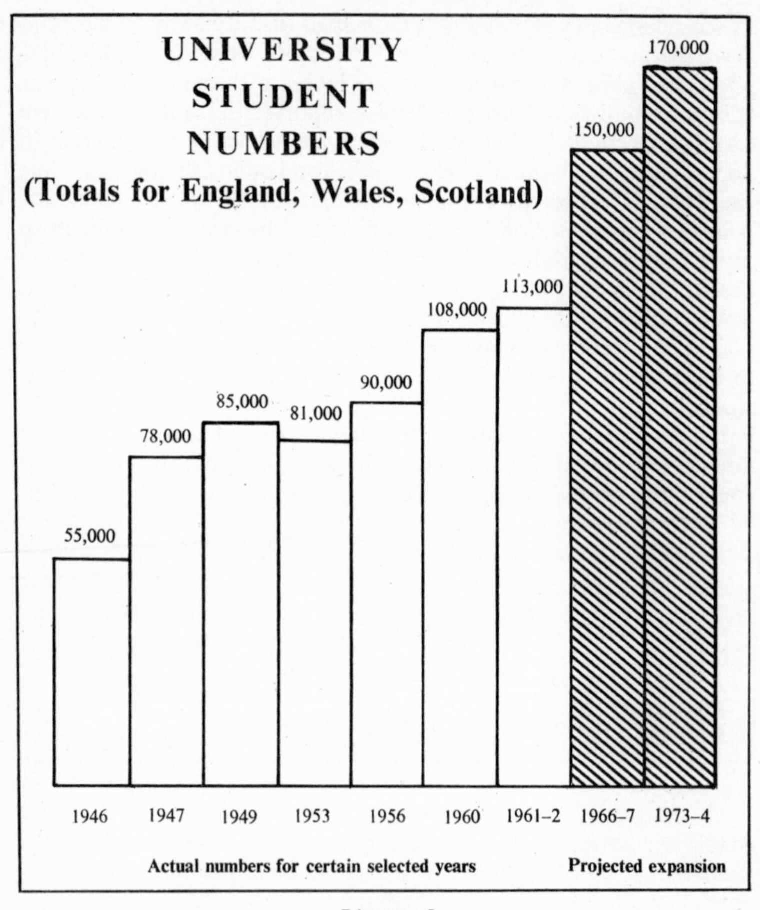

Diagram 5

CHAPLAINS AT UNIVERSITIES

The Church's ground for concern in university and technological college expansion is that these institutions have virtually ceased to be local institutions, recruiting purely locally. More and more they draw their students from the whole country or overseas. The students who come to them no longer commute from suburban homes and continue their social, family and church life in parishes where they have lived since childhood. They are in that sense uprooted. Moreover, this is a massive movement in some places, with social effects such as the creation of the bed-sitter kind of district which some town parsons have reported not without dismay. Birmingham University, for example, has fewer than 10 per cent of students living at home; as many come from overseas. It had 500 students in residence and 3,500 in lodgings in 1961. By the time its expansion from 4,610 students to 7,000 is completed in 1967 there will be 4,000 in halls of residence, but still nearly 3,000 in lodgings. The manner in which we are making these educational enclaves is itself evidence of 'massification' processes in contemporary society, with which the Church has to reckon just as much in education as in industry. The pastoral needs of these immense and transient 'parishes' of the young are grave and considerable. It is probably the last chance the Church will have of organised contact with them and only a proper expansion of the university chaplaincies can meet the situation. In the modern universities there appear to be at this moment no more than twenty-seven chaplains and assistant chaplains—about as many as in Oxford alone. Yet the probability is that we need 150 chaplains just in colleges of advanced technology. One hesitates to give a figure for the expansion of this whole college and university clerical force, but it looks as though it ought to reach 300 eventually. It needs men of academic standing and special gifts not easy to find.

Youth chaplaincies at diocesan level are hardly likely to make such demands on manpower. One full-time chaplain to every diocese would make forty-three. The larger dioceses need two or three, but this increase might balance itself against part-time appointments in smaller dioceses. It is the view of the Church of England Youth Council that if the Church is to accept the opportunities flowing from the Albemarle Report, then those appointments are necessary. The Church of England Board of Education is committed to expanding chaplaincies.

Industrial mission work at the moment of writing only appears to engage some twenty-eight clergy full-time in twenty-two dioceses, though it uses many more parsons on a part-time basis. It has the same pastoral justification as chaplaincies to universities, but it is as well an exploratory mission, essential to a Church, hitherto almost entirely based on the residential parish, to seek a pastoral relation to men and women at their place of work and a viable relationship with, and service to, an industrial and technological society at its most creative point.

In all these new fields, then, the Church is bound to increase its total pastorate. It will be calling for more men at a time when manpower is short. Though the services of the laity, part-time and full-time, ought to be increased here, it is also true that, at the moment, the Church is only believed by the world at large to be seriously committed when it entrusts these relationships to its own professional group, the ordained ministry.

WIDENING THE SCOPE

In 1961 there were 1,962 clergy in non-parochial appointments, but 496 were in cathedral or theological college posts, and some 205 were employed by church societies and 130 at other non-parochial centres of worship (religious houses and communities and royal peculiars). The number in full time teaching posts was 581; there were 436 service and hospital chaplains, making a total of 1,848. It comes down to this therefore, that the forms of extra-parochial ministry are mostly traditional ones, as Table 13 of *Facts and Figures 1962* shows. The new forms—youth, industry, chaplaincies at new universities—constitute as yet an inconsiderable fraction of the total ministry and are in no sense a real drain on the manpower available to the parochial ministry, which is understandably still the front line, the main sector of deployment. Indeed, an analysis of the scope of the ministry must lead to the conclusion that there are not enough extraparochial opportunities for men, especially for the brilliant, who ought at least for some period of their ministry to be seconded to posts where they might stretch their minds against the demands of the secular world and contribute to its needs. It does appear from what the clergy themselves say that the parochial ministry today can be inward-looking and narrowing, and sometimes harrowing for the able but frustrated: a ministry with greater scope would offer them more chances. The Church is so dominated by the beneficed living that it cannot see how to remunerate men doing other jobs—diocesan officials, university chaplains—except by finding for them small or run-down livings to keep them while they do their vital, extraparochial work. At moments when urgent decisions have to be made about vital appointments the Church can display a feebleness of indecision because it does not know how to pay the men, clerical or lay, it wants, when it finds them.

THE MINISTRY OVERSEAS

Traditionally the Church of England, like most churches of the West, supports overseas missions and sends out its ordained men. The pattern will change if the *Mutual Responsibility* programme of the Toronto Congress 1963 is operated: there will then perhaps be as much movement of men from abroad into the home provinces as movement out: at least this would be the ideal.

Evidence shows that more ordinands express a desire to serve abroad than ever actually do. All deacons ordained at home are normally asked if they would consider service overseas. In 1961–2, 580 were asked, 214, or 37 per cent, said yes. This appears to be a decline on the response of previous years, but it is still considerable. However, the Overseas Council estimated that only about seventy went to overseas posts in 1962, though in their view the proper contribution ought to be in the nature of 100 priests each year. It is impossible to be really precise, but it looks as though between 650 to 700 men ordained in the home provinces are serving overseas and (Table 21, *Facts and Figures 1962*) their average length of service is 8·5 years. In about ten years, it would appear, at the rate of seventy recruits a year, the overseas force would entirely renew itself.

The Overseas Council estimated for me that the number of men who came back in 1962 was fifty-five. Working from its own basis, and taking into account the movement in and out of England of men ordained abroad as well as men ordained here, the Statistical Unit tentatively gave me a figure for 1962 of a net 'loss' to overseas posts of some sixty men. I have accepted this as a working figure in further statistical exercises.

It seems probable that as provinces abroad grow more indigenous and autonomous, there will be less need for the old-time missionary on a life engagement and more demand for the short-service man who afterwards returns home to ordinary parish work. But the evidence to me is that there are strong disincentives here. The clergyman from abroad often finds himself a 'forgotten man' and has a struggle to get re-established and accepted. His pension rights can occasionally be affected. His standards of living may violently change. He probably needs a sabbatical term. It would seem sensible to regularise the status of men going overseas to a form of 'secondment' common to other professions and I make proposals about this later. A much greater rate of interchange should then become possible to the benefit of the whole Anglican Communion.

MACHINERY OF DEPLOYMENT AND PREFERMENT

This is very simple to describe. It does not exist. There are as many ways of moving an incumbent as there are dioceses, perhaps as there are independent patrons. As soon as one asks how are men moved from living to living in the Church one meets with the most ominous check upon the professional autonomy of the ministry. The living is not really a freehold to be transmitted to one's heirs, but a tenancy in which all rights (such as to nominate a successor) are extinguished once occupation is terminated by resignation, retirement, death or for any other reason. Moreover, the ownership of the right to present to the living (technically an advowson) may be in the hands of laity not necessarily communicant members of the Church. A man may be presented to his living through any one of a variety of channels; a private patron, a bishop or diocesan board of patronage, other clerical patrons, his university college, a religious patronage trust, the Lord Chancellor, the Prime Minister and so forth. How do these varied and often unrelated sources of deployment and preferment find their men? Where they are served by able administrators they keep careful card-indexes and conceivably confidential reports on existing incumbents and on candidates who have written to them or been recommended to them. Diocesan bishops keep lists in their desk drawers, their examining chaplains and various friends send suggestions to them, they discuss problem livings at staff conferences, they write and talk to patrons and to other bishops and consult the overseas list. After finance, staffing has the highest priority in diocesan administration. Patronage secretaries, whether of trusts or of the Crown, visit their livings, talk with local notables, interview the clergy and the bishops, sound out candidates. Assisted by an inner network of private communications sometimes rudely described, each patron does his best, often under great difficulty, to find the man he wants. The PCC is almost powerless in this, for though it has the right to be consulted and to object, it has no recourse to the material information upon which the rejected presentation was made, nor can it name a man. It cannot fare farther: it might certainly fare worse. It cannot, as the local political party executives or some free churches do, interview several candidates on the same evening and make its choice. The clergyman has still less knowledge of what goes on unless he is himself a patron. How does one get on a list? Just by writing? He could be on lists already without being aware of it. Writing, except to one's bishop, one's theological college principal, one's friend, could be bad form.

The truth is there is no central bureau or service at which comprehensive information about the clergy is registered, there is no classified clergy 'Who's Who'. Of course, there is Crockford's. But Crockford's has only limited classifications of dignitaries, chaplaincies, etc. The bulk of its material is alphabetically arranged and it has serious limitations—it gives no clergyman's age, no information about his family, no record of his secular career or accomplishments, grave deficiencies when it comes to judging a man's suitability for an appointment.

There is much evidence that the present chaos, with clergy in short supply, often makes for an unseemly scramble for names and hasty presentation of untested curates to livings. It also makes for the neglect of older, quieter, unspectacular parish priests, particularly the unmarried, and the untried. If one looks at the structure of the ordained ministry as it has grown up over the centuries, and as it has been already described, then the absence of 'staff records', 'promotion boards' and related paraphernalia is perfectly understandable. Members of independent professions do not need them: to be a member of the plateau of the profession is to have arrived. It would have been an impertinence to fix promotion machinery over a system in which an incumbent settled down for a goodly slice of years in one spot and grafted his life and service into the life of his flock, and looked for preferment beyond the rural deanery as an unlikely chance and as much of a social disaster as it was a spiritual call. Even now there is no such career ladder in the Church as one might find in industry, the BBC, teaching, or the Civil Service, for the higher posts are too few. The greater degree of movement must always be from living to living, not from grade to grade. If now there is a feeling that some central records ought to exist and to be accessible to all who need them and that the confusion of systems of presentation should be ended, it is because the ministry has long been moving away from the rugged independence once in theory possessed by more than 10,375 'corporations sole'. It has done so under pressure of social changes discussed in early chapters and for economic reasons. The original benefice income of most parishes has long been inadequate to pay its incumbents a living wage. It is supplemented where necessary, which is nearly everywhere, by subventions from the Church Commissioners and dioceses, and immediately, of course, these key bodies find themselves involved in deciding what is a living wage and in all the elaborate processes of deciding how to secure it. How they arrive at a minimum stipend and what other allowances should follow it is shown later. In fact, on the stipends side, the legal and professional independence of the clergy, even their economic independence as once expressed in the benefice, tend to get ignored. The clergy look to the whole living Church to support them. The Church in a quasi-collective sense becomes the employer, the clergyman the employee, and more and more he feels his dependent situation as servant not master. However, the more central financial policy of the Church and collective giving by the laity determine stipends, the more those who pay must be entitled to ask whether the clergy for whom the money is to be found are properly used, according to their abilities, and in the right places. The parable of the talents here pointedly applies to the Church. Yet it is impossible for the Church even to know what talents it is hiding or whether it is really using its men where they are needed in the absence of some central locus of information about them and of machinery to deploy and prefer them.

THE CLERGY AS A SOCIAL STRATUM

Does the clergy constitute a social group? Is it important to know? It is plain that in other chapters I have been contrasting the situation of the clergy in the days when social stratification was sharper than today and when it was harder to move from one class or social group to another, with that of the clergy in our more egalitarian and fluid society today. Even in the nineteenth century, the time of the middle-class breakthrough, the educational and social basis of the clergy appears to have been close to the two ruling groups—landed families and upper middle class—which was an advantage if the clergy expected social as well as spiritual authority to rest with them. It worked both ways. One means the middle class had of symbolising its own rise in the social scale was to join the Church. 'Carriage and pair do not pass the church door for more than two generations.' Yet with two classes in rivalry for political power the Church began to achieve a certain independence of both. The period of the Industrial Revolution brought forth the Wesleyan movement, the Tractarian movement, the Anglo-Catholic revival, Christian socialism, and a general concern for social justice rather than charity, and the struggle of the clergy for freedom from its own courts. The new theological colleges were an expression of the Church's concern for its own doctrinal and intellectual integrity and autonomy. The movement to free the Church from too complete identification with the Establishment reached its peak with the Life and Liberty movement and the Enabling Act of 1919. For over a century, it would seem, the Church has been moving away from the political and social establishment towards the role of one sole independent autonomous corporation, while seeking to preserve the *religious* establishment or at least to modify it only in the direction of the freedoms of the Church of Scotland. The Church moves slowly, but it looks as if it must move inevitably towards this corporate independence if it does not wish to appear to reflect the will of others or to continue to be identified with one class or ruling group and to find, as I fear it must, that no single contender for political power is committed to a purely Anglican solution of social and moral problems. Historically, these seem to amount to an effort on the part of the Church to rediscover its identity as its constitutional role (the nation on Sunday) has melted away. The effort still goes on.

Mr David Morgan, whose thesis on *Social and Educational Backgrounds of English Diocesan Bishops in the Church of England, 1860 to 1960*,[1] is discussed in the Summary of Evidence, produced a table

[1] Presented at Hull University.

of the landed and peerage connexion of bishops. He admits to some tentative conclusions and dubious connexions, for relations are not always easy to assume, but in that table (SE, Table 45) we see that though in 1860 all bishops appear to have landed and/or peerage connexions by birth and/or marriage, there has been a steady fall over the century until, in 1960, no more than twenty-three of the forty-three bishops had such connexions. They are still important therefore to the Anglican hierarchy, but not *de rigueur*.

Yet is is also significant that the description 'ruling class' is given by Mr Morgan to only twenty-one of the fathers of the 225 bishops consecrated in the century: the largest class group is 'professional' (upper professional, 20, other, 114). When it comes to 'father occupations' we discover that 95 are clergy (higher, 9, lower, 86). These researches suggest that for the major part of the century the diocesan bishop is well connected and that the family into which he is born is probably also either clerical or professional. Such a group—well connected and professional—is most certain to be interconnected with the intelligentsia, too. The diocesan bishop therefore tended to be a member of the *élite* of his time.

Across the century bishops have been public schoolboys. The leading ten public schools, Eton, Winchester, Marlborough, Shrewsbury, Rugby, Harrow, Westminster, Charterhouse, Haileybury, King Edward's, Birmingham, produced ninety-three bishops: other public schools ninety. The contribution of Oxford and Cambridge was just as dominant: between them they produced all but fifteen of the bishops in the century under analysis. Three leading colleges, Trinity, Cambridge, Christ Church and New College, Oxford, produced nearly a quarter of them.

The dominant role of the public schools and older universities is apparent in the recruitment to the ministry at the present day. In the Fayers-Heawood research analysed in the Summary of Evidence (p. 275 f.) it is shown that the Oxbridge offering of candidates to the ministry was 50 per cent greater than the offering of all the other universities put together, though of the total male students resident in English universities, Oxbridge accounted for only about a quarter. The public schools, which, on the broadest analysis, account for only about 7 per cent of all male pupils at school, offered nearly 30 per cent of all candidates. Of ordinands in training at the present time, 35 per cent have attended public or independent schools, 43 per cent grammar, high and direct grant schools, 22 per cent secondary modern and similar schools. Yet in 1961, nearly 65 per cent of all pupils went to the secondary modern schools and 28 per cent to grammar schools, and 7 per cent to public schools. Of course, it is to be expected that the largest school group of all—broadly secondary modern—will fail to make the contribution to the ministry which its numbers would justify, because it contains the '11 + failures', those whose intellectual rejection is also a social rejection. The intellectual demands of training for the ministry are beyond the majority of them: the social demands must be, too, though we are apt to forget this. Yet the Crowther Report made us aware that 9 per cent of children of the highest and 65 per cent of the second highest ability group left school at 15 or below. According to a study of National Service men by a classification of Army recruits 'half of all those in the two *highest ability groups* left school at 15'.[1] The Crowther Report surveys show that the wastage is highest among children from large families and/or from skilled and unskilled manual workers. The researches of Dr James Douglas of the Medical Research Council Unit at the London School of Economics show that in the IQ range 109–112, 59 per cent of the upper and middle class children go to grammar schools as compared with 39 per cent in the lower middle class, and 26 per cent in the manual working classes.[2] To become a member of an educational *élite* (the meritocracy, it has been called) is at least in part a social reward. Class factors are strong determinants. It is damaging for the country as a whole that there is so great a wastage from the educational system of children of the two highest ability groups. It is as dangerous for the Church, which ought to be peculiarly sensitive to losses of these kinds. Those who are disappointing intellectually and disappointed socially form the immense part of the urban millions who are so impermeable to the teaching of the Church. They are the spiritual failures, too. And they become the more unreachable if they form the impression that by class and accent the Church, and its ministry, are no more for them than the royal enclosure at Goodwood.

BIAS IN SELECTION?

The Fayers-Heawood analysis shows the presence of a strong bias towards public school candidates in Church selection procedures. The same analysis shows a bias towards Oxbridge candidates, though neither so strong nor so significant as the bias towards the public school candidates. I concede with Mr Anthony Coxon that the bias is probably an unconscious one. The selectors will certainly be moved in their selection by their own sense of what an Anglican priest should be; they will have formed their own image and certainly have

[1] *Fifteen to Eighteen*, p. 118. See Table 16, p. 119, Chap. I, Part ii, Vol. II (Surveys). See also my own report, *The Transition from School to Work* (Industrial Welfare Society, 1962), Chap. 8.

[2] Cf. *The Home and the School*, James Douglas, London, 1964.

asked themselves, 'Can I see this man in our own pulpit?' And in so conservative an institution as the Church, what a parson should be is what he usually has been down the centuries, a graduate of Oxford or Cambridge. One has to bear in mind the self-renewing, self-determining powers of the ministry considered purely as a profession, which have already been discussed: it is almost bound to wish unconsciously to renew itself in the social pattern it has always known.

Of course, this bias towards public schools and Oxford and Cambridge is as well known in other professions. The Fleming Report discovered that out of 830 bishops, deans, judges, stipendiary magistrates, highly paid civil servants, Indian civil servants, governors of dominions and directors of banks and railway companies, 76 per cent came from public schools and, of those, 48 per cent from twelve major ones. Both Labour and Conservative cabinets contain them. They are the real ruling *élite* of the country still. Bias towards Oxford and Cambridge persists in the Civil Service, too. A written Treasury answer, of 26th June, 1963, giving figures of graduates from the universities of England and Wales accepted by competitive examination into the administrative grade of the Civil Service at assistant principal level for the last ten years produced these figures:

Assistant Principal Competitions

	Normal open	*Suppl. open*	*Limited*
Oxford	194	3	3
Cambridge	149	3	1
London	35	—	5
Other universities	15	1	3

At the principal level, over four years, twenty-three graduates came from Oxford, eighteen from Cambridge, five from London, two from others. According to Mr R. K. Kelsall, figures relating to open competition results in the years 1949–52 show that compared with the pre-war results, the Oxford and Cambridge contribution has fallen from 89 per cent to 74 per cent. Nevertheless, 'Oxford's importance relative to other universities has . . . actually increased; the decline in the combined figures is entirely due to Cambridge'. He points out that British universities other than Oxford, Cambridge, Edinburgh and London have now a 10 per cent share in places gained by open competition as against a pre-war percentage of 3.[1] Church ordinations make a more representative showing.

[1] *Higher Civil Servants in Britain from 1870 to the present day*, R. K. Kelsall, London, 1955. It thoroughly analyses the class position. See also *Anatomy of Britain*, Anthony Sampson, 1962, which makes many pointed comments about the Oxbridge base of the establishment.

It would be gratuitous humbug to complain at the high percentage of men from the public schools and the older universities in the ministry. The older universities have historically the closest and longest relation to the Church of any educational institution and the greatest obligations to it: miraculously in all the social and intellectual changes that bond has never been severed. In the nineteenth century, and this, the greatest single source of the intellectual *élite*, the political and social leadership of the nation, was the public schools: their bonds with the Church were strongly forged, too, in the chapel life, in the numbers of clergy on their staffs, in the special provision they often felt obliged to make for the sons of the clergy. Indeed, we can stand the usual questions on their head and say the plight of the Church would have been poor indeed had the response to the appeal of the Church for clergy been as low from the public schools and Oxford and Cambridge as it has been from the grammar schools or the modern universities.

The questions asked at the beginning of this section can be answered. The ministry does constitute a social stratum, its centre of gravity is middle to upper class: the centre of gravity is higher upper middle to upper class for dignitaries. Patronage, just because it has gone along with landed connexions, or else is exercised by bishops, deans and chapters, Oxford and Cambridge colleges, has tended to fossilise the situation. Today English society as a whole is moving away from the domination of its life by one group, however brilliant and devoted to public service, towards a more egalitarian society. The new young people flooding from expanding grammar schools, expanding young universities, and colleges of advanced technology into every sector of our national life, but particularly into industry, teaching and the social services come from those classes traditionally least devoted to the Church. If the Church is to be a national as well as an established Church, they have to be met and understood and brought in. Were young men from those strata of society to come forward in numbers proportionate to public schools and Oxbridge, there would be no recruitment problem for the ministry, but the ministry would be socially changed in the sense that it would in its own composition be more representative of the structure of society itself. To bring in more of the secondary modern group than at present to make the thorny ascent to the ministry three things are organisationally necessary: an increased provision of pre-theological training facilities by the Church, the raising of the school-leaving age to 16, and a spread of comprehensive school facilities. Spiritually much depends on the establishment of a new and profound rapport with skilled and unskilled manual workers and their families.

CHAPTER VII

The Rewards of the Clergy

IN the course of that fascinating analysis, *Anatomy of Britain*, Mr Anthony Sampson remarks that

> in the nineteenth century the discrepancy between the bench and the clergy was grotesque. In 1906 the average income of a parson was about £150, while the Archbishop of Canterbury had £15,000 a year.

He goes on to reproduce an illuminating little table provided by Mr Kelsall[1] which suggests that the deans at least have failed to hold any lead they once had in the affluence race:

	1871	*1954*
	£	£
Permanent Secretary, Board of Trade	1,500	4,500
Town Clerk, Liverpool	2,000	5,000
Professor of Moral Philosophy, Edinburgh	502	2,100
Dean of Durham	3,000	3,000

What is the real position today? Are the parsons still so poor, the curates penniless, the bishops rich but less rich than they were? The true position, as with so many other aspects of the Church of England, is not easy to ascertain, but there is no lack of evidence as to how the Church has grappled with the financial difficulties of the clergy whose benefices are not automatically geared to the rising costs and rising incomes of an affluent society.

ENDOWED AND NON-ENDOWED INCOME

Table 84 of *Facts and Figures 1962* sets out the parochial benefice incomes of the clergy in England in 1960. This shows the main sources by which the parochial clergy are paid: the largest sum of all is endowment income, which amounted to £5,906,873. Non-endowment income amounted to £4,322,750. Thus the two major sources of clergy income begin to approach parity. The endowment income is, of course, still earmarked, as legally it must be, as the property of the particular benefice to which it belongs and to which, apart from the equalising procedures (technically 'diversions') operated in some dioceses, it naturally goes. Averaged out among 11,383 benefices it was £519 per benefice, but among the 10,232 incumbents who held the

[1] Abridged from R. K. Kelsall, *Higher Civil Servants in Britain*, p. 183.

benefices it was £528 in 1960. In the same year the non-endowment income averaged £408 per incumbent. By 1962 the ratios had already changed significantly: endowment income had risen to £593 per head; non-endowment to £530. The changing ratios point to the crux of the problem. Endowment income will remain stationary or rise only slightly, and will fall as a percentage of clergy stipend. Non-endowment income will rise both absolutely and as a percentage.

It is this second source, non-endowment income, which raises the English clergy above the direct poverty line and upon which they must increasingly depend. The main elements of this second source are (*a*) grants from diocesan stipends funds (in addition to funds raised in the diocese, the DSF receives block grants from the Church Commissioners which are dispensed at the concurrent discretion of the bishop and diocesan board of finance); (*b*) PCC and DBF contributions to rates, dilapidations, etc., or directly to stipend; (*c*) Easter offerings, fees; (*d*) expenses of office from PCC.

Indeed, eight or nine incumbents out of ten receive augmentation grants from diocesan stipends funds and over half the incumbents of the country supplement benefice income from chaplaincies and other earnings. It must be understood, however, that though the role of the diocese, through its stipends fund, is bound to increase as non-endowment income rises, this does not diminish the function of the Church Commissioners. The Church Commissioners are the principal source of the DSF. Their total distributions accounted for 75·2 per cent of clergy income in 1961 and 77·2 per cent in 1962. Nevertheless, the parish contributions, a truly independent source, continue to rise and will grow in importance.

The 1961/62 breakdowns of percentage of contributions to stipends is as follows:

Table XI. Sources of Clergy Incomes

	1961 per cent	1962 per cent
Endowments	48	49
Glebe rents	4	3
Diocesan stipends funds grants	28	28
Other diocesan grants	1	2
Parochial contribution	10	9
Easter offerings	4	4
Fees	3	3
Other sources (trust funds, patrons)	2	2
	100	100

How the main sources arrange themselves in one quite typical diocese can be shown in the following table:

Table XII. Analysis of Incumbent Stipend Averages Classified on a Population Basis (Typical Diocese)

Pop. groups	No. of benefices	Av. ben. income	Av. augmented by parish	Av. augmented by diocese	Av. net[1] income
		£	£	£	£
Under 1,000	84	461	120	266	847
1,000–5,000	110	431	180	261	872
5,000–10,000	45	390	236	256	882
10,000–25,000	17	390	273	258	921
			Diocesan average		869

[1] The figures in the whole table have been calculated after deductions such as rates, dilapidations, etc. Gross income for each group respectively would be £987, £986, £1,014, £1,088, Diocesan average £999.

It is plain enough from such a table how great the role of parish and diocese is already and how the importance of the endowment diminishes as the population density grows, while the role of the laity rises sharply, though not proportionately.

THE GREAT EQUALISER

In fact, the non-endowment elements of income constitute a great equaliser fund: without it the Church would find it impossible to fill the most poorly endowed livings. The table above shows us that the two great sources of non-endowment income are the diocese and the PCC. The more the Church struggles to raise and equalise clergy incomes the faster the non-endowed sources will have to grow, particularly parochial ones. As they become a greater fraction of the whole the more clearly it will be the case and be understood to be the case that the clergy have to be maintained by the growth of a living Church rather than by an inheritance from the past. Because at present the Church spends £17 million a year on training, stipends, housing and pensions of the ministry, of which the Church Commissioners contribute £13 million and the rest comes from the laity, the role and extent of lay giving is misunderstood. A statement to Church Assembly by the Archbishops of Canterbury and York on February 21, 1963, said, after an examination of the Church's budget: 'Here we have requirements totalling about £36 million a year. These are met from two sources, one the endowments of the Church in the hands of the Church Commissioners (13½ million) and the other the giving of the laity (21½ million through parochial channels and perhaps another £1 million through societies).' Lay giving is already decisive for the Church, in fact.[1] As the non-endowed sources of income grow, the status of the clergyman must insensibly alter *de facto* from that of the self-employed man with an independent income to that of salaried servant of the Church. Professionally the clergy might not find this easy to accept, but it is possible that a change of such magnitude could radically alter the role and self-consciousness of the laity, and bring to an end the passivity so characteristic of it in the past. Christian stewardship of money, leading to stewardship of time and talents, already points in this direction.

Although the Church Commissioners meet more than three-quarters of the stipends of incumbents and generally act as book-keepers, paymasters and arbitrators for the Church, this has not produced the imposition of a uniform policy dictated by Millbank. The uniformity is administrative only. The Church Commissioners seem to have encouraged the utmost flexibility of policy in the dioceses, many of whom have had a very hard struggle in times of rising costs and relatively static congregations to bring stipends generally to the longed-for levels above the poverty line.[2] If the function of the dioceses in fixing minima, determining allowances and raising augmentation funds is understood, what I have described as the great equalising fund is really forty-three separate diocesan funds each administered in its own way according to a policy determined locally. The irony is that the central contribution from the Church Commissioners which could determine uniform policy by its sheer weight alone cannot do so because it is geared to 11,343 separate benefice funds. The local equalising funds can only equalise locally. There is thus a double element of chance in determining a stipend—the benefice a man happens to occupy and the diocese he happens to be situated in.

As part of this survey I addressed an inquiry to all diocesan boards of finance about diocesan stipend policy at the end of 1962. It produced the following table of diocesan minimum incumbent stipends:

[1] Cf. *The Finances of the Church*, CIO, 1963, which estimates (p. 9) a total Church income of £45 million of which Church Commissioners' income is just over one third.

[2] Five Canterbury dioceses and seven York do not yet include stipend augmentation allocations in their diocesan budgets: three Canterbury and two York fail to do so for assistant curates as well. See Summary of Evidence, p. 262.

Table XIII. Minimum Stipends for Incumbents as reported by 40 Dioceses

Province	£750–799	£800–849	£850–899	£900–949	£950+
Canterbury	4	15	5	2	1
York	1	6	5	1	0
No. of Dioceses	5	21	10	3	1

It is worth noting in this table that for the whole country the largest group is in the £800–£849 range, but this is some way still from the minimum of £1,000 and a free house which is the declared aim of a number of dioceses. It is also significant that York Province which finds it harder to secure clergy has higher minima on the whole than Canterbury.

However, the minimum stipends do not tell the whole story. They merely give us the figure below which, diocese by diocese, clergy income is not allowed to fall (except for certain 'light duty' cures here and there). How high can they *rise* for parochial clergy? I have classified the highest stipends reported to me by dioceses as follows:

Table XIV. Highest Stipends Reported, analysed by Provinces

Ranges	Canterbury	York	Total
Under £1,000	1	—	1
£1,000–£1,499	6	2	8
£1,500–£1,999	10	5	15
£2,000–£2,499	6	4	10
£2,500 and over	6	2	8
No. of Dioceses	29	13	42

Of course the number of better-paid livings will be higher than the forty-two reported to me, since all I asked for was the highest example in each class from each diocese. The Church Commissioners' breakdown (1962) gives some 308 livings in the highest three classes (£1,500 and over) which is no more than 3 per cent of all livings. The highest class of all then (£2,000 and over) numbered sixty-one, i.e. $\frac{1}{2}$ per cent of all livings. The number of 'plums' is not as great as rumour would have it. They are not evenly distributed: in 1960 London had twenty-three in the highest-paid group, Southwark seven, Ely six, Birmingham six, Liverpool six: thirteen dioceses had only one each, eleven had none at all.

NET BENEFICE INCOME[1] AND TRUE INCOME

It must be said that the common category of 'net benefice income' (Crockford's gives it for example) does not fully describe incumbent income. There are some other sources. Children's allowances are among them. These vary fantastically from diocese to diocese, from £36 for the first child, £24 for each succeeding child (London) to £10 for each child under tax relief (Worcester)—or to none at all, for only twenty-five dioceses report them. The most generous appears to be Norwich, with £40 for each child under 5 and £60 for each child over 5 in full-time education. The effect of children's allowances is shown in Table 23 of the Summary of Evidence (p. 259). The table shows that in a diocese with allowances an incumbent with three children (one under 5, one 7, one 12) may gain anything from £20 a year to £160. The average gain for Canterbury province was £63 12*s*. and for York province £67 14*s*. Stipend minima which before children's allowances ranged from £750 to £950 (Canterbury province) and £800–£870 (York province) could afterwards range from £800–£1,055 (Canterbury province) and £856–£970 (York province). Children's allowances increased income differentials sharply among married men with families, and still more sharply widened the gap between the married and the unmarried, and the married with allowances and the married without. They were not an equalising factor even for the married group.

Of course, the family allowance payments were additional to the minimum stipend, or they would make no sense. Other payments or allowances could as they were made or not made effectively raise the real income, or the real minimum. Thus fourteen Canterbury dioceses and three York dioceses excluded the whole of the Easter offering in computing the minimum: in addition one Canterbury diocese excluded the first £100, another the first £50; one York diocese also excluded the first £50. Thirteen Canterbury dioceses reported that the parsonage was free of rates and dilapidations: five reported this freedom if the PCC paid. Some three York dioceses made similar arrangements. Column 9 of Appendix 1 in the Summary of Evidence (pp. 306–7) describes how really, in twenty-eight different ways, twenty-eight different dioceses made allowances of one kind or another which as a consequence automatically raised clergy stipends above the diocesan minimum. Some excluded all PCC payments to the incumbent from computation, others the first £50, or first £100 of chaplaincy fees,

[1] Net benefice income, as the Church uses the term, is *before* deduction of income tax.

others generously excluded all outside earnings, or awarded extra stipend on a points system for varying responsibilities above the average. If we take a diocese which, as far as one understands from its report, excludes nothing and has no children's allowances (No. 15, but see also 7 in SE, Appendix 1), then its minimum must stand, for married and unmarried alike, at the £800 reported. On the other hand, a married man in Diocese 2 with an Easter offering of £50, rates and dilapidations of £47, children's allowance of, say, £84, and allowed £100 outside earnings is, in fact, better off by £281 per annum, a staggering differential which has no other basis than the ability—or willingness—of the diocese to pay. *The actual difference in the minimum in these two cases, however, is only* £4. Such evidence tells us emphatically enough that there is no real comparability of stipends scales between dioceses and that the stated minimum sometimes means very little. These disparities impede movement from diocese to diocese except in an upward direction. They make it hard to estimate the real earnings of the clergy.

EXAMPLES OF INEQUALITIES

However, the same inequalities can exist *within* a diocese. Here are actual examples, first from a diocese with a standard minimum of £750:

Parish A: Minimum assured £810

		£	£
Income:			
Gross endowment income		615	
Approved letting		156	
Diocesan augmentation		195	
Fees		12	
Gross stipend		978	978
Charges: Rates	40		
Dilapidations	127	167	
Net stipend		811	
Additional income:			
Easter offering		20	
PCC contribution to expenses		27	47
Total income: Net		£858	*Gross* £1,025

Parish B: Minimum assured £750

		£	£
Income:			
Gross endowment income		245	
Diocesan augmentation		559	
Fees		45	
Gross stipend . . .		849	849
Charges: Rates	64		
Dilapidations .	35	99	
Net stipend		750	
Additional income:			
Easter offerings		140	
Expenses of office from PCC		63	
Parsonage charges met by PCC . .		99	
Other income from PCC		441	
Income from new church endowment . .		82	
Chaplaincy		60	885
Total income: Net . .		£1,635	*Gross* £1,734

Parish C: Minimum assured £810

		£	£
Income:			
Gross endowment income		660	
Diocesan augmentation		248	
Chaplaincy		50	
Fees		85	
Gross stipend . . .		1,043	1,043
Charges: Rates	80		
Dilapidations .	72		
Mortgages . . .	80	232	
Net stipend		811	
Additional income:			
Easter offerings		216	
PCC towards parsonage charges . .		212	
PCC towards income		77	
Patron's benefactor		70	
Chaplaincy		185	
Children's allowance		80	
Rural Dean allowance		75	915
Total income: Net . .		£1,726	*Gross* £1,958

Here is similar evidence from another diocese, given in slightly less detail:

Parish D: Minimum assured £844

	£		£
Income:			
Benefice income	413		
Joint parish and diocesan augmentation	480		
Emoluments grant	50		
Gross stipend	943		943
House outgoings	102		
Net stipend	841		
Additional income:			
Easter offering	80		
Chaplaincy	110		190
Total income: Net	£1,031	*Gross*	£1,133

Parish E: Minimum assured £786

	£		£
Income:			
Benefice income	301		
Joint parish and diocese augmentation	460		
Emoluments grant	40		
Gross stipend	801		801
House outgoings	40		
Net stipend	761		
Additional income:			
Easter offering	60		
Chaplaincy	156		216
Total income: Net	£977	*Gross*	£1,017

Parish F: Minimum assured £750

	£		£
Income:			
Benefice income	488		
Joint parish and diocese augmentation	440		
Special benefice grant	165		
Gross stipend	1,093		1,093
House outgoings	128		
Net stipend	965		
Additional income	—		—
Total income: Net	£965	*Gross*	£1,093

DIFFERENTIALS

It is interesting to see that, in extended answers, certain dioceses reported efforts to adjust stipends—or at least minimum stipends—to the actual burden of work or responsibility carried by each incumbent by the establishment of differential systems of payment.

1. *Bath and Wells.* The diocese has divided parishes into eight grades ranging from very small single cures (of which it has forty-seven) to largest single cures (of which it has thirty-eight): these constitute, in its own breakdown, grades A–F. Pluralities account for Grades G and H. Over the whole field the minima range from £840 for small single cures to £1,000 for the largest single cures and £1,075 for the largest multiple cures.

2. *Lincoln.* The diocese has a points sytem. Every incumbent receives a basic £650, plus Church Commissioners' annuities, and then differentials based on the following allocation of points:

(*a*) 1 point for each church;
(*b*) 1 point for each 1,000 acres to a maximum of 15,000 acres;
(*c*) 1 point for each 1,000 people to a maximum of 10,000.

Initially (1959) each point was worth £5, but now (1962) it is worth £25. By way of example, an incumbent with two churches, 2,000 population and a parish acreage of 5,000 receives £650 + £225 = £875.

3. *Ely.* The diocese has calculated minimum stipends for 1962–3 on the following basis:

One-parish charge	£800 p.a. net.
Special responsibility	£900 p.a. net.
Two-parish charge	£910 p.a. net.
Three-parish charge	£945 p.a. net.

4. *Chester.* The diocese adds differential points to send up the stipend of all those who qualify and whose stipend is £1,500 or below. A parish with two churches gets three points, with three or more churches four points; a population of 5,000 secures four points with an extra point for each 1,000 up to 20,000. A union or plurality gets seven points. Points are awarded for size of parish and parsonages expensive to heat. Currently each point is worth £12. The largest single parish gets £276 over the minimum stipend of £820: all unions get an extra £120. All incumbents of twenty years' service get an additional £20 per annum.

ASSISTANT CURATES

The stipends of assistant curates are not in the main derived from endowments. Though assisted by the Church Commissioners through the block grants to diocesan stipends funds, the ultimate sanction over the pay and employment of the assistant curate is the diocese entirely. Normally it insists that the parish employ the curate and guarantee the minimum stipend which it lays down, usually also insisting upon the provision of free housing accommodation. The parish then qualifies for diocesan grants towards the maintenance of a curate. Table 24 of the Summary of Evidence (p. 260) shows that starting stipends vary from £425 to £600 in Canterbury province and from £450 to £550 in York province. Many dioceses operate systems both of annual increments and of children's allowances. Over three years the increments raised stipends to £500 (lowest) and £675 (highest) in Canterbury province and £510 (lowest) and £675 (highest) in York province. The lowest increase was 4 per cent, the highest 36·8 per cent, both provinces considered together. The incremental system increased differentials therefore. So did children's allowances, for the hypothetical family analysed in Table 25, Summary of Evidence (p. 261). The lowest stipend after three years was £592, the highest £750, both provinces considered together (col. 4).

The built-in differentials—such as parochial endowments—which affect the income of incumbents everywhere do not exist to complicate curates' stipends. Assistant curates within one particular diocese will all receive similar incomes therefore, apart, perhaps, from differences between Whitsun offerings from parish to parish or any grants from church societies made directly to the curate. But no common policy emerges either within each province or for the whole country. It is still possible for a married curate with a child in one diocese to receive less than the starting stipend of a single man in another and very much less than a single man with three years' service. The wide differences between the percentages of increases tell the story of the current confusion of scales as effectively as the actual differences in incomes: increases after three years, for single men, vary from 4 to 36·8 per cent in Canterbury province, and from 4·8 to 25 per cent in York province; for married men in both provinces, they vary from 9 to 30·9 per cent.

COMPARABILITY STUDIES

How do clergy incomes compare with other incomes? Can one even compare them? The diocese is concerned in every case with the net benefice income—what the man actually has to spend—and this involves what the income is after rates and dilapidations are paid, no matter by whom. And we have seen from actual personal balance sheets exactly how this works. But in the secular world no such calculations are made. It is a man's gross income that counts. If out of it he has to pay rent, rates, repairs and so forth, that is his affair, not his employer's. The Church Commissioners have cut through this dilemma by calculating the *total* income of each incumbent on returns made by the clergy themselves and recording it in the Central Register of Benefice Income: and total income is net benefice income plus all those extras we have looked at. The average net total income in 1962 was £1,020 (1961, £892) as against the net benefice income of £960 (1961, £834). The net total income includes, in addition to the net benefice income, chaplaincies, public and educational appointments, stipend as curate in charge of another benefice, cemetery fees and letting of rooms. It does not include contribution towards expenses of office or additional income as a bishop or archdeacon, but it does include averaged children's allowances. It is therefore a much more exact computation than net benefice income. However, it is still *net*, that is, it is arrived at after deduction of the parson's housing costs—dilapidations, mortgage, rates, or rent and rates if there is no parsonage house. The average gross income is £1,123. The £1,020 average *net* total income includes a house free of rent and of all other outgoings. The house becomes a concealed benefit, and indeed in this the parson is quite unlike almost all other members of his congregation. And they would properly have reason to object if the income of a person *after* he had met his housing costs was compared with theirs *before* they had done so, and the parson's poverty pleaded against their affluence on this basis: or if the value of a free house were ignored altogether.

But how to assess all this? The parson fairly objects, when it comes to the parsonage, that because of his calling he *has* to live in this particular house in this particular place; he has no option.[1] And if he happens to be landed with a large rambling parsonage, then it is no asset but a liability: his income does not expand with expanding house and garden. His point is understandable. Yet still, he *has* free housing, and usually a garage and a garden, and at a time when these are more costly than ever for the ordinary citizen. He can sometimes profitably let. The Guild Churches' measure awards an extra £250 a year to a Guild Church parson without a house. The interim report (1960) of the Royal Commission on the Police valued a police house at £125 p.a. The Church Commissioners computed that the average

[1] It is not quite true: a policeman may be placed in this position, because he can't refuse to go where he is posted. A parson can refuse a living.

outgoings on a parsonage house in 1962 were £163, 14·5 per cent of gross income. It would seem reasonable to add a nominal £200 to total net income to represent the value of the parson's free house and free outgoings on the house: the average total *gross* income would then be £1,220, which is a more respectable figure in 1963. However, other professions—university staff, teachers, doctors or hospital staffs, youth service workers with a flat over the club may get accommodation free or at nominal rent. I have therefore elected to do no more than note here that to arrive at *real*, as against net, clergy incomes a factor should be added for free housing which is conservatively estimated at £200 a year. And as actual stipends, not total incomes, range from about £600 (light duty) to £4,702 (the highest I have discovered),[1] a quite astonishing range, I have shown in the comparability table overleaf three incumbent columns, one for 94 per cent of incumbents, one for the 308 most highly paid, a third for 329 most poorly paid. Otherwise the picture would be an unjust one. Two lines across the table show Royal Commission proposals about doctor's pool earnings, and average industrial earnings on a named day in 1962. It is worth noting, though the table does not include it, that the Survey, *The Employment of Cambridge Graduates*, shows that the average earnings of Cambridge graduates (of the years 1952–3) were £1,566 per annum in 1961.[2] The sources of the comparability table are the Church Commissioners, the Civil Service Pay Research Unit, *The Royal Commission on the Police, Interim Report 1960, The Remuneration of University Teachers 1961–1962,*[3] *The Royal Commission on Doctors' and Dentists' Remuneration, 1957–1960, The Times, The Economist, The Ministry of Labour Gazette, New Society*, etc., and my own inquiries.

It must be noted that if we take the 94 per cent of incumbents as most truthfully representing the general level of income for their class, the group most closely corresponding to it is the Youth Employment Officers (LA), the next is the graduate teacher group. Both the average total net income and total gross income of the incumbent group fall within the graduate teacher range. If, for the sake of argument, one were to add the incumbent's housing as an asset valued at £200 a year, then the main incumbent group would rise nearer to equivalence with the university lecturer class.

There is another way to compare incomes and that is to ask graduates (or others) what their present profession is and what they

[1] See Appendix 1, col. 11, for highest stipends in each diocese reporting. £4,702 appears in Diocese 20.

[2] Christine Craig, Cambridge, 1963, p. 35.

[3] Association of University Teachers, 1962.

Diagram 6. Clergy Earnings Compared

These logarithmic tables contrast the earnings of clergy with some 15 other professional scales. It will be seen that in terms of actual earnings, and excluding free housing, 94 per cent of the incumbents fall between £800 and £1500 per annum. Graduate teachers, Youth Employment Officers and Probation Officers are the nearest senior groups comparable. Most incumbents' earnings are above average industrial earnings.

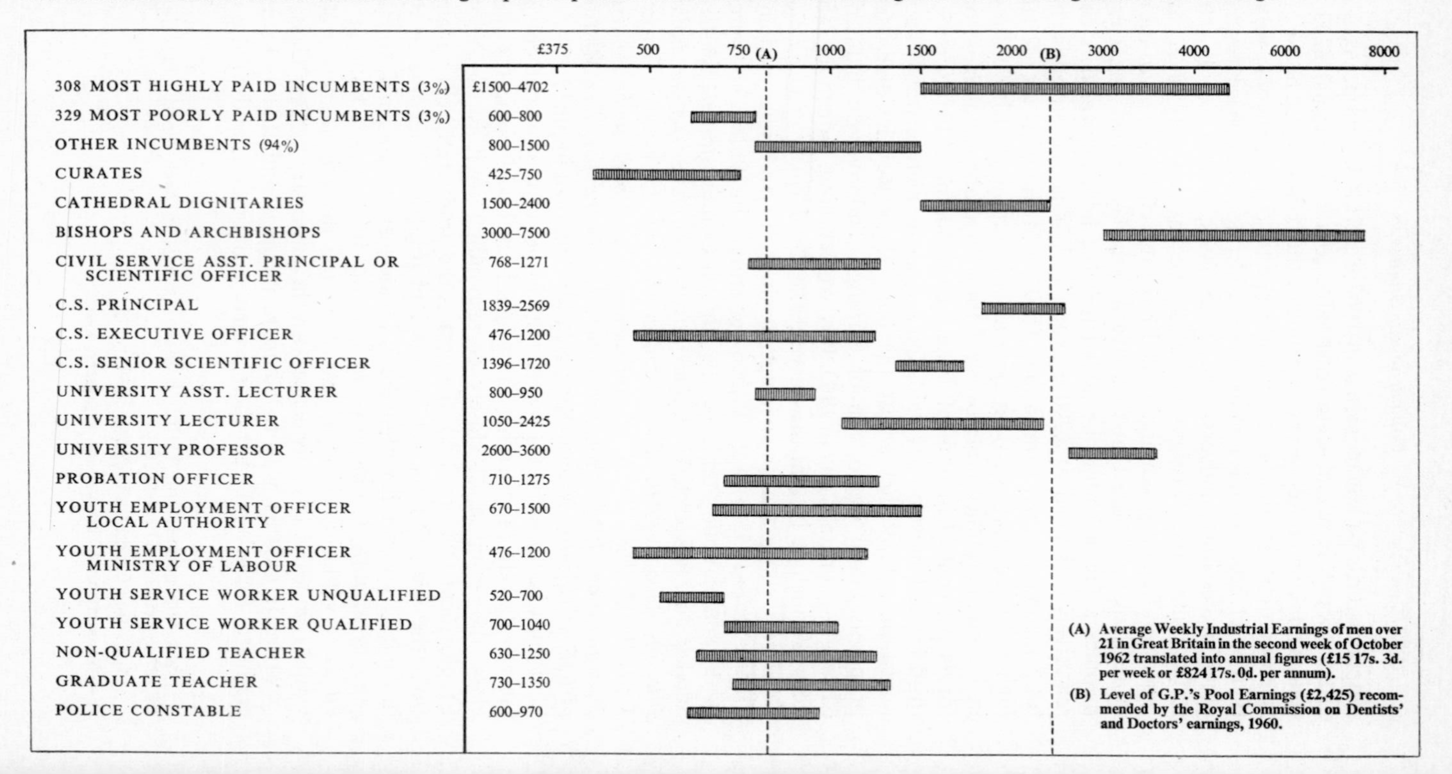

are earning. A number of exercises of this kind have been conducted. One, carried out with Cambridge graduates, includes men in the ministry and gives the percentage of each type of employment in each earnings group in 1961 of 2,149 men who graduated in 1952–3.[1] It is in part reproduced below.

Table XV. Distribution of Total Earnings by Employment Group: Cambridge Male Graduates working in the U.K.

Type of employment	Earnings group: £ per year Percentage of each type of employment								No. in group
	£ Under 1,000	£ 1,000–1,249	£ 1,250–1,499	£ 1,500–1,749	£ 1,750–1,999	£ 2,000–2,499	£ 2,500–2,999	£ 3,000 & over	
Industry	2	7	14	24	16	18	9	9	510
Distributive trades	3	5	10	23	17	21	5	16	71
Insurance, banking, finance	3	4	17	17	21	19	4	15	104
Schools	14	40	35	7	1	2	—	1	327
Universities, technical and training colleges	8	21	37	25	11	6	1	—	187
Local government	9	12	18	24	24	12	—	—	33
Civil Service	—	8	19	22	16	32	3	—	73
Churches	79	19	2	—	—	—	—	—	114
Medicine	1	13	18	38	12	12	3	3	173
Law	8	17	9	12	8	18	9	18	127
Other professions	5	10	15	15	14	16	12	13	137
Journalism, art and entertainment	19	11	8	11	15	17	13	6	47
Agriculture	35	9	7	5	5	14	8	16	59
Research establishments	1	7	12	39	19	16	4	2	93
Forces	—	6	16	24	20	24	—	—	50
Miscellaneous	10	10	21	25	14	8	6	6	46

MAKING ENDS MEET

In pursuit of stipend inquiries I sent a questionnaire (Q3) to a small sample of 245 clergy concerning their incomes: 204 replied. It is reported in SE, pp. 251–2. One hundred and seven incumbents

[1] *The Employment of Cambridge Graduates*, Christine Craig, Cambridge, 1963, p. 33. 'Churches' will, of course, include all denominations.

described their stipends as too low, and eighty-nine thought theirs adequate. However, the average annual net stipend they collectively proposed was only £1,068, no more than £100 over the present average. On the whole their proposals for their own remuneration were most modest. Thirty-three proposed a stipend of under £1,000, and the greatest number, 103, proposed one of between £1,000 and £1,249, a figure likely to be realised quite soon, if trends continue. It is already reached by average total gross income (£1,123) and exceeded if we add to it the value of free housing. But it was possible from these and other sources to see what financial problems faced the clergy, and sometimes why, for example, seventy-eight (38·24 per cent) spoke of other sources of income—private means, pensions, legacies, paid outside employment of self and wife. I have no figures for other groups in society, but it seemed surprising that more than one-third spoke of other sources of *income* rather than simply savings put aside for retirement. The figure is not altogether a trustworthy guide to the resources of the clergy, for some spoke of quite trivial sums. The more reliable guide is the thirty-eight (18·6 per cent) who spoke of private means. Seventy-seven (38 per cent) spoke of financial difficulties over the education of their children and very nearly that number thought that the Church should assist in some way (mostly by education grants) and were apparently not satisfied with the existing systems of family allowances alone. Although 103, including bachelors, said they had no problems over education of children, the figure of more than a third who had was again significant. Though the direct question was not asked, it appeared that for most of this group the financial problems were fees for preparatory or public schools. This again is a larger sector than would appear among citizens generally, though conceivably not larger than other professional groups—doctors, lawyers, university teachers—might display. It confirms what has already been said about the clergy as a social stratum if so many clergy see preparatory and public-school education as proper for their children even if they did not have it themselves. Some in remote communities felt strongly that there were really no educational alternatives for their children except the preparatory and public schools. It is not to be conceived how the fees are ever paid even for one child, on the average net total income already shown. Perhaps here private means, grandparents' legacies or covenants, and reduced fees for the sons of clergy are really decisive. Perhaps, too, we may understand why it is that sixty-six (32·35 per cent) reported that they had no holidays, and another twelve had only one week. Some said there was no possibility of finding a locum or of paying him if one did. Added to other evidence of lack of time off during the week (SE, Table 9), this amounts to renewed evidence of serious overwork, under-assistance and helpless clerical isolation. One is appalled at the thought of an East Anglian vicar taking a holiday in Wales and motoring back each week-end to take his statutory Sunday services.

The MQ replies produced some contradictory evidence. Only some 2·54 per cent of the sample mentioned private incomes—but then they were not asked about this. They *were* asked whether they had to accept paid outside employment to augment stipends, and 5·64 per cent admitted this; double the number spoke of wives who accepted paid outside employment to augment income. Roughly, the percentage of incumbents doing outside work tallies in both questionnaires. The wives going out to work are about one in seven. Incumbents usually reported teaching as their financial prop, but there were quite a few oddities, bee-keeping, goose-farming, pig-keeping, market-gardening, and so on, which called up echoes of the squarson of the eighteenth century—and at least two driving instructors. However, love of a semi-farming life was not displayed by most incumbents. No less than 395 out of 905 incumbents noted parsonage gardens as a time-consuming chore—very nearly every other clergyman. One in three of all clergy asked for help with gardens and/or churchyards and a small group (7 per cent) found it a really serious burden. With the large garden to manage often goes the large house. One hundred and fifty-one parsons, which is one in six, appeared to be wrestling with a vicarage of fifteen or more rooms: most people do on five or six.

Although some clergy still ride bicycles, and one or two move by pony along their moorland and mountain rides, and some actually walk, eight out of ten clergy have cars and almost all of their cars they themselves provide. Perhaps *two* out of every hundred clergy cars are provided by parishes, and no more than seven out of every hundred parishes pay the running expenses of the car. Only twenty out of every hundred contribute *something* to car expenses.

I have looked at several car budgets. One from an incumbent with two churches three miles apart in two parishes covering seventy square miles claims to average 120 miles per week. His total annual expenses on the car are in the neighbourhood of £250 p.a., which is not at all unreasonable. There is a diocesan grant in his case of £75 p.a. for responsibility for two parishes. If one-eighth of his annual mileage of over 6,000 was charged to private use, and depreciation annually was allowed at £92, his annual chargeable expenditure total would be £229. If the diocesan grant were purely for travelling expenses the amount on which tax relief would be due would be reduced to £154: if not, then it would stand at £229. On the lowest figure, with income tax at 7*s*. 9*d*. in the pound, his tax relief would be about £46 10*s*. p.a.—not much to offset against an annual expenditure of £250.

EXPENSES OF OFFICE

The total inadequacy of parish help in the running of clergy motors bears out the virtual complaint of parsons answering Q 3—some 112 were receiving some expenses of office, ninety-two were not. One hundred and fifty-three described parochial help over expenses of office as inadequate. The recommendations of the report to Church Assembly on Expenses of Office (13 July 1959) are clearly *not yet being fulfilled.* One of the largest votes of all in Q 3 was for expenses of office—179 out of 204 asked for them.

The expenses of office described in the report are what in other walks of life one would call business expenses—postage, stationery, telephone, transport, books, hospitality, maintenance of the 'public' parts of the parsonage house, locum tenens, and so forth. It is not possible to produce any reliable figures of clergy expenses of office. The report mentioned spoke of sums ranging annually from £60 to £500. Some clergy reported to me that they spent as much as a fifth to a quarter of their monies on expenses of office (in the region therefore of £250): this is a very hard and unfair tax upon men of moderate income and the Church has a duty to relieve them of it. The best parochial scheme I know for paying expenses of office comes to me from Esher. The parish pays for the rector's and curate's telephone rent and charges, and postage, less personal calls and stamps. It meets 75 per cent of the rector's car expenses and 75 per cent of the difference between the second-hand price of the old car and the cost of a new one every two years. It awards a sum of £190 p.a. to the rector for the cost of running his extra large rectory, part of which is used for parish purposes. It also subscribes to a supplementary pension for the rector (£50), and pays rates in full. The overall cost to the parish is in the region of £328 (1962) p.a.

STIPEND DIFFERENTIALS

On stipend differentials the clergy (Q 3) were clear in their decisions, if not united. A majority thought the differentials between bishops and incumbents and between incumbents and curates fair. One hundred and thirty-eight clergy out of 204 wanted a basic stipend for all clergy and a group almost as large (134) asked for differentials for increased responsibility. I took this to indicate that a majority of the clergy would favour reforms of the stipendiary system in these directions. Discussions at a number of clergy conferences seemed to confirm this hypothesis.

EASTER OFFERINGS

On Easter offerings I thought the clergy rather illogical. Though the greater majority wanted a basic stipend, with differentials, only ninety thought the Easter offering unfair in its incidence and only fifty-four thought it *infra dig*. One hundred believed it to be necessary and 125 wanted it as a tax-free gift, which is understandable. A rationalised stipendiary system would have to do something about a system of voluntary offering which could add as much as £4 a week to a man's income, as an example on p. 122 shows. And in any case, is it wise for a clergyman who values his independence to leave in the hands of his congregation a *monetary* method of showing its approval or disapproval of his ministry? A rational stipendiary policy would compel the transfer of Easter offerings to some common fund.[1]

PENSIONS

An explanatory memorandum of the Church Commissioners[2] said that

> In the last eight years the Commissioners have replaced a contributory pensions scheme for clergymen, producing a maximum pension of £235 a year, by a non-contributory scheme producing a maximum pension of £400, in addition to the State pension. The income limit for supplementary church pensions has also nearly doubled, so that a retired clergyman is assured of £468 a year from all sources.[3] At the same time a non-contributory pension scheme for clergy widows has been introduced and a clergyman is now assured that his widow will, from 1st October this year, have an income of not less than £350 a year.

This clearly sets out what has been done so admirably to create a reasonable pensions system for the ordained ministry, and the widows of clergy, against inflationary tendencies and other difficulties.

Some problems remain, all the same. One concerns the differentials established by *The Clergy Pensions Measure 1961* as between dignitaries and other clergy. On retirement at or after the age of 70 for forty or more years' pensionable service the Archbishops of Canterbury and York will receive £2,000 a year, the Bishops of London, Durham and Winchester £1,750 and there is then a descend-

[1] For instance, towards a fund for the Mutual Responsibility programme of the Toronto Congress.

[2] *Pensions for the Clergy and their Widows*, 1962.

[3] Now raised, 1963, to £500.

ing scale to 'Other clergy, £400'.[1] The differentials have caused much heart burning, particularly in a non-contributory scheme. Of course, opinion has been changing over pensions policy everywhere and it is now more generally accepted that what matters on retirement is not the annual sum so much as the relationship it bears to previous income. It is upon this principle, clearly, that Church Assembly legislated. It would seem sensible to say, however, that the differentials could have been far more modest and that they should only be raised beyond an agreed basis by a contributory scheme.

Clergymen still feel that though their widows may not be pensionless, they and their widows can be homeless. Clergy financial circumstances do not permit saving on the scale sufficient to buy property late in life. A number have asked for a lump sum on retirement: but a lump sum large enough to help in the purchase of property would have to be £2,000 and over. The proper solution would seem to be the provision of housing for retired clergy and their widows by the Church on a greater scale than at present. It might be linked to a regional reform of Church property administration.

Is the pension rate for ordinary clergy high enough? The clergy do not think so. 117 out of 204 incumbents proposed a pension of £500–£749, and another fifteen asked for a pension of £750–£1,000. Only twenty-one proposed a pension of under £500. Undoubtedly, rises will come as funds expand. But one final point must be made. Over pensions we have a national scheme, nationally operated, capable of proper control and national expansion. Where stipends are concerned we are still geared to the benefice system and to the local equalising methods of the forty-three different dioceses.

SOME CLERGY COMMENTS

Ex. 1. 'What is an adequate stipend? Ought it to take into account the fact that one ought to save a reasonable sum each year against one's retirement, etc? My own view is that a priest's stipend ought to be such that it could reasonably be expected to cover all eventualities—education of children, holidays, retirement (purchase, say, of cottage or small house), etc.'

Ex. 2. 'The chief thing which vitiates my work is the continual dread of failing to make ends meet, and to commence an overdraft. Total income £880, taxable income £640, with one child at college, one in Army, two at boarding school, for whom I find £250 fees, without counting clothing, fares, etc. Naturally I don't pay income tax, but I wish I did!'

[1] *Explanatory Memorandum of the Pensions Scheme, Church Assembly*, 1963

Ex. 3. 'At best I can only have one Sunday off in the year for (*a*) financial reasons, (*b*) finding priests to take the celebrations. To make up for the deficiency I slip away for a day or two in the summer months—back for Sunday. Lack of holidays is a serious cause of clerical frustration.'

Ex. 4. 'My present income of £850 should be adequate for any Christian minister, but alas, I have so many unnecessary expenses forced upon me that I live from pay-packet to pay-packet, and save nothing apart from insurance endowment policy of £20 per annum. I live in a house that costs a lot to keep warm, curtained and furnished (it has six bedrooms); and which stands in 3 acres of land with 300 yds of frontage to keep respectable. I feel that many clergy have similar unnecessary expenses. So far this winter I have spent £44 on coal and coke. It is not February yet and there is electricity on top of this.

'I get £12 p.a. for my car expenses! The tax is more than that, and there is insurance on top of that. I pay £10 a month to the bank for the purchase of the car; this will go on for the next two years. All other men covering this area for any firm with a car get free car plus all running costs. But I am never sure whether we should compare the Church's work with commercial firms. However, I think you will see what I mean by saying that the stipend of £850 is adequate; it is the expenses that make the stipend inadequate, i.e. unnecessary expenses and expenses of office. Under the present set-up we really need £1,000 p.a.'

Ex. 5. 'Income falls short of expenditure by about £200 per annum due to . . . 200 miles of motoring per week . . . large house (one woman three hours daily) and large garden (2½ acres). Partly to occupy the garden, partly to help pay for labour, partly to establish community of interest with farming and smallholding parishioners we run 3/400 head of layer poultry in deep litter, rearing ourselves from D/O chicks, and running perhaps 100 head of cockerels for Christmas market.'

Ex. 6. 'With regard to income and expenses, may I point out that the running cost of a car is in the region of £100 a year. In addition there is the capital cost of purchase. I have spent £750 in the past thirteen years in the purchase of cars, and now I am indebted to the diocese for a further £400, repayable at £80 per annum for the next five years in respect of my present car. From this it will be seen that one's income is reduced by almost £200 per annum. And what would a country parson do without a car?'

Ex. 7. 'I have three children, 10, 8 and 1. This parish, being a near slum, has quite inadequate educational facilities. With the help of grants, bursaries, reduced fees, etc., I have managed to start the 10-year-old at a boarding school. We are striving to secure financial help for the next one.'

Ex. 8. 'Living in a country village with an entirely peasant-type population meant no friends for my children. Hence expense of a nursery school (£22 per term), travelling twelve miles daily by car. This was a necessity now they are of school age. I do not wish them to be subjected to the anti-church atmosphere of the village school and to share in our own persecution. I feel I ought to send them to the private school.

'I think that provision should be made to enable the sons of clergymen to be educated at whatever type of school their ability or circumstances warrant. I think Church Commissioners should attend to this matter shortly. I hope my son will attempt and pass a scholarship to a public school—it would solve many problems in this remote area. If he passed I would have to find financial help from some source, perhaps relatives and friends, and make great sacrifices.'

Ex. 9. 'I think the Church should find money to provide accommodation for retired clergy and for clergy widows. At present even a young widow may face considerable hardship through being forced to leave the parsonage. Widows generally should be treated more generously.'

Ex. 10. 'A small scattered parish is expected to pay (i) dilaps, (ii) expenses of office, (iii) Quota, etc. These items hit the small parish *much* harder than a compact town parish, not least because our parish income is from people who are on the whole poorer and fewer in number than in a town parish. In fact, though the PCC pay expenses of office in theory, in practice I return these payments because we cannot really afford them as a parish.'

CHAPTER VIII

For and Against Redeployment

It is reasonable to say that some weighty and powerful arguments emerge from the evidence so far marshalled and displayed. The first is that the distribution of clergy is in inverse proportion to pastoral need. A pattern repeats itself time and time again: the greater the density of population the fewer relatively the number of clergy. But another pattern superimposes itself: the greater the density of population the poorer the pastoral results of the Church, the feebler its total impact. One might go further and say, the greater the density of population the more congregations approximate to ingatherings of the elect rather than to representative parochial congregations. And so the greater the density of population the more areas become mission areas against the problems of which the traditional parochial forms appear largely ineffective. All the evidence goes to show that population and house building will continue to 'explode' in coming decades. More and more parishes will fall into the network of the growing conurbations: more and more areas are bound to become mission areas as this 'massification' increases. The *central* missionary problem of the Church of England is how to carry its faith and its life with urgency and meaning into the hearts of the busy, preoccupied, harassed urban multitudes whose very pattern of life seems to estrange them from the Church. All that hitherto has been known and said about this in many brilliant studies is underlined again and again by the evidence here provided.

A second argument clamours to be heard. It concerns the state of the clergy. As great, in a sense, as the need for mission to the areas of greatest density is the need for the Church's mission to its own clergy. Any professional body faced with a charge to serve the whole populace and with a deployment of its members which makes this impossible to achieve would naturally experience distress, malaise. The clergy have to live this distress for the most part alone, in isolation, shut within their small parochial kingdoms. A certain reserve, the inheritance of centuries, separates them from their parishioners. 'To whom can I speak?' they often cry. Protocol associated with parish boundaries keeps neighbouring clergy at arm's length. Deaneries are shadowy associations in the main, preserving rather than breaking down parochial boundaries. Bishops are deflected from pastoral cares by administration: to survive they have to become organisation men. This presses more hardly upon them in the areas of greatest density. The ancient parochial system, historically justified when the parish priest was the spiritual member of both the local and national establishment, no longer protects and shows forth the *persona*, but maroons him socially and spiritually. It is probable that the success of the mission to dense urban areas depends on the prior success of the mission to the clergy, a mission which must have as its first intention the ending of the separation of the clergy from each other and their isolation from the laity: in a word to end the loneliness which eats so deeply into many spirits.

A third argument concerns the strengthening and deployment of the ordained ministry itself. We know that too many men serve too few people, too few men serve too many people. Is it possible to shift men to the regions in greatest need of clergy? Are there reserves we have yet to call up? Ought we to reconsider in the process their pay and terms of service? Such concerns are the heart of this survey, but they rank third in this present analysis, for one cannot begin even to think of redeploying men (let alone whether it is possible) unless one decides on what basis one is to do it, and unless one has a view of the impact it must make on the living men who form the clergy. A tactical exercise without troops may produce the pleasing results possible only to a purely academic exercise. Bring in the troops and put them under fire and casualties must result: the commander in the field has to decide whether the objective justifies the cost.

The first and second arguments may be taken as established by what has already been said. It is the third which must occupy us now, but with the mission needs to clergy and to the urban masses continually in mind.

THE PASTORAL EFFECTIVENESS OF THE CLERGY

Still, even before we pursue this, we have to ask one further question—what *effect* do the clergy have, pastorally speaking? So far my inquiry establishes firmly the effect of one control, population density, over pastoral results. We cannot remain perfectly happy about this, for there is obviously a second control, the ratio of clergy to population. Because of the pattern of the present distribution of clergy it so happens that (in general) where the density of population per square mile is lowest, the ratio of parochial clergy to population is highest (Hereford 1 : 1,054; Birmingham 1 : 6,607). Suppose the ratio of clergy to population were everywhere the same, what then would be the difference in pastoral results between town and country? Really to know we should have to wait for that happy day. But we have at least one study which indicates that the results would certainly not be so sharply contrasted as they are today.

In a paper entitled *A Critical Analysis of the Redeployment of the Clergy and a Possible Solution*[1] the Rev. A. B. Miskin publishes a table (discussed in Summary of Evidence, p. 267 f.) which seeks to show the pastoral effect the clergy have upon Church congregations. Upon figures supplied by the Statistical Unit he has computed the relationship between numbers of Christmas communicants and the pastoral staff. For purposes of his investigation, any full-time lay pastoral worker counted as equal in value to any full-time clergyman. But the consequence of the argument is the same—his figures tell us what influence the parson has. Column 2 of his table (SE, Table 30) shows that with one full-time worker in a living, the number of Christmas communicants is 119 when the population is 1,000. When the population is 15,000 it is 265—just over double—but with one extra worker it is 355, with two, 436. Increasing population adds ten more Christmas communicants per extra 1,000, *whereas one extra full-time worker adds eighty to ninety, irrespective of population*, though with diminishing effect per additional worker. Mr Miskin was even able to devise the formula of twenty-five basic Christmas communicants per living of 1,000 and over, plus ninety for every full-time worker, plus ten for each additional 1,000 of population. It is a formula any parish priest can apply to discover whether he and his staff are achieving the expected minimum results!

Here certainly is striking evidence for the effect of parochial manpower on pastoral results. It enables us to go on seriously to consider what consequences would attach to its redistribution.

OUGHT THE RURAL CLERGY TO BE TRANSFERRED?

It is difficult always to define a rural living but if one accepts the point made by the Rev. A. B. Miskin in another section of his paper, a realistic division between town and country livings can be made at 1,500 people. If this figure is taken as the divide, then there is one country parson for every 780 people, one town parson for every 4,700 people. Mr Miskin has taken this as his starting-point in an argument now summarised. In December 1958 there were 5,022 livings with a population of under 1,500. But of these, 2,262 were one-*church* livings with less than a thousand people: such livings constitute the 'light-duty' cures, which the Church probably ought to maintain in some way to provide for sick or ailing or elderly clergy, or clergy who because of valuable studies they might be making ought to have minimum parochial duties. At least, if they

[1] *Prism*, December 1963.

are to go, their going must wait on some other kind of provision. If these livings are retained, we are left, Mr Miskin argues, with some 2,760 livings to reorganise. If by an effort these livings were reduced by 1,000 the number of clergy freed would also be 1,000. Mr Miskin treats the redeployment of these men to a *reductio ad absurdum.* If we take the table he prepared which showed the influence of the number of workers, clergy and lay, upon the number of Christmas communicants, we are able to calculate the effect of the redeployment of this thousand, as incumbents or assistant curates in town parishes, upon pastoral figures. There would be a loss (he argues) of 22,000 Christmas communicants in the country, a gain of 100,000 in the towns: a net gain of 78,000 which is relatively insignificant against the target of 2,000,000 extra Christmas communicants, which is a reasonable first expectation.

Of course, Mr Miskin is using a formula and showing upon its basis that redeployment of this character would probably fail to do more than touch the fringe of the problem measured statistically. He misses perhaps the psychological effect these reinforcements from rural areas could have upon the laity and the hard-pressed town clergy. If they came in any wave, rather than in single spies, the effect could be dramatic, though this is an improbable event in the nature of things. What would be altered would be the number of people per clergyman: after the transfer of the 1,000 the new ratios would be, country 1 : 977, town 1 : 4,235, which only nibbles at the problem.

He raises a serious objection to the transfer *en masse* of rural clergy on grounds of age. Two out of five of rural clergy with populations of less than 1,000 were over sixty. *Facts and Figures 1962* shows the highest average ages of incumbents in dioceses like Sodor and Man and Hereford, the lowest in Manchester, Liverpool, Birmingham, Sheffield, Southwark. Sodor and Man clergy are nearly ten years older than Manchester clergy, Hereford clergy are eight years older. My own table of the pastoral results of special groups, on p. 78, shows how the average age rises more or less consistently as the pastoral cure diminishes: those with the lightest duties are eight to ten years older than those with the heaviest. Of the over-70 group thirty-four out of forty-two were rural incumbents. Of course, the *average* age of the rural clergy conceals the number of younger men in the group. They alone might be moved. Yet prudence would suggest that the country parishes ought not to be given over entirely to old men: it would make the country ministry a travesty. The ministry ought to show a clergy age structure not too dissimilar from that of the town. It ought not to be a mere *appendage* of the urban ministry. It has special problems and can be physically more exacting in winter than a town ministry.

In any case, the Church as a whole would be in grave error if it fastened all the responsibility for the misuse of manpower on the demands of small rural parishes. There are disparities almost as great in the urban area themselves.

Rural Isle of Wight has forty-six livings for its 106,000 population: with three livings vacant and four assistant clergy it had a ratio of one clergyman to every 2,255 persons: but Ryde, which is built up, still had a ratio of one to every 2,654. Old towns such as Exeter, Winchester, Canterbury, Cheltenham, Windsor, and new ones such as Weston-super-Mare have ratios just below the Ryde, Isle of Wight, figure. Norwich dropped the ratio to 1 : 1,317. Bournemouth, Bridlington, have ratios in the 1 : 3,000 class. Barnstaple, Blackburn, York, Scarborough are all under 1 : 4,000. The cathedral city ratios exclude cathedral clergy except where the cathedral is also a parish church or cathedral clergy are also incumbents of livings: if non-parochial cathedral clergy were included the ratio would drop in some cases to rural ratios. The number of City of Canterbury clergy, for example, would be almost doubled by their inclusion. Bradford diocese, with a population of 600,000 (city 290,000) is served by about 150 clergy. Two Chelmsford deaneries, Romford and Barking, with a population rising 700,000, have not more than seventy clergy at work. These are random examples, mainly based on Crockford's 1961–62 figures, but they serve to show that the unbalanced distribution is to be found everywhere in the two provinces and in areas where it is not possible to say that the acreage of parishes and the distances the clergy have to travel justify the higher ratio of clergy to population.

OTHER REMEDIES

Of course, if one cannot move clergy *en masse* from country to the towns the possibility of economies still remains. The formation of united benefices and pluralities is indeed the Church's long-standing device to stretch available manpower over more ground. There are natural physical limits to the process. How many churches can the parson actually visit Sunday by Sunday, over how great an area can his cure extend before it becomes unreal to the localities which comprise it? The evidence from bishops is indecisive, though more actually said that uniting parishes in one form or the other had gone as far as possible in their dioceses than said it had not yet gone far enough.[1] If we accept that there is a warning light here, there remains a fringe of rural parishes, comprising 1,644 livings (965 single parish ones), and taking 14·3 per cent of the clergy, which ought to be constantly under scrutiny for the actual size and product of the pastoral

[1] SE, p. 264.

cure. And where the average Sunday attendance falls below thirty per church in town or fifteen in the country there is a case for examining the total cure of the incumbent in order to see whether it really justifies the full-time services of one man old or young.

GROUP AND TEAM MINISTRIES

One much-publicised remedy for manpower shortage is a group or team ministry. Caution is necessary here, too. The experience so far of country group ministries is that they are means of serving parishes which might otherwise be without incumbents at all or else of introducing a radically new pattern of lay and ministerial life. It is conceivable that they could here and there increase the actual number of clergy at work in the area though reducing the nominal roll of incumbents. Even if they might ultimately save clergy manpower, they cannot be indiscriminately introduced or instituted by formula. The saving would be long term. Group or team ministries in town may cut down 'the plant', or what a tradesman might call the points of service, but they ought eventually to increase the total urban ministry rather than decrease it. It does not seem possible to argue a case for their introduction just on the grounds of manpower economies, though this must form one factor: to end the spiritual and social isolation of the clergy and the passivity of the laity may be more important reasons.

REMEDIES SUMMARISED

What remedies remain? The possibilities are:

(*a*) to increase recruitment to the ministry;
(*b*) to call up reserves, e.g. supplementary ministry, forms of lay service and lay ministry;
(*c*) to direct ordinands in their first and second curacies;
(*d*) to work out a diocesan staffing quota or 'manpower establishment' both for incumbents and curates and to deal with excesses or deficiencies by persuasion, pressure, incentives or actual direction.

Increasing recruitment to the ministry (*a*) would make as the years passed more and more men available to serve as curates where curacies were to be had and to fill the vacancies in existing livings afterwards. The existing pattern of the ministry would then remain unaltered, or would only slowly change. The financial cost might be high, and it would fall increasingly on the urban laity to help to support the rural clergy. The urban decay of the Church, the social and spiritual problems of clergy would remain, most probably, untouched or unsolved, the great demographic challenge unfaced. It must be said, however, that a great number of the clergy and of the laity constantly express the hope that, apart from increased recruitment to the ministry, the venerated forms and institutions of the Church will remain as they are.

At the other end of the possibilities stands (*d*) a ministry deployed under direction, involving the surrender of the freehold by individual freeholders whether incumbents or dignitaries (for a freeholder obviously cannot be redeployed unless he chooses) and a severe modification of patronage and of stipend structure. It would necessitate some deployment machinery perhaps similar to that employed by the Methodist Annual Conference. Or if these extreme measures were not resorted to for all incumbents they would be necessary for some—just the newcomers for example. The muddle which could attend partial proceedings might compel the same terms for all, or an abandonment of direction. A middle course would simply be to direct newly ordained men to their first and second curacies (*c*). An examination of what has been tried already at least teaches us something about establishment problems.

THE DISTRIBUTION OF NEWLY ORDAINED MEN

As the SE describes in detail, an Archbishop's committee set up in 1957 reported on *The Distribution of Ordination Candidates.* The report tabulated the needs of dioceses and on the basis of one curate for each parish of 5,000 to 10,000 and two for parishes over 10,000 produced an estimated deficit or surplus of assistant curates in the light of an actual distribution of some 2,628 existing men. The Bishop of Birmingham, who pursued these studies, produced an amended formula:

1 curate for parishes 5,000–9,999
2 curates for parishes 10,000–29,999
3 curates for parishes 30,000 and over

and on the basis of this, in June 1962, estimated that 4,921 curates were required, disclosing a deficiency of 2,342. He went on to show diocese by diocese how the number of men expected to be ordained in 1962 ought to be allocated on the basis of 10 per cent of need. Had this allocation actually been begun, then, in ten years or less, dependent on the size of the annual quota, deficiencies in the required number of curates would have been met. Of course, this formula had to assume that the dioceses would be capable of a proper internal distribution of their curates according to the accepted rule: this did not necessarily follow, since one in five of curates were in livings of under 5,000. Nevertheless, the point was well made in the original report and in subsequent studies that each diocese should have an establishment of curates and that men should be directed to fill the establishment as needed, a system not dissimilar after all to army postings. It was intended, however, to exclude all deacons over 40.

The plan was to be operated by common consent of the bishops for,

> What we would suggest is briefly this, that . . . each bishop should agree to ordain only a certain limited number of men in his diocese each year. This number should be based upon the number of parishes with a population of over 5,000 and over 10,000; one assistant curate being allowed for the first, and two for the second [i.e. the first formula]. The effect of this would be gradually to correct the present unequal distribution. A candidate who was unable to secure ordination in one particular diocese would be free to apply to any other diocese the quota of which was incomplete. We would emphasise the fact that if the plan we suggest is adopted it will affect the total number of curates in a diocese *only very gradually*. We are not proposing the redistribution of existing curates, only an adjustment of the number to be ordained in each diocese. The process, though gradual, will, however, prevent disaster in some dioceses which are at present living far below the percentage line.[1]

There seems to have been a partial effort to operate the first plan by mutual agreement between bishops, but a subsequent collapse. The difficulties of working such a scheme by consent of forty-three dioceses are obvious enough, but the scheme contained some strong disincentives for each group concerned—bishops, college principals, ordinands. The ordinand refused ordination in the diocese of his choice (where no doubt he would be known) was to be 'free to apply to any other diocese the quota of which was incomplete.' A chilling procedure, in the upshot like writing round desperately for a college place perhaps. In each diocese each year a proportion would automatically be 'in', a proportion 'out': the choice would be invidious, falling perhaps on Trinity rather than Advent men (assuming the quota year to run with the liturgical year). But discouraging also for bishops, who must refuse to ordain men they have chosen, encouraged and watched. Equally difficult for college principals, who have always for sound pastoral and spiritual reasons helped to guide their men to the right choice of parish and the right sort of incumbent under whom to serve their title.

Yet the intention to bring into existence a curate establishment

[1] Op. cit., p. 9.

related to pastoral needs (in this case determined on a population basis) was excellent. The report was both clear and cutting:

> We believe that the present go-as-you-please system has unfortunate effects upon not a few of our ordination candidates. It is the candidate who now interviews the bishop and a number of prospective vicars. The impression is conveyed that he is seeking Holy Employment, not Holy Orders. He is sometimes encouraged to think more of his own future training than of the Church's need. Our best men would, we are convinced, be grateful for clearer direction: and this in turn would impress on them the fact that they were not seeking employment but being given Holy Orders, and that not simply in a parish or diocese but in the Church of God.[1]

The mere fact that it was necessary to say this points to a contradiction at the heart of the ordained ministry which has already been noticed. If to be one of the clergy is to be a member of a free profession—that is, if professional status and dignity come first—then it is intolerable that a clergyman should be directed, and so lose his freedom. If, on the other hand, the pastoral needs of the whole Church come first it is intolerable if the clergy created and sustained to fulfil them are not available to be sent where they are most needed. A clear rule ought to be maintained—that the pastoral needs of the Church must come first. Yet freedom is also a good. We can add a rider to the rule, that such clergy freedoms as are consonant with this should be kept, but only such. Moreover, in applying this rider, sensitivity to the confusing ambivalence history has wished upon the social and spiritual roles of the Anglican clergyman, an ambivalence no contemporary clergyman 'invented' to fox bishops or laity, ought to restrain us from the crass psychological errors possible when plans ignore living men.

A point has to be made about the annual quota of ordained men fixed by the Bishop of Birmingham's formula: it would fill vacancies only very slowly. With this in mind I asked diocesan bishops, in December 1962, to tell me what 'actual vacancies for curates urgently needed to be filled at this moment'. Canterbury province totals were 302: York province totals 282. The figures given enabled me to calculate 'second urgency', too. The revised figures were striking. Canterbury province required as first and second urgency 415: York province 458. The undermanning of the hard-pressed northern province was painfully exemplified in these figures. The population of Canterbury province is roughly twice that of York. The need for curates for vacancies urgently in need of filling is therefore more than twice as great in York province as in Canterbury. It ought not to surprise us after the evidence of other statistics.

[1] Op. cit., pp. 8–9.

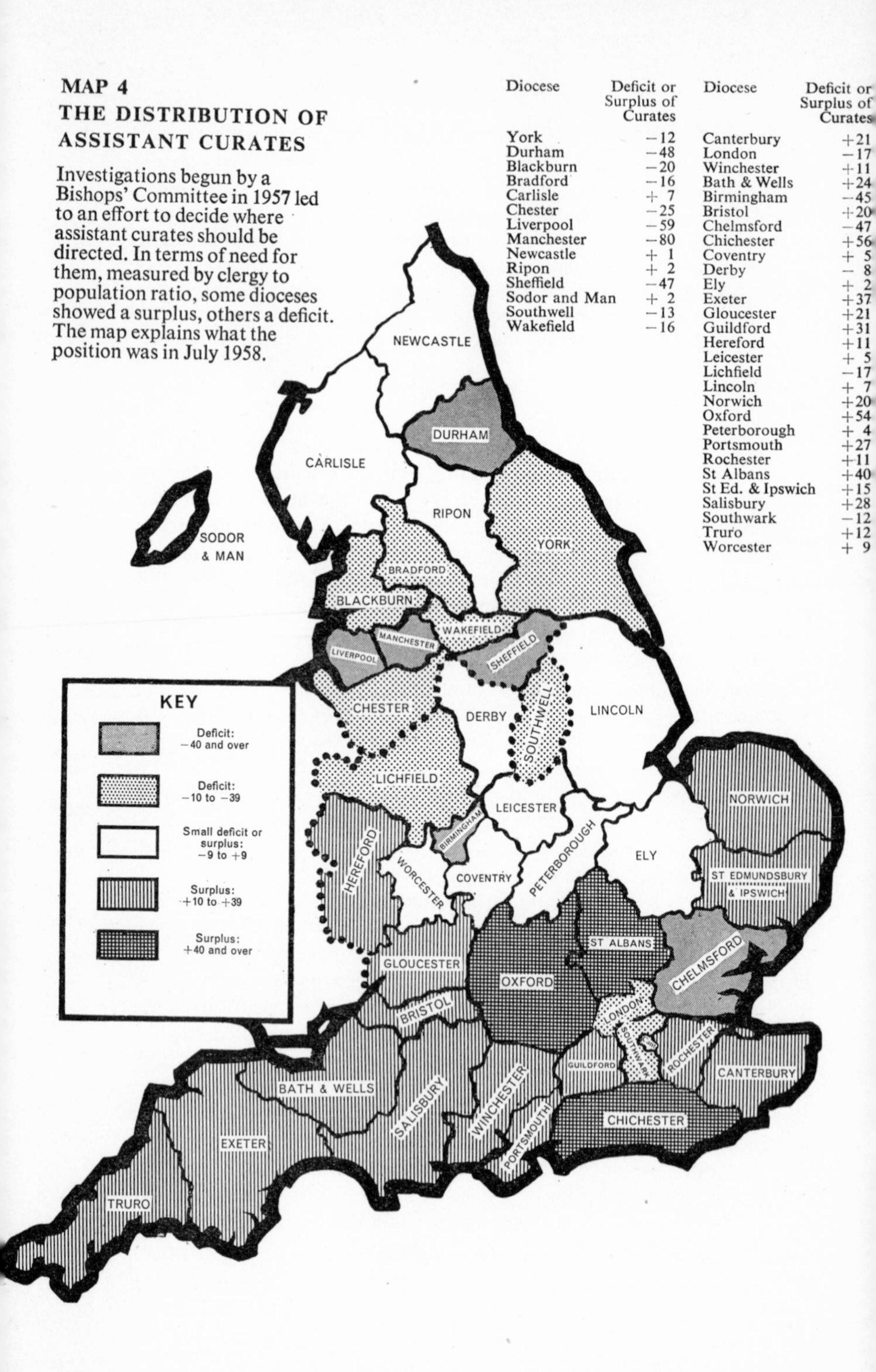

MAP 4
THE DISTRIBUTION OF ASSISTANT CURATES

Investigations begun by a Bishops' Committee in 1957 led to an effort to decide where assistant curates should be directed. In terms of need for them, measured by clergy to population ratio, some dioceses showed a surplus, others a deficit. The map explains what the position was in July 1958.

Diocese	Deficit or Surplus of Curates	Diocese	Deficit or Surplus of Curates
York	−12	Canterbury	+21
Durham	−48	London	−17
Blackburn	−20	Winchester	+11
Bradford	−16	Bath & Wells	+24
Carlisle	+ 7	Birmingham	−45
Chester	−25	Bristol	+20
Liverpool	−59	Chelmsford	−47
Manchester	−80	Chichester	+56
Newcastle	+ 1	Coventry	+ 5
Ripon	+ 2	Derby	− 8
Sheffield	−47	Ely	+ 2
Sodor and Man	+ 2	Exeter	+37
Southwell	−13	Gloucester	+21
Wakefield	−16	Guildford	+31
		Hereford	+11
		Leicester	+ 5
		Lichfield	−17
		Lincoln	+ 7
		Norwich	+20
		Oxford	+54
		Peterborough	+ 4
		Portsmouth	+27
		Rochester	+11
		St Albans	+40
		St Ed. & Ipswich	+15
		Salisbury	+28
		Southwark	−12
		Truro	+12
		Worcester	+ 9

That curates do not automatically graduate to areas of greatest need is demonstrated by the map opposite, which is based on the Bishop of Birmingham's figures. These make it possible to show dioceses with deficiencies in the number of curates against those with excesses. The distribution reveals that curates tend to flow into southern areas of relative success as against the conurbations and northern areas of greatest need. If the analysis of the diocesan distribution of curates is contrasted with three-year totals of ordained men in each diocese a startling fact emerges: *The supply relative to the need falls away strikingly as urban density increases*, as this table shows. In it, dioceses are arranged in inverse order of population density.

Table XVI. Supply of Ordinands for the Three Years 1959–1961, totalled per diocese and contrasted with actual need, 1962 (*Bishop of Birmingham's formula*)

Dioceses	Ordinations	Needs	Dioceses	Ordinations	Needs
Hereford	7	9	Canterbury	22	89
Carlisle	18	36	Derby	24	114
Truro	2	9	Coventry	33	86
Sodor and Man	1	3	Lichfield	64	228
Ely	8	21	St Albans	34	106
Salisbury	14	31	Southwell	34	108
Lincoln	28	48	Blackburn	36	113
St Eds. and Ips.	11	19	Chester	34	143
Norwich	12	27	Guildford	29	65
Exeter	32	58	Portsmouth	27	73
Bath and Wells	16	41	Bristol	27	78
Newcastle	30	104	Chelmsford	65	294
Peterborough	19	35	Durham	47	175
Gloucester	19	27	Wakefield	39	146
York	39	115	Rochester	54	150
Oxford	21	78	Sheffield	35	149
Ripon	25	89	Liverpool	50	234
Bradford	16	69	Birmingham	45	183
Winchester	24	94	Manchester	79	242
Chichester	22	92	Southwark	92	495
Worcester	17	62	London	114	508
Leicester	20	75			

Total ordinations, three years, 1,385.
Total needs, Bishop of Birmingham's formula, 4,921.

Once again therefore we are presented with evidence of the effect of increasing population density on the Church. Not only baptismal and confirmation figures fall below the average in these areas (and certainly partly through shortage of clergy), but ordination figures, too: it is a salutary lesson. The Church in the dense urban areas is failing to renew itself.

In conclusion, what the Bishop's report has done is to carry forward the work of the Commission on the Staffing of Parishes (appointed 1929, reported 1930) and to provide the first contemporary estimate of a staffing establishment for the clergy (even though of assistants only) related to population density. Precisely the same exercise is necessary at the incumbent level if some rationality is to be introduced into the present haphazard geographical scatter of men.

THE LAITY TO THE HELP OF THE MINISTRY

A first-class report to the Convocation of Canterbury in 1902, entitled *The Position of the Laity in the Church*,[1] concluded, after a long and critical study, as follows:

> The study of the Apostolic and primitive constitution of the Church, as it is set forth in Holy Scripture and in the history and writings of the first three centuries, shows, as we think, clearly the co-ordinate action of clergy and laity as integral parts of the whole body of Christ.
>
> We believe that there is a primitive distinction between clergy and laity, and that it will continue till the end of the age in which we live. This distinction is involved in the choice and commission of the Apostles; and its continuance is implied in our Lord's words to them connecting their work with His second coming (St Luke 12.41–43; St Matthew 28.18–20). But by distinction we do not understand separation as of bodies with opposing interests. We have no reason to regard the distinction as anything more than a provision for the purpose of developing the fullness of corporate life in the Church which is Christ's body, and for maintaining in it the fullness of the truth. Nay, we perceive very clearly, both from the historical and the theological portions of the New Testament, that the ultimate authority and the right of collective action lie with the whole body, the Church. We find, in fact, in this first period traces of the co-operation of clergy and laity in all the three spheres with which our report is concerned, in legislative functions, in the election of Church officers, and in judicial discipline, and we cannot but conclude that this co-operation belongs to the true ideal of the Church.

The theology seems unexceptionable, though for its time it must have been advanced thinking. But we cannot really suppose that it is a proper description of the relationship between the laity and the clergy in recent centuries. Movements of the laity have been effec-

[1] Reprinted, with an introduction by Dr Norman Sykes, Church Information Board, London, 1952.

tive, even decisive, in the church—the Reformation, nonconformism, Methodism, the growth of missions, the ecumenical movement—yet even so the relationship between clergy and laity has hardly ever been since the first centuries that of a corporate ministry. The notion of two sorts of Christians, not simply different in function but different in merit, in stature, in authority, goes back at least to the legal formalism Christianity received from the Roman Empire. When the Christian laity of Europe in medieval times and subsequently *was* 'the world' which those in holy and monastic orders 'renounced', then the laity, or the lay world, was precisely that world which tempted, soiled and corrupted, and from which those who sought spiritual perfection had to flee. To preach to the world was to preach to the laity: hence *ecclesia docens*, the teaching church, and *ecclesia discens*, the learning church. In such a perspective we can see why the church became synonymous with its members in orders, the laity synonymous with the despised world of material appetites and fleshly lusts. In this context, entering the church was, of course, equivalent to entering the ministry, certainly in England: it might be said that only such an absolute organic separation of the church from the people made possible the storms of the Reformation.

In the England of the quieter eighteenth and nineteenth centuries we see the laity as the passive receivers of a ministry socially and intellectually remote from them. The Church was simply the 'given' institution: they might be tied to it in love and devotion and particularly to the church as the sacred building, the tranquil house where they communed with God, but they were not the real providers of the Church, which, as an institution remotely and even mysteriously controlled, asked only the minimum co-operation and comprehension from them. Its liturgy was given by the law, its doctrine formulated in unalterable articles, its head was the Crown, its officers appointed, promoted and maintained by processes so tortuous and secretive that few laymen could hope to understand them, or clergy either.

Thankfully much of this has changed in this century. The laity have been brought into Church government at every level except that of convocations. Its initiatives are more and more invited. What the report said so clearly is accepted doctrine. The reasons are as much social and historical as doctrinal. The worshipping laity is no longer coincident with 'the world'. The laity and the ordained ministry are 'over against' a world which by and large does not accept either of them. If that world does not come over to the ordained ministry to be taught, how is it to be reached? At the point where the church discovers the common identity of the ministry and the laity over against a world from which both are separated, it discovers that *the laity works in that world*, has its vocations there and is strategically placed for an historic mission which the purely ministerial and hierarchical church forgot for centuries.

For these reasons the great debate is upon us. The laity has a ministry as real as that of the ordained ministry: that ministry is to 'the world', because that is where the laity *is*. Its ministry is only functionally separate from that of the ordained ministries: both together constitute the corporate pastorate of the Body of Christ in the world. Yet it cannot be said that either the laity or the ordained ministry even now look at things quite in this light. Lay service in the Church is for the most part still regarded as service in and to church organisations and auxiliaries, locally and nationally. To be a good churchman, and even more to be a good churchwoman, one is expected to give this kind of service. It is not all the lay person regards as his duty, but it is certainly an important part of the concept of living a good Christian life. 'One must support the Church'. There are two sides to the issue—church organisations give good service and good fellowship. They are necessary. But the more the laity builds itself in and around the clusters of church organisations and functions, the less effective may be its own ministry 'to the world'. Fellowship may be found this way, but not always witness. The laity can become a clericalised laity, shut off from the world by habits of thought and of social usage almost as completely as the ordained ministry is. It is even significant that some of the most acute discussions of lay functions have centred on an extension of its liturgical rather than its pastoral role: they are important functions but possibly irrelevant to its external mission.

One can only hope that the dialogue now joined between the laity and the ordained ministry will go forward earnestly and humbly. It is a matter as existential as it is doctrinal. It will work itself out in living acts, in the discovery of new forms and functions as much as in the refinements of theory; and it may take a generation thinking ecumenically to arrive at a just solution to so profound an exploratory movement of the Church's life.

If it is beyond the scope of this report to propound solutions, it is possible all the same to point to urgent needs. I have spoken of the double need of the Church—the mission to the dense urban areas and to the clergy. The Rev. A. B. Miskin, in the paper already discussed, analysed the possibility of moving the rural clergy into the towns and dismissed it in a *reductio ad absurdum*. But two important points emerged from his study. The first was that in arriving at the influence of parochial staffs upon the number of Christmas communicants lay staff was as important as clerical staff: a full-time lay worker in a parish counted for as much in pastoral influence as a full-time clergyman: in analysis they were not distinguished. It is not therefore the clerical uniform so much as the actual hours of pastoral care (mainly expressed in visiting, of course) no matter by whom which really counts. The second point he puts in these words:

> There is, however, another way of looking at the whole problem. First, we estimate the number of additional full-time workers required to bring the number of Christmas communicants up to the suggested target of 10 per cent of the population. This turns out to be about twenty-seven thousand, which is nearly twice the present (1960) total of ordained and lay parochial workers (14,791). This means on the average six additional full-time workers for every one of the four thousand odd (4,545) parishes whose population exceeds three thousand. Of course, this figure, like all averages, conceals a wide range. Thus, for one-man parishes, a parish with a population of three thousand would need two workers, while one of fifteen thousand people would need fourteen.

He asks whether to expect such a lay contribution is hopeless, and answers that perhaps it is if it means full-time workers, but if the lay people gave one or two evenings or afternoons a week to visiting, their work, he argues, might be the equivalent of a full-time worker. The 27,000 additional *full-time* workers needed can be equated with 270,000 *voluntary* workers. And he concludes that this is not out of the question, though bearing heavily on the larger single-handed parishes. He thinks such mass support is not impossible to conceive as part of a mission to England if it goes along with an actual increase in the numbers of the ministry and of full-time lay social and pastoral workers. The Church, it has already been pointed out, has more than 250,000 young people in its organisations, laity under training approaching 200,000; Sunday school teachers exceed 92,000 and there are 36,000 home members of the CEMS and so forth. It has not yet succeeded in harnessing the energies of these auxiliaries, let alone of the Mothers' Union, Toc H and student movements, for pastoral activity. Whether one accepts Mr Miskin's thesis or not, the probability is that the manpower necessary for this kind of lay pastoral service is already there.

In what forms might it be organised? One can conceive of several. A parochial lay pastorate would be the fundamental form. It should take the pattern already sufficiently tried out in such parishes as Redcar under the late Canon Hammersley and Roseworth under the Rev. Trevor Beeson—and many other places, of course—of regular lay teams of visitors. It would seem proper to group them by streets, that each street should have a leader and a deputy to whom emergencies in which the Church can give help are reported, and that the lay leaders should prepare their own visiting lists and report to the clergy what kind of 'follow-up' or other sort of help individual homes need. Organisation as basic as this does begin to restore to the Church its formative role in the community, for want of which it can perish. A lay pastorate of this kind involves a heavy lay training programme, of course. It needs also to build itself round worship as local as the team itself. And the basic locale is the house or home. Weekday house communions in each street, from time to time, and moving to each team member's house in turn, could seal in common worship the lay community linked by pastoral visiting. If generally the narrow parochial system is to give way to ministries which corporately serve a borough, a rural district, a new town or some meaningful social and political unit, it will be imperative to carry organisation as deeply as possible into the life of the neighbourhood, so that the Church becomes the Church in the street and in the homes, and not just an appendage to the vicarage. Perhaps only in this way can Christian worship become the social usage of really humble homes and therefore meaningful to them once again. It is even possible that a lay revolution has to begin with so simple an act as the saying of grace in the home before every meal. The remarkable historic tenacity of the Jewish faith must partly be rooted in religious and social usage in the family circle, particularly in the Sabbath and the sacramental meal.

There are other ways in which lay help might be mobilised:

1. Pastoral aid of lay professionals. Parishes so often number among their worshippers teachers, doctors, nurses, police officers, social workers, personnel officers, union officials and others who bring professional skills to bear upon social problems which at every point touch the Church's life. They need to be enrolled in a parish, deanery or town pastoral advisory committee. Since they mediate to special groups (hospitals, schools, prisons, factories), their work at this level has precisely the same importance as the work of street teams though less measurable in its effects. Their work would not impede the recruitment of full-time social workers, but rather watch over it and ensure professional terms of service as well as proper utilisation of such church officers.

2. There seems to be a need for the growth of a spirit of theological inquiry among the laity. I am not thinking here of the great laymen and women who in philosophy, theology, literature and poetry contribute to the thinking of the Church and enrich its life, but of the rank-and-file of the laity who will help at church bazaars, but as far as thinking goes 'leave things like that to the vicar'. All clergy initiatives about lay training are excellent, but they are still *clergy* initiatives. What are needed are lay initiatives which will give the laity courage to contribute to the great theological debates of our

times: I see this as a prerequisite to the ending of lay passivity. Perhaps the great lay organisations could convene lay conferences on the tasks of the laity as defined by the laity.

3. New constitutional forms of independent lay co-operation and action are possible. The institution of lay deanery councils in Gloucester diocese is a case in point: since there the chairmen of lay councils together with archdeacons and rural deans form the bishop's council, the views and advice of the laity can reach the bishop directly. The changed machinery has given changed status to the laity.

4. New forms of lay voluntary service. The Church needs the equivalent of that admirable organisation the Women's Voluntary Service. It needs organised volunteers to do the following: (*a*) mowing, clipping, tidying in churchyards and overlarge vicarage gardens, (*b*) cleaning, decorating, polishing in churches and church halls, (*c*) decorating vicarages, (*d*) boiler stoking and cleaning, (*e*) organising of rotas to transport parsons without cars to hospitals to visit patients or just to drive the car for tired vicars, (*f*) Sunday transport to bring folk to parish communion, (*g*) weekly voluntary secretarial help from expert typists. Scores of parsons, particularly of rural or inner town parishes where local help is scarce, are physically exhausted by a burden of simple but oppressive daily chores. A lay voluntary service to help them needs to be nationally organised and to break down to deanery level: lay volunteers are relatively easy to find within the parish for the parish. Lay mission to the home Church *wherever* it is in need and can be reached has yet to be brought to life.

SUPPLEMENTING THE PRIESTHOOD

In the decades since the first world war the Church, in its several deliberative bodies, has many times grappled with the vexed questions of who should be admitted to the priesthood, and on what terms. Traditionally the Church everywhere has made the ordained ministry a stipendiary one: those called to it become priests for life: the fact that the priesthood is also their living excludes them in practice from most other occupations. Canon law spells out the terms. The lively contemporary discussion of the nature of the full-time priesthood has taken place under haunting awareness of the Church's failure in the dense urban areas and its general pastoral decline. What ought the Church to do therefore to increase its priest-power? Admit voluntary priests or part-time priests, form new priestly orders, ordain women, create a permanent diaconate, admit laity to liturgical duties? These are the questions asked today. The ordaining of worker-priests in France and the establishment of diocesan industrial missions at home have added point to the debate. One might classify the proposals as follows: (i) worker-priests, (ii) supplementary priests, (iii) a permanent diaconate, (iv) other forms.

So far, recruitment to the worker-priest movement has been from the priesthood rather than from the workers. The movement can be described as an act of moral and social witness by part of the priesthood. The intention is that some, eventually many, priests should work where the majority work and under the same conditions. In practice, after priestly ordination, a few men, with episcopal licence, make themselves part-time priests, living not as incumbents but as workers, and dependent on their weekly wages. Their vocation is to the work-bench and their fellow workers: liturgical duties are geared to this. We have a small, devoted, selfless band of such worker-priests in England. The revision of Canon 83 (Canon Law Revision, 1959, C. 29) will safeguard their position. One can see that if the worker-priest movement grows, then at some point it will prove a source of recruitment. Men at the work-bench not ordained will seek to be ordained because they admire their comrades who are. To a limited extent this appears to be happening in Southwark diocese under the part-time scheme for training for ordination, perhaps elsewhere, too. Until it is more widespread, the worker-priest movement, effective though it is in enlarging the spiritual and social experience and outreach of the priesthood, will not be a method of supplementing it. But supplementing it would accord with a joint report (682) of the two convocations in 1955[1] which hoped for the ordination of

> a small number of hand-picked men from the ranks of industry who, after ordination, will continue to earn their living as before, and exercise an evangelistic and pastoral ministry among their fellow workers.

The industrial missions, the more widely recognised form of service to factories and workshops, do not supplement the ministry at present. They have to support their staff by incumbencies or chaplaincies. Basically their appointments are varieties of the extra-parochial ministry and at present cannot help us in the search for more men.

The supplementary priesthood on the other hand, much discussed and often proposed, was clearly formulated as a 'voluntary clergy' by the Commission on the Staffing of Parishes (1929–30) on the grounds first that it was apostolic and primitive, then—

[1] *Report of the Joint Committee on the Proposed Draft Canon 83 (and 81).*

that some priests who are still engaged in their ordinary occupations will be better able to understand the laity than those who are entirely absorbed in clerical work. . . . Thirdly, it is urged that in this way the Church could meet the overwhelming claims made upon it from all parts of the world for men to administer the Sacraments as well as to preach the Word. It is this aspect of the argument for voluntary priests that especially concerns us.

And the Commission hoped,

that the Convocations will approve of the Bishops ordaining in the next ten years a limited number of men of worth, character and intelligence who are engaged in appropriate occupations and are desirous of giving their help as priests in the Church. We recommend that these should usually be men who have resided for many years in the same place and who are not likely to move elsewhere. We think that those men, during this experimental period, should be ordained especially to help in those churches where it has been or will be found necessary to reduce the number of ordinary services.

In 1960, at the request of the Archbishop of Canterbury, CACTM appointed a working party to investigate supplementary ministries. Its report, so far unpublished, argues that of recent years ordination to the priesthood has been narrowly confined to candidates who have experienced a call to become parish priests.

The working party had no wish to restrict the numbers recruited to this sector of the ministry, already in short enough supply, but argued for the ordination of others whose gifts are not necessarily parochial—

It may not be too difficult to accustom ourselves to priests who are doctors, lawyers, farmers, civil servants or musicians, for there is already an historical precedent for such cases. But we must now accustom ourselves further to the manager, the worker at the bench, the ship's master, the journalist, the firm's welfare officer, the architect, the artist and many others.

The report proposes an increase of the priesthood by acceptance of volunteers from other professions—not as a makeshift arrangement to tide us over manpower shortage but rather as a new dimension of the priesthood altogether which will make the work of the Church more effective among the professions and in workplaces and bring a new priestly order to the rescue of the old. It would secure much needed assistance at the level of the Sunday duties of the parochial clergy, but this would be only one of many contributions. The voluntary clergy would probably be older men. They would have to be adequately trained and prepared for ordination, for professional standards for the priesthood must be maintained. Many problems would be solved if this new category of the priesthood could on ordination be enrolled in a society of secular priests, self-regulating under episcopal sanction and visitation, which could watch over the priestly as well as the secular employment of its members and enforce the standards it thought appropriate.

There are dangers inherent, of course, in my view, in a miscellaneous and undeclared priesthood outside normal ecclesiastical discipline but at work in the body politic. There is the possibility that the members of it would drift into a purely nominal attachment to Church and office: there could be bewilderment if, their priestly status previously unknown, they suddenly emerged to speak for the Church. Their status would be ambiguous if they could too easily be transferred to incumbencies. In this context the exciting and seminal notion of a new and disciplined order of supplementary priests is a very real contribution. The report warns the Church that legislation may be needed:

> If there is to be any change in the law, even if no more than a provision prohibiting members of the Society from taking office as incumbents without leave, the authority of an Act of Parliament or a measure of the Church Assembly will be required and very early in its existence the Society will have to be placed on a statutory basis.

But in conclusion the report, after considering the diaconate and the women's ministry, said, 'Our sole recommendation is that progress can now only be made by active experiment' and quoted Dr Ramsey in favour of the removal of legal and canonical barriers which might prevent someone from doing what he believes to be right.[1]

The permanent diaconate remains to be considered briefly. Interest in it rose from the need for assistance to the priest in, mainly, his liturgical duties, particularly communion. Some uncertainty arises about the wisdom of setting up a permanent diaconate if it means a second-class, relatively untrained priestly order the members of which would be mostly incapable of proceeding to the full priesthood: a status alien now (though not in primitive times) to the priesthood as a fully developed professional group in which standards must be raised rather than lowered. If readers and other laymen are in increasing numbers to administer the chalice and perhaps eventually the paten, too, against which there appear to be no real theological objections, the need for ordination of a special diaconate to assist liturgically has gone at a stroke. It looks as though the

[1] 'We would repeat the words of Dr Ramsey when he was Archbishop of York, which we quoted earlier; that what is wanted at the moment is "to remove as soon as ever possible whatever legal and canonical barriers exist, and for someone to act upon what he believes to be right".'

notion of a supplementary ministry makes sense while the permanent diaconate does not. Yet these are both groups which cannot be measured, for they do not exist: both would lighten the burdens of the clergy, but by how much we cannot yet estimate. That their establishment should be explored would seem to promise nothing but good. But a scheme for a permanent diaconate embarked on now would hardly bring relief to the clergy for several years: a supplementary ministry, because of voluntary training schemes, would not begin to have influence before five years: its total impact might take at least a decade. In addition, as it would be of service to parishes principally on Sundays its pastoral contribution might be slight. These are not reasons for rejecting either proposal, but they are reasons against delaying other reforms until we have tried them out.

LICENSED READERS

Readers of the voluntary type are growing in number, the stipendiary kind is dying (there are now only two paid readers in Canterbury province). Together they bring nearly 6,500 trained and experienced lay workers to the support of the evangelising and liturgical tasks of the clergy: it is a magnificent and quite unambiguous contribution and would seem to be the clear alternative to a diaconate receiving holy orders but which can never proceed to the priesthood. It has a useful parallel in the lay preachers of the Methodist Church and could without difficulty be amalgamated with them in the event of the longed-for union of the two churches.

One out of every three readers is licensed to his diocese. The busier he is the less service the diocesan reader is able to give to his own parish and priest. The purely parochial reader, on the other hand, seldom functions outside his local church. The diocesan reader can become a peripatetic stand-in for the priesthood: the parish reader is denied wider experience. It would seem sensible for the reader to be licensed by the bishop *to his deanery* and for the rural dean to admit him in an appropriate service. The reader would then serve in his parish and as part of the deanery team and his gifts and experience would be more easily grafted on to the pastoral work: he would then be less of a 'stand-in' clergyman, more of a lay leader. Certainly in recruitment to the readership one of the most immediate means of relief to parish clergy is to be found. Every plurality or united benefice should have at least one reader. It looks indeed as though the Church could use 10,000 readers (1962 strength 6,581). But voluntary workers cannot be deployed: they must be recruited and used locally: we cannot draft them to areas of greatest need.

WOMEN'S MINISTRY

The report of the Working Party on the Supplementary Ministry, already discussed, spoke of the parlous state of the women's ministry in the Church, the 'poor pay, pitiful pensions, no security, no prospects and no status' of most women workers. On the future of the contribution of women it spoke with anger and bitterness:

> Until the whole question of women's ministry, including their liturgical ministry, is fully explored and faced, the problems relating to the employment of women in the service of the Church will remain insoluble. But we are bound to record our judgment that the attitude of the Church towards the ministry of women even within the limits now open has been niggardly, vacillating and often insulting. The Church should regard it as one of its most pressing duties to raise the dignity of women's contribution in every possible way, by removing the hindrances, whether of ignorance, prejudice, finance or administration.

A report to Church Assembly, later in date, *Gender and Ministry*,[1] discussed the ministry of women more moderately. It spoke, in sociological terms, of the changed status and role of women in the world, and of the need of the Church in the light of them to

> re-examine its doctrine of priesthood to take into account the vast gulf which yawns between our position and that of the early Fathers of the Church. We do not question the wisdom of past ages in laying down rules to meet the social *mores* of the day. But our Lord invited us to let the dead bury their dead: our duty is to the living.

It therefore asked that

> the various reasons for . . . withholding of the ordained and representative priesthood from women, reasons theological, traditional, instinctive, anthropological, social, emotional, should be much more thoroughly examined. We note that the New Delhi Committee on Faith and Order made a similar request.

On the basis of that report, which Church Assembly accepted, the Archbishops set up a committee to inquire into just this. It is now sitting and its report must be awaited. It is to be hoped that it will consider the status and functions of deaconesses. They constitute the one *ordained* order of women, and they are full-time workers, but their status (like that of their more numerous sisters, the licensed Women Workers) still seems inferior to that of voluntary readers. All that it is necessary further to say here is that *of course* the recruitment of women would add an enormous potential to the Church, even

[1] CIO, 1962.

if at first, at least in the experience of other professions, the actual numbers of women recruited might be small. However, the Church, even if it decides upon the equal admissibility of both sexes to the ministry, may have to proceed with caution, or postpone application of the principle if it appears to be a hindrance to reunion with other churches: it may reasonably wish to move in step with other communions. There are real difficulties, not quickly to be solved whichever way the verdict of the committee and the Church goes. Nothing, however, in the rest of this report prevents application of its general proposals to an ordained ministry composed both of men and women, if the Church decides upon it.

CHAPTER IX

A Staffing Exercise

WE have reached the point where the last item, increased recruitment to the ministry in the form it now has, needs to be examined. Two considerations have to be weighed—how many clergy do we need and how are they to be found? The Bishop of Birmingham's exercise produced a notional establishment of curates by a formula based on the size of livings which exposed a deficit of 2,342 assistant clergy. Is a similar exercise practicable for incumbents? Of course, one has to say immediately that there *is* an establishment for incumbents—the number of parochial livings in the two provinces. The number of incumbents cannot exceed this. The Church's only method of adjusting its incumbent manpower to growing population is to create new parishes out of old, and so create new livings. We have seen that the parochial establishment even readjusted in that manner fails to meet the urban situation and we have to ask whether any other method of computation of necessary manpower is possible.

We cannot invent an ideal parish or living and say that its manpower ratio shall be applied elsewhere. But there is a statistically average parish and a statistically average living. The average population per living in 1958 was 3,699; in 1961, 3,814. The average number of persons per incumbent in 1958 was 4,061; in 1961 4,199. Both the average living and average incumbency therefore stand in the fifth highest population group in Table 22, *Facts and Figures 1962*, which is 3,000–4,999. The number of incumbents in charge of the 3,165[1] livings of 5,000 and above was 3,045, roughly a third of all incumbents. If one elected to bring all the livings of 5,000 or above to an incumbent-to-population ratio of 1 to 5,000, then just for that group 2,887 more clergy *of incumbent status* would be needed for parochial work. The figure takes no account of the number of assistant clergy who in this group were 1,749; if we add their number to incumbents and ask what additional staff is then necessary to keep the ratio of parochial clergy in these large parishes to 1 : 5,000 we arrive at the figure of 1,138. If, on the contrary, we accept that each incumbent with 5,000 and over ought to have at least one curate (the Bishop of Birmingham's quota), then for this group the total parochial clergy needed must be 11,864, which means a present deficit of 7,070, (say 7,100). In this sector of the Church's ministry we have at present, it is arguable, only half the men we might reasonably

[1] The latest (1961) figure for this group is 3,287, the total population of which is 30,608,032.

require in view of the depth of penetration demanded in urban areas. However, this estimate takes no account of mitigating factors, such as economies possible in the use of clergy manpower, particularly of assistant clergy now in parishes below the 5,000 density mark. In 1958 there were 573 assistants so deployed. It is improbable that more than one-third could be moved (say 200); before we elected to move them we should need to know the age structure of the group, for older, later ordained men tend to gravitate to lighter assistant cures. In fact, the movement of curates from the smaller to the larger parishes would be an exercise as unprofitable of results as moving rural clergy into the towns. Most of the objections to the one can be sustained against the other. Even supposing gains were accomplished here, other sectors of growth in the ministry would easily cancel them out: the extraparochial ministry probably *ought* to reach 3,000 in the next ten years. There is no solution to be found in proposing this particular redeployment.

Other proposals for economising in manpower look equally illusory. United benefices and pluralities are reaching the point in many dioceses where they begin to suffer from the law of diminishing returns. Economies might be made by group and team ministries, which at the most might save one man in five wherever they come into existence; but there are as yet too few of these to achieve great savings. Lay help could carry an increasing share of the pastoral burden, though the general experience is that increasing lay activity calls for an increased (and increasingly efficient) professional body to direct it. A growing voluntary organisation usually calls for a greater full-time staff.

So far the analysis takes no account of rising population which naturally calls for a ministry rising proportionately if even the present priest-to-people ratio is to be held. By how much will the population rise? No one really knows, of course, for a birth explosion is upon us, and the Registrar General's estimates are frequently revised in an upward direction. An earlier estimate predicted a home population in the two provinces of 49·5 million in 1999: a revised estimate now predicts a home population of 58·5 million for that year! If one takes the most conservative estimate (that in Table 2, *Facts and Figures 1962*), then approximately twenty-five years hence the population will have increased by 5 million, which is 12 per cent. To keep pace just with that we shall need 1,600 more parochial clergy than we have at present: experts are now sure this modest population increase will be exceeded. And if the latest prediction *is* right, then by 1988 we should need 2,880 more parochial clergy.

We have two problems, first to arrive at an agreed clergy-to-people ratio, and then to maintain it in the face of rising population.

But the *manner* in which this is done is important—a general raising of the clergy-to-people ratio could leave the present imbalance between town and country untouched. The Church's deployment problems are met only if we concentrate on the largest parishes first, leaving the small ones untouched. Hence this analysis concentrates upon what has to happen if the conurbations are to be better served by clergy. Yet, of course, such a process must reduce generally the average number of people per clergyman.

The total number of full-time parochial clergy in 1961 was 13,429. On the basis of the 1961 census population of 43,624,275 this gives us a ratio of one parochial clergyman to every 3,249. Of course, we get a slightly different ratio if we add to the parochial clergy all the clergy who are dignitaries without cures or hold other non-parochial posts in the two provinces: the 1961 total including these was 15,488, which gave a ratio of one full-time clergyman to every 2,817 persons: if we add 7,100 new parochial clergy to *this* force it would give us a total 22,588, which is a ratio of one full-time clergyman to every 1,931 people. To maintain that ratio, the clergy force will need to be 24,367 by December 1971, in the light of the latest estimates of population.

In a brilliant study which concludes the Summary of Evidence, Mr R. F. Neuss of the Statistical Unit has made and explained a series of actuarial predictions undertaken specially for this inquiry. He has, on the basis of official census figures and the statistical material gathered by his unit, arrived at an estimate (Table 50) of what is called 'the extraction rate'—that is, how many ordinands, per million males born in England and Wales in the same years as the ordinands, we may expect in the years 1963–71. He bases his calculations on the assumption that the trends observed from 1954 to 1962 will continue at the same rate of increase. His prediction is that the ordinands in the 23–39 age group will rise from 519 in 1963 to 699 in 1971 and in the 40–69 age group from 122 to 131 per annum over the same period (Table 52). This gives us new, though hypothetical, controls to juggle with. We may expect rising population, we may also expect a rising number of ordinations. Between 1961 and 1966 the home population is expected to rise by nearly 1·5 million (43·9 million to 45·4 million) and the number of ordinations to increase (all ages) from 632 per annum to 713: in the next quinquennium the population will rise by just over 1·6 million (45·4 million to 47 million) and the annual number of ordinations is expected to rise from 737 to 831 (see Tables 55 and 52). There is reason to expect more priests. Will there be enough?

The diagram by Mr Neuss (p. 163) and col. 2 of Table 55 show that in the current quinquennium the full-time clergy force at home will rise by 1,492, and in the next by 1,960, an average rise of (say) 300 per annum in the first five years and 400 per annum in the second. These are healthy and encouraging increases and upon these we can proceed to reconsider the manpower situation. Before I tabulate these there are certain points to be made. Mr Neuss's calculations take account, of course, of annual losses from the full-time force through death, retirement, service overseas and other causes, and on the other hand what gains the full-time clergy force may expect from missionaries returning home or from men ordained abroad coming here to serve. These are vexing totals to arrive at. The average total wastage for the three years 1960–2 was 544, but

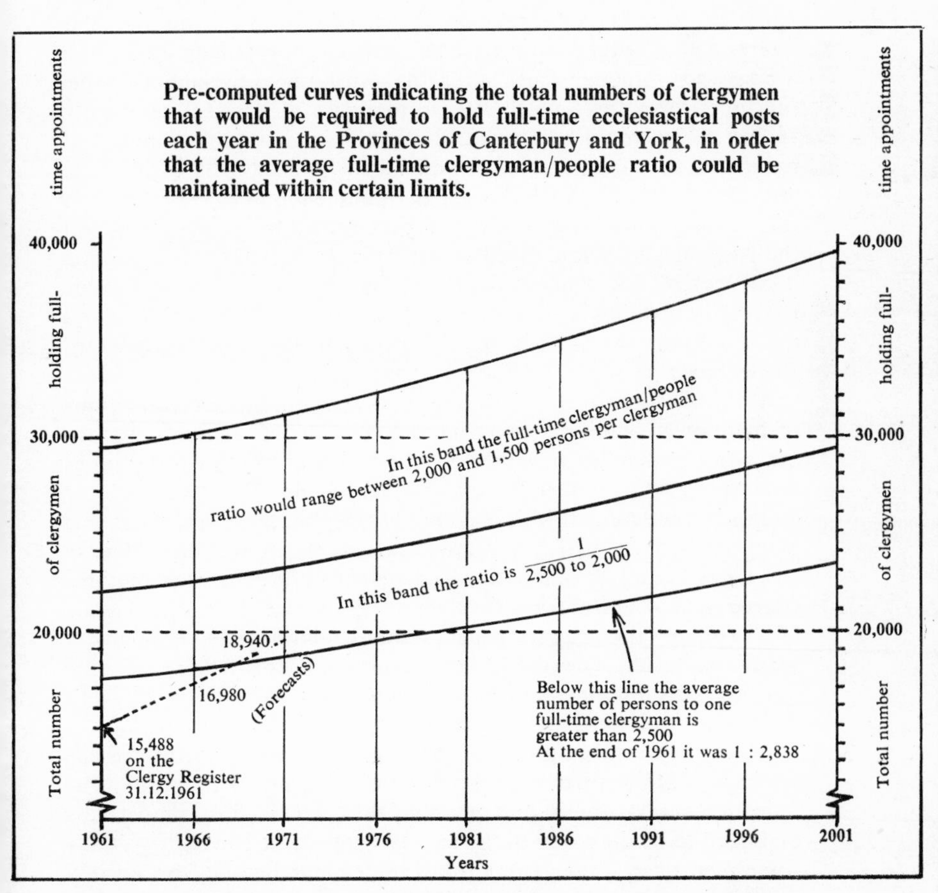

Diagram 7. Forecast of Clergy Numbers in Relation to Exploding Population.
(Source SE, Table 55)

the wastage is expected to fall now that the average age of all the clergy is decreasing.

In the tabulation opposite I have used round figures from item 3 on, because from that point it is an argument which is set out. It does not pretend to be an exact statistical analysis.

There is another way of looking at the manpower problem in the present quinquennium. We may expect, on Mr Neuss's prediction, to have 16,980 full-time clergy by 1966 (Table 55). To keep the present ratio we need only 16,113. In that sense, if his prediction proves correct, we may be argued to have 'gained' 867 clergy by then. But the maintenance of the present ratio covers only items 13 and 14 of Table XVII: it allows nothing for items 15 and 16. These total 4,050 in five years. Therefore the improvement in recruitment figures would reduce the deficit, but only to approximately 3,200. In the second quinquennium—to 1971—recruitment should raise the full-time clergy force to 18,940: to maintain the present ratio only 16,703 clergy would be needed. But in the second quinquennium, if hypothetically all annual losses and gains and needs stay as they are, and if all the needs stated for the first quinquennium have been met in full, we shall still need another 4,050 clergy and we should be, on the basis of prediction, 1,813 short. Averaged for the whole decade under review the annual shortage even on this more favourable basis of reckoning is hardly likely to be less than 500. In the first quinquennium the deficit would be 640 annually—which agrees with the estimate on line 18 of the table opposite.

It is important to stress the hypothetical nature of my tabulations of manpower requirements. I have done no more perhaps than to indicate the manner in which future and more exhaustive studies might proceed.

It is interesting that Mr Neuss predicts within the current decade a rising recruitment which will lower the average age of the ministry and allow for rising population and reduce eventually the clergy-to-people ratio. The Church can take a small satisfaction in this when a few years ago the prognostications about the future of the ministry were grim indeed. The picture in these terms is nevertheless of a static ministry, just holding its own, incapable even of providing the additional curates immediately required by item 1, and remote from the fulfilment of the Bishop of Birmingham's estimate of need to rescue the hard-pressed urban priesthood. The alternative I propose in the tabulated breakdown is an increase of the total ordained ministry by one-third to be deployed in the areas of greatest urban density. Only some such effort on the part of the whole Church could conceivably make a dent in the vast urban indifference with which the Church is faced. But even such an apparently ambitious scheme would take

Table XVII. Establishment Needs at Several Hypothetical Levels

(*a*) *Total Breakdowns, 1963–71*

Item	Number
1. Shortage of assistant curates on the basis of filling urgent vacancies (SE, Table 28)	863
2. Shortage of assistant curates on the basis of Bishop of Birmingham's formula (SE, Table 36)	2,342
3. Incumbent shortage on the basis of reducing existing cures in the 5,000–20,000+ group to a maximum cure of around 5,000 souls each	2,900
4. Assistant curate shortage on the basis of one curate to each of the 2,900 new incumbents	2,900
5. Existing assistant curate shortage in present 5,000–20,000+ group simply on basis of one curate to each existing incumbent	1,300
6. Items 3, 4, and 5 totalled indicate total hypothetical shortage of parochial ministry	7,100
7. Total 1961 establishment of parochial clergy	13,400
8. Additional establishment required on basis of 3, 4, 5	7,100
9. Non-parochial clergy working full time in England, approximately	2,100
10. Total full-time clergy force needed by 1971, approximately	24,400
11. Actual 1961 force, approximately	15,500
12. Deficiency, say	8,900

(*b*) *Annual Breakdown to the end of 1971*

Item	Number
13. Minimum annual increase required for the full-time clergy force in the light of rising population	80
14. Minimum annual number required to make good losses,[1] say	475
15. Minimum annual number to meet increases in extra-parochial ministry, say	100
16. Additional annual increment to overcome present parochial shortage of 7,100 in ten years	710
Total	1,365
17. Average of expected ordinations, all ages, per annum, say	725
18. Estimated annual deficiency	640
19. On this basis the average annual ordinations should be	1,365

[1] These must rise as the total clergy force rises, but not substantially enough in the first quinquennium to affect the estimate.

ten years before it reached numerical completion: a whole new long-term plan of expansion is called for if the Church is really anxious about the deployment of its clergy in terms of pastoral need. It must be noted that in the breakdown proposed, livings below 5,000 population have been ignored. No transfers or redeployment have been proposed. There are several justifications for this. Such ministries would certainly not escape the effect of other pastoral reforms and therefore of indirect redeployment. The smaller livings, those of the lowest population groups, are already subject to considerable pressures, dictated by manpower shortage, to unite. The smaller the cure on the whole the greater the age of the incumbent. The town ministries need an influx of the youngest men. The deflection of curates from the smallest cures would be automatic if means were found to deploy all newcomers into the towns. Finally, it is good policy to try to lift the manpower ratio of the densely populated urban cures to the level of at least the average ratio rather than to redeploy in the sense of bringing those above it down. A policy of expansion is more hopeful and stimulating than that of rationing, which depresses men and produces bad feeling.

What results might we expect from the urban activities of 7,000 additional parochial clergy? The Rev. A. B. Miskin somewhat schematically redeployed 1,000 rural clergy in the towns and argued that they would produce an additional 100,000 Christmas communicants there. On that basis 7,000 would produce 700,000—still only a third of the way towards the target of 2 million Christmas communicants necessary to bring the total number to 10 per cent of the population. If his statistical computation of the ratio of staff to communicants is a reasonable one, then (if clergy alone are the staff) my figure of clergy shortage is inadequate. It would be reasonable to expect, however, that additional clergy would generate that lay activity necessary to lift the total pastoral care of the Church to the level that would bring at least 10 per cent to church. In that case, my estimate might stand, though it could hardly be reduced: and 10 per cent is only a beginning.

What should we *do* with such an addition to the number of the clergy? The exercise was doubly hypothetical in that it depended on the elimination of all cures over 5,000 souls and so on the creation of many new parishes or livings—theoretically 2,887. If this were actually accomplished, then the urban areas would be further fragmented into still less meaningful parochial units. For this reason I used the phrase 'clergy of incumbent status'. Many, even most, of the additional clergy would have to be used in groups or teams in which their status ought to be more than that of an assistant curate. This we must presently pursue. The important point here is that a wholesale fragmentation of the larger parishes would be a disaster and the additional clergy would therefore have to be deployed through new ministerial forms, or not recruited.

Battles have many times been lost because generals deployed troops which existed only on paper. Where would the additional men come from? How would we expect to double the number of ordinands? How could we train them?[1] How could we pay for them? (Doubling the number in training would at present estimates raise the charge upon central church funds to approximately £800,000 per annum.) Even if we ask for supplementary clergy to lighten the load, they, too, will have to be trained in some manner: they cannot be brought in without some financial burden.

Even if it had the resources, the Church is unable to go to the market-place and bid for its manpower as a social service or an industry might do, though it might and clearly intends to call men more vigorously. Withal it must leave an inner voice to speak to men and not seek to usurp it. Nothing, on the other hand, prevents it from declaring its ministerial needs and planning how to use them, and praying that by the grace of God they may be fulfilled. In the proper spirit, nothing prevents us from asking where the required men might come from. Many studies today are directed to discovering what happens to sixth-formers and graduates—where they go to, what jobs they show preferences for. It is possible to examine what, as we have seen, statisticians and others speak of in their own language as an 'extraction' ratio, by which they mean the discovery of a ratio between, say, the total male population and annual rate of entry into certain industries or professions. Recruitment to a particular profession can often be expressed as a proportion of the total field or recruitment, whatever that may be. Recruitment to the ordained ministry does appear as a ratio of total male population, or of the number of male confirmands. However, an extraction rate conceals a fallacy. It is this: one can understand an extraction rate maintaining itself with some constancy once established, but what establishes its magnitude *ab initio*? If, for example, a century ago ordination was unthinkable without graduation, then the extraction rate to the ministry had meaning only in relation to the total number of men graduating year by year. If that could be expressed as a proportion of total male population, then the number ordained each year could also be so expressed. The proportion would, however, hide the fact that the real ministerial potential was unknown, for an academic barrier automatically prevented large groups of the population from making any offering to the ministry at all: their

[1] Theological college places have increased by about 25 per cent since 1951: but, 1963, we have only 1,703 places and an annual turnover of about 500 men.

potential could never be tested. The rate of applications for commissions in the Army before 1914 could have and perhaps has been expressed as a ratio of the then male population between 18 and 40: the expansion of the officer cadre between 1914 and 1918 showed that it bore no real relation to officer potential. The cut-off line was artificially determined by class, social connexions, and income group. In the same way one can speak of a rate of offering to the ordained ministry and express it as a proportion of the male population, but it is meaningless if social usage prevents one from discovering the ministerial potential of the whole male population.

The discussion of the clergy as a social group or stratum shows that social usage is an element in determining the total offering to the ministry. It is probably less emotional to think of it apart from class and to ask, why is there a high offering to the ministry from the sons of clergy, why is there a high offering from public schools? In both these groups, membership of the Church is obviously an important part of social usage as well as of individual faith. It is part of one's public duty and social responsibility to go to divine worship, to join in public or family prayers, to be baptised, to be confirmed, with great seriousness and solemnity to consider all religious vows and obligations, including married ones, to avoid the kind of personal life which would bring one into headlong collision with one's public way of life. From such a group the rate of offering is bound to be higher than from classes of society which, equally Christian, lack a sense of public commitment. It happens that in England this double sense of personal faith and public religious obligations has very roughly a class connotation—the public schools, Oxford and Cambridge, the professions, landed families. A further element is added by the deservedly high intellectual prestige of the public schools and ancient universities. From them, such has been their sense of public service, the Civil Service and the colonial administrators of the past and many schoolmasters have in the main been recruited, as well as the ordained ministry. But there is nothing sacrosanct about the pattern. If the public schools retained their Christian usage, but recruited their pupils from the poorest in the land, and not from the rich, we might have exactly the same extraction rate. The experiences of Ireland, France, Italy and Mexico suggest that you can have a largely peasant priesthood if peasant boys go as boarders to seminaries where Christianity is the lived daily life.

In fact, though in the Anglican priesthood public school (i.e. upper class) background is strong, and stronger still in the hierarchy, it is not a social 'given' from which there is no escape. A movement of social usage away from the Church in the families and institutions of the rich would lower the rate of offering from that quarter: on the other hand, a change towards religious practice in other groups or classes of the population could increase their rate of offering to the ministry. Without in the least seeking to lower the rate of offering from public schools and Oxford and Cambridge we need to raise the rate from grammar schools, technical schools, secondary modern and comprehensive schools, colleges of technology and the new universities. A shift of a few per cent would give us the additional ministry my establishment exercise demands. If, for example, grammar schools had, in the decade 1953–62, offered candidates at the same rate as public schools, we should have had 2,323 candidates from them instead of 993. If the secondary modern groups had offered at *a quarter* of that rate we should have had an additional 805 candidates from them—altogether in that period more candidates than CACTM could have handled. But, as we have seen, candidates do not come forward simply because they have, so to speak, a percentage entitlement. The ministry must seem to them an opening under God for their talents, their creative impulses, and their longing to serve their fellow men. In that first-class investigation into *Technology and the Sixth Form Boy*,[1] promoted by the Gulbenkian Foundation, and carried out in several countries, students were given a list of occupations to place in order of choice from the point of view of pay, prestige, intelligence. 'Clergyman' was not a profession in the list, though 'schoolmaster' was. Doctors, nuclear physicists and solicitors appeared highest in rank: doctors leading. It is an instructive result telling us much of the longings of young people for service, for the doctor unlike the pure scientist or technologist is the healer. Obviously much work needs to be done by the Church to show forth the duties, satisfactions and sanctity of the ministry. There are some efforts the Church might make—highest priority to chaplaincies at the new universities and colleges of advanced technology, special conferences of church men and women working and teaching in these fields, residential conferences and week-end schools for grammar-school boys only, and separately for secondary-modern and comprehensive-school boys, too.[2] Steps towards reunion would certainly create new and improved opportunities to teach in and speak to the pupils of LEA schools: barriers here are falling anyway. A new link is forged when the parson's children go to the LEA schools. Perhaps a greater task still is demanded of the Church in

[1] Oxford University Department of Education, 1963. See also *Arts and Science Sides in the Sixth Form, A Report to the Gulbenkian Foundation*, also Oxford University Department of Education, 1960.

[2] As more and more of this group move into the GCE or equivalent streams more and more of them will acquire at least the minimum academic qualifications for entry into the non-graduate level of the ministry.

the light of its present almost unconscious social structure, and that is to shift the centre of its thinking and feeling towards the centre of the national life. This demands a great spiritual struggle in a church so dependent on and so attached to the social forms and institutions of a quite different past. To be blunt, the men are probably there, waiting, but not in the places we are looking.

Even given these new rates of offering, are the men available? One has only to look at the advertising pages of the more responsible newspapers and reviews to become aware of the hunger for qualified manpower. Both schools and universities are demanding more men with the qualifications also required by ordinands. The Association of University Teachers put out a statement[1] saying that if the university staff-to-student ratio of 1: 8·2 is to be maintained and the accrued wastage of 4·5 per cent per annum to be replaced, a total recruitment of 6,700 is required between now and 1966–7; however, the AUT regard the Government's target of 150,000 students by 1966–7 as an underestimate. Their own estimate of 170,000 students demands 9,600 additional staff. If we consider church demands against the number of industrially employed male persons with qualifications in science and technology (229,940, census 1961) and male teachers (144,218, census 1961), a ministry of 25,000 to 30,000 male persons is slight indeed, a drop in the bucket. The Church ought not to be prevented from reaching this total because of the pressure of other manpower demands. Its present recruitment from grammar and other secondary schools or from redbrick universities cannot represent its real potential, and an examination of the types of employment taken by university graduates shows that material rewards are far from being the only rewards graduates consider when taking posts.[2]

[1] 1st August 1963.

[2] Of the 2,149 male graduates reported on in *The Employment of Cambridge Graduates*, by Christine Craig, the second largest group was in teaching. Only one group had lower average pay than the teachers and that was 'Churches'. See Table XV, p. 129.

CHAPTER X

A Blueprint for the Reconstruction of the Ministry

THERE is no doubt that what the evidence urges upon us is a reform of the ministerial structure and of the pastoral machinery of the Church, or rather not one single reform, but an interlocking series of reforms; in fact, an operation of the utmost delicacy and complexity. Though the difficulties stare us in the face, the alternatives are chilling—to do nothing, which means to abandon the nation to its religious decline and the clergy to their isolation, or to attempt a few piecemeal reforms which may save face but leave the central missionary problem to the conurbations unresolved. The crux of the whole problem of deployment seems to me this—though short of manpower the Church cannot use the clergy it has as effectively as it ought to: it is a bad steward. It needs more clergy, but it has no moral right to ask for them unless it can deploy them effectively. It cannot, one would have thought, remain content with what is virtually the self-deployment of the clergy upon an archaic pattern. At the same time it does not want a harassed, servile, or timid clergy as the price of reorganisation: as a profession the clergy needs to be raised in standards and stature, not lowered. Considered as a corporate body, the Church needs the same control over its organisational life as it is beginning to insist it must have over its liturgical life. Conceived of as a total corporation, not just the clergy, it must, if it can, bring the laity into a joint ministry with the clergy. The clergy and the laity together form a minority over against a society which has largely abandoned regular Christian practice.

We need, then, to seek to see the shape of a new kind of corporate ministry to England: it may be possible to describe its main features.

DEPLOYMENT

If the manpower problem were to be tackled by the acquiring of corporate powers by the Church to move clergy on a considerable scale from small cures to large ones, that is mostly from the country to the towns, the result would simply be confusion. The rights inherent in the freehold could not easily be abrogated: the simple abolition of them would be costly and the Church might find itself involved in labyrinthine legal undertakings which would infinitely delay the missionary tasks. When accomplished such a transfer, the evidence shows, would be inadequate. The results would not be worth the bitterness they might cause. Though a modification of the freehold seems necessary, a headlong abolition is not proposed. The more urgent task would seem to be both to increase recruitment to the ministry and to change what would be described in other callings as 'the terms of engagement'. In the first place it should be a condition of CACTM grants for training that an ordinand should accept direction for five years, roughly the present period of his first two curacies. If the condition attaches to CACTM grants rather than to ordination pure and simple, this leaves it free for the older man or the volunteer to the supplementary priesthood to be ordained to serve in his home town or diocese without affecting the situation of the younger ordinands on whom the main burdens of the parochial ministry must fall. There ought to be no question of a quota of ordinands for each diocese, beyond which it will not go. Negative provisions are perilous. It is sensible for bishops to ordain as many as they approve *to serve their titles anywhere they may be directed.* As to how they might be directed I will at this moment defer. Ordinands at present under training might be asked *voluntarily* to accept direction in this manner, since for them it was not a condition of entry. This first simple step would begin the creation of a new body of clergy under a new dispensation more adapted to the urgent missionary tasks of the Church.

What might happen after the five years of direction? The young clergyman should then be free to go where his sense of duty or his inclination calls him, but he will have served his prentice years in the areas of greatest need: many men will undoubtedly forge links of loyalty with the parishes and dioceses they first serve. Ultimately, however, no good purpose is served by then feeding the prentice priest into the existing system of freeholds and patronage. The evidence about the freehold is overwhelming: it is not really possible to maintain the clergy today as though they were minor eighteenth-century landed gentry. What to some is a guarantee of their freedom is to others a prison from which they can neither be pushed out nor climb out. They can be left there in their loneliness and frustration. This happens to far too many. Others who are offered the chance to move, move too soon. For them the freehold is a disposable affair not valued highly. The plea the Archbishop of York has made for longer incumbencies is to the point here.

However, if instant abolition of the freehold is not proposed, what might be done? It would seem proper to transform the freehold into a leasehold which gives an incumbent while he holds it the same protection as a freehold, i.e. he cannot be dispossessed of it except through legal processes or voluntary surrender. What would be necessary would be legislation which ensured that as each living fell vacant, then (unless earlier by voluntary surrender) the benefice became a leasehold instead of a freehold: if the process of transformation is not to be unduly prolonged, there ought to be an absolute term, i.e. each freehold shall be transformed into a leasehold as it falls vacant, or within a term of ten years, whichever comes first. The leasehold would give an incumbent an opportunity to move on, and would give his ordinary the power, which he badly needs, to move a man on for his own or the parish's good, or because reorganisation demands it. The existing disciplinary powers are invidious and largely inoperable and unoperated. In any case the real problem is not the obstinate misfit, but the clergyman who is 'sitting down to it', one who has grown old or tired or complacent, or inured to failure. He needs to move on to fresh ground, but no charge of refusal to fulfil his duties could be lodged against him with any hope of success. A reasonable tenure would be ten years, with opportunity to renew for not more than half that time. The powers of patrons and of the PCCs would not necessarily be disturbed by this measure. One procedure, however, would have to be guaranteed, that at the end of seven years of a leasehold incumbency the clergyman should be seen by his diocesan in order that his future movements might be discussed and plans made: this procedure has often been recommended. The leasehold system could not be operated without it. Nothing, of course, would prevent an earlier surrender of the leasehold, though there might be less opportunity to make it, or to consult about it, for preference in movement would of *necessity* have to be given to men nearing the end of their tenure. This would have to be insisted upon, though not to the exclusion of earlier movement or the ministry would lose its newly acquired flexibility.

It would seem to be part of such a system that proper records of the clergy should be kept in a central directory of clergy and that such card index records as CACTM now keeps of every ordinand's background, education, secular qualifications and experience should be continued to cover the rest of a clergyman's career. They might be added to the material already kept in the Central Register of Clergy organised by the Statistical Unit. Thus we should for the first time really know about our clergy—a responsibility we have to history anyway. Confidential reports on clergy should not be part of its cards or files. The same directory should have equally systematic information about parishes and extraparochial posts and be able to circulate information about vacancies, actual or pending. It would seem a necessary professional freedom that a man nearing the end of his tenure should have access to these lists and be able to apply for vacancies, after his 'tenure interview' with his bishop, either directly or through his bishop, at least in default of other methods of making his talents and experience personally known. The circulation of lists of 'open information' (i.e. of 'Who's Who' type) of men about to move would be a gain: it would be available solely to those who would have the duty to study such lists. The list of returning clergy that was circulated by the Overseas Council is a model in this respect.

DEPLOYMENT AND THE PAROCHIAL SYSTEM

Much has been said of the failure of the parochial system to adapt itself to present pastoral needs and of its cruel tendency to isolate the clergy. So far the discussion of the deployment of the clergy has turned on the parochial system as it is. Are changes needed? What changes are *possible* as well as necessary? First let it be said that a total transformation of the parochial system is neither immediately feasible nor practicable. The old has to be allowed to live and the new has to be allowed to grow alongside it. The most important thing is to create new forms of ministry to introduce into areas where the old parochial system has broken down. These define themselves: (i) isolated rural areas suffering depopulation and/or loss of clergy and of natural leaders, (ii) decaying downtown areas and inner suburbs, (iii) rapidly developing fringes of great conurbations. The classification of parishes as in decay or as suffering social change made earlier shows, however, how numerous these areas can be, *perhaps one-third of all our parishes*. The kind of problems they present are easy to describe. The Hilborough group of nine parishes in Norfolk, for example, presented a picture of extreme neglect. The majority of the livings had been vacant for a considerable time, one for five years. Buildings were not being maintained. No regular pastoral work had been done. Some churches subsisted on an average income of less than ten shillings a week in collections. Congregations were down to a few elderly people or children. The area covered by the nine parishes was thirty-six square miles, with seven villages each with about 250 population and two hamlets of fifty each. Because of the difficulty of finding men, and the absurdly small cures, the area was destined to become a religious desert. The Bishop of Norwich called into existence a team ministry under the Rev. Hugh Blackburne to handle the nine parishes as a group. This it is doing with vigour and pastorally the area is recovering remarkably. Right at the other end of the scale of population density, East Manchester group ministry was called into existence to deal with a changing area in which twelve churches at first served 60,000 people, then 30,000 and eventually will serve only 20,000 under rebuilding and planning projects.

The new parochial instrument the Church has brought into existence is the group or team ministry. The acceptable definition of a group ministry is several parishes run together by their separate incumbents; of a team ministry, one parish run by clergy working as equal members of a team. In fact, the pattern varies from place to place and the definitions do not easily hold. In the Hilborough group there is one rector for the nine parishes: his team consists of two, an assistant priest and a deacon; the team members live in separate rectories in different villages. Only the rector in this case enjoys the legal status of an incumbent. The East Manchester group is unique in being a voluntary association of incumbents of four or five adjacent parishes: it involves no sacrifice, its promoters say, of freehold by the clergy or of its individual incumbent and PCC by the parish, although a representative group council speaks for all PCCs.

The famous South Ormsby experiment[1] in group ministry covers what were fifteen small ecclesiastical parishes with twelve churches. The group's area is approximately seventy-five square miles and the population just over 1,100. The parishes, originally served by six elderly incumbents, are now covered by the rector, an assistant priest, a deacon, a deaconess, and a licensed reader. The Brinton group of twelve parishes in Norfolk is also a group ministry in the sense that all members are incumbents of neighbouring parishes who have agreed to run their parishes together. To make this possible every incumbent is also licensed to serve as assistant curate in every other parish in the group; he therefore serves everywhere as of right, not just of courtesy. Other groups, such as that of the Ford Estate, Sunderland, are informal and unofficial and have no legal entity. Hatfield has the legal basis of Hilborough—rector, two priests-in-charge, three assistant curates, a full-time lay youth worker. Each priest-in-charge has a territorial responsibility, but all clergy freely interchange. Hemel Hempstead, also a new town ministry, has a vicar and seven assistant curates each serving as a priest-in-charge. Groups vary therefore from the most informal to the legally tight form of Hatfield or Hemel Hempstead: and the tight structure is not new. It exists in all those towns where in times past the central church established daughter churches, served by priests-in-charge appointed by the rector. A bishop writes:

> Technically, any who are licensed to a group without being beneficed will have the legal status of a curate. What we are really concerned to get accepted is the concept that in such a team ministry, if the junior members of the team are not instituted and do not hold a freehold, it does not mean that they are of the status of junior men under training, but rather of partners in the team, who will have delegated responsibilities of their own.

[1] *The South Ormsby Experiment*, A. D. Smith, London, 1960.

The rector of the Stevenage group ministry wrote in 1961:[1]

> A neighbourhood church is served by a priest-in-charge, for such is his courtesy title, though he is in fact licensed as a curate to the parish church. This is at once unfair and undesirable, for inevitably he is no different in official status from a newly ordained curate serving his title in a parish. His entry in Crockford states that he is a curate. He may leave his present position after ten years in orders 'promoted' (in official circles) to what may be quite a small benefice.

The point is clearly made that because of the existing parochial system the members of a group ministry (all incumbents) have equal status, but members of a team ministry cannot be given it. What is unquestionably needed is a new parochial form to permit group or team ministries formed of clergy on an equal basis to come into existence. To create these permanently it is requisite to unite the benefices, in order that one freehold (or leasehold) may be created, and then permit that freehold to be held and enjoyed by a corporate body (a corporation aggregate having perpetual succession), namely a college of clergy of which all members except those under training would have equal rights and of which the chief or head or leader would properly be called a dean: perhaps 'town dean' where this might be appropriate, to distinguish him from a rural dean: but rector of the college might also be appropriate. Such a college would resemble in some measure cathedral chapters or colleges. The parochial area of such a college ought sensibly to be called, because of its size and importance, a 'major parish'. Thus, without destruction of the parochial system, there would come into existence major parishes run by colleges of clergy side by side with minor ones (the existing corporations sole) run by individual incumbents. A truly corporate ministry would thus come legally alive for the first time in the parishes since early monastic days.

The legal form is ultimately necessary even for the most friendly and co-operative of loose group ministries. Fatigue, loss of interest, movements of clergy, the attitude of patrons, the obstruction of sequestrators can cause a voluntary group to decline. Because the parishes remain legally untouched, the clergy of one group tell me they are tied in a decaying area to maintaining twelve churches, ten rectors, ten schools and old halls, fifty-seven organisations. They are aching to plan their own area, but pastoral reorganisation goes on over their heads: they cannot *claim* a right to be consulted. Because of leap-

[1] *Diocesan Memorandum concerning the Clergy serving in a large Town Parish under one Incumbent*: Rev. E. W. B. Cordingly, now Bishop of Lynn. See also *Unity in Itself, The Stevenage Experiment in Group Ministry*, Derek W. Price, London, 1963, which fully discusses the problem.

frogging rights of presentation they fear 'turns' will fall to unsympathetic patrons and the group unity will be destroyed. The old legal forms cannot really cater for group and team ministries.

Provision ought to be made for full-time layworkers to be members of the college, perhaps, to meet legal requirements, with non-voting rights on the property side of the corporation. The legal rights of the PCC need not be affected. One major parish means one legal PCC but if the area of the major parish is a large one, provision might have to be made for 'ward' organisation feeding delegates to a small central PCC. Of such a parish all full clergy members would have the status of vicars or incumbents. The clergy of such major parishes would have to be subject to the same 'leasehold' or terminable tenure as incumbents generally.

It would clearly be a tactical error to push areas into the form of a major parish without preparation. Therefore, the existence of looser forms, or alternative forms, is of value. For many areas there should be phasing, in any case: one begins with an unofficial group ministry and out of joint pastoral efforts, area acts of worship, new forms of lay consultation, one develops an official 'Brinton form' of joint service: out of such a loose federation it would be possible to proceed, at the right moment, to the establishment of a major parish. In fact, though many areas are now waiting for such an institution as the major parish, others simply need as a start that much closer clergy and lay co-operation in the spiritual and pastoral life which must spring from a lively deanery. The deanery which gets together its clergy regularly, and provides regular social occasions for clergy wives, can do much to relieve clergy loneliness. If upon the chapter and the ruri-decanal conferences were placed as a matter of first obligation the discovery and establishment of forms of inter-parochial co-operation, we might see springing up those *ad hoc* voluntary efforts the English are so good at improvising.

There is yet another parochial change waiting upon legislation. The growth of industrial missions, and the expected expansion of university and college of technology chaplaincies, have created or will create from time to time establishments or institutions which will be doubly served—by the incumbent of the parish they are in, and by an appointed chaplain. It should be legally permissible for diocesan bishops to designate, as the opportunity arises, such institutions as 'extraparochial places' on the lines of the Guild Churches Act, so that where the pastoral obligation falls can be clearly stated. A major parish ought to include specialist ministers such as chaplains or industrial missioners as members of the college. The incumbent of a minor parish cannot be expected to be able to serve equally well in every field: but he must not be able to block those who can. But if chaplaincies are separated decisively from minor parishes, and no major parishes exist, then direct forms of payment for chaplains must be instituted.

DIOCESAN POWERS AND PASTORAL REORGANISATION

The initiatives in the hands of diocesan bishops are always considerable, so, too, are their powers of persuasion. But patronage and the freehold place strict limits upon the means at a bishop's disposal. A whole series of measures of Parliament and of Church Assembly give powers for the initiation of schemes for united benefices and pluralities: among the most important are the Pastoral Reorganisation Measure, 1949, the Union of Benefices Measure, 1923/52, the New Parishes Measure of 1943, the Reorganisation Areas Measure, 1944/54, and the Benefices (Suspension of Presentation) Measure, 1953. A commission is now sitting upon pastoral reorganisation measures and will presumably shortly complete its work. What one supposes it will seek to do is to reduce the many different measures to some sort of order. The Benefices (Suspension of Presentation) Measure gives the bishop power, after consultation with the parochial church council and with the consent of the patron and the bishop's pastoral committee, to suspend presentation to the living for five years, and then a further five years. He may exercise his power within twelve months of a vacancy occurring. The Measure is an extremely valuable instrument in the reorganisation of difficult areas and in the formation of new kinds of parochial ministry. Individual parishes can be kept suspended until a group of them is free and a team simultaneously appointed to work to an agreed plan. But the life of the Measure ends in 1965, and will need to be reviewed if even the minimal pastoral planning is to be continued by the Church.

It must be assumed that the Commission will have regard for the existing pastoral reorganisation machinery provided by such acts as the Pastoral Reorganisation Measure, 1949, and related measures by which new parishes and benefices can be created, others dissolved, parish boundaries altered, churches declared redundant, extra-parochial places created and so forth. Without them no pastoral committee, no diocesan bishop, could function. We have to ask, are new powers needed? At the end of the war, faced with so much destruction and so many ruined churches and parishes, the Church took to itself the special powers of the Reorganisation Areas Measure, 1944, for ten years. The Amending Measure of 1954 extended by three years the period during which proposals could be presented under the Measure. The Measure therefore extinguished itself in 1957. Its powers were unique and for the first time in history gave the Church the opportunity to replan whole areas. Pt. I gave power to diocesans to create 'ecclesiastical reorganisation areas' and Pt. II [4–(1)] gave power to form new benefices or parishes, to dissolve or alter old benefices, to demolish and dispose of old churches and parsonage areas and to endow and staff new benefices in new ways, all without let or hindrance from existing rights of freehold or patronage. Changing social conditions, particularly movements of population, have created areas as much devastated by such changes as earlier areas were devastated by war. It seems to me that a bishop needs to have power again to define such areas and to replan them accordingly. I can see need therefore for a restoration of the powers of the Reorganisation Areas Measure of 1944, but with a differently worded justification simply if 'it appears to the committee that as the result of planning or replanning schemes, or other social and industrial changes, the number and situation of the population has so changed as materially to affect pastoral supervision or the general effectiveness of the ministry of the area'. To make such new areas effective adjacent *good* parishes might have to be grouped with decaying ones and therefore the Pt. I [2(b)] clause about a contiguous or adjacent parish ought perhaps to be in the plural.

In the creation of such new areas it is important that existing freeholds or rights of patronage should not stand in the way, or if suspended, not be re-established in such a way that new and inexpugnable 'properties' are created which would hamper long-term solutions of freehold or the patronage. In any measure a clause might be necessary giving power to transfer the rights of presentation which remain after promulgation of a 'Reorganisation Area' Order to the bishop and/or diocesan board of patronage or similar body for a period of ten years or longer if agreed with the patrons of the old livings. But at the end of such a period it should be possible for more than one course to be open: e.g.—

(*a*) for the rights of patrons to be re-established if such in the view of the bishop or patronage board is both equitable and pastorally desirable;

(*b*) for the bishop's powers to be renewed for a further five years;

(*c*) for the creation of a college of clergy as the corporate body responsible for the whole area with the right of presentation to vacancies in the college exercised jointly with the bishop and/or board of patronage;

(*d*) always saving that presentation, no matter how or by whom exercised, is to a pastoral cure not exceeding ten years and renewable for a further five years only by consent of all parties properly concerned—PCCs, the clergyman himself, the bishop and board of patronage;

(*e*) upon the formation of a college of clergy to run the reorganisation area it ought to be assumed that the reorganisation has been completed: the area might then be designated a 'major parish', and the dean of the college described as 'town dean' or 'rector' and his colleagues as 'vicars'.

THE SHAPE OF THE MINISTRY: (A) PASTORAL CARE OF THE CLERGY

I have proposed new conditions of entry into the ministry involving direction for the first five years of service, then movement at will into a parochial system in which a 'leasehold' has been substituted for a freehold, and a new parochial form, the major parish, run by a college of clergy, is to be established. All these make possible the growth of a new ministry side by side with the old. The promise of so great an ultimate transformation of the ministry compels us to look at its total shape. It would certainly force the Church into quite a new and much closer concern for its ordained men. In the present, and the past, to reach an incumbency was, as we have seen, the peak of ministerial life: no one except the incumbent himself was really *compelled* to think of what happened after that. If, however, the old independence is brought to an end by the substitution of the leasehold for the freehold, then new problems arise. Every diocese will have to concern itself with its 'job-structures' as a whole and more conscientiously watch over the shape of individual ministries. This will be still more necessary if recruitment grows at the rate asked for in the previous chapter: it would be fatal not to have a place to which to move a man who ought to move on, and wants to: it would be absurd not to know what to do with one's new recruits. It could happen *at present* that a badly understaffed diocese would be embarrassed by a flood of men of incumbent status: its capacity to absorb them, however much it needed them, would be limited by the number of benefices at its disposal. It could turn away wanted men. So there has to be a double reshaping—one of the pattern of the ministry, the other of the 'job-structures' in dioceses, including, of course, the extraparochial outlets. It goes without saying that this presupposes financial and property reorganisation, too.

A first aspect to study is the pastoral care of men in the ministry. It has three stages: (i) curacy period, (ii) incumbency period, (iii) retirement and old age. I will take them in turn.

Curacies. It seems most important that a man just down from theological college should be placed where he can best be trained. A college principal is closer than the best bishop to a man under training. It is pastorally necessary that the principal should advise and help to place a man in a parish where his first steps can be guided by a 'teaching' priest. Colleges build up understandable traditions about these transactions, but they can manifestly conflict with manpower needs and this would seem to be one reason why the allocation of ordinands under the scheme described in *The Distribution of Ordination Candidates*, 1957, failed to work. If, however, men are to be directed in their first five years, direction to the first curacy on manpower grounds could again conflict with the need for training. Clear principles need to be laid down:

(*a*) an ordinand is to be directed to an area, but

(*b*) in his first two years primarily in the light of his need for training,

(*c*) in the three years remaining, on the basis of manpower demands.

The two needs are not incompatible, of course, but the successful parishes least need clergy but most easily train them, the decaying parishes most need clergy but least easily train them. Bishops have said to me that they could not send deacons to certain badly staffed parishes most in need of them, because the overwork, frustration or despair of the present incumbents would be ruinous to the new men. If, however, major parishes are brought into existence in such bad areas they could easily become first-class training centres, making special provision for beginners as Portsea did, and many group and team ministries now are doing, and providing, at least for the unmarried, a communal life in a clergy house. The two needs would be less incompatible if in every diocese lists of teaching or training priests and parishes were compiled (and regularly revised) and if the priests were kept in simple and unbureaucratic relation with the training needs of the diocese by visits from the Director of Post-Ordination Training. Then training possibilities would be better known and understood in dioceses to which it is necessary to direct men and the difficulties inherent in transfer at the end of two years to an entirely new set-up would be avoided. However, even now, not all deacons go (or even ought to go) to places with a reputation for training. As recruitment grows, training parishes will be oversubscribed. An alternative is necessary: one would be to place a deacon under a clerical director of studies who is not the incumbent he is serving under. The director would have an agreed claim on the curate's morning studies and attendance at conferences and lectures and serve both as an intellectual and a spiritual guide. Suitable older clergy in lighter-duty parishes who have kept their minds alive might be enlisted for these duties and find new justification for their ministry in them. A deacon with three direct sources of training and support—his actual parish life, post-ordination training, independent intellectual and spiritual direction—could be as well served in the understaffed diocese which needs him as in a good training parish of the older sort. In any case if we are to direct men to understaffed dioceses this must inevitably face those dioceses with a strong challenge to develop first-class training schemes and the best pastoral care of the young men entrusted to them. It also seems possible to devise sensible schemes for consultation between college principals and bishops or their chaplains about the placing of ordinands.

Good public relations are essential. Ordinands should know why direction is imperative. It should be personally explained to them before selection. A poster showing the 'league position' of dioceses in terms of manpower ought to be prepared annually and circulated to colleges and churches and kept constantly in display.

It would also be pastorally most valuable if young men entering the ministry regarded their first five years as 'the celibate years' in gift to the ministry at the point of greatest need and delayed marriage till afterwards.

Incumbents or priests of incumbent status. We have commented on the professional 'plateau' created by the benefice system. A man can reach full professional stature at his first incumbency, perhaps even by 25, today often long before 30. On this plateau he remains immobile, short of the preferment possible only to the 3 per cent. For forty years or more he will go on doing the same tasks, though probably in a succession of parishes. He can be left too much alone, enjoying only tenuous contacts with other clergy, and isolated from the laity. As the years go by, in the necessary absence of a system of professional promotion, the incumbency can become a desert in which a man's inner life dries up: or else he finds his life fulfilled in tasks other than those for which he was ordained—teaching, farming, local government, hobbies, the garden. He goes on in his fifties, because there is nothing else to do. But he may have nothing left to offer. Whatever happens to other proposals, it is feasible to draw the clergy more closely together corporately, on the lines of the following proposals:

I. The rural dean should become 'the bishop in little', leading his team, admitting readers, directly concerned with the pastoral care of the clergy, their families and wives.

II. The office of rural dean should not be a freehold or leasehold. It should circulate among the clergy in order that as many as possible should have experience of a wider ministry. The present term, usually five years, is sensible. Total service in the office ought not to exceed two such terms.

III. A monthly meeting of the chapter appears a minimum requirement: it should include (and normally does) worship and a meal: studies should be promoted and papers read from time to time.

IV. The rural dean and chapter should be charged with the task of promoting formal and informal group ministries and joint meetings and activities of adjacent PCCs. Even the informal group should meet weekly.

V. The leadership of the bishop of a diocese involves not only policy-making but administration, too. It is impossible to free him entirely from this. But ways have to be devised to spare him excess of administration in order to release him for his pastoral and evangelistic duties: some proposals will be made presently.

VI. There should never be less than two suffragan bishops in a diocese, each with a clearly defined area of pastoral care. This need not prevent the appointment also of assistant bishops without attachment to areas, though it might involve clear decision as to whether an assistant was assistant to a suffragan or to the diocesan at the centre.

VII. The suffragan with a territorial responsibility would be simply representative 'helper' of his bishop not 'chief in superintendency', i.e. not taking the place of the bishop. The relationship of territorial suffragans to archdeacons would have to be determined afresh. As an archdeaconry is a legal division of a diocese for administrative purposes, it would be convenient for a suffragan to have authority in one or more archdeaconries. There is a case to be argued for uniting the offices of archdeacons and suffragans. It need not detain us, nor affect the present proposals.

VIII. What is argued generally here is that without impediment to the direct relation of bishop to every corner of his diocese some decentralisation of pastoral care is urgently necessary. (Exactly the same kind of decentralisation is necessary in existing big parishes and the newly proposed major parishes. Pastoral care will have to be taken down to ward or neighbourhood and street level and worship to some extent 'decentralised' through the house church and house communion.) It is only through diocesan decentralisation that the much-needed systematic pastoral care of the clergy can be undertaken under the present system. The new dispensation I have proposed will be inoperable without it.

IX. Yet these modest reforms are far from being all that is necessary. The principle of a sabbatical year is well established in academic circles. Teachers can be seconded by local authorities for refresher courses. Doctors can take courses to bring them up to date.

That a man who as his profession or way of life is giving himself continually to other people needs to pause, reflect and study for a period longer than a holiday is generally accepted. The clergy do not often get this opportunity and never as an established professional right. They are not even well served over holidays. In this, too, the freehold is a limitation: who will provide the statutory services if a locum cannot be found, *or paid for*? And no one except the incumbent has the responsibility to find one.

I believe we have an obligation to give the clergyman in his early fifties, the years of spiritual drought, the opportunity for at least *a sabbatical term* away from parochial duties. That part of the term might be rest or travel is reasonable: that a large part should be spent in collegiate life with other clergy and with laity is imperative. Reading and seminar work in such a college would be as important as attendance at lectures. I believe it is desperately important that every clergyman should have such an opportunity of renewal, without resignation of office, at least once in a lifetime, and that during it his status should be safeguarded and his parochial duties undertaken for him without financial loss to himself. The Anglican colleges which already exist, St Augustine's College, Canterbury; William Temple College, Rugby; Moor Park, Surrey, might welcome the opportunity to serve in this manner. Perhaps a new collegiate institution is needed which might serve other urgent purposes for the Church, too. The growth of a new corporate life among the clergy would make the establishment of a 'sabbatical rota' easier: major parishes would have no difficulty in arranging periodic releases. For those less fortunately placed it is not impossible to visualise help directly from the diocese as the manpower situation improves: young priests might be ready to give one year of their early ministry to serve a series of locums for men sent away for their sabbatical periods.

Family problems would be created: they might cause us to increase our pastoral care of clergy wives: they do not strike me as insuperable. On the St Augustine's courses I have attended the wives often go, too.

Old age and retirement. The Church is richly endowed with a separate corps of elderly clergymen: the clergy, as the diagram on p. 96 shows, have a more prolonged professional life than other professional men now that in other professions the retiring age of 65 is well established. The elderly clergy render a service of great value and the pastoral results and work scores they show in Table IX do not suggest that they are less hardworking or less successful on the whole than other groups.

However, there are problems. One, of course, is that under the present system it is hard for the elderly clergyman to move. Parish church councils even of small cures usually prefer a young clergyman to an older one: certainly they feel that a constant succession of elderly clergy is not good for the parish. It is wrong to regard rural cures simply as the final stations of a ministry the best years of which have been spent elsewhere. It has been argued in this report that the age structure of the rural ministry should bear some relation to the general age structure. If the proposed system of 'leasehold' benefices is established, every diocesan will face the problem of placing in new livings and under new conditions men already well into their sixties. It is not a new problem, but at the moment under the freehold it has a 'built-in' solution: the man who ought to move but cannot stays in his parish until he retires or dies. This solution by neglect will no longer be possible under a leasehold system.

Some remedies suggest themselves:

(*a*) Though it is probably wise that there should be no compulsory age of retirement, the penalties in the shape of reduced pension which attach to retirement at 65 should be steadily diminished as funds permit, until 65 rather than 70 is the full pensionable age. The Church would then be in line with other professions, except that retirement would still be voluntary.

(*b*) At 70 freehold (under the present system) and leasehold (under the new) should automatically be extinguished for the holder of every cure or dignity: licence to continue beyond 70 for annual or biennial renewable terms should be granted by the bishop or archbishop.

(*c*) Where possible a proportion of small single-church parishes should be preserved for some considerable time to come to house and provide light-duty cures for clergy too advanced in years or poor in health to fulfil bigger tasks. But a cure should never have only the elderly or ailing.

(*d*) It should be made possible for elderly clergymen voluntarily to return without loss of status, stipend or dignity to the role of an assistant curate.

(*e*) Major parishes in town or country in control of their own housing facilities might make permanent provision for one or two elderly or retired clergy on a part-time basis.

(*f*) The practice of providing homes for retired clergy in places where they may still give help pastorally or in divine worship ought to be encouraged.

(*g*) The complete break which compulsory retirement creates in other professions, i.e. from full professional life to complete professional death in one day, ought to be avoided at all costs for the clergy, whose vows are life vows and not terminable contracts.

THE SHAPE OF THE MINISTRY: (B) STIPENDS AND PROMOTION

There appear to be in general two kinds of professional status. The first is where status is fulfilled by becoming a qualified officer or person, and then carrying on one's profession in independence: a general practitioner, a family solicitor, a barrister, are of this group. The second kind is where one becomes a qualified person, but can carry on one's profession only through a statutory authority or corporate body: examples of such are probation officers, youth employment officers, child care workers. For them the career possibilities are slight: to move on they must change official status and become, say, administrators. The teaching profession resembles both sorts: master or teacher status is the fulfilment for most. But promotion to headships of department, or to headmasterships, and seniority and special duty pay relieve the contours of the professional plateau.

The ordained ministry has points of resemblance with them all. The curate is like a junior master not yet on a permanency at full rates, but the incumbent is rather like a G.P. (except in the level of his earnings). But his capital is not involved and he can move if an offer comes along, and there are mild promotion possibilities (a better-paid or more congenial living, preferment, differential pay in some dioceses for added responsibility): and in this he more nearly resembles a schoolmaster. However, he suffers from disabilities which impede few other professional men (except to some extent doctors and barristers). He cannot canvass his abilities or experience; he cannot apply for promotion however worthy he may think himself; he cannot apply for other livings going vacant (or at least it is not good taste to do so).[1] The Church does not provide a 'career' structure as industry does: it would look askance at the parson who appeared to make his own. Yet in the course of events men do get transferred, preferred, translated. Someone, somewhere, has lists: someone has made decisions. No one can be quite sure on what grounds decisions have been made, or who precisely had a hand in them. The Church has a 'closed' system of promotion. In the absence of an 'open' system, those passed over, those long ignored or neglected, those conscious of unused and even unrecorded abilities which no one seems to require, come to believe in wire-pulling, grapevines, 'old-boy-net' and all the secret forms of career promotion which flourish the better in the absence of an open system. There is no evidence that these actually are more the vices of the ministry

[1] Though the advertising of vacant posts and livings goes on in Church newspapers and by circulating lists.

than of other professions. In any case can one ever know? At what point do friendly inquiries and name-canvassing among bishops and their staff become 'old-boy-net'? But overlooked men can hardly be blamed for thinking they do exist. However, there is much evidence that bishops are baffled by staff problems. They find themselves unable to draw on the whole talents of the Church, because there are no means by which they can learn of them. The inadequacy of the Church's system of promotion and preferment is the cause of bitterness among the clergy. Many have said to me that they find it hard to speak of their acute disappointment, even to their bishop, without seeming to advertise themselves as career-minded, or else as misfits.

I have already suggested one remedy for this in the shape of an open central directory of clergy. The time has come to ask whether a more open ministry generally is not to be preferred to the present one if by such we more effectively deploy men as well as remove grounds of grievance. An open ministry, in the sense meant here, would be one like the teaching profession in which terms of entry, of advancement, of increments, of transfer were easily ascertainable: the structure of the profession could be 'shown'.

The elements of such an open system would be:

(*a*) a uniform stipendiary system,
(*b*) a uniform system of increments and allowances,
(*c*) recognition of seniority and special responsibilities,
(*d*) an open system of promotion,
(*e*) control by the Church of its staffing needs (i.e. its establishment).

I will take each in turn.

A UNIFORM STIPENDIARY SYSTEM

Already, of course, by the establishment of diocesan minima and uniform systems of allowances dioceses are producing locally uniform systems. There can be nothing *in principle* against the uniformity becoming regional or provincial or national as well. The process of establishing diocesan scales ought in the course of time inevitably lead to national scales. Indeed, we have them already, much though they are criticised, for pensioned men. Now that the Church Commissioners administer one great common benefice fund we are already half-way to a 'unification of benefices'. The subdivision of its product into parochial benefices is a bow to history and to property rights, but no longer essential to the proper allocation of the income from the fund. Benefice income is today the shadow of local rights, not the substance. The local benefice does not enjoy the capital gains or even necessarily increased interest, nothing beyond the original terms of the endowment. These other accumulated benefits are pooled and disbursed in the form of more general awards to the Church's living agents. It would be good sense to legalise—and complete—the process so far halted half-way and to unify all benefices into one common stipendiary fund by means of which one agreed stipendiary system could be created. The moment to do so in each parish might be when a freehold becomes converted to a leasehold or within ten years of a named date: the benefice would then be legally absorbed into a common fund.

The actual systems of awards to clergy vary so much from diocese to diocese that a uniform system of benefice payments from the Church Commissioners would still leave many fantastic differences between clergyman and clergyman, diocese and diocese. (We have seen that the absence of a benefice system has not produced uniform stipends for curates.) Agreements between dioceses would be necessary on family allowances, allowances for special responsibility, inclusion and exclusion of income in computing what amount has to be augmented, and so on, before a uniform stipendiary system could come into force. This means the establishment of machinery to negotiate stipends. I propose that this should be set up on a regional basis—four or five dioceses together—in the first instance, because it might be reasonable to maintain some regional differences in stipends related to regional differences in cost of living and for other organisational reasons which will presently appear. Nevertheless, all regional efforts at uniformity should keep in step with each other. This means advice and help from a central board charged ultimately with the task of negotiating a national scale with permitted local differences.

UNIFORM SYSTEMS AND CLERGY STATUS

Every diocese adopts an incremental system where assistant curates are concerned and discovers no sinister product as a result. It is as necessary to negotiate a uniform incremental system for assistant curates regionally as it is to negotiate a uniform regional stipendiary system for incumbents.

However, the unification of benefices and the negotiation of agreed rates for beneficed and unbeneficed clergymen would present an opportunity to bring to an end the legal distinction between these two classes of men which has no real parallel anywhere else. In *Unity in Itself*, an account of the Stevenage experiment in group ministry, the Rev. Derek Price is as clear and emphatic as a man could be about the damage which could be done to group ministries (and the personal consequences to a man) by the fact that a priest-in-charge of 10,000 souls (in Stevenage for instance) is technically 'only' a curate. A member of my proposed college of clergy in a major parish would, as things are at this moment, be 'only' an assistant curate. It is obvious that the ranks of the unbeneficed clergy will grow with group ministries and the hoped-for rise in the extraparochial ministry, and the present distinction between the two classes will grow more and more false. The time finally to end the distinction will be when the unification of benefices is accomplished; that is, within ten years. At that moment, when no man is left with a purely local title in Church property, clergy should be divided into two groups only: assistant curates for the first three years after ordination, staff priests thereafter. The term vicar or even incumbent might still be used of the leaseholder of a living, or a member of a college of clergy: probably tradition will compel this anyway, but the distinction between beneficed and unbeneficed clergy would disappear. All would be salaried men.

Then with one direct line of ministerial service, the incremental system so well established for assistant curates could be extended to all priests and related to the rewards of other professions. Because curates' increments seldom have a life beyond five years (the men move on into incumbencies) I suggest that there should be a junior stipend scale for the first three years, at the end of which a man would reach the senior scale—something near the present diocesan incumbent minimum, whatever his post. Beyond that *as a minimum* there should be at least one seniority increase at the end of ten years in the ministry and another at twenty years in order that long service and increased cares and responsibilities may be charitably recognised. Parishes, parochial and extraparochial posts should be graded according to responsibilities and duties, but with some severity, so that only the really heavy duties are rewarded and uniformity of scales not destroyed. The points system instituted by several dioceses could be a useful guide. Family allowances and other special allowances should be of one and the same kind and rate from the beginning of a man's ministry to the end. It would be an idealistic and unprofitable exercise to propose here what they should be. The technicalities are considerable and must be in the first case negotiated regionally and related to diocesan ability to pay them. It is important, however, that negotiated scales should have a reasonable life before further increases or deductions are permitted: reconsideration every five years would seem to be sensible and practicable. Church Commissioners, diocesan boards of finance, parishes faced with rising quota demands all need to avoid an inflationary stipends system. The payment of the clergy has very high priority, but it is not the only financial burden the Church has to carry: the stabilisation of stipends for agreed terms can grant the Church freedom to tackle other tasks.

It is not realistic to recommend an actual stipend for the clergy. Any such figure would rapidly fall out of date. It *is* possible to say that as a professional group the clergy are poorly paid, but that the severe poverty most of them suffered about ten or fifteen years ago has been mercifully brought to an end. It is reasonable to recommend what *levels* should be aimed at: the basic starting stipend for the proposed senior scale (incumbent level) should not fall below the yearly average of industrial earnings. Where these differ from region to region they could form the basis of regional differences in stipends. We know that between the basic minimum of diocese after diocese and real earnings there is a gulf fixed. The average basic minimum for the two provinces is £827 (see Appendix One), the average real earnings are £1,020. These exclude free housing. In terms of *real* earnings as against basic minima, clergy earnings should not be allowed to fall below graduate teachers' salaries or to rise much above them. Clergy after twenty years' service should be at the top salary scale for graduate teachers. As teaching in LEA schools is a poorly paid profession, these are modest proposals. However, caution as well as modesty is necessary. The Church must not place itself in the position of using monetary awards as an incentive to enter the ministry. The stipendiary system must be economically neutral. If the Church accepts this principle, then it must accept, too, to gear salaries to scales close to the salaries of teachers or of members of the various social service professions. *They* will have to be pacemakers. Another principle of great importance also emerges: clergy today are greatly embarrassed to have to preach sacrifice to and ask for funds from parishioners much poorer than they are. Too high an income separates them socially from their flock: too low an income impedes their work and feeds a sense of bitterness and inferiority. It seems proper that industrial earnings should form the bottom rung for them—university lecturer and graduate teacher round about the top for the average incumbent. Granted this, and free housing and lifelong security, the clergyman's position is not unfavourable—either under the old dispensation or the new one proposed here.

Some of the clergy find any talk of rewards objectionable, despite scriptural sanction for paying them. The Church must continue gladly to welcome men who as members of religious orders or of the Company of Mission Priests will find means of living on a minimum far below what the Church would dare to offer to a priest with family or other responsibilities, and of contributing the balance of stipend to other causes. There is a case for the voluntary poverty of clergy *within an order which will sustain and discipline them*, but not for inflicting an involuntary poverty on clergy for want of will to do otherwise. The two positions must never be confused if we are to avoid a kind of double-think about clergy pay.

PENSIONS

A system of determining a national scale of pensions already exists. It will simply be necessary to relate it to the new stipendiary system proposed. Other professional pension systems should be studied as models. It has been argued (pp. 133–4) that differentials in pensions, though not in principle unreasonable, could have been much more modest than they actually are. In any case it would seem proper that those receiving higher pensions should help to pay for them. An equitable solution to this vexing business would be to guarantee to every clergyman irrespective of office or dignity a basic non-contributory pension and to make available beyond that a second supplementary pension towards which all those wishing to participate would make an annual contribution out of income and related to it. Though the basic pension would remain the same for all, the supplementary pension would vary for each contributor according to his previous income and so automatically provide a differential.

AN OPEN SYSTEM OF PROMOTION

One must distinguish between two aspects of promotion or preferment; the first concerns the Crown prerogative in the appointment of bishops and dignitaries, the second relates to the more general run of clergy appointments not subject to the Crown. As to the first, a commission is at present sitting and its report must be awaited. *À propos* of it one may hazard the remark that control over its senior appointments, a control not necessarily elective, is probably vital to the corporate identity of the Church. Perhaps one has also to confess that after reading Anthony Sampson's *Anatomy of Britain* it is impossible any more to use the phrase, 'It's odd but it works', without blushing.

Here the more general notion of promotion must concern us. One may perhaps by-pass the conceivably endless discussion about the ethics of promotion by saying that something quite modest is under discussion—how men get moved to posts of greater challenge, greater responsibility, and sometimes greater reward.

It is obvious that if the proposed uniform stipendiary system and a uniform pattern of ministry are adopted at least one of the safety-valves of the existing system, the occasional good fortune of being offered a living better financially and in other ways, will disappear. The interest attaching to transfers will remain, but the stipendiary advantages will go. An incremental system, with at least two seniority increases, provides some compensation. What is also needed is some more general increase of promotion possibilities. It is already clear that the office of rural dean will have a new importance and that in the 'town dean' (or rector or senior incumbent) of the college of clergy of a major parish a new office of major importance will be created. I recommend that promotion to the office of rural dean or 'town dean' or rector of a college of clergy should carry a stipendiary increase at least equal to the first proposed seniority payment: in addition that appointment to a rural deanship should qualify the holder for additional staff in the form of one (or one more) curate or assistant priest and one paid lay administrative or social worker (at preference). It would seem proper that the chapter of a rural deanery should have statutory rights in the appointment of the rural dean. The Recommendations to the Convocation of Canterbury[1] are excellent, and are here repeated:

> As soon as possible after the occurrence of a vacancy in the office of Rural Dean, the Archdeacon giving fourteen days' clear notice should call a meeting of the clergy of the deanery (beneficed or licensed under seal) who should by secret ballot either (*a*) select three of their number for nomination to the Bishop of the Diocese, and the Bishop should appoint one of the nominees to the vacant office, or (*b*) elect one of their number to the office subject to the Bishop's right of veto. In the case of the exercise of the veto a fresh election should be held.

These proposals seem unexceptionable so long as it is within the right of the chapter to choose which system it will prefer to operate. The first, which is semi-elective, has much to commend it in that it introduces the bishop as a positive rather than a negative contributor to decisions.

One dilemma remains. The Canterbury Convocation Report recommended a three-year term of service for rural deans, renewable once, and then disqualifying the holder for service again until after three more years: I suggest a five-year term, renewable only once. Both suggestions rule out the kind of tenure which exists under the existing freehold or would exist under the proposed leasehold. It appears to be the general will that this office should circulate: it is an important means of training senior clergy for wider responsibilities. But what happens to the improved staff and stipendiary status

[1] The Committee appointed to inquire regarding *The History, Functions and Manner of Appointing of Rural Deans in the different Dioceses of the Province (1948)*.

proposed for the rural dean when he surrenders office? I suggest that he forfeits the right to extra staff which are, as it were, deanery staff, not personal staff, but retains his stipendiary increase. This will mean that a body of senior clergy who have once served as rural deans will be in receipt of extra seniority pay while they remain in the livings in which they served. On change of post or living the additional stipend should only be sustained if hardship would seem to result without it. It is an important principle that rural deans should not ultimately be financially worsened for having served: care for them will also create the broader promotion plateau of which the Church, under the new dispensation, would stand in need.

THE DEAN OF A COLLEGE OF CLERGY

The dean of a college of clergy serving a major parish will, unlike the rural dean, be a leaseholder of his office for ten years. The office of rural dean is *in addition* to his other pastoral cares and would remain so under the new dispensation unless (and this has much to recommend it) a rural deanery transforms itself into a major parish, in which case the status of every clergyman member would simultaneously change. Therefore one does not need to propose an elective office for the dean of a college in the same way as for a rural dean, though there ought not to be anything to prevent a change of posts within a college if every member approved it. However, if the dean of the college has a leasehold of his office, it is important that the college should have the right to present in confidence to the bishops or patrons the name of a suitable and acceptable successor from among their own members or any eligible clergy anywhere and the same right as a PCC anywhere has to object to an unsuitable successor. Parallel PCC rights would not be affected. The college's power should apply to the filling of any place in the team. The effect of these proposals would be to secure, in practice, maximum consultation before the making of appointments.

ADMINISTRATIVE PROBLEMS INVOLVED

It is obvious that the recommendations made so far for an increase of the ministry, more rational deployment and greater pastoral care of men, for new parochial forms, a more uniform stipendiary system and a more rational structure for the ministry are piling up administrative and organisational problems for the Church. It would be reckless to pursue these recommendations without pausing to ask whether the machinery exists to carry them out and if not what new machinery is necessary and whether it can actually be created.

One is not helped in this examination by the picture which constantly emerges of the Church as a system of checks and balances rather than as a unified organisation. Mr Anthony Sampson in the endpapers of his *Anatomy of Britain* illustrates the establishment of the nation as a series of interlocking and overlapping circles (with the Church as a peripheral circle), and his text illustrates his theme that there is *not* one centre (the Crown or Parliament), with everything fitting concentrically around it, but many different centres of power and initiative, each only vaguely responsible to the others and not one in absolute control. This is true of the Church, too, except that we might argue that Parliament, though it has abdicated day-to-day supervision, is in final control of church affairs. Leaving aside Parliament, four controlling bodies, Church Assembly, the two Convocations, and the Church Commissioners are autonomous centres of authority, statutorily separated, and likely to remain so in the absence of true synodical government for the whole Church. But each diocese is also a true centre of power in a Church in which the pattern is essentially and properly episcopal. Provincial powers, except through convocations, are shadowy by contrast. Each parson, too, is a corporation sole who is secure in his freehold so long as he fulfils his statutory duties: he is himself a centre of power therefore. In spiritual matters there is a flow of authority—convocation to diocesans to priests: in legal, administrative and financial business there is a triangular movement—between Church Assembly, Church Commissioners, and dioceses. Authorities such as Church Assembly boards accept powers delegated by dioceses and dioceses receive legal powers from Church Assembly.

If we leave aside the Church Commissioners, a civil service created by the State for the Church, but with no legislative power, the final sources of administrative power are the Church Assembly, which has parliamentary powers, and the dioceses. Any decisions about the shape of the ministry and its deployment must be agreed between them. But forty-three dioceses can deploy in forty-three localities; they cannot deploy nationally. Church Assembly departments could deploy nationally and locally, but at the cost of surrender of, or substitution for, diocesan powers. Is the only alternative to diocesan schemes a nationally operated deployment run, as it would then have to be, from Westminster? Though I believe that the Church needs to become a unified and integral corporation, master in its house, the dangers of excessive centralisation ought to be avoided if they can be, particularly over so sensitive an operation as the direction and deployment of men. I have already indicated the need to establish regional consultation to agree stipend levels, increments and allowances for groups of dioceses. A similar need exists for deployment, too. It would greatly facilitate direction, deployment and redeployment of manpower if groups of dioceses could establish joint staffing machinery to:

(*a*) survey the needs of their joint area upon a staff establishment basis agreed at Church Assembly level,

(*b*) to bring together a better balance of rural and town livings,

(*c*) to facilitate the movement of men from diocese to diocese within the region and outside it,

(*d*) to co-operate with a central directory of clergy by the collection and dissemination of 'job information' and of clergy records.

It would seem sensible if some, or all, of the functions of diocesan boards of patronage devolved upon the regional machinery. These boards have a somewhat muted history since their establishment under the Benefices (Diocesan Boards of Patronage) Measure 1932. So great is their sense of acting *under* their diocesan bishop that they appear not really to fulfil an independent function. But this raises the long-deferred problem of patronage. Is it really possible to deploy men, or to give the ministry a new look, under a system in which the decision of a patron in the placing of a man is paramount?

PATRONAGE

The origins of patronage have so often been described that no point would be served by any re-examination of them here. Patronage places upon the shoulders of lay persons and various institutions, clerical or otherwise, the responsibility for finding and presenting clergymen to livings. The association of advowson and freehold was inevitable when putting a man securely in possession of all the rights of the living was the only way of protecting him and others. Most of the historical justifications have gone: an advowson today is a property without value: other justifications of the freehold slowly diminish. It can be said to be a spiritual protection; it no longer guarantees an economic one. Even the argument that it provides a lay element in appointments is weak today. Diocesan bishops, parochial clergy, deans and chapters, own twice as many advowsons as private patrons. Colleges, trusts and religious societies own about as many. The lay significance shrinks year by year as private patrons surrender rights of presentation, or seek the bishop's help. While ecclesiastical patronage is simply another way of making the Church responsible for appointments (which it ought to be anyway) other forms of patronage (colleges, lay persons, societies) have less to commend them. As the Church is an established church and the Crown its titular head, there cannot be any objection in principle to Crown appointments to certain livings. Objection could only be sustained if they stood in the way of a general reform of patronage. Perhaps while the Crown remains responsible for senior appointments it ought to have a role in more general parochial ones, too. But if the constitutional interest of the Crown is obvious, patronage by private individuals, by colleges, by religious patronage trusts defies any justification except the pragmatic one that men might be found this way and in no other. It is the oddest principle indeed that compels a college to offer livings to its members: and an irrationality which does the Church moral harm if a patronage society or religious trust owns advowsons and uses them to determine parochial appointments of the colour of churchmanship it approves. One can imagine the outcry in the press if it were discovered that a political party 'owned' the right to make civil service appointments in order to ensure placing men of the right political colour in key posts! Such a dubious system of empire-making within the Church could only have grown up because the Church was never properly master of its house.

Patronage also creates endless legal confusion. A title of patronage belonging to trustees or private owners seems often incorrect and legal justification difficult. Where joint or successive ownership or a 'trustee' system operates the difficulties of legal title increase. Many so-called trustees are not legally trustees, but beneficial owners, for no proper trust deeds exist. Deeds of conveyance, I have been assured, are as necessary as deeds of appointment of new trustees: in one diocese ninety-one titles are said to be out of order. Reform cannot be long delayed for the good of the Church's soul.

A simple act of cancellation of patronage, without alternative machinery, would create more problems than it would solve. What appears to be needed is the transformation of patronage into a staffing or appointments system in line with the more general openness of ministerial structure proposed in the report. This would preserve in principle the lay element and even make it more effective: such new machinery might be brought into relationship with proposed regional machinery for the negotiation of stipends. But we are already, as I have said, in danger of duplicating machinery. The national and regional bodies needed to determine clergy establishments at various levels and ratios, to cope with problems attendant on the transformation of patronage into a system of staff or appointment boards, and actually to direct men for the first five years of their ministry, must be kept to a minimum. Such bodies should have statutory powers. Yet they should not in any sense supersede or harass the episcopal government proper to every diocese, though they must lift some loads from episcopal shoulders. Is it possible to devise such machinery?

THE NEW MACHINERY

What appears to be needed at Westminster is a *Clergy Staff Board* or Staffing Committee responsible to Church Assembly. Whether it should be part of a transformed CACTM or function independently is something which might be decided at a later stage: whatever its formal structure it would need powers of direct action. In the most general terms it would act on the one hand as a staff planning body for the whole country and a clearing house on staff information, and on the other, exercise the statutory powers which the acceptance of this report would necessitate to transform patronage into a more open and systematic appointments advisory system. The second mandate would give rise to many legal problems and it might be practicable to have a separate board or committee to manage them: this I discuss later. However, it would seem imperative to secure that the patronage system is transformed under, and related to, a general staffing plan: too great a separation of powers might be disastrous.

A second group of bodies is needed in the shape of *Regional Boards*. How many we may need and the area they might cover are matters I will for the moment defer. They would have one first, but presumably temporary function, to secure diocesan agreement on stipend scales and systems of allowances for curates and incumbents, and to plan the phases by which uniformity might be achieved. Beyond that they should act as staff planning bodies and clearing houses for their region and local agents in the transformation of patronage. Each regional board would be represented upon the central board and upon the regional board each diocese would be represented: but the regional boards would be autonomous, not simply agents of the central board. They would have the right to act by powers transmitted to them in two ways—statutory authority and the agreed delegation of powers by dioceses.

Might we, on the basis of these preliminary definitions, attempt a more exact description of the powers of both bodies?

THE CLERGY STAFF BOARD

The duties of the board should include the following:

(i) To keep the parochial and extraparochial staff needs and recruitment of the ordained and supplementary ministries continuously under review.

(ii) To publish triennial estimates and such other surveys and findings as it thinks necessary to keep the Church informed.

(iii) To advise and assist dioceses and regional boards on staff problems and on staff quotas and on the proper clergy-to-people ratios it is advisable to maintain: to plan with college principals and diocesan bishops the system of direction of ordinands.

(iv) To receive and register the reports, accounts and copies of deeds of all patronage societies and trusts (including colleges) which are independent of ecclesiastical control and discipline: to advise them and Church Assembly on any legal action necessary to broaden their basis or to devolve their rights on regional or national bodies.

(v) To request, under statutory powers given to them, the archbishops to nominate representatives or trustees to patronage bodies when good sense and equity seem to require a broadening of their basis.

(vi) To require patrons to clear up their legal titles to presentations, in default of which to surrender the right to bodies the board shall name, by an appointed day.

(vii) To supervise the establishment and direction of a central directory of clergy.

(viii) To advise on the transfer of advowsons to regional or diocesan boards or other properly constituted authorities.

(ix) To advise regional and diocesan boards on the stipends policies which should be pursued in the common interest of the whole Church.

(x) To advise about the adjustment of ecclesiastical boundaries to civil boundaries.

REGIONAL STAFF BOARDS

The first purpose of a regional board, it has already been argued, would be to secure agreement between the dioceses it represents to a common stipendiary policy. The second would be to act as the staff or establishment advisory council for the region, producing regional plans or estimates as the central board would produce national ones. The third would be to organise with dioceses the placing of directed men. The fourth would be to act eventually (or by an appointed day) as the corporate patron (*a*) of all livings or (*b*) of such livings as were not already under ecclesiastical or Crown control in the region. Probably (*b*) is sufficient patronage responsibility to begin with. The devolution of Crown livings upon regional boards might have to wait upon decisions about the ultimate form the establishment is to take. It might not be wise to seek to break up the constitutional establishment in piecemeal fashion. Nevertheless, though I see a great difference in principle between patronage in the hands of the Crown and in the hands of party trusts or private persons, there is not a great deal of difference in operation. It is the case, I think, that the regional boards would never be completely effective unless *all* presentation for their region (except royal peculiars) was in their trust. I believe that both the State and the Church are peculiarly unimaginative when it comes to other forms the establishment could take. Nothing in principle commits the State to patronage in the Church when it has vanished everywhere else. Its constitutional relation to the Church could be expressed by the appointment of senior civil servants to the central and regional staff boards. It might be prepared to second civil servants with establishment experience to act as secretaries of the regional boards, in order to get them going. It is important, however, not to delay the setting-up of the new machinery until the constitutional establishment problems are settled. It is important, too, to work to secure a named day on which all patronage outside the boards is extinguished. The regional boards ought to have power to accept the duties and powers of diocesan patronage boards (which would then dissolve) where the diocese was ready to surrender them. It would have to have power to draw in private patronage in the region and to take it over in exchange for the representation of private patrons on the board. Some thought will have to be given to the constitutional means to ensure this.

The authority of the diocese would be by no means impaired by the action of a board upon which it was, after all, represented and to which it was delegating powers. A division of powers proclaims itself. The bishop would have precisely the same legal, pastoral and spiritual rights in relation to the board as he has already to patrons when they present men to livings. The pastoral shape of the diocese would be under his control—the formation of united benefices and pluralities, the creation of major parishes, of reorganisation areas, of new deanery group forms and so forth. But many bishops have written or spoken to me of the labours which are theirs already in filling vacant livings and advising patrons, and hesitate at the thought of the tasks that would fall on them if the whole of patronage were to come into their hands.

The boards, finding, sifting, presenting men, and apprised of the staff needs of the whole region, responsible for an overall plan, would lighten the burdens of bishops immensely and prove a formidable ally in the solution of the Church's manpower difficulties.

Yet there is another important aspect of the board's work which must not be overlooked. It will supervise and arrange the direction of men in their first five years of ministerial service. It will be of psychological advantage if it is able to call *first* upon its own regional ordinands: these men may then move within the region of their ordination and this is important so far as it involves their local patriotism. It is also a stimulus to each region to become self-supporting in its recruitment to the ministry, a possibility no dense urban diocese on its own yet possesses.

ARE THERE ALTERNATIVES?

Of course, one does not make such considerable recommendations lightly or without asking whether simpler alternatives are possible. We have to recall, though, the nature of the crisis which prompted both the survey and the recommendations—the acute shortage of clergy, and its unequal distribution, the continual decline of the effectiveness of the Church in urban areas until presently, obviously, it will be unable to renew itself; the loneliness, isolation and malaise of the clergy. If cures are to be sought for these grievous wounds they will probably have to be heroic, they will certainly have to be organisational—good organisation is good stewardship—so that alternatives must appear to provide effectiveness in the same field as the recommendations already made or they are useless.

Is it possible to dispense with regional boards, for instance? The answer is yes. Their powers could be divided between the central board and diocesan boards of patronage. Truly regional planning, over great conurbations, would be lost however. But the difficulty of securing agreement between forty-three separate dioceses on all the matters discussed would almost certainly mean that to get things done the powers of the central body would have to be increased or would prove self-enhancing. Just this increased centralisation is what many clergy say they dread. If there is to be effective planning, and if the manpower challenge is to be met, there must be either increased central powers, or new regional ones, or both.

It is possible to argue that instead of several regional boards there should be only two, one for the province of Canterbury, and another for York. This is a perfectly reasonable proposal for York province, but the size and population of Canterbury province is such that one foresees that a provincial board would be more than half-way to a national board. Its regional *raison d'être* would vanish.

Would the burden of manpower planning and simultaneous patronage reform be too great for newly formed central and regional boards? This is an important objection: it could be true. An alternative might be to name a date by which all patronage except Crown and ecclesiastical patronage had to be surrendered to bodies named to receive the advowsons. Statutory powers could be granted either to an *ad hoc* legal commission or to the Church Commissioners who could perfectly well undertake this dissolution within the statutory period. By the end of this period the regional boards (and other bodies, if this was thought to be wise) would be the residual legatees of all patronage without themselves having to struggle to organise it. I make this an alternative recommendation.

Similarly, though the task of securing an agreed regional stipends policy might not prove very difficult, it would certainly prove distracting. Therefore an *ad hoc* regional commission to bring this about, or alternatively a national commission to secure a uniform stipends policy for the two provinces, might be given a brief life to negotiate these ends, surrendering powers to the central board or regional boards when they are accomplished. I state these as reasonable alternatives.

In the end it does not seem possible for the missionary challenges the Church now faces to be met without new organisational forms, parochially, regionally, nationally. The organisation is not the end, but the spiritual function of the Church in the ministering of the sacraments and the preaching of the gospel *is*. If the organisation impedes this function it ought to go: but this applies to old organisation just as much as to new. Some organisation there must be.

It could be argued that what is proposed here, regionally and nationally, is some sort of super-bureaucracy which will escape episcopal direction or ecclesiastical control. Need this really be so? The central board would be directly responsible to Church Assembly: regional boards would be required to report to it, too: all would be representative. But we have an excellent and traditional remedy for the danger that regional boards will escape episcopal control, and that is to make each region a province under an archbishop. Then the regions would be provided with a spiritual authority and direction precisely related to their area of manpower and stipendiary authority. The primacy first of Canterbury, then of York need not be affected: one might even have provinces and 'archprovinces', in fact, and the old historical pattern therefore maintained. One could see, indeed, how such a provincial reorganisation might free the Archbishops of Canterbury and York, to some extent, for leadership of Church Assembly and for a more effective role in relation to the reunion of churches and the growth of the Anglican Communion. Synodical government in Canterbury and York provinces makes some sense, but eight or so separate synods would hardly do so. The creation of new provinces might therefore clear the way for true synodical government for the whole Church. I ask that this be considered.

WHAT MIGHT THE REGIONS BE?[1]

Purely tentatively, for more demographic study and ecclesiastical inquiry is necessary before any decision can be made, I suggest the following groupings of dioceses for consideration.[2]

N.W. Group: Carlisle, Blackburn, Liverpool, Manchester, Chester, Sodor and Man. (Population: 7·0 million.)

N.E. Group: Newcastle, Durham, Ripon, York, Bradford, Wakefield. (Population: 5·9 million.)

Central Group: Sheffield, Derby, Southwell. (Population: 3·0 million.)

Midlands and Eastern Group: Leicester, Lincoln, Peterborough, Ely, Norwich, St Edmundsbury and Ipswich. (Population: 3·3 million.)

West Midlands Group: Lichfield, Birmingham, Coventry, Worcester, Hereford. (Population: 4·8 million.)

London and Home Counties Group: Oxford, St Albans, Chelmsford, London, Southwark, Rochester. (Population: 12·3 million.)

South West Group: Gloucester, Bristol, Salisbury, Bath and Wells, Exeter, Truro. (Population: 3·6 million.)

Southern Group: Winchester, Portsmouth, Guildford, Chichester, Canterbury. (Population: 4·2 million).

My intention has been to include one or more expanding conurbations in each grouping and to relate the almost purely rural dioceses to urban or industrial ones, so that staff planning is able to utilise both kinds of areas. Certainly the groupings avoid as far as possible linking the rural dioceses together in opposition to the urban, which ought to be prevented at all costs. The weaknesses of my tentative groupings are in the placing of the following dioceses, Oxford, Rochester, Southwell and Winchester. The division of Oxford into three dioceses would simplify planning.

THE EFFECT OF REGIONALISATION ON DEPLOYMENT

Opposite is an interesting table which sets out the differing contributions the proposed eight regions have been making to ordinations. Columns 2 and 3 taken together show that some regions—those of the Midlands and the North—can do more than replace their existing curate force in six years by their own regional ordinations: the first five actually provide themselves with a theoretical

[1] Canon Eric Waldram Kemp, DD, in the Bampton lectures for 1960, published as *Counsel and Consent*, London, 1961, makes interesting proposals on p. 220 *et seq.* for as many as 85 dioceses in England and Wales, grouped into provinces. His findings and his maps deserve close study in relation to my own proposals.

[2] The figures in brackets are 1963 populations.

'surplus'. This surplus would enable them to make a small annual reduction of the quota proposed for their dioceses by the Bishop of Birmingham (cols. 6 and 7). The three southern regions, however, could not replace their force in six years: on the contrary they would have a deficit. They could make no contribution to the quota figure provided for them in col. 6.

The table has limitations explained in the notes on page 204, but it shows very plainly that, though the northern regions are short of clergy, their contribution to clergy manpower is far superior to that of the southern regions. They, in fact, at present can only make good their own manpower deficiencies by drawing men from the North at the end of their first curacies. Only regional controls and the power to direct men for the first five years could really prevent this. All in all, and accepting the hypothetical nature of the figures in col. 5, the analysis seems a powerful argument for the creation of regional boards.

Table XVIII. An Examination of the Ability of the Eight Proposed Regions to Renew and Increase their Existing Establishment of Curates

Region	Distribution of curates 1958	Estimated ordinations over 6 years (1959, 60, 61 × 2)	Surplus to 1958 establishment	Deficit on 1958 establishment	Total curates needed: Bishop of Birmingham's formula	Deficit (col. (5) minus col (1))	Ability in % p.a. to reduce deficit in col. (6).
	(1)	(2)	(3) +	(4) −	(5)	(6)	(7)
1. NW	291	436	145		771	480	5·0
2. NE	309	392	83		698	389	3·6
3. Central	137	186	49		371	234	3·4
4. Midland E	181	196	15		225	44	5·7
5. Midland W	244	332	88		568	324	4·8
6. London & Home Counties	800	760		40	1,631	831	
7. SW	279	220		59	244	35 *surplus*	
8. South	338	248		90	413	75	
Totals	2,579	2,770	380−189 (191)		4,921	2,342	

Explanation of Table XVIII:

Col. (1) gives the distribution of assistant curates, region by region, in 1958.

Col. (2) gives the actual ordinations of curates for the years 1959, 1960 and 1961, in each region, *multiplied by two* in order to show what the total new recruitment might be in six years. In six years, of course, the curate force completely changes, for few curacies go beyond six years. Therefore in six years it is probably completely replaced. The NW region shows up over 400 ordinations in six years against an establishment of less than 300; the southern 248 against an establishment of 338. Col. (3) deducts col. (1) from col. (2) to arrive at a surplus to establishment figure. Col. (4) deducts col. (2) from col. (1) to arrive at a deficit. Col. (5) gives the total number of curates required by the Bishop of Birmingham's formula (see SE, p. 272, and Table 36).

Col. (6) produces a deficit by deducting col. (1) from col. (5), or a surplus by deducting col. (5) from col. (1).

Col. (7) tells us in percentages what is the annual ability of each region to reduce the deficit in col. (6) in terms of figures shown in cols. (3) and (4), i.e. it seeks to show what power each region has to grow in curate strength. For example, the table shows the NW region to have a deficit of 480 curates (col. 6). But it also achieves in six years (col. 3) a surplus to its 1958 establishment of 145; an average surplus therefore of 24 per annum. Clearly in an effort to reduce the deficit of 480 a staff planning board would count on this annual figure of 24 as a first contribution to its needs over and above the 1958 figure: 24 is 5 per cent of 480: therefore the NW region has a theoretical power (other things being equal) to reduce its deficit by 5 per cent per annum. In the South, however, the position is reversed. There the regions have ordination deficits considered in terms of the 1958 establishment and cannot by their own recruitment cover their 1958 needs, let alone the deficit exposed by the new standards laid down by the Bishop of Birmingham's formula. They can only meet either situation by bringing in curates from other regions.

CHAPTER XI

Some Additional Proposals

THE LAITY

THE role of the laity is so immense in the reforms proposed that another exercise is necessary to study them. If this report is in principle accepted, I recommend that this be undertaken. It would seem to me that the whole of my recommendations would prove worthless if an increase in the ordained ministry led simply to a retreat of the laity from responsibility and joint ministry. Every proposal for major parishes or new rural deanery forms should be invalid unless it provides for lay training and lay responsibilities—lay street groups, house churches, independent lay initiatives. I have already made proposals for lay voluntary service in aid of the hard-pressed ministry in the field of car-driving, church care, and secretarial services. Something else is needed, however, and that is a lay maturity, and this not simply in the form of lay status in areas previously reserved for the clergy—e.g. lay persons on deanery chapters or the chapters controlling major parishes, if this is legally feasible, but lay independence, too. If the clergy can meet in independent chapter without the laity, then this privilege should be available to the laity, too. Purely lay chapters, or councils, of jointly constituted bodies should be permissive from the diocesan conference down to the PCC. However, it is important to consider the whole role of the laity afresh and from every angle as part of the common ministry, hence my recommendation for further study.

SERVICE OVERSEAS

It is to be expected, even apart from the Toronto Congress *Mutual Responsibility* plan, that short-term service in provinces overseas will increase, long-term service will decrease, and that more men ordained overseas will serve here. How can service overseas, which naturally attracts younger men, be reconciled with the direction of ordinands so strongly urged in the previous chapters? Two alternative proposals suggest themselves:

1. That each regional board be allowed a quota of overseas places to fill, and for which it would seek volunteers.

2. That the period of service overseas should follow the five years of direction at home (though the engagement might still be made through the regional boards).

It would seem to be imperative that a man going overseas should, if he wishes, be 'seconded' by his regional board, on the books of which he would remain and which would accept responsibility for his reappointment on his return. Similarly, it is proposed that incoming priests ought to be 'on loan' to regional boards which would watch over their placement and replacement.

CHURCHES AND PARSONAGE HOUSES

It is clear that the parochial system has the effect of tying an area to a church, to an actual consecrated building that is. The church hall and parsonage house are outliers of the church. Social and demographic changes make churches redundant: the creation of new reorganisation areas, or of major parishes, would often have little effect unless redundant churches and parsonages could be disposed of in a lawful manner, with full accountability, but with the minimum of time-wasting and legal obstruction. As a problem quite independent of this report, in any case, it must be the concern of the Pastoral Reorganisation Commission: it does seem as though a new 'drill' is desirable. The sale of useful but redundant sites, or their redeployment for social or cultural ends, could be a valuable support, financial and otherwise, for the general purposes of this report.

In general, parsonage houses fall into two classes, those which are reasonable in size and in garden responsibilities and therefore constitute an asset in the shape of free housing and the basis of a good home life, and an important second group the members of which are too large. It consists of houses of fifteen rooms or over —according to MQ returns 17 per cent of the whole. Here the advantages of free housing are cancelled out. Maintenance of the parsonage becomes a financial burden: as gardens grow proportionately with the size of houses, at this level they become a time-waster, or a physical burden, too. There is a case to be made, and it becomes stronger if ever the freehold is abolished, for placing nominal ownership of all parsonages and other church houses in the hands of diocesan boards (or the proposed regional boards or new ones appropriate to the tasks). The appropriate board would have the right (subject to whatever legal limitations are thought proper) to dispose of property or to rebuild or to divide it, to use it for the housing of other living agents or officers of the Church—curates, social workers, industrial missioners, readers, churchwardens—or for club and committee work. They would have the obligation to maintain it structurally and the incumbent or other tenant would have a lease holder's common obligation to keep it in reasonable tenantable repair. I ask that this should be considered.

THE FREEHOLD FOR BISHOPS AND OTHER DIGNITARIES

It would be invidious for the freehold to be abolished for incumbents and retained for bishops and other dignitaries. For all full-time cathedral clergy and for archdeacons I recommend a leasehold tenure of ten years, renewable for five, and with the same interview obligations laid upon the diocesan bishop at seven years. Bishops tend to become bishops in their early fifties: a leasehold tenure of ten years might leave them no place to go forward to of comparable opportunity just before retirement. It might also involve them in interruption of their pastoral duties in order to concern themselves about the next post. I recommend a tenure of fifteen years, renewable for five. As with incumbents, their leaseholds would terminate at seventy.

CATHEDRALS AND PAROCHIAL RESPONSIBILITIES

In many areas where cathedrals are not already parish church cathedrals, the cathedral itself might form the basis of a corporate parochial ministry such as a major parish. This possibility should be kept in mind in diocesan reorganisation plans. The new and apparently satisfactory staffing basis established by the Cathedrals Measure, 1963, might have to be supplemented by clergy with purely parochial duties.

THE NEED FOR RESEARCH

This report by its very nature has placed new emphasis upon the relationship between the Church's ministry and social, demographic and economic factors in the world at large. There is a need for a constant re-examination of this relationship in order to discover what it can tell us of our tasks and the way we ought to set about them. This is the field, to some extent, of 'the sociology of religion' or of 'religious sociology'. Both descriptions are a little suspect and 'social and religious studies' might be a title less exposed to criticism. Whatever the title, we need a small research unit continually devoted to studies of attitudes and to statistical and demographic surveys of the kind opened up by this report and suggested by Canon Boulard's *An Introduction to Religious Sociology*. The research unit should be centrally placed and financed, able to send out field workers, empowered to programme itself, and to advise and feed information to dioceses, central and regional boards. It should work side by side with the indispensable Statistical Unit, but in independence.

A STAFF COLLEGE

The possibility of a new college to provide for clergy eligible for sabbatical terms has already been canvassed. The Church also seems badly to need a staff college which could:

(*a*) hold courses in administration for all sorts and conditions of clergy,

(*b*) run short courses for training parochial secretaries and administrative assistants,

(*c*) run clergy and lay seminars on church organisation and strategy,

(*d*) provide, in addition to permanent staffs, residential fellowships of two or three years' duration, for lay or clerical members of the Church of England, with the intention that they shall present publishable surveys and studies upon urgent problems of church strategy, organisation and sociology. If a condition of each fellowship was that the holder should give a modest number of lectures each year, research fellows then would give additional strength to the teaching staff.

It would be admirable and exciting if some clergy sabbatical courses could be held in a staff college. This would provide opportunity for the necessary continuous dialogue between the strategists and the front-line men.

FINANCIAL CONSIDERATIONS

The principal financial resources of the Church lie in the hands of the Church Commissioners and the parishes. The 'channelling' functions of the dioceses ought not to disguise from us where the real strength lies. The diocese is a channel for both parish and Church Commissioner funds. The proposals of the report ought to permit some simplification of the labyrinthine financial operations of the dioceses and the Commissioners and so bring useful economies. The reorganisation of the stipendiary system would eliminate a system of payment first of all based upon benefice income, then upon its various augmentations. It would be appropriate if, when the stipendiary system becomes uniform, a block grant system of payments from the Church Commissioners could be introduced. Each diocese could then meet from that block grant, plus its own augmentations, the stipends of all pastoral agents, incumbents, curates, social workers: a stipulated percentage of the grant could be available for secretarial and administrative workers.

Increasing stipends, new regional machinery, an increasing number of ordinands to train and to place in posts, will face the Church as a whole with an escalating budget. It is already suffering from the many inflationary tendencies of the times. Yet it has great resources in its own endowments and property and in lay generosity which, as stewardship campaigns show, is capable of quite new levels. I see no reason to be pessimistic about its capacity to pay for what its duty must compel it to do. A drawing together in a budgetary sense of the Central Board of Finance and the Church Commissioners would be sensible: a regionalisation of many of the functions of the Church Commissioners might help to dispel the mistaken notion, which many people hold, of the Church as a great financial empire. If the bill for the proposals of this report is too great for the Church to face, but the reforms are necessary, then a national home missionary appeal might provide a trial run in which the Church could show its strength and its determination.

CHAPTER XII

A Summary of the Principal Recommendations

(*The recommendations are summarised in the order in which they appear in the report. The order below is therefore not related to their importance and is not a classified one. The reader is asked in every case to refer back to the context in which each recommendation is argued: the relevant page numbers are given in brackets.*)

1. The formation of a parochial lay pastorate is urged: street organisation based on house communions is recommended (151).
2. Pastoral advisory committees of teachers, doctors, social workers and others are recommended, serving parishes, rural deaneries or towns (152).
3. A spirit of theological inquiry among the laity is asked for, and lay initiatives over lay training (152).
4. A lay voluntary service on the lines of the Women's Voluntary Service is recommended (153).
5. It is recommended that readers should be licensed by the bishop to the rural deanery and admitted to office by the rural dean in an appropriate service (157).
6. It is recommended that the Church give highest priority to chaplaincies at the new universities and Colleges of Advanced Technology (169).
7. It is proposed that it should be a condition of CACTM grants that an ordinand accept direction for the first five years of his ministry. Ordinands at present under training might be asked voluntarily to accept direction (172).
8. It is recommended that every freehold shall be transformed into a leasehold as it falls vacant, or within a term of ten years, whichever comes first (172).
9. A tenure of the leasehold of ten years, renewable for five, is suggested (173).
10. In his seventh year the incumbent of a leasehold should be interviewed by his bishop in order that his future may be planned (173).
11. CACTM records, with other sources, including the material in the Central Statistical Register of the Clergy kept by the Statistical Unit, should be expanded into an open central directory of the clergy (173). The directory should make available to authorised persons lists of vacant parishes and of men about to move (173–4).

12. A new parochial form is proposed, a *major parish* run by a college of clergy all of whom would enjoy 'incumbent status'. Single incumbent parishes would then become *minor* parishes (176).
13. Full-time lay workers, with certain safeguards, should be members of the college (177).
14. PCC rights need not be affected by the establishment of a major parish, but a delegate PCC based on ward organisation is suggested if the parish area is a large one (177).
15. Looser forms of group and team ministries are recommended (177).
16. It is recommended that a diocesan bishop should have power to designate a university, college, or other such place an 'extra-parochial place' (177).
17. It is recommended that to a diocesan bishop should be restored the power now lapsed under the Reorganisation Areas Measure (1944) to declare an area a reorganisation area. Some modification of the description of such an area is proposed (179).
18. Suggestions are made for resolving patronage and freehold problems in the reorganisation areas and for bringing an area legally to an end under this designation by the formation of a major parish (179–80).
19. It is proposed that clear principles should be laid down about the direction of newly ordained men, i.e. that they shall be directed for the first two years as to training and for the next three on the basis of pastoral needs (181).
20. Lists should be kept of training parishes: they should be visited by the Director of Post-Ordination Training (181).
21. Where training parishes are not available, it is suggested that deacons should be placed under the care of clerical directors of studies (181).
22. It is recommended that the authority and status of the rural dean be raised, making him 'bishop-in-little'. Suggestions for strengthening the office and the rural deanery follow (182–3).
23. It is proposed that there should never be less than two suffragan bishops in a diocese, each with a territorial charge, and that the relationship of suffragan bishop and archdeacon should be worked out afresh (183).
24. A sabbatical term for every clergyman in his early fifties is proposed (184).
25. It is proposed that ultimately 65 shall be the age of voluntary retirement on full pension (185).

26. And at 70, freehold or leasehold shall automatically be extinguishable for every office, but renewable annually or biennially under licence (185).
27. It is asked that some small single-church cures be retained for elderly men or others (185).
28. And that elderly clergymen should be able to return to the status of curates without loss of dignity or stipend (185).
29. Major parishes are asked to make provision for housing and employing elderly clergy (185).
30. An *open* ministry is argued to be necessary in which terms of entry and advancement are known (186–7).
31. It is suggested that benefice funds be pooled to create one common stipendiary fund (188).
32. And that the distinction between beneficed and unbeneficed clergy be brought to an end (188). The clergy should be divided into two groups only: assistant curates for three years; staff priests thereafter (189).
33. Regional machinery is proposed to negotiate one common stipendiary system (188). All would become salaried men (189). Senior scale would be reached after three years (189). Scales should be reviewed every five years (189).
34. The regional machinery should be given help from a central board charged with negotiating a national scale (188).
35. Two seniority increases are proposed in stipends, one after ten years', the second after twenty years' service (189).
36. Parishes should be graded, it is urged, according to responsibilities and duties, and a points system introduced as a basis for differentials (189).
37. The basic starting stipend for senior staff should not fall below average industrial earnings, it is argued, nor rise much above graduate teacher pay. Top scale should be reached after twenty years (190).
38. A solution to the problem of pension differentials is tentatively advanced: (*a*) a basic non-contributory pension for all clergy alike, (*b*) a supplementary (and voluntary) pension scheme on a contributory basis so arranged as to provide a pension 'differential' related to previous income (191).
39. The office of rural dean should carry a stipend increase at least equal to the first seniority payment. The rural dean should qualify for extra staff (192–3). He should be appointed for a five-year term renewable only once (192). Unless he changes his living he should not forfeit his extra pay on resignation, but he should no longer be entitled to extra staff (193).

40. The college of a major parish should have the right to present nominations for a dean of the college to the bishop or patrons and the same right as a PCC to object to an unsuitable presentation. The same power should apply to the filling of any place in the clergy team (193).
41. It is proposed that joint staffing machinery should be established regionally. It should take over the functions of diocesan boards of patronage (195).
42. Patronage should be transformed into a staffing or appointments advisory system (196).
43. It is recommended that a clergy staff board responsible to Church Assembly be set up. It should seek to plan staff requirements for the whole country and to supervise the transformation of patronage. Its possible duties are set out (197–8).
44. Corresponding regional boards are proposed (197). Their duties are set out (198-9).
45. It is important to secure a named day on which all patronage outside the regional boards is extinguished (199).
46. Private patrons might be represented on the regional boards (199).
47. Alternatives to regional boards are considered (200).
48. Alternative bodies to handle the dissolution of patronage are considered (200–1).
49. Alternative means of securing common regional stipends policies are considered (201).
50. Tentative proposals are made for eight regional groupings (202). It is asked that consideration be given to making them provinces (201).
51. An inquiry into the role of the laity is asked for (205).
52. Proposals for major parishes, etc., should be invalid unless they provide also for lay training and lay responsibilities (205).
53. Independent lay chapters are proposed (205).
54. It is recommended that regional boards be given a quota of overseas places to fill, or else that overseas service should follow the period of direction (205).
55. Men going overseas should be seconded by regional boards. Incoming priests should be seconded to them (206).
56. Diocesan or regional boards should have nominal ownership of all parsonages and other church houses (206).

57. It is recommended that bishops and cathedral clergy, and other dignitaries, should have their offices transformed into leaseholds. The tenure of bishops would be for fifteen years, for archdeacons and cathedral clergy ten years, both renewable for five. Their leaseholds would terminate at 70 (207).
58. It is suggested that the cathedral might form the basis of a corporate parochial ministry to a town (207).
59. A research unit is proposed (207).
60. A staff college is proposed. Its tasks are outlined (208).
61. Block grants to dioceses for the payment of living agents should take the place of the existing system (208).
62. It is suggested that some of the work of the Church Commissioners might be regionalised (209).

SUMMARY OF EVIDENCE

I THE SURVEY

II RELATED RESEARCH

TABLE OF CONTENTS

LIST OF TABLES

APPENDICES

I THE SURVEY

HOW THE SURVEY HAS BEEN CONDUCTED

My first and principal task was to be fact-finding, but it was left open to me to make recommendations if I saw fit. I began the task on 1st February 1962. CACTM appointed an advisory committee, and to this committee and to the Council I have reported as often as possible during the course of the survey. To CACTM Council, of course, my final report is now submitted.

The period of actual research lasted for fifteen months from February 1962. Writing began May 1963.

I thought that it was most important to consult as widely as possible by visit, interview and questionnaire, so that clergy, laity, and every sort of interested body might contribute evidence and proposals if they had them to give. Despite the burden it imposed upon an improvised organisation, this has been done. Though there was a constant search for material in newspapers, journals, books and reports, the main load of inquiry had to be carried by questionnaires and letters of inquiry, of which the principal ones have been, in order of their dispatch:

1. A pilot questionnaire, to fourteen incumbents in the Battersea deanery and thirty-six friends in holy orders, dated 3rd May 1962, and to fifty incumbents in the Newcastle diocese on 26th May 1962. Upon results of this the Main Questionnaire (3, below) was based. This is described as Q 1 or 'pilot scheme' in the report.

2. A letter of inquiry dated 28th May 1962 to diocesan bishops of both provinces asking for information about: (i) group ministries; (ii) the state of rural deaneries; (iii) the growth of extraparochial ministries, and for copies of manpower reports and any social or religious censuses and surveys in the diocese. This is described as L 1.

3. A questionnaire, dated 7th to 16th July 1962, to a 10 per cent sample of parishes (prepared by the Statistical Unit of the Central Board of Finance) seeking information about the parochial responsibilities and the shape of the professional life of each recipient. This is described as the Main Questionnaire (MQ).

4. A questionnaire, dated 5th December 1962, to a 2 per cent sample of incumbents on clergy incomes. This is described as Q 3.

5. A questionnaire, dated 7th December 1962, to diocesan boards of finance on diocesan stipends policies for incumbents and assistant curates. This is described as Q 4.

6. A letter of inquiry, dated 10th December 1962, to diocesan bishops asking for further information on manpower problems. This is described as L 2.

7. A letter of inquiry, dated 14th February 1963, to all deans and provosts asking for a picture of the staffing situation in cathedrals and for views on cathedral staff stipends. This is described as L 3.

8. In addition, on 4th March the Central Board of Finance itself directed an inquiry to a selected number of dioceses on diocesan lay and clerical staff and passed the results on to me. This is described in the report as Q 5.

Inquiries on a smaller scale, by individual letter rather than questionnaire, have been sent to not less than fifty bodies at home and overseas. They posed questions, or invited information or asked for counsel. They include nine religious communities, seven lay organisations, five home and overseas missions, fifteen patronage societies, five clergy charities, and various boards concerned with the extraparochial ministry. A special inquiry has been made to overseas provinces of the Anglican Communion about such things as payment, deployment, freehold, patronage, outside England.

Consultation with the laity was much more difficult: broadcasting a questionnaire did not seem feasible. Direct consultation with the laity has been attempted instead and meetings with laity have been held through the media of PCCs, parish meetings, or conferences in London (3), Caversham, Cambridge, Norfolk, Newcastle, Rochester, Portsmouth, Wadhurst, Wakefield. At some of these the lay members retired into discussion groups and produced written reports at the time or later. I have also spoken to clergy conferences when opportunity presented itself, notably in Smethwick, Leeds, Birmingham, Newcastle, Portsmouth and Westminster, and to students at theological colleges and those engaged in post-ordination training. I mention these in order to show that the maximum possible consultation has been undertaken. I will now set out the substance of the questionnaires and their results.

THE PILOT SCHEMES (Q 1)

The pilot scheme was a trial run for the Main Questionnaire described below. It was intended to test two things: (*a*) whether a questionnaire could be devised which could be searchingly directed at the nature and problems of the professional life of the clergy, (*b*) whether the clergy would be prepared to answer it. The trial run was with three groups: (i) personal friends who were incumbents; (ii) by agreement with the Bishop of Newcastle, a 25 per cent sample of the incumbents of his diocese (chosen because of its reasonable balance of urban and rural parishes and its remoteness from the metropolis); (iii) the clergy of the Battersea deanery in Southwark diocese (where to some extent I could judge the value of replies through my own long experience of the borough).

The response was as follows:

Table 1. Pilot Schemes' Returns—May/June 1962

Groups	Ques. sent	Ques. returned	%
Friends	36	30	83
Battersea deanery	14	12	86
Newcastle diocese sample	50	42	84
	100	84	av. 84

As the total response was 84 per cent I felt that this indicated that the clergy as a whole would be prepared to answer a similar questionnaire. The replies had indicated that the questionnaire needed some modifications, but with those made I believed that it would serve as the kind of courteous probe into clerical professional life I had been seeking to devise.

Seven of the incumbents who appeared in the Newcastle pilot scheme reappeared as members of the Statistical Unit's 10 per cent sample for the Main Questionnaire. They were not asked to fill in a questionnaire twice, but their pilot scheme replies were analysed *also* under the Main Questionnaire breakdown.

MAIN QUESTIONNAIRE (MQ)

A. *Nature of the Sample*

The questionnaire which is set out below was dispatched in July 1962 to a 10 per cent stratified random sample of parishes prepared for me by the Statistical Unit. A problem was set by the number of parishes inevitably falling within the sample at which there was no incumbent. Should substitutes for these be sought, or should the 'no-incumbents' be regarded as in themselves deployment evidence? As time was also a factor and as delays would have produced further vacancies, I decided not to seek substitutes but to take note of the vacancy figure: of the total sample arranged of 1,462, 139 parishes were without incumbents, i.e. 9·5 per cent of the whole. A further reduction in the number sent occurred because thirteen clergy holding parishes in plurality had been included for both livings. Five clergy (friends) who had been approached for Q 1 were also dropped. The total number dispatched was 1,387, of which 905 were received back completed and subsequently studied and analysed. The final summary is set out here.

Table 2. Questionnaires Sent and Returned July/December 1962

	Nos.	%
1. Total in the sample prepared by CBF	1,462	
Deduct withdrawals (13 duplicates, 5 already in pilot schemes)	18	
Deduct parishes from which no return was possible (livings vacant, incumbents deceased, retired, resigned or letters returned 'not known' by GPO)	139	
Deduct returns from wrong parishes	7	
Valid sample	1,298	
2. Of valid sample of	1,298	100
Questionnaires completed and returned	905	69·8
Refusals	39	3·0
Letters in lieu of returned questionnaires	10	·8
Too late for classification	2	·1
Did not reply	342	26·3
3. Completed and returned questionnaires as % of 10,370 incumbents (*Facts and Figures 1962*, Table 9)		8·73
4. Returns from pilot schemes as reported in Table I	84	
5. Excess to sample questionnaires returned (Returned from the wrong parish 7, miscellaneous 9, Hemel Hempstead group ministry 7)	23	
6. MQ, pilot schemes and excess to sample returns total and as a % of 10,370 incumbents	1,005	9·7

It will be seen that the Main Questionnaire actually analysed gave an 8·73 per cent sample of all the incumbents, a satisfactory figure. If the excess to sample questionnaires are added, then 9·7 per cent of incumbents was reached, a percentage very close to the original 10 per cent planned for the exercise.

B. *Reasons for Refusing*

The reasons which recipients of questionnaires advance for refusal to fill them in are always interesting, though difficult to classify. As far as they can be classified, they are as follows:

Table 3. MQ: Reasons for Refusing

	Reason	
1.	Opposed to the inquiry	12
2.	Not prepared to co-operate in another statistical exercise	16
3.	Too busy	5
4.	Perplexed by the questionnaire	3
5.	Miscellaneous	3
		39

C. *Checks on the Accuracy of MQ Figures*

Page 1 of the Main Questionnaire asked for certain facts and figures, as many of which as time allowed were subsequently tabulated and analysed. Question 3 asked for the number of Easter communicants (EC) 1962 and Q 4 for the average Sunday attendance, all services (ASA). Both these figures have proved of significance in measuring the pastoral effectiveness of the Church's ministry, as I shall subsequently show: Sunday attendance figures have not previously been collected and analysed in this way. Question 3 was less precisely worded than it ought to have been, for it did not indicate how to deal with sick communicants and others within the octave. Nevertheless most incumbents replied to the question without demur and their figures made possible the plotting of diocesan averages per 1,000 of the population. These are shown in the lower curve of the graph on p. 54. As a contrast to this I plotted the figures of diocesan averages of Easter communicants taken from the Central Board of Finance table, p. 60, of *Facts and Figures 1962*. The table is based on figures for 1958, i.e. four years earlier than mine, and is also calculated on Easter communicants per 1,000 population age 15 and over, whereas my figures are based on total populations as reported by incumbents. It is this second fact (plus exaggerated MQ population returns) which gives the CBF curve a higher mean than that of the curve plotted from MQ figures. Then, too, the CBF figures are not a sample, *but are based on total returns*, in which theoretically the limits of error ought to be nil. In view of these differences the correspondence between the two curves is a remarkable tribute to the accuracy of the returns made to me by incumbents and to the value of the sample.

A further check on EC figures became possible in the late summer of 1963, when returns from the biennial CBF questionnaire to incumbents enabled a comparison to be made between figures taken from the Parochial Returns of Membership and Finance 1962 and figures from MQ returns. Not all my 905 returns gave EC figures, not all parochial returns gave them either: it was only possible therefore to check 728 MQ returns. For this group, analysed in eight population brackets, my MQ Easter communicant returns were 100·45 per cent of the Easter communicants according to parochial returns. This satisfactory reconciliation of my EC figures with the official ones concealed two discrepancies: in the smallest parochial population groups, i.e. those of 299 and under and those between 300 and 999, the degree of error was as high in the first as 250·80 per cent and 132·09 in the second. However, there proved to be an explanation in part satisfactory for a discrepancy nowhere else repeated. It is in these population groups that pluralities are most to be found and though theoretically the sample was of sample *parishes* the incumbents had mostly made returns to me for their *livings* and there proved to be no way of breaking up figures returned for a *living* to isolate the return for the required sample parish. Hence the exaggeration in this group was only an apparent one, not a real one, and the deviation diminished in influence as sample parish populations rose. However, although the two small population groups accounted for 22·5 per cent of the 728 parishes analysed in this exercise they *only accounted for 1·6 per cent of the total population.* Statistically, the discrepancy is negligible therefore and reliance upon the EC figures of MQ returns is confirmed. If the EC figures are reliable then logic suggests the ASA figures ought to be, too. The diocesan averages are to be found graphed (Graph 2, p. 56) and in contrast with confirmees of 15 or over per 10,000 of the population (CBF figures). The extraordinary conformity between the two curves provides a second proof of the reliability of MQ returns. It also suggests that every ten years a church re-creates its congregation in terms of new members, but that the rate of loss is very high.

D. *Inaccuracy in Population Returns* (*MQ*)

In one field the MQ figures were proved unreliable. In the summer of 1963, when my own statistical work was largely completed, the 1961 census populations of ecclesiastical parishes became available to the Statistical Unit. I had asked (MQ, Q 2) for parish populations (and more frequently got populations of livings) and analysed and averaged those per diocese. It proved possible now, at a late hour in the preparation of the report, to contrast, individually and collectively, MQ population returns with the census figures. One fact was immediately demonstrable—incumbents had not proved accurate in estimating the populations of their cures. Some individual parishes had returned a remarkable increase where the census showed a decrease. Some showed a remarkable decrease when the census showed only a slight one. Some, more proficient, were within a hundred or two in their estimates of population change. A spot check showed that the average overestimate in the Chelmsford diocese was 34·8 per cent; in Chichester 19·2 per cent; in Ely 31·6 per cent; in Guildford 44·7 per cent. The overall percentage error of 52, is, of course, quite serious. The question was—was the degree of error so serious as to invalidate all the statistical exercises so far undertaken? All my EC and ASA averages *per 1,000 population* had been, of course, based upon incumbents' population returns and not upon census 1961 figures, for these had not then been available. The consistency of the graphs based on my returns and contrasted with CBF parochial returns tended to suggest that if my figures were out, the deviation must be a fairly uniform one, i.e. that the invalidation was not total.

I was encouraged to hope for this by the fact that everywhere clergy had exaggerated the sizes of their cures: of no diocese as a whole was the opposite true.

The most immediate observable effect was that exaggeration of the population size accompanied by *accuracy* of EC and ASA returns depressed the averages of the pastoral effectiveness of the parishes surveyed by as much as 62 per cent over the whole country. On the basis of the 1961 census results fifty-four people out of every thousand of all ages are Easter communicants: my MQ returns showed only thirty-five per thousand. The ASA averages per 1,000 population for the whole country need also to be increased by 60 per cent. In my main abstract, where all the contrasting figures are set out (Appendix 3) it is shown as 31·1 per thousand. It is therefore probably more truly 50. Dioceses most remote from conurbations and social and economic changes, proved most accurate in estimating populations, industrial and heavily urbanised dioceses least accurate: therefore the pastoral results are more depressed for the densely populated dioceses than for rural areas.

On p. 77 f. of the report, and again in the Summary of Evidence, an analysis of special groups, abstracted from the MQ, is made. In Table IX of the report the groups are arranged in population density discrepancy between the incumbents' returns of their population and the 1961 census figures. However, a spot check has shown that the reductions made to each group in column 4 would tend to be uniform and the ranking therefore would, as far as can be seen, remain substantially unaltered. Most of the important findings and relations of the table would not be challenged—average age, ASA per clergy, Sunday score, weekday score. Special Group 3 (line 2 in Table IX) 'Largest Reported Parishes' is based upon single-handed parishes *reported by incumbents as having 10,000 population and over.* The 1961 census showed that only fifty-six of the ninety-five parishes were validly so described. A new analysis of MQ returns was then made to isolate a similar group of large single-handed parishes solely upon the basis of the 1961 census. A cut-off line of 7,500 gave ninety-one single-handed parishes of this population and over.

It is now possible to contrast the three groups, the original ninety-five reporting 10,000 and over, the actual fifty-six with this population, the ninety-one single-handed parishes of 7,500 or over. Here are the contrasted returns.

Table 4. Three MQ Groups with Large Parochial Populations Contrasted

Sample	Av. pop. per living	ASA per clergy	ASA per 1,000 pop.	EC per 1,000 pop.	Sunday score	Wkday score	Av. age
1. Ninety-five as in line 2 Table IX	14,065	246	17·8	18·9	5·16	15·17	48·8
2. The ninety-five re-assessed on basis of 1961 census figures	10,410	246	23·67	25·32	5·16	15·17	48·8
3. Fifty-six actually 10,000 pop. or over (1961 census figures)	12,680	233	17·39	18·78	5·10	14·85	50·8
4. Ninety-one with actual 7,500 pop. or over (1961 census)	11,099	230	21·57	25·45	5·13	14·67	49·9

An examination of these figures shows that the group of ninety-five which supposed that it had populations of 10,000 and over came very close in results, and even in population averages, to the fifty-six really in this population group according to 1961 census figures. The ASA per 1,000 and the EC per 1,000 show only fractional differences. The reassessment of the ninety-five, on the basis of their corrected population figures, shows that, because the population has been overestimated by 26 per cent, the pastoral showing in ASA and EC is depressed by almost the same percentage, 25–26 per cent. If therefore time permitted a reassessment of all the groups in Table IX, what would probably occur for all of them would be a rise in the pastoral results correlated to the percentage correction in the population. It does not appear that the trends illustrated by the table would be much affected.

I have asked myself why, when other figures appeared to be so correct, almost every incumbent misjudges the size of his cure. The first answer is that he is as dependent as the rest of us on official figures and the last he could have had access to were 1951 census figures—eleven years before my questionnaire; eleven years of great social change. The population figures in Crockford's could not have been of great help to him, since they, too, are dependent on the census. Diocesan year-books sometimes give population, sometimes not: quite often their figures are out of date. Let us be frank, few ordinary citizens could give with reasonable accuracy the population of their boroughs or villages.

Then, too, the figure first given to a parson on his induction to a living may be remembered and changes go unnoticed or unnoted. People often tend to exaggerate the population changes brought about by new building: nearly everyone assumes that new building in place of old increases population, whereas usually it reduces the density of population per acre. In one sense the exaggerations of population are a tribute to that sensitivity to social change which parsons have shown and I have classified in other ways. Since all my exercises show how important is the relation between pastoral results and population density, the failure of the MQ population returns to reach even a reasonable degree of accuracy points to this —the responsibility for giving the incumbent an accurate account of the size of his cure ought to rest firmly on diocesan or central authorities. For many reasons, we cannot expect him to know. In the end I have elected with these explanations to allow Table IX and related figures to stand, and set out in Appendix 3 the 1961 census returns and 1962 CBF parochial returns against MQ figures: a complete check is therefore possible.

The population exaggerations I have revealed in no way affect the general arguments of the report, or its conclusion, or specific recommendations. The original figures are quite valid in the revelation of the trends in which the report is interested. Urban failure and rural success, or vice versa, where based on my MQ population returns, are somewhat exaggerated, but are not overthrown. One recommendation of the report is strengthened by just this evidence. The Church needs a consistent system of gathering information, such as the Statistical Unit has set up, and it needs to test its own material against information supplied by the civil authorities: but it also needs persistent research into backgrounds and demographic changes which only a permanent research unit could provide.

However, in order to attempt to adhere to the time-table set for this report I have not thought it proper to hold it back for a complete statistical re-analysis of MQ returns against the 1961 census figures. If the Church Assembly feels that it is a justifiable undertaking and approves it, it will be quite possible to make a revision of MQ returns in the light of 1961 census figures.

E. *The Text of the Main Questionnaire*

Page 1

FACTS AND FIGURES

1. Name of parish: ....
2. Population: .... Size of parish (if known): ....
3. Number of Easter communicants, 1962: ....
4. Average Sunday attendances, all services: ....
5. Number on Electoral Roll, Annual Meeting, 1962: ....
6. Total number of churches, including mission churches, for which incumbent is responsible: ....
7. Number of church schools: Primary..........; Secondary ....
8. Number of church organisations using church and/or church hall each week: ....
   Number of other organisations using the church hall each week: ....
   Number of vicarage meetings: ....
9. Full-time staff (the post, not the name):
   Clerical (1) Incumbent .... Lay (1) ....
   (2) .... (2) ....
   (3) .... (3) ....
   Part-time staff:
   Clerical (1) .... Lay (1) ....
   (2) .... (2) ....
   (3) .... (3) ....
10. Number of voluntary lay workers (in Sunday schools, clubs, societies, etc.): ....
11. Are you compelled to accept outside employment to augment your income? ....
12. Are you married? ....If so, does your wife:
    (*a*) help in the parish? ....
    (*b*) take up paid employment to augment the family income? ....
13. Please state your age: ....
    and length of service in the Ministry: ....
14. Have you a car? ....
15. Who provided it?.......... and pays running costs? ....
16. How large is your vicarage? ....

Page 2

TIME-TABLE

17. Sunday services (in which incumbent is involved): ....
Sunday school and/or 'Children only' services (if incumbent is involved): ....
Average number of Sunday preachings: ....
Club work or other Sunday duty: ....

18. Normal weekday duties of incumbent:
((It is quite understood that during the great church festivals, or weeks of special duty like cemetery duty, the pattern will completely change. But if it is impossible to fill this in as it stands, a slice from your diary, or a note about the normal pattern of your week, will be much appreciated.)
Mon. Morning: ....
Afternoon: ....
Evening: ....
Tue. Morning: ....
Afternoon: ....
Evening: ....
Wed. Morning: ....
Afternoon: ....
Evening: ....
Thu. Morning ....
Afternoon: ....
Evening: ....
Fri. Morning: ....
Afternoon: ....
Evening: ....
Sat. Morning: ....
Afternoon: ....
Evening: ....

Page 3

COMMENTARY

19. Which day do you take off? ....
Is it strictly kept? ....

20. Are you able to secure a period of relaxation each day? ....
How long? ....

21. Do you have too little to do? ....
On Sundays? ....
On weekdays? ....

22. Roughly how much *time* each week are you able to give to:
    (*a*) serious reading? ....
    (*b*) prayer? ....
    (*c*) meditation? ....
    (*d*) pastoral visiting? ....
    (*e*) sermon preparation? ....
    (*f*) class teaching and/or private instruction? ....
23. To which of these above would you like to give more time? ....

    ....
24. How much *time* each week do you *have* to give to:
    (*a*) parish administration, including secretarial work of any description? ....
    (*b*) parochial meetings and societies (other than services)? ....

    ....
    (*c*) services? ....
    (*d*) day-school teaching? ....
    (*e*) extraparochial work, such as diocesan or deanery jobs? ....

    ....
    (*f*) chaplaincies, both paid and unpaid? ....
    (*g*) public duties (if any)? ....
    (*h*) other chores, religious or secular, including manual ones? ....

    ....
25. For which of the above do you most need help? ....

(*add sheets if necessary*)

Page 4

26. Are your lay workers reliable? ....
    and capable of functioning without supervision? ....
27. What parish work has grown during your tenure? ....
28. What has diminished during your tenure? ....
29. What are you conscious of having failed to develop? ....

    ....
30. Have you, alone or in conjunction with other parishes, a long-range plan for the development of the parish? ....
31. Are you able to plan your work, or is your life 'organised' for you by callers, correspondence, the daily post? ....

(*answer at length if necessary*)

32. Most parishes seem unique. Do please add sheets to explain the parish situation and/or your life and work if the questionnaire appears inadequate in any way. ....

    ....

F. *The Breakdown of the Material*

1. Of the first page only answers to Questions 1 and 2b (size of parish) were neither extracted nor analysed.

2. Answers to Questions 3, 7 (*a*) and (*b*), 8 (*a*), (*b*), (*c*), have been extracted but not analysed.

3. The remaining answers (to Questions 3, 4, 6 and 9, 10, 11, 12, 13, 14, 15, 16) have been extracted and analysed.

4. The statistical answers to Questions 2, 3, 4, 6, 9, 12, 13, tabulated or analysed on a diocesan basis, are given in Appendix 3.

5. The returns on Question 10 though extracted and analysed were dropped. 'Voluntary lay worker' proved too vague a term to yield results comparable from parish to parish. One example of the inadequacy of the term came from the incumbent who gave a nil return for Question 10, but later casually mentioned a team of 24 lay visitors.

6. The answers to Question 12 (*a*) were tabulated (see below), but the answers to 11 and 12 (*b*) yielded the following information (not all of it asked for):

Table 5. Outside Incomes of Clergy and Wives

	York	% of sample	Cant.	% of sample	Totals	% of sample
Clergy accepting paid outside employment	14	5·04	37	5·9	51	5·64
Clergy mentioning private income	9	3·24	14	2·23	23	2·54
Clergy wives accepting paid employment	27	—	83	—	110	—
Clergy wives mentioning private income	2	—	3	—	5	—
Chaplaincies, paid and unpaid	49	17·64	80	12·77	129	14·26

The numbers of clergy wives accepting paid employment have to be set against the number of married clergy: this shows that in Canterbury province 15·8 per cent, in York 11·3 per cent, and over the two provinces 14·4 per cent of the wives of married clergy go out to work: more would, I was frequently told, but for responsibilities with growing families.

7. The answer to 12 (*a*)—'Does your wife help in the parish?'—produced almost a 100 per cent return from married clergy: the few exceptions involved invalid or elderly wives, those with a very young family, or those fully committed in professional careers. It is not felt necessary therefore to mount a statistical demonstration that the ministry of a married clergyman is in this sense at least a team ministry.

8. Question 14 ('Have you a car?') produced the incidental information that only four clergy in the sample in Canterbury province and three in York went about by pedal bicycle still. The clergy have become motorised. Tabulated the results are as follows:

Table 6. Provision of Clergy Motor-cars

Province	Total	Provided by incumbent	Provided by parish	Cost shared	Expenses		
					Inc.	Parish	Shared
Canterbury	516	499	11	6	377	37	102
York	206	201	2	3	151	9	46
Total	722	700	13	9	528	46	148
	% of 905	% of 722			% of 722		
	79·78	96·95	1·80	1·25	73·15	6·37	20·48

9. When it came to Question 16 all that I thought it was necessary to extract was the number of clergy who seemed grossly overhoused. Those with fifteen rooms or over in the province of York were 34, in Canterbury 117, a total of 151. Those constitute together 17 per cent of the total sample.

10. Though this concludes the summary of the treatment of answers extracted from p. 1 of the Main Questionnaire, certain other incidental information which was tabulated might be included here. It was soon clear from remarks made in reply either to Questions 18, 24 (*h*), or 25, and sometimes to all three, that the vicarage garden (and/or churchyard) was as much a problem for many incumbents as the over-large vicarage or rectory. Garden comments were therefore separately tabulated and analysed, and added to answers on clergy houses (Question 16), with this result:

Table 7. Clergy Gardens and Houses

	Nos.	% of sample
Clergy noting gardening as a time-consuming chore	395	44
Those of the above finding it a really serious physical burden	65	7
Those asking for help with gardens	278	31
Clergy houses with fifteen rooms or over	151	17

The comments of incumbents made it plain that their concern over time and energy spent in gardening reflected an important post-war social change—the disappearance of the humbly paid odd-job man, of the jobbing gardener, from society. It is no longer possible to knock on a cottage door as heretofore and 'get Alf to do it' for half a crown. But then all those vast rectories and vicarages, too, were meant to be run by two or three housemaids and a pantry boy, with a groom and a gardener as outside staff. This race has vanished more swiftly than any other from the social scene.

11. Questions 17 and 18. These two were designed to arrive at the shape of a parish priest's professional life. That they could do so was pure hypothesis. Has a parish priest's life a particular shape? Ought it to have? I was simply seeking guidance here through study of what incumbents might tell me. Analogies with other professions were not very helpful. The doctor is under obligations to his patients, but it would be unprofessional of him to seek out new ones. The parish priest is under statutory obligations to his congregation: he must provide the minimum services for them: beyond those and the maintenance or supervision of the parish machine (PCC, etc.) he is free to make his own programme. But this programme morally should include 'getting out' among his parishioners whether or not they come to church, or whether or not he feels he is wanted by them. The degree of energy or zeal—or time—an incumbent applies to this part of his programme is understandably his own affair and he might reasonably object that exercises in comparability are not possible in this sphere. Yet a study of payment and deployment involves inevitably some attempt to assess the demands and pressures on the clergy. At what point does a man become so underemployed that he ought to be moved or so overworked that he ought to be helped? Ought degrees of overwork or underwork to be recognised in stipends structure? Answers to those questions had to be attempted: it was hoped that analysis of the answers to Questions 17 and 18 would assist me to do so. In the upshot the sub-question about Sunday preachings did not greatly help, but the remaining sections did show whether *on Sunday* the parish priest was fully extended or not, i.e. whether he was working a one-, two- or three-session day. A fully extended Sunday, the pattern showed, consisted of something like this—two or three morning services, baptisms and Sunday school in the afternoon, evensong and youth club in the evening. Such a Sunday scored 6 in the tabulated breakdown. Though conservatively, even severely marked, in fact, fifty-eight, 6·4 per cent of incumbents (forty-five Canterbury, thirteen York), scored 7 for their Sunday duties. In all, 193 (133 Canterbury, 60 York), scored 6 or more on

Sundays, giving a percentage of 21·3 men fully extended on Sunday duties.

These high Sunday scores could not be attributed solely to pluralities and united benefices, for of the 193:

Those with one church constituted	37·3 per cent
Those with two churches constituted	34·7 per cent
Those with three churches constituted	21·8 per cent
Those with four or more constituted	6·2 per cent.

The average Sunday duties score was worked out per diocese and provincial and national averages established as follows:

Average Sunday duties scores, Canterbury	4·78 per cent
Average Sunday duties scores, York	4·83 per cent
Average, both provinces	4·80 per cent.

12. Question 18 was, in similar spirit to Question 17, directed to the discovery of the weekly pattern of work. Arguing that no man could work more than a three-session day (though, in fact, some parish priests appeared to achieve a four-session day!), I sought the details of the weekday work pattern of the incumbents in the sample, awarding a score of one for each session filled: the total possible weekday score then being naturally 18, a figure actually achieved by thirty-two or 3·5 per cent of incumbents who replied, and even by 8·8 per cent of those with a Sunday score of 6 or over! In scoring a work-session, 'gardening', 'running the children to school', 'shopping', 'watching Panorama', and such were not allowed to count, but 'study', 'sermon preparation', 'preparing the church for Sunday', 'cleaning the church hall', 'marriage interview', 'youth club', 'visiting', 'confirmation class', 'case problem', and so forth were. Again the marking was conservative, even severe. Teaching in the church school was accepted as a normal duty, but teaching which ranked as a separate paid employment not incumbent on the parish priest—WEA classes or a teaching post with the LEA and so forth—was not. The line was sometimes hard to draw; the incumbent was always given the benefit of the doubt. An effort was made to check the weekday score by reference to the times reported under Question 24.

The average weekday and Sunday scores diocese per diocese are given below, with provincial and national averages:

Table 8. Average Sunday and Weekday Scores of Clergy by Dioceses

Canterbury Province		
Diocese	Sunday	Weekday
Canterbury	5·21	13·8
London	5·02	13·8
Winchester	4·81	12·8
Bath and Wells	4·74	12·9
Birmingham	4·5	14·5
Bristol	5·12	14·4
Chelmsford	4·99	14·9
Chichester	4·55	14·0
Coventry	4·77	13·3
Derby	4·36	14·4
Ely	4·43	14·9
Exeter	4·56	14·3
Gloucester	4·98	13·3
Guildford	5·35	14·0
Hereford	5·1	13·3
Leicester	4·4	13·7
Lichfield	7·86	15·3
Lincoln	4·43	13·5
Norwich	4·42	13·3
Oxford	4·68	14·3
Peter-borough	4·71	14·2
Portsmouth	5·09	14·8
Rochester	4·24	13·7
St. Albans	5·15	14·3
St. Ed. and Ips.	4·59	12·9
Salisbury	4·4	14·7
Southwark	4·99	14·9
Truro	4·44	14·5
Worcester	5·2	15·0

York Province		
Diocese	Sunday	Weekday
York	5·34	14·2
Durham	4·9	14·0
Blackburn	4·5	15·6
Bradford	4·5	14·7
Carlisle	5·4	13·3
Chester	4·77	14·2
Liverpool	4·65	16·4
Manchester	4·64	14·5
Newcastle	5·2	15·3
Ripon	4·73	15·0
Sheffield	4·91	14·8
Sodor and Man	4·0	16·0
Southwell	4·88	14·3
Wakefield	5·13	14·9

Provincial averages:		
Canterbury	4·78	14·1
York	4·83	14·7
Both provinces	4·80	14·3

The above figures are shown again on Graph 4, p. 76.

13. Question 19 was thought vital, since the clergy's working week does not follow the pattern most citizens enjoy. In a way he is always on duty and the week-end can be his busiest time. It seemed sensible to inquire whether a day off was secured during the week: for much the same reason it was reasonable to ask of a man who, like a doctor, is always on call, whether he manages a period of relaxation each day. The tabulated answers are:

Table 9. Time Off for the Clergy

Province	Those Taking full day off	Regularly	Those taking half day off	Regularly	Those taking hour or more rest daily
Canterbury	437	168	10	2	332
York	196	62	7	4	146
All	633	230	17	6	478
% of sample	70	25	2	—	53

14. Question 21 was designed to provoke the incumbent into looking back at his answers and checking them against the direct question which echoes what the unthinking man in the street often feels—that the parson, even if busy on Sundays, has nothing to do in the week. It is interesting that six reported too little to do on Sundays *and* weekdays: the round total of forty saying yes to one or other or both is equivalent to 4·42 per cent of the sample. Ought one to have asked the antithetical question 'Do you have too much to do?' Clearly not. It would have become, like the question 'Does your wife help in the parish?' a leading question provoking an almost unanimous yes. Few of us are immune to the suggestion that we are working too hard.

15. Questions 22, 23, 24, 25 were aimed basically at the overworked incumbent. It was hoped that an analysis of Questions 22 and 24 would roughly confirm the pattern of duties set out in 17 and 18. But more than this was expected. The incumbent, as we know, is both the pastor and spiritual leader of his congregation and stands also in a pastoral relation to all the people of his parish. Traditionally the English parson is a man of learning who has contributed generously to science and literature, not simply to theology. How seriously can the pattern of his spiritual and pastoral duties or his necessary reading and study be disturbed by administrative pressures, public occasions and other chores?

Time has so far prevented as thorough a study of the answers as I could wish. Only answers to 22 (*a*) and (*d*) have been both extracted and analysed: they are of outstanding importance, of course, and less subject to personality factors than 22 (*b*), (*c*), and (*e*). Of the Q 24 group (*a–h*) only (*a*) has so far been exhaustively treated. The findings from these three are most remarkable: they show, averaged per diocese, not only that the administrative curve climbs with increasing density of population, but that the curve is corelated with the other two, visiting and reading. The results are shown on Graph 3, p. 74.

Table 10. Analysis of Preferences, Q 23, 'To which of these would you like to give more time?'

Preference	No. 1st pref.	% of 905	No. 2nd pref.	% of 905	Combined 1st and 2nd	% of 905
Serious reading	535	59·12	60	6·64	595	65·55
Prayer	85	9·39	291	32·15	376	41·57
Meditation	28	3·09	80	8·84	108	11·94
Visiting	117	12·93	119	13·15	236	26·07
Sermon preparation	19	2·10	55	6·08	74	8·18
Class teaching, etc.	27	2·93	28	3·09	55	6·08

Table 11. Order of Preferences, Q 23

1st pref.	No.	%	2nd pref.	No.	%	Combined 1st and 2nd	No.	%
Reading	535	59·12	Prayer	291	32·15	Reading	595	65·55
Visiting	117	12·93	Visiting	119	13·15	Prayer	376	41·57
Prayer	85	9·39	Meditation	80	8·84	Visiting	236	26·07
Meditation	28	3·09	Reading	60	6·64	Meditation	108	11·94
Teaching	27	2·98	Sermon preparation	55	6·08	Sermon preparation	74	8·18
Sermon preparation	19	2·10	Teaching	28	3·09	Teaching	55	6·08

The combined results for the first three seem most weighty and revealing, though the whole complex of results deserves more study. While it is only negative evidence, it might be remarked that the idea of having more time for sermon preparation arouses little enthusiasm.

Question 24 produced the following results:

Table 12. Analysis of Preferences, Q 24, 'For which of these do you most need help?'

Preference	No. 1st pref.	% of 905	No. 2nd pref.	% of 905	Combined 1st and 2nd	% of 905
Parish administration	310	34·25	31	3·24	341	37·68
Parochial activities	66	7·29	49	5·41	115	12·68
Services	55	6·08	46	5·08	101	11·16
Day school teaching	1	·11	1	·11	2	·22
Extraparochial work	3	·33	5	·55	8	·88
Chaplaincies	7	·77	4	·44	11	1·21
Public duties	0	·0	4	·44	4	·44
Other chores	210	23·20	79	8·73	289	31·93

Table 13. Order of Preferences, Q 24

1st pref.	No.	%	2nd pref.	No.	%	Combined 1st and 2nd	No.	%
Parish administration	310	34·25	Chores	79	8·73	Parish administration	341	37·68
Chores	210	23·20	Parochial activities	49	5·41	Chores	289	31·93
Parochial activities	66	7·29	Services	46	5·08	Parochial activities	115	12·71
Services	55	6·08	Parish administration	31	3·24	Services	101	11·16
Chaplaincies	7	·77	Extraparochial work	5	·55	Chaplaincies	11	1·21
Extraparochial work	3	·33	Chaplaincies	4	·44	Extraparochial work	8	·88
Day school teaching	1	·11	Public duties	4	·44	Public duties	4	·44
Public duties	0		Day school teaching	1	·11	Day school teaching	2	·22

The combined order of preferences is perhaps the most illuminating of these tables. It must be related to what are virtually protests about gardening chores given on p. 232. It suggests at the least that the incumbent finds it easier to cope with liturgical duties than with the weekly grind of parish chores such as secretarial and financial work, cleaning, gardening, stoking, and the round of meetings and societies which mount as his pastoral work becomes more effective.

16. Page 4 of MQ (Q 26 to 32 inclusive) was not designed to produce statistical information, but to give opportunity for those extended answers which are so much more rewarding as objects of study than bare facts and figures. All that has been thought of value in the extended answers has been extracted and, as the report shows, assessed in other ways. Nevertheless, unexpectedly, some of the most useful statistical material emerged from the answers to page 4.

I therefore instituted a system of classifying the returned questionnaires on the basis of their evidential value. This yielded the following results:

Table 14. Questionnaires Classified by Types of Evidential Value

	No.	% of sample
1. Parishes reporting considerable social change	278	30·73
2. Incumbents providing personal deployment evidence	186	20·55
3. Incumbents submitting extended detailed diaries	56	6·19
4. Incumbents submitting stipend evidence	45	4·95
5. Incumbents submitting a case history	20	2·21
6. Incumbents reporting ideal set-up	7	·77

At the same time as these categories were established a further classification was made into rural (R), suburban (S), and town (T), parishes (with a fourth group of mixed, e.g. R+T or R+S, since a few suburban parishes gave evidence of a completely rural tail and certain town parishes reported the existence of a rural enclave, such as a mission church or daughter church: the mixture was sometimes the consequence of uniting benefices).

The results of this breakdown are as follows:

Table 15. Further Classification of Parishes

Province	Rural	Suburban	Town	Mixed	Totals
Canterbury	287	169	152	19	627
York	92	77	103	6	278
All	379	246	255	25	905
Totals as % of 905	41·88	27·18	28·18	2·76	100

An attempt was also made to isolate within these categories parishes which from the general tenor of the answers it was permissible to regard as (*a*) busy and successful, (*b*) in decay.

Their numbers proved to be:

Table 16. Distribution of Successful and Decaying Parishes

Type	Rural	Suburban	Town	Mixed	Totals
Successful	5	38	14	0	57
Decaying	21	12	69	0	102
All other	354	198	172	22	746
Totals	380	248	255	22	905
The same expressed in per cent:					
Successful	1·32	15·33	5·49	0	6·29
Decaying	5·53	4·84	27·06	0	11·26
All other	93·15	79·83	67·45	100	82·45
	100·00	100·00	100·00	100	100·00

A further exercise suggested itself—an examination of the relation between 'social change', 'decaying', 'successful', categories. Altogether eighty of the 'decaying' parishes and twenty-one of the 'successful' were also classified under 'social change'. The remaining 177 of the 'social change' parishes were neutrally classified as R, S, T or Mixed. The analysis is as follows:

Table 17. Social Change Parishes Otherwise Classified

Province	As decayed				As successful				As neutral					Totals
	R.	S.	T.	Total	R.	S.	T.	Total	R.	S.	T.	Mixed	Total	
Canterbury	15	8	27	(50)	1	13	3	(17)	57	33	26	12	(128)	195
York	6	2	22	(30)	0	4	0	(4)	15	23	10	1	(49)	83
All	21	10	49	(80)	1	17	3	(21)	72	56	36	13	(177)	278

A ratio of rather more than one in four of the parishes experiencing social change also passing through some form of parochial decay is a highly significant one, of course, and suggests that social change has an important bearing on parochial stability. The figure, eighty, is a trifle under 80 per cent of the total number of parishes (103) so classified. Conversely of the 'successful' category of parishes (fifty-six) only twenty-one were classified under social change—just 37·5 per cent. Other figures stand out: ninety-four of the 'social change' parishes are rural ones, though only twenty-one of them are also classified as in decay: 61·25 per cent of the total of decaying parishes are town parishes: this is over one in three of all town parishes: by far the highest category of 'decaying' parishes also classified under 'social change' is the town parishes (forty-nine). What appears to emerge here is a special group subject both to urban decay and to urban renewal. In the 'successful' category the suburban parishes achieve singular success. They constitute thirty-eight of a total of fifty-six 'successful' parishes.

I accept that the forms of classification just described involve subjective judgments, or at least judgments not easy to reduce to a formula. They cannot inspire the same confidence as the more purely statistical analyses I have embarked upon. Nevertheless they are all classifications made on the basis of what the incumbents have told me in extended answers or else in important figures, or both. As results, they have fallen into patterns of significance and a closer analysis of what I think they portend, and a justification of the procedure, will be found in the main report.

In order to make further study of the Main Questionnaire returns easier I pencilled a comment at the end of each return as to whether an incumbent was possibly overworked or possibly underemployed. Though in the nature of things this was a purely tentative conclusion, it amounted to a preliminary classification of men. It produced these results:

Table 18. The Classification of Incumbents

Category	Canterbury	York	Totals
Hypothetically overworked	51	48	99
Hypothetically underemployed	81	15	96
The above as % of 905:			
Hypothetically overworked	5·63	5·30	10·93
Hypothetically underemployed	8·95	1·66	10·61

This concludes the study of the forms of classification. It leads to a consideration of the necessary further breakdown of Main Questionnaire results.

FURTHER BREAKDOWN OF THE MAIN QUESTIONNAIRE

A. *Demographic Problems*

At this point it was necessary to ask further questions of the mounting mass of evidence. Had it anything at all to say, for instance, about deployment? One of the first facts which emerges from *Facts and Figures 1962* is that the effectiveness of the Church's ministry varies in inverse ratio to the degree of urbanisation or industrialisation of a diocese or of a parish. This does not appear to be a consequence of, or only of, say, failure to deploy the clergy in some rough relationship to population: it has deeper roots in the social pattern, the way of living of great conurbations. But it does help to define areas of greatest failure and therefore of greatest need. One figure from the Main Questionnaire had unexpected value—the 'average Sunday attendance' (ASA). Almost every returned questionnaire gave this figure, sometimes with a detailed breakdown. It is obviously a figure over which many a parish priest ponders as one measure (not the only measure of course) of the impact of his ministry. I had included the question originally to guide me about the extent of a man's parochial charge, believing it to be a more useful guide than the number of Easter communicants or the electoral roll, both of which I asked for by way of contrast. I was agreeably surprised to find it so useful a congregational and social pointer. But how to demonstrate its value?

The crucial breakdown of dioceses has always seemed to be not one based on their area, total population, or number of parishes but on the relative density of population. True, this has one disadvantage, it masks the ratio between rural and urban areas within a diocese, which must affect all statistical breakdowns, but it remains a good index just the same of the degree of urbanisation in any given diocese. It was this index I used, plotting against it the various sets of figures the Main Questionnaire had given me, of which the ASA, averaged per diocese, under these categories, *per 1,000 population, per living, per church, per clergyman,* yielded the most arresting pointers.

1. Graph 2 shows that, as the already known facts of the influence of urbanisation show, the ASA per 1,000 population falls as the density of population rises.

2. Graph 1 demonstrates that the Easter communicant figures from the Main Questionnaire fall into the same pattern and that so do the Central Board of Finance EC figures per 1,000 of the population aged over 15 for 1958.

3. Graph 5 contrasts the ASA per 1,000 with the ASA per church.

B. *Human Problems*

The graphs above focus attention on the areas of greatest failure and greatest need. They tell us where to concentrate manpower. What of the human problems they create? Graph 3 shows how the time that incumbents give to certain social duties is inexorably affected by the same demographic pattern. It plots three diocesan averages arrived at from answers to 22 (*a*), 22 (*d*), 24 (*a*), i.e. time spent on:

(1) visiting,
(2) serious reading,
(3) parish administration.

The graph shows in brief that, as population density rises, the time spent on visiting and serious reading falls, while the time spent on parish administration rises.

Graph 4 examines the weekday and the Sunday score of incumbents again with the intention of asking for the effect of population density on the man. It shows that the weekday score and the Sunday score rise with increased density of population. Of the ten most densely populated dioceses, six are above average for Sunday score, and eight above average for weekday score.

What of the other human problems the sharp differences in pastoral results so far exposed must presumably create? The facts of underemployment and overwork did not seem to yield themselves to some statistical yardstick as simple as the ASA: at least I could discover none and I elected therefore to isolate and study certain groups which were by definition susceptible either to overwork or underemployment. They were, hypothetically in the 'overwork' end of the spectrum:

1. Those with the maximum possible weekday score (Wk. sco. 18).
2. Those with 6 or over Sunday score (Sun. sco. 6+).
3. Clergy running single-handed the largest parishes (Largest rep. s.h.p.).
4. Clergy running single-handed three or more churches (1 man to 3+ ch.).
5. Rural deans (sample of forty only from my returns).

And, hypothetically again, at the 'underemployed' end (with which older clergy and the ill and disabled are included for comparison purposes, since one is entitled to assume that they have lighter duties):

6. Clergy with parishes of 450 population or less (Par. 450—).
7. Clergy with ASA of thirty or less per church (ASA 30—).
8. Clergy of 70 or over (Clergy 70+).
9. Ill or disabled clergy.
10. Case histories.
11. Those reporting too little to do (TLTD).

In addition, by the forms of classification already described, I had already isolated two groups in this very field of inquiry, which demanded the same sort of investigation. They are as follows:

12. Hypothetically overworked (OW).
13. Hypothetically underemployed (UE).

The thirteen groups constitute the following table:

Table 19. Numbers and Percentages of Special Groups

No.	Group	Incumbents	% of 905	Total clergy	% of 1,374½	Total churches	% of 1,566
1	Weekday sco. 18	32	3·5	68+2 pt	5·0	70	4·5
2	Sunday sco. 6+	193	21·3	321+5 pt	23·5	384	24·5
3	Largest rep. s.h.p.	95	10·5	95	6·9	121	7·7
4	1 man to 3+ ch.	80	8·9	80	5·8	258	16·5
5	Rural deans	40	4·4	78+2 pt	5·8	73	4·7
6	Parishes 450−	48	5·3	49+1 pt	3·6	86	5·5
7	ASA 30−	98	10·8	100	7·3	251	16·0
8	Clergy 70+	42	4·6	45+2 pt	3·3	57	3·6
9	Ill or disabled	21	2·3	31	2·3	33	2·1
10	Case histories	20	2·2	27	2·0	40	2·6
11	TLTD	40	4·4	44	3·2	82	5·2
12	OW	99	10·9	170	12·4	179	11·4
13	UE	96	10·6	97	7·1	171	11·0

The groups overlap, of course—for example, seventeen with a Sunday score of 6 or more have also a weekday score of 18, and twenty-nine of the same group are single-handed clergy with largest parishes. Of those with a Sunday score of 6 or over *and* a weekday score of 18, five are single-handed clergy with largest parishes—hypothetically the most overworked group of clergy in the two provinces.

The cross-references are as follows:

Table 20. Special Groups Cross-references

	Group	1	2	3	4	5	6	7	8	9	10	11	12	13
1	Weekday sco. 18	*32*	17	9	1		—	—	—	—	1	—	17	—
2	Sunday sco. 6+	17	*193*	29	34		4	16	7	—	2	—	38	10
3	Largest rep. s.h.p.	9	29	*95*	5		—	1	—	—	2	—	27	—
4	1 man to 3+ ch.	1	34	5	*80*		6	41	2	—	4	8	4	14
5	Rural deans												(14)	(2)
6	Parishes 450−	—	4	—	6		*48*	28	8	5	3	9	—	25
7	ASA 30−	—	16	1	41		28	*98*	12	5	3	19	1	36
8	Clergy 70+	—	7	—	2		8	12	*42*	1	1	4	1	9
9	Ill or disabled	—	—	—	—		5	5	1	*21*	1	2	—	3
10	Case histories	1	2	2	4		3	3	1	1	*20*	1	4	—
11	TLTD	—	6	—	8		9	19	4	2	1	*40*	—	17
12	OW	17	38	27	4	(14)	0	1	1	0	4	0	*99*	—
13	UE	—	10	—	14	(2)	25	36	9	3	—	17	—	*96*

When all the overlappings have been eliminated the total number of incumbents in all the special groups is 535, an astounding figure. If the number of rural deans not also in any of the other special groups, which is fifteen, is deducted (because this group is a sample only) then we are left with the figure of 520, which is 57·5 per cent of all the incumbents in the MQ sample. More than half therefore of all incumbents fall into groups isolated because they appear at first sight to illustrate overwork or underemployment. One group (2) is ambiguously placed: Sunday score of 6 or more can more easily go along with overwork or underemployment of its members on weekdays than membership of any other group: its averages, however, place it in the overwork sector. One notes, too, that twenty-five out of forty rural deans are in special groups: therefore one assumes that the pressures on them are greater as a whole than on ordinary clergy.

Though special groups are chosen for the capacity to illustrate either overwork or underemployment, further consideration compels us to qualify this severely. A Sunday score of 6 or over, or one priest to three churches or more will certainly indicate a busy Sunday, but not *necessarily* overwork on weekdays. Then, too, the over-70s and the ill and disabled are light-duty groups: the case histories are priests with personal problems. The value of such groups as these is really purely comparative. A further refinement of the analysis gives us therefore *three* classes:

		% of 905
1. Overwork (Groups 1, 3, 12)	179	19·8
2. Underemployment (Groups 6, 7, 11, 13) ..	183	20·2
3. Neutral (Groups 2, 4, 8, 9, 10)	158	17·5
	520	57·5

The final breakdown therefore gives us almost one member of the overwork category for one member of the underemployed. It is an interesting and important deployment conclusion that one clergyman in five is overworked, possibly heavily, and one in six is a member of a group seeming to present special problems either of a pastoral or personal nature, one in five is presumably underemployed.

The mere existence of these groups, collectively so large, itself says something about the human problems of the ministry: but it is possible to do more—to ask how the pastoral results in each group measure up to the averages for the two provinces separately and as a whole. Here are two comparisons:

1. The ASA per 1,000 population for the whole sample is 31·1. Groups 1, 3, 5, 9, 10, 12 fall below this. Groups 2, 4, 6, 7, 8, 13 above.
2. The ASA per clergyman for the whole sample is 154·2. Groups 5, 6, 7, 8, 9, 10, 13, fall below this: Groups 1, 2, 3, 12 are above.

In general the same pattern is to be observed for the Easter communicant figures, too. If we turn to Table IX on p. 78 of the report it is possible to study the general pattern into which the findings arrange themselves.

As in earlier graphs and tables, the arrangement of these special groups of pastoral results against population density is remarkably illuminating. The pastoral averages—ASA per clergyman, ASA and EC per 1,000 population, and the work indices of the clergy arrange themselves in a predictable fashion. The ASA per clergyman falls with falling population density, the ASA and EC per 1,000 rise in the expected manner. The Sunday duty and weekday work indices fall fairly consistently with falling population density. Even where the group steps out of rank in one or other rising or falling curve, this is equally predictable. Thus it is not unexpected that the man with three churches (usually brought to him by uniting benefices or creating pluralities) will show a Sunday duty and a weekday score higher than the average for his population density rank. Equally it is to be expected that the 'solo' men (Group 3), the single-handed parsons with large livings, will yield an ASA per 1,000 below expectation for their population density group. Perhaps, too, we should expect that Group 7—the ninety-eight parishes with an ASA of less than 30 —will put up poorer overall results than even Group 6, the forty-eight parishes with populations of under 450. For it looks as though Group 7 is one exhibiting so attenuated a congregational life that we are really catching dying churches in this particular statistical net. It is perhaps confirmed by the fact that the Sunday duty and weekday work indices for the parsons of this particular group accord with their density group expectations: we cannot therefore easily attribute their pastoral results to laziness. The complete analysis appears in Table IX of the report and should be studied there.

One or two other points may be made:

Group 10, Case histories: In all respects except ASA per clergy this group is close to normal. It cannot therefore be argued to consist of men who have failed.

Group 5, Rural deans: Though they show a working week fractionally above normal, their pastoral scores appear depressed ones. We may presume overwork therefore.

Group 8, Age over 70: It appears that elderly clergymen stand up well to comparison with other groups.

Group 2, Sunday score 6+: The group will include those churches which provide more services than the statutory three, as well as those with the heaviest Sunday social duties. The multiplication of services will tend to inflate the ASA, hence its out-of-rank position in column 6, Table IX.

Group 12: These consist of ninety-nine incumbents originally pencilled 'overwork' in a hypothetical way. The overall results of the group confirm this judgment. The group shows the highest but one weekday score and the third highest Sunday score. Its hard work appears actually to pull ASA and EC averages above expectation for population rank and close to the national averages.

Group 13: Again the hypothetical judgment is confirmed. Only two groups stand below it in Sunday score—those with confessedly too little to do, and the ill or disabled. Only those with too little to do and those with parish populations of 450 or under are below them in weekday score. Pastoral results are poor, too.

Such a ranking, linking pastoral results and personal work indices so closely with population densities, cannot be accidental. It reveals to us social or demographic factors as (with some exceptions) the principal causes of a man's overwork or underemployment, rather than his personal inclination.

A further breakdown of the more important information yielded by study of the special group may be summarised as follows:

Group 1. Weekday scores of 18: 32 livings.

- (*a*) The average Sunday score of the group was 5·7, as against the national average of 4·8. 11 of the group had Sunday scores of 6 or 6½, 6 had scores of 7.
- (*b*) 9 had three or more churches to serve: 20 altogether had more than one church.
- (*c*) 17 needed more time for serious reading and 17 asked for help with parish administration.
- (*d*) 5 were rural deans.
- (*e*) 14 had been classified on various grounds as overworked.
- (*f*) The average age of the group was 53.

Group 2. Sunday scores of 6 or over: 193 livings.

- (*a*) Of these 58 had Sunday scores of 7 or over.
- (*b*) 27 reported single-handed parishes of 10,000 or over.
- (*c*) 17 had weekday scores of 18: 91 (47·2 per cent) had over average weekday scores.
- (*d*) 54 (28 per cent) had three or more churches but the greatest group, 72 (37·3 per cent), had only one church.
- (*e*) 116 asked for more time for serious reading and 74 for help with parish administration.
- (*f*) 18 were rural deans.
- (*g*) 38 had been classified on various grounds as overworked, 9 as underemployed.
- (*h*) The average age was 50.

Group 3. Largest reported single-handed livings: 95 livings.

(*a*) 5 had parishes of three or more churches, and therefore re-appear in Group 4: 17 had two churches.

(*b*) 62 asked for more time for serious reading and 47 asked for help with parish administration.

(*c*) 3 were rural deans.

(*d*) 25 were classified on various grounds as overworked, one as underemployed.

(*e*) The average age was 49.

Group 4. One man to three or more churches: 80 livings.

(*a*) Of these, 67 had three churches; 10 had four churches; one had five churches; two had six churches.

(*b*) 7 livings had an ASA of less than 30 per church.

(*c*) 48 asked for more time for serious reading, 19 for help with parish administration.

(*d*) 5 were rural deans.

(*e*) 5 were classified on various grounds as overworked; 13 as underemployed.

(*f*) The average age was 51.

Group 5. Rural deans: 40 livings.

(*a*) This group is a 4·4 per cent sample of my own sample, extracted to secure a cross-section of the pressures upon rural deans.

(*b*) 20 of them had one church, 10 had two, 10 had three or more.

(*c*) 9 had chaplaincies.

(*d*) 9 only had a regular day off, though 24 reported that they attempted it: 19 reported regular daily rest.

(*e*) 19 asked for more time for serious reading, and 19 for administrative help.

(*f*) 6 were classified as overworked, 3 as underemployed.

(*g*) 3 had a weekday score of 18, 7 of 17: 18 had a Sunday score of 5 or over. The average weekday score was 14·71 and Sunday score 5·05, as against the national averages of 14·3 and 4·8 respectively.

(*h*) The average age of group was 56.

Group 6. Parishes with a population of under 450: 48 livings.

(*a*) 19 livings had one church; 23 livings had two churches; 5 livings had three churches; one living had six churches.

(*b*) The average weekday score was 11·8 and Sunday score 3·97: in 31 cases insufficient information was given to permit calculation of a weekday score.

(*c*) 21 asked for more time for serious reading, 6 for help with parish administration.

(*d*) 2 were rural deans.

(*e*) 1 was classified as overworked on Sunday, 21 as under-employed.

(*f*) 7 were in bad health: 8 were 70 or over.

(*g*) The average age was 58.

Group 7. ASA 30 or less per church: 98 livings.

(*a*) 251 churches were covered by these livings: therefore an ASA per church of 17·6 worked out at an ASA per clergyman of 44·6.

(*b*) There were 37 churches (in 16 livings) with an ASA of 26 to 30; 162 churches (in 67 livings) with an ASA of 11 to 25; 52 churches (in 15 livings) with an ASA of 10 or under.

(*c*) 51 asked for more time for serious reading, 16 for help in administration.

(*d*) 5 were rural deans.

(*e*) Two were classified as overworked, 30 as underemployed.

(*f*) 12 were over 70, two over 80, 12 were ill or convalescent or presented case histories.

(*g*) Weekday score averages were 12·72.
Sunday score averages were 4·56.

(*h*) The average age of incumbents in this group was 55.

Group 8. Incumbents over 70: 42 livings.

(*a*) 3 were rural deans, one an assistant bishop.

(*b*) 1 was classified as overworked (a town parish of 5,300 population and an ASA of 400 with one retired clergyman to assist), 8 as underemployed (though in the circumstances 'on light duties' would be more appropriate).

(*c*) There were 7 with parish populations of over 5,000: in only one such case was any other clergy help forthcoming.

(*d*) The average age of the whole group was 74.

Group 9. Ill or disabled: 21 livings.

(*a*) 8 were permanently disabled.

(*b*) One had too little to do on weekdays.

(*c*) 3 were classified as underemployed.

(*d*) One was a rural dean.

(*e*) 12 were rural incumbents.

(*f*) 9 had two or more churches.

(*g*) 5 had curate or other clergy to assist.

(*h*) 12 had parish populations of 2,000 and under, 9 had parish populations of 5,000 and over.

(*i*) The average population per living was 4,830 as against the national average of 7,483 (MQ figures).

(*j*) The average age was 58.

(*k*) Clergy were not asked in MQ to declare whether they were ill or disabled. The group consists only of those who volunteered the information; therefore the percentage (2·3) of the sample of 905 must not in any way be regarded as indicative of the degree of illness or disablement suffered generally by the clergy.

Group 10. Case Histories: 20 livings.

(*a*) 6 livings were over 10,000 population.

(*b*) 3 were classified as overworked: one as underemployed.

(*c*) 9 asked for more time for serious reading, 8 for help with parish administration.

(*d*) The average weekday score was 13·5, Sunday score 4·34, as against national averages of 14·3 and 4·8 respectively. 7 gave insufficient information to enable a weekday score to be allotted.

(*e*) 13 were from rural parishes.

(*f*) 15 were clergy working single-handed.

(*g*) 12 reported a weekly day off; only one that it was regularly kept.

(*h*) The average age was 54.

Group 11. Too little to do: 40 incumbents.

(*a*) 6 reported too little to do on Sundays and weekdays, 13 on Sundays only. Canterbury province had 8 reporting too little to do on Sundays, 26 on weekdays, 5 both; York, 5 Sundays, 7 weekdays, one both.

(*b*) The average weekday score was 12·3 and Sunday score 4·28, against the national average of 14·3 and 4·8 respectively. The weekday average is unreal, for 22 gave insufficient information to enable a weekday score to be allotted.

(*d*) The same marked difference appeared in ASA. The ASA for Canterbury province was 60 per living, of York 128: Canterbury had 14 livings with 50 or under ASA per living; York only 3. The average ASA per living for the whole group was 75·6. I note that one priest reporting too little to do on Sundays had two curates.

(*e*) The average age was 55.

Group 12. Hypothetically overworked: 99 livings.

(*a*) 51 of these livings were in Canterbury province; 48 in York.

(*b*) 17 had a weekday score of 18; 38 a Sunday score of 6 or more; 27 were single-handed in parishes of 10,000 or over.

(*c*) 14 were rural deans.

(*d*) One had an ASA of 30 or less, but he was the chaplain of a very large hospital.

(*e*) 4 were case histories.

(*f*) 50 had one church; 26 had two churches; 12 had three churches; 8 had four churches; two had five churches.

(*g*) The average age was 50, but six were 65 years or over.

Group 13. Hypothetically underemployed: 96 livings.

(*a*) 81 of these livings were in Canterbury province, 15 in York.

(*b*) 10 had a Sunday score of 6 or over; 14 had three or more churches; 25 had population of 450 or less, 36 had an ASA of 30 or less per church; 9 were over 70, 17 confessed to too little to do.

(*c*) Two were rural deans.

(*d*) The 96 livings were staffed by 97 clergy; they totalled 171 churches—not quite two to each man.

(*e*) The average age was 56.

CONCLUSION

Finally, it has proved possible to mount some of the results of the Main Questionnaire in chart form. They are set up in Appendix 4. Here the whole sweep of pastoral problems of the Church of England as MQ reveals them are ranged against the population density table taken from *Facts and Figures 1962*.

The breakdown of the main pastoral results is also given with national, provincial and diocesan averages, and census 1961 figures in contrast in Appendix 3.

QUESTIONNAIRE 3

Clergy Incomes (Q 3)

Questionnaire 3 was directed on 5th December 1962 to a random sample of 2 per cent of incumbents in both provinces in order to seek their attitudes and counsel over stipends and stipend policy in the Church.

In all, 245 questionnaires were sent out, 204 replies received and analysed. The replies received represent a return of 83·3 per cent; they constitute a sample of 1·97 per cent of 10,370 incumbents.

The text of the questionnaire was as follows:

Questionnaire to Incumbents about Clergy Incomes

1. Do you feel that your present stipend is (*Please tick*)
   too low?...................... adequate?...................... too high?......................
2. Do you feel that the pension you will receive is
   too low?...................... adequate?...................... too high?......................
3. Would you care to state in figures what you would consider to be at this moment
   (*a*) a fair annual net stipend?......................
   (*b*) a fair annual net pension?......................
4. At what age would you *like* to retire?......................
5. Do you consider the Easter offering to be
   (*a*) unfair in its incidence as between parish and parish?
   (*b*) *infra dig?*
   (*c*) necessary?
   (*d*) unnecessary?
6. Would you like to see the Easter offering
   (*a*) abolished?
   (*b*) compounded for a fixed annual sum?
   (*c*) regarded as tax-free gift?
   (*d*) turned into a parish offering for the diocesan stipends fund?
7. Are you involved in financial problems over the education of your children, or do you expect to be?
8. If your answer is Yes, do you feel the Church should assist in some way?...................... Could you indicate how?......................
9. Do you believe that the present differences between stipends of, say, bishops and incumbents are fair and equitable?
10. Or between assistant curates and incumbents?

11. In place of the present system would you prefer to see
    (*a*) a basic stipend paid to all priests of the Church of England?
    (*b*) with differentials for added responsibility or specially hard work?
    (*c*) with provision for expenses of office?
    (*d*) and payment of family allowances?

12. (*a*) Do you have sources of income other than your stipend?
    (*b*) Can you say what the sources are?

13. (*a*) Can you afford a proper holiday each year?
    (*b*) How long?
    (*c*) With or without clerical duties?

14. In 1959 Church Assembly accepted a report which recommended that clergy should receive expenses of office.
    (*a*) Are you receiving expenses of office?
    (*b*) From?
    (*c*) Is the contribution adequate?

15. Do you consider the present system of dilapidations deductions fair?

16. Have you any other comments on your own or the Church's financial problems?

Analysis of Replies

Of the sixteen questions, only the last, which involved extended answers, is not reported in the tabulations below.

Questions 1 and 2: Present stipends and pensions:

	Too low	*Adequate*	*Too high*	*Totals Answering*
1. Stipend	107	89	0	196
2. Pension	149	29	1	179

Question 3: Stipends and pensions.

(*a*) The average annual net stipend proposed was £1,068 3*s*.

(*b*) The average annual net pension proposed was £545 6s.

(*c*) 1 incumbent proposed a net stipend of £2,000;
13 incumbents proposed a net stipend of £1,500–£1,999;
13 incumbents proposed a net stipend of £1,250–£1,499;
103 incumbents proposed a net stipend of £1,000–£1,249;
33 incumbents proposed a net stipend of under £1,000.

163 83·2 per cent of 196 answering Q1.

(*d*) No incumbents proposed a net pension of over £1,000.
 15 incumbents proposed a net pension of £750 to under £1,000;
 117 incumbents proposed a net pension of £500–£479;
 21 incumbents proposed a net pension of under £500.

153 85·5 per cent of 179 answering Q2.

Question 4: Retiring age.

		% of 178 answers
6	proposed a retiring age of between 60 and 64	3·4
76	proposed a retiring age of 65	42·7
9	proposed a retiring age of 66–69	5·0
56	proposed a retiring age of 70	31·5
5	proposed a retiring age of between 71 and 80	2·8
26	hoped never to retire	14·6
178		100·0

18 gave no answer.

Questions 5 and 6: Easter offering.

			% of 274 answers
5 (*a*)	90	thought the offering unfair in its incidence between parish and parish	32·8
(*b*)	54	thought it *infra dig*.	19·7
(*c*)	100	believed it to be necessary	36·5
(*d*)	30	considered it unnecessary	11·0
	274		100·0

			% of 238 answers
6 (*a*)	51	proposed that it be abolished	21·4
(*b*)	40	wanted it compounded for a fixed annual sum	16·8
(*c*)	125	wanted it as a tax-free gift	52·5
(*d*)	22	as a parish offering to the diocesan stipends fund	9·3
	238		100·0

Table 21. Easter Offering Cross-references

Qs. 5 and 6	1	2	3	4	5	6	7	8
1. *Unfair*	*90*	31	41	19	26	28	50	15
2. *Infra dig.*	31	*54*	14	14	30	18	16	14
3. *Necessary*	41	14	*100*	2	8	18	84	4
4. *Unnecessary*	19	14	2	*30*	20	6	9	8
5. *Abolish*	26	30	8	20	*51*	9	12	10
6. *Compound*	28	18	18	6	9	*40*	20	2
7. *Tax-free*	50	16	84	9	12	20	*125*	3
8. *Diocese*	15	4	4	8	10	2	3	*22*

Questions 7 and 8: The education of children.

77 said that they had financial problems over education;
103 said not;
67 felt the Church should assist;
21 thought not.

Of the 65 making proposals which could be classified,

38 proposed education grants from the Church;
16 proposed children's allowances;
2 proposed higher education grants;
2 proposed a church boarding school;
4 proposed higher stipends.

Questions 9 and 10: Stipends differentials.

Between bishops and incumbents—97 thought them fair, 69 not fair, 21 answers not classifiable.

Between incumbents and curates—100 thought them fair, 67 not fair, 12 answers not classifiable.

Question 11: Attitudes to stipends policy.

(*a*) 138 approved a basic stipend for all clergy (67·6 per cent of 204);
(*b*) 134 asked for differentials for responsibility, etc. (65·7 per cent);
(*c*) 179 wanted expenses of office (87·7 per cent);
(*d*) 149 wanted payment of family allowances (73 per cent).

Table 22. Cross-references on Stipend Theories

Q. 11, a–d	1	2	3	4
Basic stipend	*138*	108	129	116
Differentials	108	*134*	129	114
Expenses of office	129	129	*179*	145
Family allowances	116	114	145	*149*

Question 12: Private incomes.

78 had other sources of income (38·2 per cent);
111 had none (54·4 per cent).

The additional sources of income reported were private means 38; pensions 15; legacies 13; paid outside employment 8; wife's paid outside employment 5; savings 3; lettings 2.

Question 13: Holidays.

66 had no holiday, which is 32·35 per cent of 204;

12 had one week 59 had two weeks 33 had three weeks 24 had four weeks	Of the total of 128, 105 had holidays without clerical duties.

Question 14: Expenses of office.

112 were receiving some expenses of office; 92 were not. 106 were receiving them from the PCC, 3 from diocese, 1 from endowment, 2 not specified. 36 said the contribution was adequate, 153 that it was not; 5 answers were unclassifiable.

Question 15: Dilapidations.

128 thought the present system fair, 52 thought not; 14 answers were not classifiable.

QUESTIONNAIRE 4

Diocesan Stipends Policy (*Q 4*)

Questionnaire 4, sent to the secretary of every diocesan board of finance, with a copy to his bishop, on 7th December 1962, was designed to provide the material for an analysis of diocesan stipendiary policy at the end of 1962. Forty-three questionnaires were sent out; forty-two were returned.

The text of the questionnaire is given below. It has four parts: Questions 1 to 8 ask for facts about incumbents' stipends; Questions 9 and 10 ask for views on the working and rationalisation of that policy; Questions 11 to 13 ask for facts about stipends for assistant curates; Question 14 invites an extended answer. Answers to Questions 9, 10 and 14 are excluded from the tabulated breakdown, but are dealt with in the report. The tabulated breakdown is set out in Appendices 1 and 2.

Questionnaire to Diocesan Boards of Finance

(a) Incumbents

1. Has the diocese established a minimum stipend for incumbents?.................... How much per annum?....................

2. Are you able to give the figure of the lowest stipend?....................
And the highest?....................

3. Has the diocese a minimum stipend target above that which it is at present able to guarantee?.................... Please state the figure ....

4. If a diocesan policy over stipends has been decided upon, please attach a document describing it, or summarise it here.

5. Has a family allowance policy been adopted?....................
If yes, please say how it operates.

6. Is the diocese able to make grants for cases of special hardship?.................... What is the maximum grant?....................

7. (*a*) Have differentials in stipends been established for livings or posts of special difficulty or responsibility?....................
(*b*) Would you favour such a policy?....................

8. Does your diocesan budget include allocations for augmentation of stipends of:
(*a*) incumbents? ....
(*b*) assistant curates? ....
(*c*) stipendiary lay workers? ....

9. Over the last decade a system has operated generally which bases stipends on these three ingredients:
(*a*) the endowment income attached to the benefice,
(*b*) the amount voluntarily contributed by the parish,
(*c*) an augmentation grant calculated by the DBF.
Have you any evidence of dissatisfaction with this procedure on any grounds?

10. Various ways of 'rationalising' stipend policy have been suggested to me:
(*a*) A stipends scale nationally arrived at and applied (in order to obviate differences between dioceses).
(*b*) A basic stipend for all priests of the Church of England, irrespective of office, with family allowances and expenses of office added (presumably this would need to be determined nationally, too).

(*c*) Stipends geared to a cost-of-living index.
(*d*) Stipends determined regionally after proper study of earnings in professions held to be comparable (teachers, doctors, social workers, civil servants, solicitors).

Would you care to comment, please?

(*b*) *Assistant Curates*

11. Does the diocese lay down a minimum stipend for assistant curates? If yes, how much is it in the first curacy? .... How much in the second curacy? ....

12. Is it left to the incumbent and the PCC to give effect to this or does the diocese underwrite it?

13. If there are any special diocesan grants to assistant curates, please give figures for
Family allowances..................... Housing ....
Expenses of office..................... Other ....

(*c*) *General*

14. Have you any general comments about clergy stipends?

Further Breakdown of Incumbents' Stipends

Some points of interest arise from Appendix 1. The first is that considerable differences between the incomes of incumbents are reported. The highest stipend was £4,702—'a solitary plum' was the comment made—only three were £3,500 or over. No effort was made by me to discover how many highly paid benefices existed in each diocese, but simply from the forty-two examples in the answers to Question 2b I was able to compile Table XIV of the report.

The breakdown suggests that the strongest higher-paid class throughout the country will be the third one, £1,500–£1,999, with the fourth a runner-up. The possibility for the less-well-paid parson of eventual preferment into this group must constitute what the sociologists tend to call a professional 'incentive'. At the same time the existence of these five groups points to widespread differentials within the incumbent group itself, differentials almost as considerable as those which divide incumbents from bishops and other dignitaries, and this bears on the problems confronting any authority seeking to rationalise or make more equitable the whole stipendiary system.

Appendix 1 also yields the information that eighteen Canterbury dioceses and seven York report systems of family allowances. These vary fantastically. The lowest—it depends on the number of children

—would appear to be either the diocese reporting £20 per annum for the first child only or those reporting £10 for each child per annum. The highest is an allowance of £40 for each child under 5, and £60 thereafter per child per annum until the end of university or equivalent training, which substantially raises the stipend for the married man with family in that diocese.

If we suppose for each diocese the same fictitious parsonage family of three children, one under 5, one of 7, one of 12, the effect of the various children's allowances in relation to minimum stipend can be more clearly seen in Table 23 opposite.

It will be noted from the new order of dioceses established for each province that on the whole those most generous with the minimum stipend are also most generous with the children's allowances, though there is one important exception (19). It can be seen, too, that (upon this fictitious basis) the gap between the highest and lowest pay is increased, not diminished, by children's allowances. On plain minimum stipends there is a difference of £200 between the top and bottom of the whole table: with family allowances added this rises to £255—more than 25 per cent.

Classification of Minimum Stipends

It is worth noting that nineteen of the Canterbury dioceses have a minimum between £750 and £849 and only eight have £850 and above. In York the minima stand higher: i.e. eleven of the thirteen York dioceses replying had minima standing between £800 and £899. The classification appears in Table XIII of the report.

For the whole country the largest group is in the £800–£849 range.

Stipends of Assistant Curates

Page 3 of Questionnaire 4 asked in Questions 11 and 13 for the minimum stipends and special allowances paid to assistant curates. The results are set out in Appendix 2.

Stipends for curates, unlike those for incumbents, normally stipulate increments for years of service, for priesting and for marriage. The effect of these increments is shown for single men in eighteen dioceses in Canterbury province and eleven in York province which provided evidence, in Table 24 below. Table 25 shows how the married curate with one child benefits by various increments: the eight dioceses in Canterbury province and the five in York province were the only ones from which sufficient details were received in time to make the calculations possible.

Table 23. Dioceses Reporting Children's Allowances for Incumbents[1]

Diocese No. as in *Facts and Figures*	Minimum stipend order	Allowance for three children	Totals (2) and (3)	New stipends Order in each province	
				Diocese No.	Stipend
(1)	(2)	(3)	(4)	(5)	(6)
Canterbury province:	£	£	£		£
3	750	+ 50	800	3	800
26	750	+ 60	810	26	810
16	790	+ 36	826	16	826
29	800	+ 30	830	29	830
1	800	+ 60	860	1	860
12	800	+ 65	865	21	860
19	800	+160	960	2	864
21	800	+ 60	860	12	865
2	804	+ 60	864	6	870
28	820	+ 60	880	25	880
17	825	+ 60	885	28	880
25	825	+ 55	880	17	885
6	850	+ 20	870	11	900
11	860	+ 40	900	13	930
9	870	+ 90	960	9	960
13	900	+ 30	930	19	960
14	925	+ 75	1,000	14	1,000
5	950	+105	1,055	5	1,055
Average	£828 17*s.*	+£62			£890 17*s.*
York province:					
40	800	+ 88	888	35	856
35	820	+ 36	856	32	875
32	825	+ 50	875	41	885
41	825	+ 60	885	40	888
30	830	+ 60	890	30	890
38	850	+ 50	900	38	900
36	870	+100	970	36	970
Average	£831 8*s.*	+£63 9*s.*			£894 17*s.*
All average	£829 11*s.*	+£62 8*s.*			£891 19*s.*

[1] Diocese 18 reported children's allowances but no minimum stipend, hence its omission.

Table 24. Increments of Assistant Curates, Single

No. in this table	Minimum starting stipend	Total increments over 3 yrs.	Stipend after three years	% increase
(*a*) Selected instances from Canterbury province:				
	£	£	£	
1	504	72	576	14·3
2	500	30	530	6·0
3	500	50	550	10·0
4	525	75	600	14·3
5	600	75	675	12·5
6	480	30	510	6·3
7	425	75	500	17·6
8	500	90	590	18·0
9	500	150	650	30·0
10	525	50	575	9·5
11	475	80	555	16·8
12	500	70	570	14·0
13	450	75	525	16·7
14	475	175	650	36·8
15	500	20	520	4·0
16	475	45	520	9·5
17	500	150	650	30·0
18	500	80	580	16·0
Average	£496 7*s*.	£77 7*s*.	£573 13*s*.	15·6
(*b*) Selected instances from York province:				
	£	£	£	
19	500	50	550	10·0
20	550	30	580	5·5
21	500	75	575	15·0
22	525	25	550	4·8
23	450	60	510	13·3
24	525	110	635	21·0
25	500	60	560	12·0
26	500	125	625	25·0
27	550	125	675	25·0
28	500	100	600	20·0
29	500	45	545	9·0
Average	£509 2*s*.	£73 4*s*.	£582 5*s*.	14·4
Average both prov.	£501 3*s*.	£75 15*s*.	£576 19*s*.	15·1

Table 25. Increments of Assistant Curates, Married

(Supposing a man married on being ordained, with one child born before the end of three years)

No. in this table	Commencing stipend	Increments and allces 3 yrs.	After three years, child allces incl.	% increase
(*a*) Selected instances from Canterbury province:				
	£	£	£	
1	560	60	620	10·7
2	600	150	750	25·0
3	550	130	680	23·6
4	550	150	700	27·3
5	625	80	705	12·8
6	475	117	592	24·6
7	520	100	620	19·2
8	550	170	720	30·9
Average	£553 15*s.*	£119 13*s.*	£673 8*s.*	21·6
(*b*) Selected instances from York province:				
	£	£	£	
9	600	60	660	10·0
10	575	55	630	9·6
11	500	95	595	19·0
12	550	90	640	16·4
13	525	70	595	13·3
Average	£550	£74	£624	13·4
Average both prov.	£552 6*s.*	£102 2*s.*	£654 8*s.*	18·5

How the commencing stipends are grouped is shown in the classification below. The lowest minimum curate's stipend is £325 less than the lowest minimum incumbent's stipend (light-duty cures excluded): the highest curate's stipend is only £150 below it: curates on their maximum may in more than one diocese approach or even conceivably surpass the incumbent minimum elsewhere. However a differential of £300 seems to be in general maintained for the principal group of twenty-two dioceses. But comparisons would be more worth while if it were possible to discover what relation the incumbent's stipend bears to his real earnings.

Table 26. Commencing Stipends of Assistant Curates

Province	£425–449	£450–499	£500–549	£550–599	£600–649
(*a*) Assistant Curates, Single:					
Canterbury	3	7	14	3	1
York	1	1	8	2	0
	4	8	22	5	1
(*b*) Assistant Curates, Married (where reported):					
Canterbury	—	1	3	5	5
York	—	—	2	3	1
	—	1	5	8	6

Concluding Note

A final point has to be made. A diocese must budget annually for its expenditure: if it is to exercise control over stipend policy and stipend augmentation it ought to include augmentation estimates in its budget. Five Canterbury and seven York dioceses reported, in answer to Question 8a, that their budgets did not include allocations for augmentation of incumbents' stipends; three Canterbury and two York reported similar failure to make budget allocations for the stipends of assistant curates.

This concludes analysis and discussion of Questionnaire 4.

QUESTIONNAIRE 5

Diocesan Staffs, Clerical and Lay (*Q 5*)

The Central Board of Finance sent a questionnaire to a selection of dioceses (twenty-six) on 4th March 1963, asking for an analysis of the whole range of diocesan staff appointments, clerical and lay.

The breakdown asked for was as follows:

(*a*) Into clerical and lay members of staff;

(*b*) then whether the members were (i) wholly paid by the diocese, or partly paid; (ii) where they were wholly or partly unpaid by the diocese, how the balance was met, i.e. by canonry or benefice income, etc.; (iii) how many, both clerical and lay, were honorary and unpaid.

The tabulated results of the Q 5 answers are as follows:

Table 27. Staffs of twenty-six dioceses

(*a*) Analysis of how the clergy staffs of twenty-six dioceses are paid:

Province	Wholly by dio.	Partly or wholly by benefice	Total full-time	Part-time pd. by dio.	Hon. & unpaid	Totals
Canterbury	48	58	106	16	65	187
York	7	32	39	5	26	70
	55	90	145	21	91	257

(*b*) Similar analysis of lay staffs of twenty-six dioceses:

Province	Wholly paid by diocese	Part-time paid by diocese	Honorary and unpaid	Totals
Canterbury	226	63	54	343
York	73	25	30	128
	299	88	84	471

This concludes the statistical analysis: further comment will be found in the report.

GENERAL LETTER OF INQUIRY TO DIOCESAN BISHOPS (L 1)

This early letter of inquiry, dated 28th May 1962, had really the intention of opening up survey problems with diocesan bishops, and the answers naturally are not susceptible of tabulation or statistical analyses. The letter asked for information under, principally, the following headings: 1, religious censuses or social surveys; 2, group or team ministries; 3, the state of rural deaneries; 4, manpower reports; 5, extraparochial ministries. Thirty-seven replies were received.

The responses were as follows: ten had instituted censuses or surveys or knew of them; twelve had group or team ministries or were about to begin them; fifteen had asked for manpower reports or knew of them; eleven reported growth of the extraparochial ministry, usually in connexion with university or youth, or industrial mission chaplaincies; sixteen had matters of interest to report about the state of rural deaneries, of which five declared emphatically in answer to the direct question that their rural deaneries were not 'powerhouses'. (It is unwise to assume that those bishops who did not reply to this point believed that their rural deaneries were.)

A SECOND LETTER OF INQUIRY TO DIOCESAN BISHOPS (L 2)

A second letter of inquiry, dated 10th December 1962, asked for the counsel of diocesan bishops on four important matters, to wit: 1, the number of 'hardcore' vacant livings (i.e. livings habitually vacant for an abnormal length of time); 2, 'the number of actual vacancies for assistant curates urgently needing to be filled at this moment'; 3, whether the bishop favoured a system of 'allocation' of newly ordained men on a quota system; 4, whether it was thought that the amalgamation of benefices (whether united benefices or pluralities) had gone far enough in the bishop's diocese. In addition to these the letter sought the confidential views of the bishops on such matters as the system of patronage and the parson's freehold. These, in any case, are hardly in the form that permits tabulation: the others are. Here then is a statistical summary of the answers to some questions from the forty-one replies received:

	Provinces		
	Canterbury	York	Totals
1. 'Hardcore' vacant livings reported[1]	52	18	70
2. Assistant curates vacancies:			
First urgency	293	264	
Add estimate for two dioceses	9	18	584
Second urgency	110	156	
Add estimate for two dioceses	3	10	279
Totals	415	448	863
3. In favour of allocation of men	10	5	15
Against	15	6	21
Doubtful or no answer	3	1	4
4. Believed united benefices and pluralities had gone as far as possible in the diocese	6	4	10
Not far enough	6	2	8
Undecided or no answer	16	6	22

The total number of curates required breaks down as follows:

[1] Four dioceses in Canterbury and two in York spoke of 'hardcore' problems but gave no figures. One in each province did not answer.

Table 28. Curates Required as a Matter of First Urgency, December 1962

Canterbury:		York:	
Canterbury*	9	York	11
London	30	Durham	23
Winchester	12	Blackburn	19
Bath and Wells	0	Bradford	20
Birmingham	8	Carlisle	10
Bristol	9	Chester	25
Chelmsford	20	Liverpool	40
Chichester	23	Manchester	20
Coventry	6	Newcastle	32
Derby	28	Ripon	15
Ely	0	Sheffield*	18
Exeter	6	Sodor and Man	2
Gloucester	12	Southwell	30
Guildford	14	Wakefield	17
Hereford	7		
Leicester	3		282
Lichfield	20		
Lincoln	7		
Norwich	7		
Oxford	6		
Peterborough	7		
Portsmouth	4		
Rochester	10		
St Albans	27		
St Edmundsbury and Ipswich	1		
Salisbury	7		
Southwark	8		
Truro	2		
Worcester	9		
	302		

* Canterbury and Sheffield figures are estimated on the basis of their proportions of total home population and of parishes of 10,000 pop. and over.

LETTER OF INQUIRY TO DEANS AND PROVOSTS (L 3)

In February 1963 I addressed a letter of inquiry to deans and provosts asking for information about clerical manpower as on 1st March 1963, including:

1. The clerical staff of the cathedral, full-time or part-time.

2. How many cathedral posts were used to provide the diocese with an official.
3. Whether the cathedral had any terminable canonries.
4. Whether the canonries are being used as once they were to provide theologians and others with opportunities to think and write.
5. What views were held about the remuneration of cathedral staffs.

The tabulated answers to Questions 1–3 inclusive are given below:

Table 29. Cathedral Staffs, 1st March 1963

Province	Deans and provosts	Residentiary canons	Minor clergy
Canterbury	29	93	41
York	13*	44	19
Totals	42	137	60

* In Sodor and Man the Bishop is the Dean of the pro-cathedral.

Of the above cathedral clergy 58 held the following posts:

Province	Assistant bishops	Arch-deacons	Other diocesan officers	Profes-sors	Princi-pals	Totals
Canterbury	5	20	5	5	2	37
York	2	8	9	2	—	21
Totals	7	28	14	7	2	58

If the minor clergy are excluded, the number of cathedral clergy becomes 179: no less than 32·4 per cent of these clergy held other posts or dignities on 1st March 1963.

II

RELATED RESEARCH

1. THE RELATIONSHIP BETWEEN STAFF AND NUMBERS OF COMMUNICANTS

(Rev. A. B. Miskin)

On the 15th December 1961 the Rev. A. B. Miskin, ARSM, FRICS, wrote to the *Church of England Newspaper*, arguing that 'the number of Easter communicants per full-time agent is independent of the number of persons under his care', and that therefore the assumption that the greater the population of the parish the greater the number of people who are brought to Christ is not justified. On what he called the scanty figures available in *Facts and Figures 1959* he

worked out the number of persons per full-time worker (incumbent, assistant clergy, Church Army workers, etc.). This gives the average population of what might be called a 'reduced parish'. Similarly, for each diocese, the number of Easter communicants per 'reduced parish' was found. It was very nearly 153—rather higher in the province of York and rather lower in Canterbury. What was unexpected was that this figure—153—was independent of the population of the 'reduced parish'. The correlation (by the Chi squared test) was only about 25 per cent. In other words, provided the number of people under one person is not less than about 900, the number of Easter communicants will be independent of the population of the parish.

This, if proved, was an important finding, bearing upon the whole deployment problem. The General Secretary of CACTM, Mr W. H. Saumarez Smith, and Mr R. F. Neuss of the Statistical Unit, both took up the matter directly with Mr Miskin, and when I started the research the matter was handed to me. Mr Miskin has gone on with this study with my encouragement and gratitude, using later figures from *Facts and Figures 1962* and the figures of Christmas communicants supplied by Mr Neuss, rather than Easter figures, as the area of research. More and more incumbents tend to argue that Christmas communicants figures are more reliable than Easter ones as an index of the parochial congregation for the simple reason that in the age of the motor-car many more people are away at Easter than ever before.

Mr Miskin defined his research as follows:

The purpose of the analysis is to find the influence on the number of Christmas communicants per living of each of the following, separately:

(i) Number of full- or part-time workers in the living;
(ii) Population of the living;
(iii) Number of places of worship in the living.

Although it is more work, I am finding the *partial* regression coefficients, i.e. the influence of any one of the three factors above while the other two remain constant. For example, one could thus get an estimate of the increase of number of Christmas communicants in a living if they get one additional full-time worker (curate, Church Army captain or sister, etc.) while the population and number of places of worship remain unchanged.

Mr Miskin and I agreed a weightage which could be given to the parochial workers whose descriptions appear in Table 12 (cols. 14, 15, 16, 17) and Tables 55 and 56 of *Facts and Figures 1962*. It is as follows:

(*a*) *Full-time clergy* 1

(*b*) *Laymen:*

Church Army full-time	1
Church Army part-time	½
Readers unpaid	0
Readers paid	1
Officials of societies	0
Lay workers voluntary	1
Lay workers paid	1

(*c*) *Women workers:*

Church Army full-time	1
Church Army part-time	½
Deaconesses	1
Moral welfare workers	¼
Diocesan workers	½
Parochial workers	1
Others incl. Religious	½

Using the statistics of *Facts and Figures 1962* as his data and other statistics supplied by the Statistical Unit and by me, Mr Miskin pursued his investigations. His own account of his findings is published in *Prism*, December 1963. His tables of the influence of full-time workers on communicants is given here:

Table 30. Average Number of Christmas Communicants per Living

Population	Number of full-time workers in the living		
	1	2	3
1,000	119	—	—
2,000	130	220	—
3,000	140	230	311
4,000	151	241	321
5,000	161	251	332
6,000	171	261	342
7,000	182	272	353
8,000	192	283	363
9,000	203	293	373
10,000	213	303	384
12,500	239	329	410
15,000	265	355	436

The table obviously shows that population has little influence on communicants—ten extra per extra 1,000—but that one extra full-time worker produces from eighty to ninety. These are actual computed results, not hypothetical ones. The formula produced by Mr Miskin's exercise is twenty-five basic communicants per living of 1,000 and over, plus ninety for each full-time worker, plus ten for each thousand of population. His paper goes on to ask whether a transfer of priests from small rural livings to the towns would lift urban areas from their pastoral depression. And he shows, by what is virtually a *reductio ad absurdum*, that this would not prove effective. His significant arguments are discussed in the Report (p. 139 f.). He concludes that only massive lay pastoral activity could bring, say, the additional two million communicants the Church can reasonably expect to attract, as the first step in the reconversion of England.

2. SMALL SINGLE-CHURCH PARISHES

(Rev. A. B. Miskin)

The Rev. A. B. Miskin also undertook an analysis of single-church parishes with a population under 1,000, and tabulated according to the ages of incumbents. The results for both provinces are as follows:

Table 31. Ages (31.12.59) of All Incumbents of Single-church Parishes of Population under 1,000

Age groups	Canterbury	York	Totals
80 or over	20	1	21
75–79	51	8	59
70–74	139	30	169
65–69	206	60	266
60–64	180	54	234
55–59	198	48	246
50–54	175	48	223
45–49	148	16	164
40–44	79	25	104
35–39	42	11	53
30–34	21	3	24
Under 30	3	0	3
Totals	1,262	304	1,566
All incumbents	7,561	2,814	10,375
Incumbents in small one-church parishes	17%	11%	15%

Properly these livings can be considered as lighter charges than the normal and it is interesting therefore that only about half of them in each province are occupied by older men. However, the diocesan incidence of these parishes is of as much importance as their provincial totals: thus the heavily urbanised dioceses are poorly served with them: e.g., Birmingham has 4, Liverpool 5, Southwark 7, Manchester 8, Guildford 10, Portsmouth 10, Derby 11 and Wakefield 11; whereas Oxford has 114, Exeter 94, Bath and Wells 90, Norwich 88. The significance of this, in deployment terms, is that the highly urban areas have far fewer light-duty parishes into which to move ailing or older clergy. As changes go today very much by diocese—a man moves in his own diocese more easily than in and out of dioceses—this presents a problem. The full diocesan table is given here:

Table 32. Single-church Parishes of under 1,000 Population by Dioceses

Canterbury province: 1,262 parishes			
Canterbury	37	Leicester	30
London	25	Lichfield	65
Winchester	27	Lincoln	58
Bath and Wells	90	Norwich	88
Birmingham	4	Oxford	114
Bristol	15	Peterborough	43
Chelmsford	69	Portsmouth	10
Chichester	43	Rochester	33
Coventry	18	St Albans	40
Derby	11	St Ed. and Ipswich	58
Ely	58	Salisbury	61
Exeter	94	Southwark	7
Gloucester	49	Truro	39
Guildford	10	Worcester	35
Hereford	31		
York province: 304 parishes			
York	48	Manchester	8
Durham	13	Newcastle	21
Blackburn	31	Ripon	15
Bradford	12	Sheffield	15
Carlisle	63	Sodor and Man	6
Chester	34	Southwell	22
Liverpool	5	Wakefield	11

There is some evidence that fatigue, illness and breakdown cause clergy to retire too early. In pursuit of this probability Mr Miskin produced these two tables from Tables 45 and 54 of *Facts and Figures 1962.*

Table 33. Age of Retirement of All Retired Clergy Alive on 31.12.59

Age at retirement	No.	%
Under 60	302	8·6
60–69	1,127	32·1*
70 or over	2,077	59·3
Total	3,506†	100·0

† Excluding 69 whose ages at retirement were not known.

Table 34. Losses in Manpower in Years 1956–9

Age at retirement or death	Retired	%	Died before retirement	%
Under 60	59	4·0	149	26·7
60–69	406	27·4*	217	39·0*
70 and over	1,014	68·6	191	34·3
Totals	1,479	100·0	557	100·0
Ages not known	8		9	

Note. These figures—especially those 'starred'—show very clearly how clergy over 60 need light-duty parishes. When one remembers the financial loss (in Church and National Insurance pensions) if one retires before 70, clearly sickness and/or fatigue in most cases is responsible for causing retirement before 70.

At the moment only 27 per cent of all incumbents aged 60 or over are in light-duty parishes.

Mr Miskin's two tables above, and his conclusions are illuminating, even startling. Whether as a consequence we need to retain the light-duty parishes for older clergy, or to lower the voluntary retirement age, or to provide for them to move to lighter duties in new ways, or all three, are matters discussed in the report.

3. THE DISTRIBUTION OF ORDINATION CANDIDATES

(The Bishop of Birmingham and others)

In 1957 the then Archbishop of Canterbury, Dr Fisher, set up a committee under the chairmanship of the Bishop of Manchester to study the distribution of ordination candidates. It reported in 1957, and its report *The Distribution of Ordination Candidates* was 'circulated to diocesan bishops only and confidential'. In effect it is a deployment study, and the present Archbishop, Dr Ramsey, courteously withdrew the confidential limitation placed upon it in order that its evidence might be made available for this report. Basically the report produced a formula for judging whether a diocese was adequately staffed with assistant curates or not. It argued that it was reasonable for a parish of between 5,000 and 10,000 population to have one curate, for a parish of over 10,000 to have two. On the basis of this formula and of the actual distribution of 2,628 curates the report published a table which in Column 9 gave the 'deficit or surplus of curates based on such expectations'. An amended version of the formula, produced by the Bishop of Birmingham, who continued the work begun by the committee, awarded notionally one curate for parishes of from 5,000 to 9,999, two curates for those of 10,000 to 29,999 and three curates for those of 30,000 and over. A cyclostyled report, *The Distribution of Curates*, using this latter basis was circulated in June 1962. It gave 2,242 parishes between 5,000 and 9,999 population; 1,290 in the 10,000–29,999 group and 33 in the 30,000 and over group. The total number of curates required by this second formula was 4,921 against the existing provision of 2,579—a deficit of 2,342. However, the mere *total* of deficiencies does not indicate the *real* deficiencies in terms of the distribution required by the formula, i.e., were the existing curates where they ought to be? A similar investigation in 1958 directed by the Bishop of Birmingham revealed that 495 assistant curates were then distributed among 8,402 parishes of under 5,000 population—that is, from the point of view of the Archbishop's committee just about one in five of the assistant curates was wrongly deployed.

Table 35 opposite gives the July 1958 estimate of distribution of assistant curates and of shortage. Table 36 shows the breakdown diocese by diocese in terms of the second formula (which necessarily discloses a higher deficiency figure) and an actual allocation to each diocese (roughly in the region of 10 per cent of the need of each diocese) of the 530 deacons the Bishop expected to be ordained in 1962. This quite rigorous and systematic theoretical effort to deploy manpower was unfortunately stillborn for reasons discussed in the report: but it did succeed in exposing the manpower situation and exercising a persuasive power on the theological college principals. The Bishop of Birmingham produced one other interesting set of figures—the actual number of men ordained diocese per diocese in 1959, 1960, and 1961. These are set out and contrasted with national needs in Table XVI on page 147.

Table 35. Distribution of Assistant Curates

Summary of diocesan replies to questionnaire of July 1958.*

(*a*) *Existing distribution, analysed on population:*

(i) In 8,402 parishes of under 5,000	495
(ii) In 2,053 parishes of 5,000/10,000	984
(iii) In 927 parishes of over 10,000	1,100
	2,579
Diocesan estimates of shortage in forty dioceses	1,438
Similar shortage assumed in other three dioceses	100
Estimated total number of curates required	4,117

(*b*) *Existing distribution analysed on kinds of parishes:*

(i) Single benefices with one church	1,163
(ii) Single benefices with two or three churches	910
(iii) United benefices	120
(iv) Benefices held in plurality	67
(v) Benefices used for training	29
(vi) Rural groups of benefices	22
(vii) Urban groups of benefices	3
(viii) Conventional districts and special areas	227
(ix) Special diocesan or parochial capacity	38
Total	2,579

* The diocesan replies do not quite accord with the 1959 statistics set out in columns (3) and (17) of Table 22, *Facts and Figures 1962*.

Table 36. Hypothetical Distribution of Curates

Total number of curates needed in each diocese. Group A parishes, 5,000–9,999—one curate; Group B parishes, 10,000–29,999—two curates; Group C parishes, over 30,000—three curates.

Diocese	A	B	C	Curates needed	Quota 1962
Canterbury	51	19	0	89	9
London	240	131	2	508	55
Winchester	48	23	0	94	10
Bath and Wells	29	6	0	41	4
Birmingham	50	62	3	183	20
Bristol	44	17	0	78	8
Chelmsford	76	100	6	294	32
Chichester	52	20	0	92	10
Coventry	35	24	1	86	10
Derby	54	30	0	114	11
Ely	19	1	0	21	2
Exeter	40	9	0	58	6
Gloucester	19	4	0	27	3
Guildford	42	10	1	65	7
Hereford	7	1	0	9	1
Leicester	31	22	0	75	8
Lichfield	77	68	5	228	25
Lincoln	23	11	1	48	6
Norwich	17	5	0	27	3
Oxford	38	20	0	78	8
Peterborough	19	8	0	35	4
Portsmouth	22	24	1	73	7
Rochester	48	51	0	150	16
St. Albans	43	30	1	106	11
St. Ed. and Ips.	17	1	0	19	2
Salisbury	21	5	0	31	3
Southwark	192	144	5	495	54
Truro	7	1	0	9	1
Worcester	30	16	0	62	7
York	48	32	1	115	12
Durham	93	41	0	175	19
Blackburn	74	18	1	113	12
Bradford	39	15	0	69	8
Carlisle	22	7	0	36	4
Chester	83	30	0	143	15
Liverpool	89	71	1	234	26
Manchester	136	53	0	242	26
Newcastle	30	34	2	104	12
Ripon	37	26	0	89	9
Sheffield	55	44	2	149	16
Sodor and Man	3	0	0	3	1
Southwell	56	26	0	108	11
Wakefield	86	30	0	146	16
No. of parishes	2,242	1,290	33		
No. of curates	2,242	2,580	99	4,921	530*

* Actually 632 deacons were ordained in 1962, of whom 139 were over 40.

4. THE FAYERS-HEAWOOD RESEARCH

(Rev. H. D. F. Fayers and Mr Geoffrey Heawood)

Mr Geoffrey Heawood, when General Secretary of CACTM, kept close and careful notes of the background and attainments of candidates who appeared before the selection boards of which he was a member, notes which became more systematic as time went on. At my request the Rev. H. D. F. Fayers examined and tabulated these records and my tabulation of his final figures is presented below.

Corrected Results Fayers-Heawood Research 1954–62

A. *General*

In the period covered by the records of these ninety-four CACTM boards the total number of candidates for ordination was 1,921, of which 1,525 were accepted fully or conditionally, and 396 not recommended or not yet recommended. For analysis purposes the fully or conditionally recommended are regarded as accepted for training; the not recommended or not yet recommended (and the few 'no decision') as rejected. The summary of the boards examined is as follows:

Table 37. Selection Boards attended by Mr Heawood

Year	Total boards	No. of boards in sample	Total candi-dates	Candi-dates in sample	Total R	Sample				
						R	CR	NYR	NR	ND*
1954	39	11	785	223	597	136	51	12	23	1
1955	43	11	891	220	692	136	44	16	22	2
1956	43	12	893	241	641	154	36	29	21	1
1957	43	13	893	270	672	180	26	27	36	1
1958	44	13	922	263	714	161	45	30	27	—
1959	45	15	964	320	757	216	48	32	24	—
1960	46	11	954	231	708	134	35	29	32	1
1961	44	5	873	93	646	44	28	8	11	2
1962	46	3	899	60	673	42	9	3	4	2

* R = recommended: CR = conditionally recommended: NYR = not yet recommended: NR = not recommended: ND = no decision.

B. *Backgrounds*

The candidates offering themselves over the whole period had the following backgrounds:

Table 38. School and University Backgrounds of Ordinands

(*a*) *Schools*:

	No. of candi-dates	% of 1,921	Accepted	% of Col. 1	Rejected	% of Col. 1
Public schools	557	29·0	478	85·82	79	14·18
Grammar schools	993	51·7	796	80·16	197	19·84
Sec. Modern, technical, ele-mentary, etc.*	355	18·5	242	68·17	113	31·83
Details not given	16	·8	9	56·25	7	43·75
	1,921	100·0	1,525	79·39	396	20·61

*Includes three privately educated.

(*b*) *Universities* (i.e. those who were at university at the time of the selection conference, or had already graduated):

	No. of candi-dates	% of 1,921	Accepted	% of Col. 1	Rejected	% of Col. 1	Col. 3 as % of total univ. offer.	Col. 5 as % of total univ. offer.
Oxford and Cambridge (A)	301	15·67	278	92·36	23	7·64	53·98	4·47
All other univer-sities (B & C)	214	11·14	191	89·25	23	10·74	37·09	4·47
	515	26·81	469	91·07	46	8·93	91·07	8·93

(*c*) The category 'All other universities' can be further broken down, labelling Oxford and Cambridge as 'A', candidates from London, Durham, Glasgow and Edinburgh were labelled 'B', and candidates from all other universities as 'C'. Line 2 of (*b*) above therefore breaks down as follows:

	No. of candi-dates	% of 1,921	Accepted	% of Col. 1	Rejected	% of Col. 1	Col. 3 as % of total univ. offer.	Col. 5 as % of total univ. offer.
'B' university	103	5·36	89	86·41	14	13·59	17·28	2·72
'C' university	111	5·78	102	91·89	9	8·11	19·81	1·75
	214	11·14	191	89·25	23	10·74	37·09	4·47

C. *Further Breakdown*

The figures for the ninety-four CACTM boards were then broken down into three-year periods. The last period is regarded as incomplete, for the summary above gives only five boards attended by Mr Heawood in 1961, and three in 1962.

Table 39. Further Breakdown

(*a*) *Schools:*

Type of School	1954–6			1957–9			1960–2		
	Total	Acc.	Rej.	Total	Acc.	Rej.	Total	Acc.	Rej.
Publ. No.	195	169	26	257	222	35	105	87	18
% a. or r.	100	86·7	13·3	100	86·4	13·6	100	82·85	17·15
Publ. as % of total sch. candidates	28·51	30·35	20·48	30·13	32·85	19·76	27·34	29·80	19·50
Grammar No.	356	293	63	446	354	92	191	149	42
% a. or r.	100	82·30	17·7	100	79·4	20·6	100	78·0	22·0
as % of total sch. candidates	52·05	52·62	49·60	52·29	52·40	52·0	49·74	51·9	45·7
All others No.	117*	86	31	150†	100	50	88	56	32
% a. or r.	100	73·5	26·5	100	66·67	33·3	100	63·5	36·5
as % of total sch. candidates	17·11	15·45	24·42	17·58	14·80	28·25	22·29	19·20	34·80
Details not given: No.	16	9	7						
% a. or r.	100	56·3	43·7						
as % of total sch. candidates	2·34	1·60	5·50						
Totals	684	557	127	853	676	177	384	292	92

*Including two privately educated. †Including one privately educated.

(*b*) *Universities:*

	1954–6			1957–9			1960–2		
	Total	Acc.	Rej.	Total	Acc.	Rej.	Total	Acc.	Rej.
'A' Nos.	121	116	5	125	115	10	55	47	8
% a. or r.	100	95·58	4·42	100	92·0	8·0	100	85·45	14·55
'A' as % of total un. candidates	63·02	67·05	26·33	54·38	54·0	58·8	58·70	56·6	80·0
'B' Nos.	30	23	7	52	47	5	21	19	2
'C' Nos.	41	34	7	53	51	2	17	17	—
'B' & 'C' total as % of total un. candidates	36·98	32·95	73·67	45·62	46·0	41·2	41·30	43·4	20·0
Totals	192	173	19	230	213	17	93	83	10

It will be seen that the percentage of rejections within the 'A' group rises in this series:

4 : 8 : 15

while the 'A' share in the *total* universities candidates accepted falls in this series:

67 : 54 : 57

The first fall in the series is accompanied by an actual decline in numbers accepted from 'A' of only one. Therefore the percentage decline has to be attributed to a rise in the numbers from other groups rather than a falling away of candidates from 'A' universities. 'B' and 'C' numbers rise absolutely from the first triennium to the second: the figures for the third triennium fall, inevitably (and with all other groups), for Mr Geoffrey Heawood attended only five boards in 1961 and three in 1962, as against an average number of boards attended in each of the seven previous years of 12·3. However in ratio the 'B' and 'C' figures of candidates for the last triennium represent an increase: the series of three triennial periods expressed in percentages of the total university offering within the sample is:

37 : 46 : 41

Their acceptances rise in this series:

33 : 46 : 43

while the percentage of rejections steeply falls whether expressed as percentage of the whole university offering, or of its own group offering.

D. *Comment*

(*a*) Over the total period analysed the Oxford and Cambridge offering was approximately 50 per cent greater than the offering of all the other universities of England put together, though in 1960–1 of the total male students resident in British universities Oxford and Cambridge only accounted for 25·41 per cent.

(*b*) The total offering of schools was for the nine years

Public 557—29 per cent.
Grammar 993—52 per cent.
Secondary Modern and all others 355—19 per cent.

Yet in 1961, for example, the public schools only accounted for 7 per cent of male pupils at school, while the grammar schools accounted for 28 per cent and secondary modern, technical and other LEA schools accounted for 65 per cent.

The figures below illustrate this:

Universities 1960–1:

Total figure for men	81,330	
less Scotland and Wales	18,002	
	——	63,328
of which Oxford men	7,685	
of which Cambridge men	8,111	
	——	15,796

which is 25 per cent of the total male resident students.

*Schools 1961**

		% of total attendance
Headmasters' conference schools ..	98,000	7
Grammar schools	407,000	28
Secondary Modern and Technical, etc. ..	935,000	65
	1,440,000	100

* Approximate figures.

E. *Bias?*

It is relevant to the study of the clergy as a particular social stratum to ask whether there is bias in the selection of ordination candidates. It is evident that if more public school and Oxford and Cambridge candidates come forward for ordination than candidates from the other schools and universities, then the selection figures will reflect this, which is just what they do. Their offering is at a higher rate, proportionately, than the offerings of other groups. This is not a factor which selection boards could change or would wish to change. However, bias which is a mere reflection of self-selection at a stage beyond reach of selection boards is not the issue. Is there preference shown to one group rather than another when men reach the board? In the case of Oxford and Cambridge men the figures would seem to show that as their rejections rise and acceptances fall during the decade under examination (while the reverse is sharply true of men from other universities) any bias towards them has been neutralised during the decade, or is very slight.

In the case of public school candidates this neutralisation or reversal of bias is not established. Public school *rejections* rose in this series 13 : 14 : 17, while grammar school rejections rose, too, in this order 18 : 21 : 22; their acceptances fell slightly as a percentage of total acceptances. Public school candidates clearly more than hold their own in the decade, for whatever reason.

The Fayers-Heawood figures were made available to Mr Anthony Coxon for his study of the backgrounds and attitudes of ordinands which is reported on in the next section. He will make further use of them in a more refined analysis in his thesis. However, he subjected the hypothesis that 'there is significant bias towards public school and Oxford and Cambridge candidates with respect to the selection procedures of CACTM' to Chi-square tests, on which he will enlarge in his thesis, and showed me his workings and reported to me as follows this interim conclusion, which I accept:

'Allowing for other predictable contingencies, we can summarise the results of the research on this as follows:

'(1) In all possible combinations of school types of candidates in respect of selection procedures, there is consistent, strong bias towards the public school candidate.

'(2) In all combinations of university-type, and in relevant combinations with non-university candidates, there is consistent bias towards the selection of the Oxbridge candidates; but this bias is not so strong, nor so persistently significant, as is bias towards the public school candidate.

'The most important results of the study of this hypothesis are that it allows for the higher proportion of candidates applying from these sources, and that the bias which is demonstrably present when this has been fully allowed for cannot be explained in any way by reference to the requirements of CACTM. It should also be pointed out that this pattern is also reflected in the selection procedures of other professions.

'Study of the *trend* in bias in selection procedures shows that although bias toward Oxbridge candidates is decreasing slowly, but consistently, this is by no means the case in bias towards public school candidates.'

5. ORDINANDS AND THEIR BACKGROUNDS

(Mr Anthony P. M. Coxon)

Simultaneously with my survey, Mr Anthony Coxon has been conducting an inquiry (*Ordinands' Survey*, 1962) into the training of Anglican ordinands, under the Department of Social Studies of Leeds University. He has courteously made available some of his findings in advance of the completion of his thesis. These throw light on backgrounds and areas of recruitment of ordinands at present in theological colleges and by and large appear to confirm the data derived from the Fayers-Heawood analysis. It is, for example, remarkably interesting that of the 494 ordinands in training (a 30 per cent sample) who answered Mr Coxon's questionnaire 35 per cent had attended public or independent schools; 43 per cent grammar and high schools (including direct grant schools); 22 per cent secondary modern, all age elementary and similar schools, or were educated abroad.

The table which follows breaks down these groups proportionately to the number of returns from each theological college:

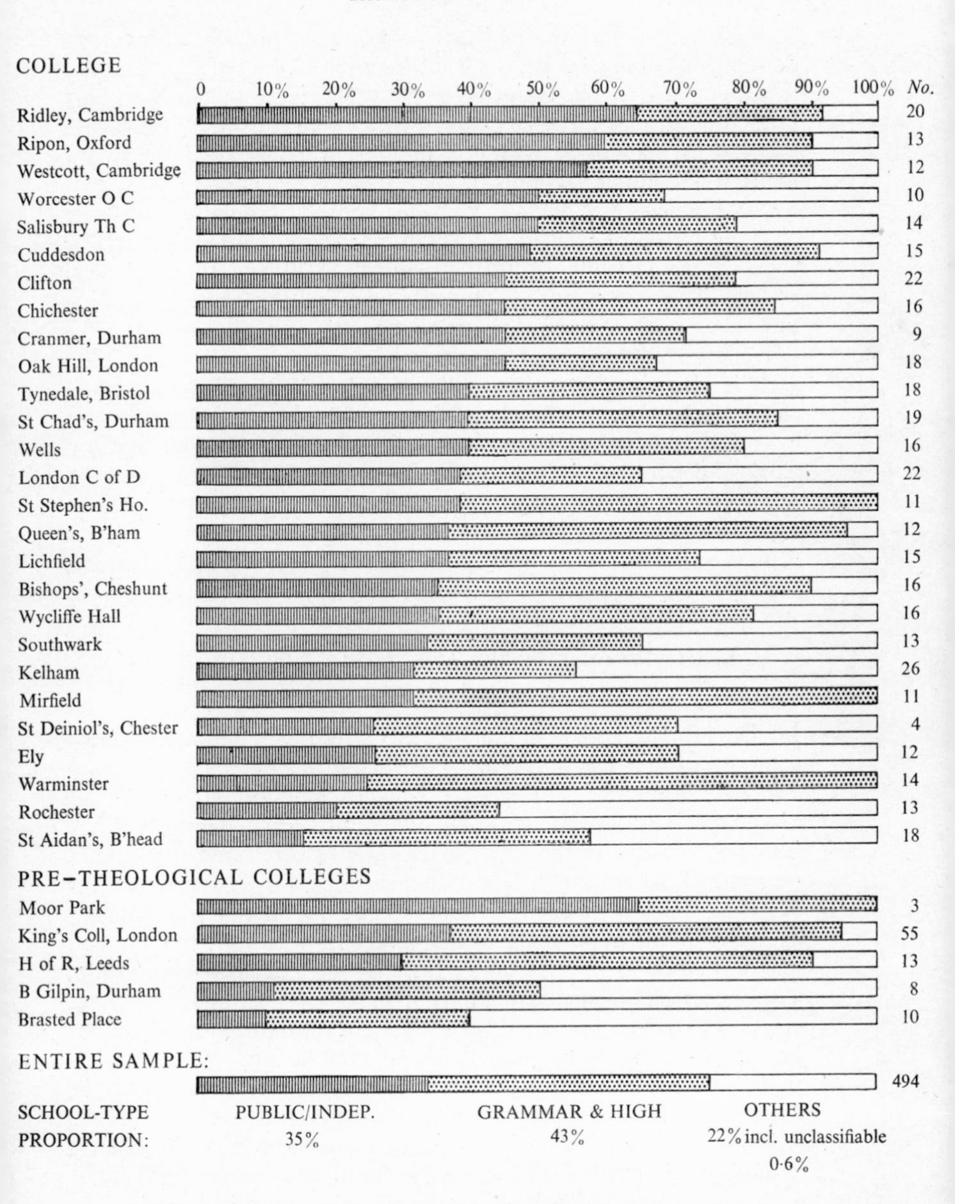

Table 40. School Backgrounds of Ordinands

However, despite the high percentage from public and independent schools, only 1·2 per cent put themselves, by self-definition, in the upper classes. The majority, 67 per cent, placed themselves safely in the middle class. The 26 per cent who opted for the working class accords in magnitude with the number who attended secondary modern and similar schools, though there is evidence to show that a working-class boy tends to consider himself automatically middle class by virtue of education at grammar school and university, or some other institute of further education, including theological college. Theological college students who feel this sense of moving into a new class are simply repeating the general experience of university students from back-street backgrounds.

It is also significant that of the sample of 494, 29 per cent had clerical relations. As the clergy form nowhere near 30 per cent of the adult manpower of the country, it is a tribute to their pastoral work and personal influence that three out of ten ordinands have relatives who are clergymen. Of the largest groups of the occupations of fathers of the 494, ninety were administrators or managers, forty-four clergymen, thirty-nine members of other free professions, twenty-one of the forces or the police, fifteen in teaching.

6. DIOCESAN BISHOPS AND THEIR BACKGROUNDS

(Mr David H. J. Morgan)

Mr David Morgan has, simultaneously with this inquiry, completed a thesis entitled *The Social and Educational Backgrounds of English Diocesan Bishops of the Church of England, 1860 to 1960*, and he has kindly made available to me some of his statistical conclusions. They bear out findings in the Fayers-Heawood research and throw light on some of Mr Anthony Coxon's conclusions. Mr Coxon shows, for example, that the possession of a father or a relative in the ministry exercises a strong influence in the choice of vocation: three out of ten ordinands at present under training have such a relationship. The importance of such a relationship in bishop-making is even more startling. Mr Morgan noted (in a table not reproduced here) that of bishops consecrated between 1860 and 1960 (a total of 225) no less than ninety-five had *fathers* who were Anglican clergy—that is, 42 per cent. No other profession approaches this degree of influence in bishop-making. Fathers in other professions were thirty, in business twenty-five, in Parliament fourteen, in the armed services fourteen.

Mr Morgan's figures bear out the predominant role played by the public schools in the recruitment to the ministry. It is clear from the Fayers-Heawood research that the public schools have been and are the most important field of recruitment for the ministry: the social importance of this has yet to be estimated. But a public school background, common in the ministry, is *de rigueur* for bishops, as the following table of schools attended shows:

Table 41. Schools Attended by Bishops, 1860–1960

Category	1860/79	1880/99	1900/19	1920/39	1940/59	1960	Total Bishops
Leading 10†	11	14	16	25	25	10	93
Other major	0	0	1	3	7	7	17
Minor public	1	5	5	4	2	9	24
Day public	5	3	13	11	16	11	49
Others	3	12	10	7	8	6	39
Private tuition	5	2	5	1	1	0	13
Not recorded	3	0	0	1	2	1	7
Total schools	28	36	50	52	61	44	242

†The leading ten, in order of importance, are Eton, Winchester, Marlborough, Shrewsbury, Rugby, Harrow, Westminster, Charterhouse, Haileybury, King Edward's (Birmingham). All accounted for four or more bishops (Eton contributed 25).

His second table (below) emphasises the predominant role of Oxford and Cambridge in bishop-making and within those universities the quite special part (almost 25 per cent) played by three colleges. His third table repeats the analysis for theological colleges: there it is shown that four theological colleges trained between them in the last century rather more than 25 per cent of the bishops. However, Wells was founded in 1840, Cuddesdon in 1854, Ridley in 1879, Westcott in 1881, and it is not until the first decades of this century that they appear in Mr Morgan's figures as bishop-makers. From that time their influence grows. Of the fifty-eight bishops instituted in the last duodecade, 1940–59, nineteen came from these four colleges. The number jumps to thirty-one in 1960, a fact which points to their growing influence. The final table on the ages of bishops shows that it is more difficult now than 100 years ago to become a bishop under 50 and that there has been a strong growth of bishops in the 50–60 age group: the average age is falling slightly.

Table 42. Universities attended by Bishops, 1860–1960

Categories	1860/79	1880/99	1900/19	1920/39	1940/59	1960	Total Bishops
Leading three colleges*	10	7	12	11	14	4	55
Cambridge	14	13	19	19	17	20	94
Oxford	13	15	22	25	37	19	114
Others	1	3	1	5	5	5	18
Total (universities)	28	31	42	49	59	44	226

* Trinity, Cambridge, Christ Church and New College, Oxford.

Table 43. Theological Colleges attended by Bishops, 1860–1960

Categories	1860/79	1880/99	1900/19	1920/39	1940/59	1960
None recorded	27	28	38	37	25	4
Cuddesdon	0	0	1	4	11	7
Ridley	0	0	0	2	6	7
Westcott	0	0	0	0	0	12
Wells	0	0	2	3	2	5
Others	0	1	1	1	14	8
Total (colleges)	27	29	42	47	58	43

Table 44. Ages of Bishops at Six Dates

Age groups	1860	1880	1900	1920	1940	1960
30–35	1	0	0	0	0	0
35–40	0	0	0	0	0	0
40–45	2	1	0	0	0	0
45–50	4	0	1	5	1	2
50–55	4	4	3	4	8	13
55–60	1	4	9	10	5	9
60–65	1	6	3	6	9	6
65–70	4	4	4	5	10	9
70–75	3	5	8	7	6	3
75–80	4	2	2	1	4	1
80–85	0	0	1	0	0	0
Total	24	26	31	38	43	43
Average	59·9	63·3	64·4	61·1	63·7	59·8

Mr Morgan has also essayed the difficult task of estimating the peerage and landed gentry connexions of the episcopacy by birth and marriage. This has produced the following somewhat tentative table. Its importance for determining the nature of the episcopacy as an *élite* is unmistakable.

Table 45. English Diocesan Bishops: Landed and Peerage Connexions by Birth and Marriage

Year*	Category†						
	Peerage by birth	Peerage by marriage‡	Landed by birth	Landed by marriage	Landed/ peerage birth and marriage§	Total peerage/ landed con-nexions‖	Total bishops
1860	8	1	7 (0)	11 (0)	12	27 (108·0)	25
1880	4	5	5 (2)	14 (0)	8	28 (103·7)	27
1900	5	10	7 (1)	7 (1)	7	29 (93·5)	31
1920	8	7	6 (1)	7 (1)	6	28 (73·7)	38
1940	5	4	6 (0)	9 (2)	5	24 (55·8)	43
1960¶	0	2	11 (5)	10 (2)	4	23 (53·5)	43
Total**	25	24	36	53	36	138 (75·4)	183

*Year, that is, in which all the bishops discussed were diocesan bishops.

†Categories include all relationships, as well as some rather dubious possible landed connexions which will be excluded in the final thesis: figures in brackets, cols. 4 and 5, indicate the possible number of these.

‡Where bishops married twice into nobility, both connexions are recorded.

§That is, bishops who were both sons of gentry/peerage and married daughters from these categories.

‖Figures in brackets, col. 7, show total of peerage/landed connexions as a percentage of the total number of diocesan bishops for each year.

¶Not to be taken too seriously. Overweighted by these 'possible' landed connexions. See note †.

**Adjustments made for bishops who appear on two dates, hence avoiding double counting.

7. THE DISTRIBUTION OF PATRONAGE

(The Rev. Michael Daniel and others)

One important aspect of the deployment of the clergy is the distribution of patronage. I sought by various inquiries to discover its pattern. What would appear to be a simple matter of counting, turns out not to be so, for a variety of reasons. I passed over the material I had gathered to the Rev. Michael Daniel, who generously sought to reconcile three different analyses for me: when after examination it was seen to be impossible because, *inter alia*, tables based on advowsons differ considerably from those based on livings, it was decided to show the three different tables as they are without comment except perhaps to say that they reveal the confusion which exists and which the report discusses. Col. A in the table below is based upon *Church of England Year Book*, 1963 figures, Crockford's, and my own direct inquiries; col. B on an advowson analysis made of Crockford's by Mr O. H. Woodforde of the Church Commissioners' staff; col. C. on an analysis of Crockford's made by Mr Peter Whiteley.

Table 46. Distribution of Patronage

Patronage	A	%	B	%	C	%
1. Crown and its officers	780	7	726	6	748	6
2. Diocesan bishops	3,500	30	4,116	33	4,115	35
3. Deans and Chapters	700	6	672	5	653	6
4. Parochial clergy of mother church	1,200	10	1,062	8	1,035	9
5. Diocesan boards of patronage	200	2	318	3	315	3
6. Colleges, etc.	850	7	875	7	772	7
7. Religious patronage trusts and societies	1,830	16	1,859	15	1,690	14
8. Private patronage	2,570	22	2,109	17	2,512	21
9. Joint and misc.			783	6		
	11,630	100	12,520	100	11,840	100*

* Decimal points have been eliminated and so percentage columns do not exactly total 100.

8. THE ROSEWORTH SURVEY

(The Rev. Trevor R. Beeson and others)

The Report discusses a house-to-house survey organised by Anglicans and Methodists in the Roseworth Estate, Stockton-on-Tees. Here are the details: first, of the simple inquiry form filled in by the canvasser on the doorstep and then of the results as they affect particularly the Church of England.

A. *The inquiry form:*

PARISH SURVEY

Road.. Number..
Name of Family..

	Church	Bapt.	Conf.	Attend
Mr				
Mrs				
Children over 15				
....				
....				
Children under 15				
....				
....				
....				

(Canvasser to add comments)

B. *Survey results:*

i. Declared religious denomination of 2,189 households:

(*a*)	Church of England	1,328
(*b*)	Roman Catholic	405
(*c*)	Free Church	294
(*d*)	Mixed Church of England/Roman Catholic	101
(*e*)	Mixed Church of England/Free Church	53
(*f*)	Jehovah's Witnesses or no professed belief	8

ii. Place of baptism of individuals

		No.	%
(*a*)	Church of England	5,312	65
(*b*)	Roman Catholic	1,800	22
(*c*)	Free Church	1,060	13
(*d*)	Unbaptised	18	—
		8,190	100

iii. Number of individuals who have been confirmed in the Church of England 731

iv. Number of active Church of England families i.e. where at least one member of the family (over 15) attends church fairly regularly (at least thirteen times a year) 142

v. Number of Church of England families in which at least one member of the family (over 15) attends occasionally 44

vi. Number of individual members of the Church of England (over 15) who attend church regularly 182

vii. Number of individual members of the Church of England who attend church occasionally 75

viii. Ages of those over 15 who attend church regularly or occasionally:

(*a*)	15–24 years of age	69
(*b*)	25–44 years of age	119
(*c*)	45–64 years of age	56
(*d*)	65 and over	13

ix. Number of children under the age of 15 who attend church or Sunday school 360

x. Number of individuals who attend church, but live outside the parish boundaries 14

xi. Occupations of the congregation

(*a*) Unskilled	71
(*b*) Semi-skilled	51
(*c*) Skilled	114
(*d*) Semi-professional	21
(*e*) Professional	Nil

xii. Number on the Church Electoral Roll 135

9. AN ACTUARIAL PREDICTION OF THE NUMBERS AND AGE STRUCTURE OF THE CLERGY IN THE CHURCH OF ENGLAND FOR 31ST DECEMBER 1966 AND 1971

(A Paper by Mr R. F. Neuss, DFC, FSS, Head of the Statistical Unit of the Central Board of Finance)

CLERGYMEN IN THE CHURCH OF ENGLAND

Three categories are covered by the prediction below. They are:

Category 1

Numbers of clergymen expected on the Central Statistical Register of the Clergy; comprising (*a*) all Anglican clergymen expected to be engaged in ecclesiastical work, or living in retirement in the dioceses of the Provinces of Canterbury and York, whether or not they were ordained in the forty-three English dioceses, and including (*b*) home clergymen who may be serving or residing abroad at the predicted dates.

Category 2

Numbers of clergymen expected on the register in the Provinces of Canterbury and York, comprising those defined in (*a*) above.

Category 3

Numbers of Anglican clergymen on the register expected to be engaged in full-time ecclesiastical work in the Provinces of Canterbury and York, whether or not they were ordained in the forty-three English dioceses.

PREDICTED TOTAL NUMBERS

Category	*31 Dec. 1966*	*31 Dec. 1971*
1	21,200	23,200
2	20,000	21,800
3	16,980	18,940

2. It must be emphasised that these forecasts have been based entirely on the assumption that throughout the period of the prediction there will be a continuance of the trends so far discernible from study of the actual statistics of:

(*a*) the numbers and age analyses of the clergy on the Central Statistical Register of the Clergy at 31st December 1961;

(*b*) analyses of ordinations from 1954 to 1962 inclusive;

(*c*) inward and outward migration;

(*d*) losses through death and retirement and other causes, as recorded for recent years by the Statistical Unit of the Central Board of Finance;

(*e*) the relationships of some of these statistics to the Registrar General's published figures for many years past of the numbers of males born in England and Wales, and to his projections of the total populations of the two countries up to the 30th June 2001.

3. That is to say, the work has proceeded quite objectively; bearing only on the evidence collected from well-established facts and the logical inferences deduced from the arrangements of the figures in accordance with the ordinary laws of mathematics and statistical practice. However, whenever an experience over recent years has disclosed a rising or falling trend it has been presumed that it is reasonable to provide for it to continue at the same rate. Of course, this is a matter of opinion, because there can be no certainty that the forces that have operated in the past will continue to influence the position in the same way in the future.

4. Even though the starting premises may be sound, the error of any prediction is very likely to increase in magnitude the farther one tries to forecast ahead of the original data. It is fairly certain that the estimated figures for the end of 1966 will not be found to be much at variance with the facts eventually to be obtained for that date; but it has to be appreciated that any major changes of policy (such as enlarging the recruitment of younger ordinands; the re-deployment of the ordained ministry at home and overseas; lowering the age of retirement, etc.) that may be implemented after the publication of this report, could prove the forecasts for the end of 1971 to be substantially understated. Indeed, it is to be hoped that this will be the case; for although the numbers of the clergy are now rising, the current rates of increase are still insufficient when considered in relation to the continuing expansion of the size of the population (see Table 55 and Diagram 7 on page 163) and are still less adequate if the ratio of population to clergy is to be reduced.

HOW THE PREDICTIONS WERE MADE

Stage 1. Estimation of Future Ordinations

The Basic Data

5. Statistics of the numbers of ordinations in the Provinces of Canterbury and York going back annually from 1961 to 1872 were published in Table 36 and Diagram XII on page 38 of *Facts and Figures about the Church of England 1962*. Those figures were compiled for each year from Advent to Michaelmas and there is no available analysis of them to show the ages at which the men were ordained as deacons. That table shows that the highest total of ordinations was 757 for the year 1886, and that since the end of the Second World War the numbers rose from 158 in 1946 to 626 in 1961.[1]

6. For the purpose of making an actuarial prediction of the likely numbers of the ordained ministry in the future, accurate details of the ages of all the clergy must be obtained, and from information provided by CACTM, or by the deacons themselves, the Statistical Unit has compiled the following table wherein the analysis is computed on a calendar-year basis.

Table 47. Age Structure of Deacons Ordained by the Church of England, 1954–1962

Extracted from the Central Statistical Register of the Clergy

Age groups	1954	1955	1956	1957	1958	1959	1960	1961	1962
(1)	(2)	(3)	(4)	(5)	(6)	(7)	(8)	(9)	(10)
Under 25	31	33	33	20	34	50	57	56	66
25–29	232	242	255	263	279	274	324	312	310
30–34	54	48	65	59	60	80	78	90	68
35–39	28	20	20	27	30	31	34	32	49
40–44	22	32	27	29	25	24	33	34	44
45–49	26	28	32	25	23	21	18	35	30
50–54	21	19	25	22	24	18	25	16	24
55–59	10	9	16	13	15	10	9	18	12
60–64	13	17	16	11	9	19	17	7	17
65–69	3	6	4	7	4	5	3	4	10
70–74	1	1	2	3	2	2	1	—	2
75 and over	—	—	—	1	—	—	—	—	—
Under 40 yrs.	345	343	373	369	403	435	493	490	493
40 yrs. and over	96	112	122	111	102	99	106	114	139
Totals	**441**	**455**	**495**	**480**	**505**	**534**	**599**	**604**	**632**
Average age	33	33½	34	34	33	33	32½	32½	33½

[1] For the years ended Michaelmas 1962 and 1963 the numbers of ordinations were 605 and 653 respectively (Table V, Statistical Section, *Church of England Year Book*, 1964).

7. Simple forecasts of the numbers of future ordinations may be computed for any age grouping from these figures without reference to any other factor than the straight line which best fits the data given for these nine years. Such a trend line was calculated by the method of least squares, the object of which is to determine the co-ordinates of a line which, when plotted on a graph, is positioned between the actual values observed during the period so that the vertical distance between each observation and the trend line will be a minimum. For example, taking the totals ordained at all ages under 70 years as items measured by the y axis and 1958 as the middle of the time scale, when $x = 0$, the equation of the trend line is:

y^t (the computed number of deacons aged 23–69) $= 525{\cdot}\dot{5} + 24{\cdot}6x$

and by substituting the number of years between 1958 and the year for which an estimate is required as the value of x in this equation, the following results are obtained:

Years	1963	1965	1967	1969	1971
x =	5	7	9	11	13
Estimated number of deacons aged 23–96	649	698	747	796	845

8. Of course, all these 'forecasts' are liable to errors, since they are merely points farther along the assumed trend line and, like the original data, it may be expected that sometimes the actual numbers of ordinations will be above the estimates while others will be below them. By somewhat tedious calculation it is possible to measure the probable range of the error for each prediction, but this is of little practical use, especially in this exercise where it is necessary to carry the predicted numbers for further calculations with other sets of figures towards the ultimate evaluation of the whole manpower estimates. On the average, the accumulation of such errors can be expected to be relatively small, because the tendency will be for one to cancel out another, provided that the overall trend between the interpolated figures and the extrapolated ones is constant, as has been assumed *ex hypothesi.*

9. The preceding two paragraphs have been included mainly for the purpose of introducing the use of the least squares method of fitting a trend line to a series of figures. The mathematics involved in the method may be found in any reputable statistical textbook and it is not therefore necessary to set out here the large volume of working calculations which led to the results now reported. It will

be observed from what follows that such figures obtained by the simple process in paragraph 7 were not in fact utilised, except to provide a rough check on the subsequent results which are given in Table 52. If the simple forecasts of paragraph 7 are compared with those in the last line of Table 52, it will be seen that the former are progressively larger than the latter which have been calculated by reference to an additional argument, that is, to a better degree of refinement. Nevertheless, the differences are not large, and the lesson is a good example in support of the popular adage 'one can prove anything with figures'!

10. There must be a large variety of factors which influence the numbers of men who are called for service in holy orders in the Church of England, and there are other forces that determine how many of each age will be ordained deacons in any one year. Although it is impossible to measure the strength of these forces individually, as we do not know what they all are, we may obtain indications of the resultants of the combined effect of them all. These indications, or index numbers, can be calculated by relating the numbers in each age group ordained in any one year to either (*a*) the total number of males in that age group in the population, or (*b*) the total number of males born in the same years as the ordinands; and expressing each result as a proportion of every million males born (or living in the case of (*a*)).

11. Although plan (*a*) has the advantage that the denominators consist of all living males of each age, it suffers from the complication that each population is affected by migration, and this makes accurate estimation of future populations very difficult. Since the predictions of ordinations would have to be made by applying appropriate index numbers to the corresponding estimated populations for future years, and would be affected by errors in the allowances for migration, this method has been rejected and plan (*b*) adopted. But there is also a snag attached to (*b*), because not all the boys born will be alive when their compatriots of the same epoch become clergymen of the Church of England. However, since the rates of mortality for each age group are only slightly declining, this factor will not have much effect on what may be termed 'the ordination extraction rates per million of the male generative populations of England and Wales'.

12. In Table 48, therefore, these rates in respect of the years of ordination 1954 to 1962 have been set down, but in order to save space separate tabulation has not been given of all the individual totals of the five years' male births from which the rates were

computed by reference to the numbers of ordinations in the appropriate age groups for these nine years which are in Table 47. Table 51, however, begins with these totals for the ordination year 1962, and from these the following examples show how the rates were obtained for Table 48 on p. 294.

Ex. 1. From Table 47, in 1962 there were 310 deacons ordained ages 25 to 29. These were born in the years 1933 to 1937. From the Registrar General's Statistical Reviews the numbers of male births in England and Wales were:

1933	296,729
1934	306,874
1935	307,552
1936	310,605
1937	313,618
Total	1,535,378 or 1,535 thousand for col. 3 of Table 51.

Therefore, the 1962 ordination extraction rate per million males born in England and Wales twenty-five to twenty-nine years before is:

$310 \div 1{\cdot}535378 = 201{\cdot}90$ for col. 3 of Table 48.

Ex. 2. From Table 47, in 1962 there were 630 deacons ordained ages 23 to 69 inclusive. These were born in the years 1893 to 1939. The sum of the numbers of male births for these 47 years is 19,057,789. Therefore the 1962 ordination extraction rate per million males born in England and Wales twenty-three to sixty-nine years before is:

$630 \div 19{\cdot}057789 = 33{\cdot}06$ for col. 14 of Table 48.

Comments on Table 48

13. Four encouraging facts emerged during the computation of the rates for Table 48:

(i) Over the nine years 1954/62 the ordination extraction rates per million of the generative male populations *increased for all age groups;* the largest increases being in the age groups 23 to 25, and 40 to 44, where for both groups the rates for 1962 were more than double those for 1954.

(ii) The highest rate in *every* ordination year occurred in the 25 to 29 age group.

(iii) Whereas the rates for all ages between 23 and 44 have generally increased from year to year, the rates for ages over 45 have fluctuated above and below the rates for the middle year (1958) of the period of observations.

(iv) The general rise in the rates for all age groups has been achieved despite the fact that during the period the total numbers of appropriate generative male populations have been contracting. This is evident from Table 49, which shows that there were over 20 million

Table 48. Numbers of Clergymen ordained by the Church of England in the years 1954 to 1962 per million males born in England and Wales in the same years as those who entered each age group of the English diaconate

Evaluated from the Central Statistical Register of the Clergy, and from the Registrar General's Statistical Reviews

Years of ordination	Proportions of every million males born in England and Wales who were ordained as deacons in the following age groups:—												
	Under 25	25–29	30–34	35–39	All under 40	40–44	45–49	50–54	55–59	60–64	65–69	40–69	All under 70
(1)	(2)	(3)	(4)	(5)	(6)	(7)	(8)	(9)	(10)	(11)	(12)	(13)	(14)
1954	47·33	135·12	25·89	15·10	**54·66**	9·79	11·01	8·80	4·27	5·69	1·32	**6·84**	**21·78**
1955	51·73	143·61	24·51	10·36	**55·22**	14·51	11·93	7·95	3·83	7·36	2·66	**8·01**	**22·63**
1956	54·00	154·12	34·62	10·19	**61·09**	12·51	13·80	10·45	6·79	6·93	1·77	**8·70**	**24·77**
1957	33·13	160·84	32·57	13·36	**60·78**	14·11	10·89	9·24	5·49	4·74	3·09	**7·82**	**24·10**
1958	55·34	174·95	34·06	14·50	**66·73**	12·85	10·15	10·10	6·30	3·87	1·75	**7·37**	**25·64**
1959	80·89	174·19	46·59	14·86	**72·57**	12·94	9·34	7·62	4·19	8·10	2·19	**7·20**	**27·32**
1960	91·31	209·15	46·29	17·36	**84·76**	17·10	8·16	10·65	3·77	7·24	1·30	**7·76**	**30·91**
1961	88·61	203·10	54·40	17·04	**85·96**	17·32	16·21	6·90	7·52	2·97	1·73	**8·45**	**31·46**
1962	104·10	201·90	41·59	27·05	**87·78**	21·77	14·60	10·45	5·04	7·18	4·31	**10·19**	**33·06**

Table 49. Males born in England and Wales

Nine 47-year periods

Periods	Totals
(1)	(2)
1885 to 1931	20,202,635
1886 to 1932	20,063,233
1887 to 1933	19,899,492
1888 to 1934	19,754,763
1889 to 1935	19,615,143
1890 to 1936	19,474,530
1891 to 1937	19,346,078
1892 to 1938	19,198,805
1893 to 1939	19,057,789

Table 50. Predicted index numbers of ordinations by the Church of England per million males born in England and Wales in the same years as the deacons to be ordained in the years 1963 to 1971, in age groups

Calculated on the assumption that the trends observed from 1954 to 1962 will continue at the same rates of increase

Age groups in the years of ordination	Values of the trend lines that best fit the observed 'ordination extraction rates' 1954 to 1962, *vide* Table 48		Predicted index numbers of ordinations per million males born in England and Wales, as classified in Table 51								
	Trend value for 1958 when x = 0	Annual trend increment	Calculated values of the equations of the least squares trend lines ($y^t = a + bx$) when the value of x for the following years is:								
			x = 5	6	7	8	9	10	11	12	13
	a	b	1963	1964	1965	1966	1967	1968	1969	1970	1971
(1)	(2)	(3)	(4)	(5)	(6)	(7)	(8)	(9)	(10)	(11)	(12)
23 & 24	67·3817	7·6684	105·72	113·39	121·06	128·73	136·40	144·06	151·73	159·40	167·07
25–29	174·6929*	9·4836*	215·70	222·36	228·51	234·14	239·27	243·87	247·97	251·55	254·62
30–34	37·8349	3·1633	53·65	56·81	59·98	63·14	66·30	69·47	72·63	75·79	78·96
35–39	15·5373	1·3945	22·51	23·90	25·30	26·69	28·09	29·48	30·87	32·27	33·66
40–44	14·7682	1·0735	20·14	21·21	22·28	23·36	24·43	25·50	26·58	27·65	28·72
45–49	11·7876	0·2399	12·99	13·23	13·47	13·71	13·95	14·19	14·43	14·67	14·91
50–54	9·1284	0·0377	9·32	9·35	9·39	9·43	9·47	9·51	9·54	9·58	9·62
55–59	5·2451	0·1135	5·81	5·93	6·04	6·15	6·27	6·38	6·49	6·61	6·72
60–64	6·0091	−0·0536	5·74	5·69	5·63	5·58	5·53	5·47	5·42	5·37	5·31
65–69	2·2370	0·1214	2·84								
23–39	69·9507	4·7305	93·60	98·33	103·06	107·79	112·53	117·26	121·99	126·72	131·45
40–69	8·0368	0·2035	9·05	9·26	9·46	9·66	9·87	10·07	10·27	10·48	10·68
23–69	26·8519	1·4517	34·11	35·56	37·01	38·47	39·92	41·37	42·82	44·27	45·72

*With the exception of the age group 25–29 years it has been assumed that a straight line provides the best estimate of the probable trend of the rates over the period of the prediction. But it appears that a curved line is more representative of the observed rates for the age group 25–29. Accordingly, a parabolic line was used in order to obtain the figures for this group in columns 4 to 12 above; the equation of this line being $y^t = a + bx + cx^2$, the value of $c = -0{\cdot}2565$. (y^t being the calculated rate which corresponds with an observed rate y.)

Table 51. Total numbers of males born in England and Wales, 1893–1951 classified to show the sizes of the generative populations that will yield candidates by age groups for ordination as deacons by the Church of England from 1962 to 1974

Figures in thousands, extracted and totalled from the Registrar General's Statistical Reviews

Years	Total numbers of males born in England and Wales, the survivors of whom will be within the following age groups respecting the years of columns 1 and 16, and from whom the Church of England may expect to ordain deacons from 1962 to 1974													Years of birth	Years	x
	23 & 24	25–29	30–34	35–39	23–39	40–44	45–49	50–54	55–59	60–64	65–69	40–69	23–69			
(1)	(2)	(3)	(4)	(5)	(6)	(7)	(8)	(9)	(10)	(11)	(12)	(13)	(14)	(15)	(16)	(17)
1962	634	1,535	1,635	1,812	**5,616**	2,021	2,055	2,296	2,381	2,366	2,322	**13,442**	**19,058**	1893 to 1939	1962	4
1963	628	1,557	1,595	1,762	**5,541**	2,069	1,945	2,267	2,377	2,380	2,326	**13,363**	**18,904**	1894 to 1940	1963	5
1964	609	1,566	1,573	1,717	**5,465**	2,086	1,854	2,248	2,362	2,388	2,346	**13,283**	**18,748**	1895 to 1941	1964	6
1965	633	1,570	1,549	1,685	**5,437**	1,958	1,930	2,205	2,347	2,390	2,348	**13,178**	**18,615**	1896 to 1942	1965	7
1966	689	1,557	1,536	1,654	**5,436**	1,877	1,963	2,159	2,319	2,393	2,356	**13,066**	**18,502**	1897 to 1943	1966	8
1967	740	1,579	1,535	1,635	**5,490**	1,812	2,021	2,055	2,296	2,381	2,366	**12,931**	**18,421**	1898 to 1944	1967	9
1968	738	1,613	1,557	1,595	**5,503**	1,762	2,069	1,945	2,267	2,377	2,380	**12,799**	**18,302**	1899 to 1945	1968	10
1969	772	1,685	1,566	1,573	**5,596**	1,717	2,086	1,854	2,248	2,362	2,388	**12,655**	**18,251**	1900 to 1946	1969	11
1970	876	1,723	1,570	1,549	**5,719**	1,685	1,958	1,930	2,205	2,347	2,390	**12,515**	**18,233**	1901 to 1947	1970	12
1971	853	1,849	1,557	1,536	**5,794**	1,654	1,877	1,963	2,159	2,319	2,393	**12,365**	**18,159**	1902 to 1948	1971	13
1972	775	1,966	1,579	1,535	**5,856**	1,635	1,812	2,021	2,055	2,296	2,381	**12,200**	**18,056**	1903 to 1949	1972	14
1973	735	2,013	1,613	1,557	**5,918**	1,595	1,762	2,069	1,945	2,267	2,377	**12,014**	**17,932**	1904 to 1950	1973	15
1974	707	2,001	1,685	1,566	**5,959**	1,573	1,717	2,086	1,854	2,248	2,362	**11,840**	**17,799**	1905 to 1951	1974	16

Note. As all the figures have been given to the nearest 1,000 births some of the totals may not exactly tally with the sums of the entries in the lines of the table.

males born twenty-three to sixty-nine years before 1954, from which source deacons could be ordained at ages under 70 years. Whereas the corresponding source for the 1962 ordinations was reduced to just over 19 million.

It should be noted that by 1974 the corresponding total of males born twenty-three to sixty-nine years before that year will have decreased to just over 17¾ million (see col. 14 of Table 51).

14. After observing the actual rates experienced from 1954 to 1962, the next step was the calculation of the trend lines for each age group, and this was performed by the method of least squares as briefly described in paragraphs 7 to 9. The values thus obtained for a and b in the equation $y^{t} = a + bx$ are given in cols. 2 and 3 of Table 50. Subsequently, by substituting the appropriate value of x in each equation the extrapolated or predicted rates for each age group were obtained in respect of each year from 1963 to 1971; these have been tabulated in cols. 4 to 12 of Table 50 above.

15. In section (iv) paragraph 13 it is pointed out that the *total* numbers of the generative populations have been getting smaller and will continue to do so throughout the period of these forecasts. It will be noticed, however, from Table 51, that for the youngest age groups (cols. 2 to 4) there will be *an expansion* in the sizes of the numbers that will yield candidates for ordination. This is a most encouraging feature, because the expectancy is that, *providing the Church of England maintains its efforts to attract and train candidates for the ministry*, greater numbers of young men will become clergymen. This will be the main factor which will lead to a reduction in the overall average age of the active ministry, and thus enable its total strength to be enlarged more rapidly over the years ahead by reason of the longer periods of individual expectation of service in holy orders.

16. The basic information assembled in Tables 50 and 51 provides the means whereby predictions may be made for each age group of the most probable numbers of deacons to be ordained by the Church of England during the next decade, assuming that the trends observed over the previous nine years will continue. Thus, to estimate for a required age group, take the appropriate four-figure number given in Table 51 for the ordination year and, treating the comma in it as the decimal point, multiply those figures by the corresponding index number from Table 50. For example, the likely number of ordinations ages 25 to 29 in 1964 is $1{\cdot}566 \times 222{\cdot}36 = 348$ approximately. In paragraph 8 attention was drawn to the range of uncertainty inherent in each computed estimate, but it was suggested that generally the

total of the accumulated errors can be expected to be small, because some of the estimates will be above the true numbers and others will be below them. In arriving at the final totals of new ordinations, given in Table 52, the computed numbers for each individual age group down to the smaller total of the numbers computed for either (*a*) the sum of the large composite age group, *i.e.* (23 to 39) + (40 to 69) or (*b*) the entire age range (23 to 69) have been proportionately reduced. By thus cautiously restricting the forecasts to the lowest of the aggregate predictions each year, it is hoped that they may prove to have been conservatively estimated, but not greatly below the true results.

Table 52. Predicted numbers of ordinations by the Church of England, 1963–1971

Age groups	1963	1964	1965	1966	1967	1968	1969	1970	1971
(1)	(2)	(3)	(4)	(5)	(6)	(7)	(8)	(9)	(10)
23–39	519	537	560	586	607	631	654	677	699
40–69	122	124	125	126	128	129	130	131	131
All ages	642	662	686	713	737	761	785	809	831

Notes: 1. These numbers have been calculated by the application of the predicted ordination extraction rates given in Table 50 to each million of the relevant generative male populations of England and Wales which are given in Table 51.

2. An arbitrary one or two have been included in the totals of all ages for ordinands over 70 years of age.

Stage 2. Allowances for Migration

17. For each of the nine years under consideration in connexion with the forecasting of the total numbers of the clergy at the end of 1966 and 1971, the annual intakes from new ordinations are bound to be supplemented by other numbers of clergymen who come from abroad (Scotland and Wales, as well as countries overseas) to join the full-time ordained manpower of the Church of England. We may also expect others to return home, either to rejoin the active ministry or to reside in retirement within the dioceses of the provinces of Canterbury and York; and some, who are able to do so, will continue to exercise their orders as part-time priests and occasional preachers.

18. On the other hand, every year there will occur losses from the full-time establishment for the English provinces, on account of clergymen leaving for service abroad in other dioceses and provinces of the Anglican Communion. Some of these will be our own ordained men departing overseas for periods of missionary work, and others will be clergymen ordained abroad who resign their present eccle-

siastical appointments in our provinces, in order to return to their original dioceses, or to take up pastoral work elsewhere. According to past experience, a small allowance also has to be included for a few losses from the Church's active ministry for some who relinquish their orders, or resign their ecclesiastical posts upon returning to secular employment, or whose services are lost to the Church of England through causes other than death or retirement.

19. While searching through the customary analyses which the Statistical Unit has made every year since the Central Statistical Register of the Clergy was created, it was found that it is not yet possible to determine precisely the complete picture as regards inward and outward migration. However, it is hoped to improve this aspect of the records in due course. For this study, therefore, it has been necessary to rely largely on the migration figures from the analyses made of the register for the three years 1960 to 1962. Consequently, for the calculation of the projections of the full-time ordained ministry in the provinces of Canterbury and York, in addition to the predicted annual numbers of ordinations, average numbers for certain age groups have been carried forward for each year; and this allowance represents a constant intake of eighty-six immigrating clergymen per annum; the averages from the 1960-62 experiences being:

	Age groups									
	25 to 29	30 to 34	35 to 39	40 to 44	45 to 49	50 to 54	55 to 59	60 to 64	65 to 69	Totals
Numbers of clergy ordained abroad joining full-time ministry of the provinces of Canterbury and York	—	4	6	10	12	9	7	3	—	51
Numbers of Canterbury and York ordained clergy returning home to rejoin full-time ministry of the provinces of Canterbury and York	1	3	5	7	6	5	4	3	1	35
										86 p. a.

20. Likewise, on the basis of the analyses for 1960 to 1962, a constant deduction was made for each year 1962 to 1971 to represent the numbers of emigrating clergymen who will probably leave the full-time ministry of the provinces of Canterbury and York, including seven or eight per annum who depart through causes other than death or retirement; the average deductions being:

	Age groups										
	Under 25	25 to 29	30 to 34	35 to 39	40 to 44	45 to 49	50 to 54	55 to 59	60 to 64	65 to 69	Total
Numbers of clergy emigrating from the full-time ministry of the provinces of Canterbury and York	1	14	26	14	12	15	12	7	5	1	**107 p. a.**

Stage 3. Retirement, and Mortality before Retirement

21. The largest causes of wastage from the numerical strength of the active ministry of the provinces of Canterbury and York are the deaths and retirements of clergymen from their full-time ecclesiastical work; this is shown by the statistics for the past six years:

	1957	1958	1959	1960	1961	1962
Numbers of clergymen who died before retirement from the full-time ministry	146	160	114	139	122	141
Numbers of clergymen who retired from the full-time ministry	339	431	383	317	289	310

22. The calculation of the 1966 and 1971 predictions for the total numbers expected in the full-time ordained manpower of the provinces of Canterbury and York (category 3) was made by a different procedure from that used for the predictions of the total numbers of clergymen in categories 1 and 2 (defined in the first paragraph). In order to compute the numbers of probable survivors on the full-time strength of the two home provinces at the ends of those years, an 'all-in' wastage rate was computed for each quinary age group. This was done by taking the averages for the three years 1960–62 of the total wastage from the full-time strength, i.e., deaths before retirement, retirements, departures abroad, losses from other causes; and relating each average to the actual numbers of full-time clergymen enumerated in the relevant age groups at 31st December 1961.

23. From these rates, probabilities were calculated of the numbers out of 10,000 starting at age 23 expected to be remaining on the full-time strength at the middle age of each subsequent quinary group. Finally, by the application of these probabilities to the numbers on the full-time register at the end of 1961, and to each of the predicted intakes of new ordinations plus the constant eighty-six

immigrants for the years 1962 to 1971 inclusive, the ultimate grand total numbers of clergymen expected in category 3 were obtained for the 31st December, 1966 and 1971. These totals are given in col. 2 of Table 55 and are illustrated in Diagram 1 on p. 94 of the report.

24. The summations of the total intakes and the total losses forecasted in respect of the full-time ordained manpower of the provinces of Canterbury and York amounted to:

Predictions

	Between 31 Dec. 1961 and 31 Dec. 1966	Average p.a.	Between 31 Dec. 1966 and 31 Dec. 1971	Average p.a.
Total intakes	3,765	753	4,353	871
Total wastages	2,273	455	2,393	479
Differences = net gains to the full-time strength	1,492	298	1,960	392

Stage 4. The Total Mortality of the Clergy

25. The work involved in the production of predicted total numbers of the clergy in the other two categories, 1 and 2, is not affected by the retirement statistics because no attempt was made to separate the estimated numbers into working or retired. Such a division would be of no value, for at present there is no compulsory age of retirement for the clergy. In any case, there is no indication that when a clergyman resigns a full-time post he does not intend to undertake further ecclesiastical work, and so it is very difficult to discover when he decides fully to retire. The question that mainly arises, therefore, concerning these total predictions, is how to estimate the total numbers of deaths; and the forecasts, consequently, are not concerned with whether the deaths occur before or after retirement.

26. It was necessary, therefore, to determine the rates of clergy mortality. These were produced by relating the average numbers of deaths of all clergymen, recorded by the Statistical Unit for the years 1960 to 1962, to the total numbers living on 31st December 1961, as enumerated by the analyses of the Central Statistical Register of the Clergy. From this data the following abridged life table was eventually compiled, and here we are indebted to the Government Actuary for his Report on Life Tables, 13th September 1956, published in the Registrar General's Decennial Supplement,

England and Wales, 1951. This is a most useful guide to the best method of constructing a life table.

Table 53. Abridged Life Table, 1960–62, Church of England Clergy

Age x	l_x	Years $\mathring{e}_x$
23	10,000	51·0
25	9,992	49·1
30	9,967	44·3
35	9,937	39·4
40	9,901	34·6
45	9,829	29·7
50	9,684	25·2
55	9,451	20·7
60	8,957	16·8
65	8,035	13·3
70	6,683	10·5
75	5,096	7·9
80	3,118	6·4
85	1,767	4·6
90	670	3·3
95	154	2·7
100	23	2·4

Notes

1. This abridged life table is based on the total number of clergymen enumerated at 31st December, 1961 from the Central Statistical Register of the Clergy, and the average numbers of deaths that occurred during 1960, 1961 and 1962.
2. The column 'l_x' shows the number of clergymen in the Church of England who probably would survive to the exact age x out of 10,000 commencing at age 23 who were subject throughout their lives to the mortality rates observed 1960–62.
3. The colume '$\mathring{e}_x$' shows the 'expectation of life', i.e., the average after lifetime of a clergyman at age x, assuming that he is subject to the same rates of mortality.

Stage 5. The Predictions for Categories 1 and 2

27. In addition to the predicted numbers of new ordinations, a constant net allowance of forty-one clergymen was included in the estimates for categories 1 and 2; these represent the average annual net gains expected as changes to the total numbers on the register each year that will no doubt occur through inward and outward movements of the clergy. This allowance was estimated as follows:

Number of clergymen ordained abroad expected to enter the provinces of Canterbury and York	51	
Number of clergymen originally ordained by the Church of England and believed to be alive, but not yet traced and not included on the register at 31st December 1961	25	
		76
Deduct:		
Number of clergymen ordained abroad at present on the register, working or residing in the provinces of Canterbury and York, but expected to leave the home area ..	28	
Number of clergymen expected to be removed from the register through causes other than death, migration or retirement	7	35
Net estimated annual addition to the register		41

28. By the application of the probabilities of the numbers expected to survive to subsequent quinary age groups (given in Table 53) to the total numbers of clergymen living at 31st December 1961, and to each of the predicted numbers of new ordinations plus the constant forty-one net additions to the register for the years 1962 to 1971, the grand total numbers of clergymen expected on the register by the 31st December, 1966 and 1971 were obtained.

29. The summations of the total intakes and the total wastages thus forecasted in respect of the total numbers of clergymen to be accounted for in the Central Statistical Register of the Clergy in the Church of England, category 1, amounted to:

Predictions

	Between 31 Dec. 1961 and 31 Dec. 1966	Average p.a.	Between 31 Dec. 1966 and 31 Dec. 1971	Average p.a.
Total intakes	3,540	708	4,128	826
Total wastages	2,176	435	2,128	426
Net gains	1,364	273	2,000	400

The accumulated total number on the register is therefore predicted to increase from 19,836 at 31st December 1961
to 21,200 at 31st December 1966
to 23,200 at 31st December 1971.

In the 1961 enumeration the total includes 3,962 of 70 years and over.
In the 1966 estimate the total includes 3,500 of 70 years and over.
In the 1971 estimate the total includes 3,150 of 70 years and over.

These figures are illustrated in Diagram 1 on page 94 of the report.

30. The estimates for the remaining pair of predictions, namely, those in respect of the likely numbers of the clergy expected to be within the provinces of Canterbury and York, category 2, were produced on the assumption that the present numerical relationships between the totals of categories 1 and 2 will not materially change.

31. It is observed that:

(i) of the grand total of 18,969 clergymen registered at 31st December 1959, category 1, there were 18,148 resident in the two provinces, category 2, that is 94·67 per cent of the grand total;

(ii) of the grand total of 19,836 clergymen registered at 31st December 1961, category 1, there were 18,749 resident in the two provinces, category 2, that is 94·52 per cent of the grand total.

Table 54. Clergymen in the Church of England, 1901–71

Provinces of Canterbury and York

Years	Total nos. of clergymen in the two provinces	Age Groups					
		22 to 34	35 to 44	45 to 54	55 to 64	65 to 74	75 and over
(1)	(2)	(3)	(4)	(5)	(6)	(7)	(8)
1901	23,670	4,789	5,896	4,946	3,889	2,761	1,389
1921	22,579	2,417	4,396	5,408	5,422	3,221	1,715
1951	18,196	1,768	4,252	3,141	3,505	3,396	2,134
1961	18,749	2,865	2,758	4,722	3,357	2,802	2,245
1966	*20,000	3,480	3,280	4,040	4,600	2,320	2,280
1971	*21,800	4,380	4,080	3,490	5,010	2,900	1,940

Table 54a

Years	Total nos. of clergymen in the two provinces	Proportions per 100 in Age Groups					
		22 to 34	35 to 44	45 to 54	55 to 64	65 to 74	75 and over
(1)	(2)	(3)	(4)	(5)	(6)	(7)	(8)
1901	23,670	20·23	24·91	20·90	16·43	11·66	5·87
1921	22,579	10·70	19·47	23·95	24·01	14·27	7·60
1951	18,196	9·71	23·37	17·27	19·26	18·66	11·73
1961	18,749	15·28	14·71	25·19	17·90	14·95	11·97
1966	*20,000	17·40	16·40	20·20	23·00	11·60	11·40
1971	*21,800	20·09	18·72	16·01	22·98	13·30	8·90

Table 54b

Years	Populations in the two provinces	Total nos. of clergymen in the two provinces	Approx. average ages	Average nos. of persons to one clergyman in the Church of England	Total nos. of clergymen over the age of 65	Total nos. of clergymen below the age of 65	Average nos. of persons to one clergyman below the age of 65
(1)	(2)	(3)	(4)	(5)	(6)	(7)	(8)
1901	30,654,239	23,670	49	1,295	4,150	19,520	1,570
1921	35,389,993	22,579	53	1,567	4,936	17,643	2,006
1951	41,329,643	18,196	55	2,271	5,530	12,666	3,263
1961	43,624,275	18,749	54	2,327	5,047	13,702	3,184
1966	45,389,000	*20,000	53	2,269	4,600	15,400	2,947
1971	47,053,000	*21,800	51	2,158	4,840	16,960	2,774

*Predicted figures (August, 1963) see Note 3 below.

Notes. 1. The statistics on the first three lines of each table above are taken from Table 17 of *Facts and Figures about the Church of England, 1962*, but they originated from the censuses of England and Wales, and so they represent the numbers of persons resident in the two provinces at the dates when the censuses were taken, who described themselves as clergymen of the Church of England. (The said Table 17 gives the comparable statistics for each decade before 1901 back to 1851.)

2. The figures for the year 1961 have been obtained from the analysis of the Central Statistical Register of the Clergy at the 31st December, 1961.

3. All figures for the years 1966 and1971 have been predicted by the Statistical Unit of the Central Board of Finance, actuarially by reference to:
(a) the clergy mortality rates 1960–62; (b) the rising trends of the numbers of ordinations in age groups per million males born in England and Wales;
(c) by the addition of notional rates of annual intakes of clergymen ordained in other provinces and dioceses of the Anglican Communion;
(d) plus estimates of the numbers of clergymen returning home after serving or residing abroad;
(e) minus allowances for departures abroad and losses through other causes.
The estimates for (c), (d) and (e) were made on the assumption that the rates experienced during the three years prior to 1963 are likely to continue throughout the period of the prediction.

4. Column 2 of Table 54b: the first four statistics are the populations enumerated at the censuses for the ecclesiastical area of the provinces of Canterbury and York; for 1966 and 1971 the home populations of the two provinces have been estimated, as at the 31st December, by the Statistical Unit from the projections of the total populations of England and Wales prepared by the Government Actuary's Department, published in Appendix E of the Registrar General's Quarterly Return No. 456.

But the percentage has probably reduced slightly, because during the two years larger numbers have been added to the register of clergymen living abroad who have only recently been traced. (There are, no doubt, others yet to be located; this explains the allowance made for them in paragraph 27.) Consequently it has been presumed that 94·34 per cent of the 1966 estimate of 21,200 for category 1 will be in category 2, that is 20,000; and that 93·97 per cent of the 1971 estimate of 23,200 for category 1 will be in category 2, amounting, in round figures, to 21,800.

Stage 6. Comparison with Other Information

32. Having reached these figures for the Provinces of Canterbury and York, it would be interesting to compare the forecasts with the facts for some years past. Accordingly, the three tables on the previous page, and Diagram 2 on page 95, have been prepared. These speak for themselves, so no comment is necessary.

33. Finally, it has been necessary to make certain adjustments to the Government Actuary's estimates of the future populations of England and Wales, in order to extend the estimates of the Church of England's populations to the year 2001. These figures appear in Table 55 and this statistical exercise is concluded by illustrating in Diagram 7 on p. 163 the very great need of the Church of England for a continuing enlargement of the full-time ordained ministry in order that in the years ahead the proportion of clergymen to the population may be substantially increased.

Table 55. Total Numbers of Full-time Clergymen Required in Relation to the Increasing Population of the Provinces of Canterbury and York, 1961–2001

According to the predicted average no. of persons to one full-time clergyman at 31st Dec.:				Pre-computed numbers of clergymen that would be required for the full-time ordained ministry, in order to maintain the full-time clergyman to people ratio in England at an average of:		
Years	Total nos. of the full-time clergy	Estimated home populations of the two provinces	Average nos. of persons to one full-time clergyman	1 : 2,500	1 : 2,000	1 : 1,500
(1)	(2)	(3)	(4)	(5)	(6)	(7)
1961	15,488	43,952,000	**2,838**	17,581	21,976	29,301
1966	16,980	45,389,000	**2,673**	18,156	22,695	30,259
1971	18,940	47,053,000	**2,484**	18,821	23,527	31,369
1976		48,706,000		19,482	24,353	32,471
1981		50,385,000		20,154	25,193	33,590
1986		52,746,000		21,098	26,373	35,164
1991		54,402,000		21,761	27,201	36,268
1996		57,309,000		22,924	28,655	38,206
2001		59,358,000		23,743	29,679	39,572

Notes. 1. Column 2: The total numbers of the full-time clergy at the 31st December, 1966 and 1971 are predictions.
2. Column 3: The estimates of the home population of the Provinces of Canterbury and York at the 31st December of each quintan year were calculated from the mid-yearly projections of the total populations of England and Wales prepared by the Government Actuary's Department, published in Appendix E of the Registrar General's Quarterly Return No. 456.
3. See Diagram 7 on p. 163.

APPENDICES

APPENDIX 1. ANALYSIS OF Q4 (INCUMBENTS)

(a) CANTERBURY PROVINCE—DIOCESAN SCALES FOR INCUMBENT STIPENDS

Stipends				Family allowances		Stipends	
Diocese (1)	Minimum (2)	Easter offerings (3)	House (4)	(5) (6) (7) (8)*	Other allowances (9)	Actual lowest (10)	Actual highest (11)
1	£800			£20 per child if near minimum (inc. with £800 and three children gets £60 or £820, £40)		£800	£2,000
2	£804	Excluded	Free of RD	£36, £24, £24, during full-time educ.	Up to £100 outside earnings	£804	£2,300
3	£750	Excluded		£30, £10, £10, until 21 if no other income	Special benefice grants to poor parishes	£795	£1,500
4	£800	Excluded	Free of RD	None	First £100 chaplaincies or other earnings, 50 per cent after. Differentials	£800	£1,500
5	£950	Excluded	Free of RD	£35 per child until end of university or training (no means test)	Extra £50 stipend for two churches	£950	£2,272
6	£850	Excluded	Free of RD	£20 first child only	First £75 of chapl. fees. Any PCC contributions, cemetery fees	£850	£1,388
7	£775			None		£775	£2,400
8	£825	Excluded	Free of RD	None	First £100 of all fees	£650 (L/D)	£3,500
9	£870			£40, £30, £20, until leave school		£720	£3,188
10	£800		Free of RD if PCC pays	None yet, but one coming	Extra £100 for UB or PL	£700 (L/D)	£1,220
11	£860	Excluded		£40 per family until youngest is 16	All PCC payments excluded Chaplaincy excluded	£860	£2,653
12	£800		Free of RD	£35, £15, £15		£800	£1,350
13	£900	Excluded	Free of RD	£10 each child at Christmas	Chaplaincy incomes, etc., Extra for 2 churches £50, for three, £100, etc., up to £500	£900	£3,600
14	£925		Free of RD if PCC pays	£25, £25, £25, up to 18 for children of all clergy	Extra £100 for UBs and PLs. Additional benefice income excluded to £500	£925	£1,600
15	£800	Included	No answer	None	Differentials	£800	£985
16	£790	No answer	No answer	£12, £12, £12, to leaving school	No answer	£790	£1,817
17	£825	No answer	Free of RD	£20, £20, £20, to 18 if still at school	Extra £25 for mission churches and £75 for plurality. PCC grants excluded	£825	£3,155
18	None	Excluded up to £100	Free of RD if PCC pays	£20, £20, £20, to 18	Points differentials	£736	£1,500
19	£800	Excluded	Free of RD	£40 for each child under 5. £60 for each child over 5 in full-time educ.	Parish contributions up to £100 expenses excluded	£800	£1,279
20	£800	Excluded	Free of RD if PCC pays	None	Plus £50 for UBs, etc. First £50 of chaplaincy, etc., fees excluded, PCC grants totally, additional benefice income. First £50 from educ. appoint.	£400 (L/D)	£4,702
21	£800	Excluded	No answer	£20 for each child to 19 where income does not exceed minimum	Extra £50 of £75 for differentials. Fees excluded	£800	£2,130
22	None	Excluded	Free if PCC pays	None	Educ. earnings	£900	£1,592
23	£850	Included	No answer	None	PCC expenses of office excluded	£900	£2,100
24	£875	Excluded	Free of RD	None	Extra £100 for UBs, PLs Chapl. excluded	£875	£1,900
25	£825	Excluded	Free if PCC pays	£10 rising to £20 at 8–11, £35 at 12–18 (means test)	Extra £75 for UBs, PLs Contributions made by parish excluded, new benefice income excluded	£825	£1,346
26	£750	Excluded	Free of RD	£20, £20, £20 each child to 18	Extra £60 two or more churches. First £100 fees, all lets, PCC grants excluded	£750	£1,958
27	£800	Excluded	No answer	None	No answer	£800	£1,500
28	£820	No answer	Free of RD	£20 each child under 16 or being educated	Extra £100 for UBs, PLs	£820	£1,000
29	£800	Excluded	Free of RD	£10 each child under tax relief	Extra £50 for UBs, PLs All non-ben. income	£800	£1,600

(b) *YORK PROVINCE—DIOCESAN SCALES FOR INCUMBENT STIPENDS*

Stipends				Family allowances		Stipends	
Diocese (1)	Minimum (2)	Easter offerings (3)	House (4)	(5) (6) (7) (8)*	Other allowances (9)	Actual lowest (10)	Actual highest (11)
30	£830	No answer	No answer	£30 per child towards fees	Four differential grades £830–£880–£905–£930	£830	£1,500
31	£850	No answer	No answer	None		£850	£2,008
32	£825	Excluded		£20, £15, £15 up to 18		£825	£1,650
33	£900	No answer	93 out of 132 PCCs pay full RD, all pay some	None	Extra £50 for over 5,000 population or 10,000 acres; UBs, PLs, 10 big benefices £1,000	£900	£1,300
34	—	No answer	No answer	No answer	No answer	—	—
35	£820	No answer	Free if PCCs pay RD	£36 per child 9–18	Extra £250 UBs, PLs (if PCCs pay RD), PCC expenses excluded, Chapl. excluded, long service awards extra. Differentials	£820	£2,244
36	£870	No answer	No answer	£50 per child 7–18	No answer	£870	£2,847
37	£850	Up to first £50 excluded	No answer	None	First £50 chapl. fees, first £50 expenses of office, all cemetery fees. UBs, etc., extra £100	£850	£2,300
38	£850	No answer	No answer	£25 per child while educated from 5 years	No answer	£850	£2,667
39	£780	Excluded	No answer	None	Extra £70 UBs, PLs. Practically all non-endowment income ignored	£650 (L/D)	£1,634
40	£800	Excluded	Free if PCC pays	£40, £24, £24 to end of school	No answer	£800	£1,693
41	£825	No answer	No answer	£25, £20, £15	No answer	£855	£1,195
42	£800	Excluded	Free if PCC pays RD	None	Extra £100 for special parish if PCC pays half. All PCC grants, chapl. excluded	£830	£1,950
43	£850	No answer	No answer	None	No answer	£850	£2,300

* 5, 6, 7 and 8 are a summary of sections numbered in this way in a larger unpublished abstract.

ABBREVIATIONS

RD = rates and dilapidations

UB = united benefice

PL = plurality

L/D = light-duty

Note. These tables should not be taken as a guide to prevailing stipends and allowances but rather as evidence of the complexities of the stipendiary system. The rates and conditions are those reported in operation at the end of 1962 or in the first quarter of 1963. Many have changed much since. The tables have been checked and re-checked but it is still possible that the summaries fail to do justice to the obscurities and nuances of so many varied systems of payment.

APPENDIX 2. ANALYSIS OF Q4 (CURATES)

(a) CANTERBURY PROVINCE—DIOCESAN SCALES FOR ASSISTANT CURATES

Diocese (1)	Minimum (2)	Rising by (3)	Children's allowances (4)	House (5)	Extras (6)
1	£445 S £545 M		£20 p.a. each dep. child	Free or £85	
2	£504	£24 to £576	£36, £24, £24 in full-time educ.	Free	Spec. res. £60–£120 p.a.
3	£500 S £560 M	£10 to £550 (£610M)	£30, £20, £10 p.a. in full-time educ.	See col. 6	£50 deducted from M stipend if house free
4	£500 S £600 M	£550 for priest to £575 in two years (or £650–£675 M)	£50, £25, £15, £10		
5	£525	£25 to £675	£50 per child	Free or £80 p.a.	
6	£600	£25 to £700 max. on second curacy	£20 for first child	Free	
7	£480	£10 to £530	£30, £20, £10	Free	
8	£425	£25 to £525	£45 per child		
9	£500 S £550 M	£30 to £680 (or £730 M)	£40, £30, £20 until leave school	No	
10	£500 S £550 M	£50 when priested then to £650 or £700	None yet	Free	
11	£450	+ £50 when priested	£30, £20, £10		
12	£470 S £520 M		£35, £15, £15		
13	£525 S £625 M	£575 for priest rising to £675 M	£30, £20, £10	Free	
14	£500 S £600 M	To £600 (or £700 M)	£25, £25, £25 up to age of 18	Free	
15	£500 S £550 M	+ £25 when priested	£30, £20, £10	Free or £75	
16	£475	£525 S priest £550 M + £30 after two and + £50 after four years	£12, £12, £12, to end of school	Free	+ incidental forms of help
17	£550	None	£20 per child to end of school	No	
18	£500 S £525 M	+ £50 when priested then £10 p.a. for five years	£20 per child		+ £50 for curates of town daughter churches
19	£525 S £600 M		£40 for each child under 5, £60 for each child over 5 in full time educ.	Free	
20	£450 S £520 M	+ £25 when priested then £25 to £550 S, £620 M	£25, £25, £25 to 16	Free	Whitsun offgs.
21	£560 S £610 M		£20 each dep. child to 19 if on min.	Free	
22					
23	£550				
24	£475	+ £50 when priested, then + £75 + £50 to £700	None	Free or £75	
25	£500	+ £20 when priested	£10 for 5–7 years old, £20 for 8–11 years old, £35 for 12–18 years old	Free or £120	Whitsun offgs.
26	£475	£15 to £550	£40, £10, £10	Free	Whitsun offgs.
27	£440 S £490 M	+ £30 in second curacy	£35, £10, £10	£50 in lieu	
28	£500 S £550 M	+ £50 when priested, then by £50 to £650, £700 M	£20 per child to end of school	Free	
29	£500	+ £50 when priested, then by £15 to £595	£30, £20, £10	No	

(b) YORK PROVINCE—DIOCESAN SCALES FOR ASSISTANT CURATES

Diocese (1)	Minimum (2)	Rising by (3)	Children's allowances (4)	House (5)	Extras (6)
30	£500	+ £25 when priested, then £25 to £550		Free or £70 if M	Marriage allce £12 deacon, £24 priest
31	£550 S £600 M	£10 increment p.a.	£30, £20, £20	If free deduct £50	Whitsun offgs.
32	£500	By £25 to £575, then by £50 to £625	£20, £15, £15 to 18		
33	£525 S £575 M	+ £25 when priested	£30, £20, £10	Free or £50 if M	
34					
35	£450 S £500 M	By £20 to £540 (or £590 if M)	£35, £25, £25		
36	£525	By £20 to £565 and by £50 to £750	£30, £20, £10		
37	£500 S £550 M	+ £20 when priested, then by £20 to £600 (or £650 M)	£30, £20, £10 under 16	Free if M	Whitsun offgs. Spec. res. allce
38	£446 S £550 M		£32½, £19½, £13 usually to 16	Free	Whitsun offgs. Differentials
39	£500	+ £50 when priested, then by £75 to £625	None	No	
40	£550	+ £50 when priested, then £675 after two years	£40, £24, £24 to end of school	Free if M	+ £50 post of spec. res.
41					
42	£500	By £25 to £550 then £50 to £650	None	Free or £70	
43	£500 S £525 M	+ £25 when priested, then by £10 to £575 (or £600)	£25 per dep. child	Free	

ABBREVIATIONS

S = single

M = married

spec. res. = special responsibility

Note. These tables should not be taken as a guide to prevailing stipends and allowances but rather as evidence of the complexities of the stipendiary system. The rates and conditions are those reported in operation at the end of 1962 or in the first quarter of 1963. Many have changed much since then. The tables have been checked and re-checked but it is still possible that the summaries fail to do justice to the obscurities and nuances of so many varied systems of payment.